# In Levittown's Shadow

Historical Studies of Urban America

*Edited by Lilia Fernández, Timothy J. Gilfoyle, and Amanda I. Seligman*
*James R. Grossman, Editor Emeritus*

RECENT TITLES IN THE SERIES

Sean Dempsey, *City of Dignity: Christianity, Liberalism, and the Making of Global Los Angeles*

Claire Dunning, *Nonprofit Neighborhoods: An Urban History of Inequality and the American State*

Tracy E. K'Meyer, *To Live Peaceably Together: The American Friends Service Committee's Campaign for Open Housing*

Mike Amezcua, *Making Mexican Chicago: From Postwar Settlement to the Age of Gentrification*

Arnold R. Hirsch, *Making the Second Ghetto: Race and Housing in Chicago, 1940–1960, With a New Afterword by N. D. B. Connolly*

William Sites, *Sun Ra's Chicago: Afrofuturism and the City*

David Schley, *Steam City: Railroads, Urban Space, and Corporate Capitalism in Nineteenth-Century Baltimore*

Rebecca K. Marchiel, *After Redlining: The Urban Reinvestment Movement in the Era of Financial Deregulation*

Steven T. Moga, *Urban Lowlands: A History of Neighborhoods, Poverty, and Planning*

Andrew S. Baer, *Beyond the Usual Beating: The Jon Burge Police Torture Scandal and Social Movements for Police Accountability in Chicago*

Matthew Vaz, *Running the Numbers: Race, Police, and the History of Urban Gambling*

Ann Durkin Keating, *The World of Juliette Kinzie: Chicago before the Fire*

Jeffrey S. Adler, *Murder in New Orleans: The Creation of Jim Crow Policing*

David A. Gamson, *The Importance of Being Urban: Designing the Progressive School District, 1890–1940*

Kara Murphy Schlichting, *New York Recentered: Building the Metropolis from the Shore*

Mark Wild, *Renewal: Liberal Protestants and the American City after World War II*

Meredith Oda, *The Gateway to the Pacific: Japanese Americans and the Remaking of San Francisco*

*A complete list of series titles is available on the University of Chicago Press website.*

# *In Levittown's Shadow*

## Poverty in America's Wealthiest Postwar Suburb

TIM KEOGH

The University of Chicago Press
Chicago and London

Publication of this book has been supported by Furthermore: a program of the J. M. Kaplan Fund.

Furthermore:
a program of the J.M.Kaplan Fund

The University of Chicago Press, Chicago 60637
The University of Chicago Press, Ltd., London

Published 2023
Printed in the United States of America

32 31 30 29 28 27 26 25 24 23    1 2 3 4 5

ISBN-13: 978-0-226-82773-5 (cloth)
ISBN-13: 978-0-226-82775-9 (paper)
ISBN-13: 978-0-226-82774-2 (e-book)
DOI: https://doi.org/10.7208/chicago/9780226827742.001.0001

Library of Congress Cataloging-in-Publication Data

Names: Keogh, Tim (Historian), author.
Title: In Levittown's shadow : poverty in America's wealthiest postwar suburb / Tim Keogh.
Other titles: Historical studies of urban America.
Description: Chicago ; London : The University of Chicago Press, 2023. | Series: Historical studies of urban America | Includes bibliographical references and index.
Identifiers: LCCN 2022056872 | ISBN 9780226827735 (cloth) | ISBN 9780226827759 (paperback) | ISBN 9780226827742 (ebook)
Subjects: LCSH: Suburbs—New York (State)—Long Island—History—20th century. | Poverty—New York (State)—Long Island. | Poor—New York (State)—Long Island—Social conditions—20th century. | Discrimination in housing—New York (State)—Long Island—History—20th century. | Economic assistance, Domestic—United States—History—20th century. | Equality—Economic aspects—New York (State)—Long Island. | Suburbs—New York (State)—Long Island—Economic conditions—20th century. | Long Island (N.Y.)—History—20th century.
Classification: LCC HT352.U62 N745 2023 | DDC 307.7409747/21—dc23/eng/20230111
LC record available at https://lccn.loc.gov/2022056872

♾ This paper meets the requirements of ANSI/NISO Z39.48-1992 (Permanence of Paper).

*To the most beautiful, smartest, and creative person in the whole world—*
*Aila, I love you*

# Contents

# Introduction

Morning began with a snap. The cat broke a rat's neck next to Dorothy Daniels's couch, waking her from a troubled night's sleep. The tan-and-white feline was Ms. Daniels's best defense against the vermin terrorizing her family each day. "I hear them squeaking when I go to sleep," Ms. Daniels told a reporter. She had tried patching the football-sized hole in her kitchen, but the rats found other ways into the house. They couldn't forgo the feast of dirty pots and pans strewn across the floor. She didn't have functioning cupboards to store the wares, so that's where she had to leave them. She didn't have much space at all: just two bedrooms, living room, and kitchen built atop a concrete slab. Her six children split the bedrooms, while she slept on the couch in the bare living room, next to the TV atop a crate and the home's lone chair.

The cat's murder was a good alarm anyway. Dorothy Daniels woke at 5 a.m. each day to make breakfast for the kids before a small white van crawled down the block. The van picked up women to clean more fortunate people's homes and watch their kids. Dorothy could expect $8 for a hard day's work in the 1960s. This was the equivalent of $58 today, close to the current federal $7.25 hourly minimum wage. But that was after the van driver's $4 charge, a quarter of her pay. She, like her neighbors, didn't own a car, and there wasn't reliable bus service, forcing her to rely on the van's monopoly. The rhythms of low-wage work determined everyone's lives in the neighborhood. The only days people stayed home were on the first and fifteenth of the month, when the welfare checks arrived. Families then scrambled to buy groceries, and most importantly, catch up on rent.

James Northrop collected the rent. He owned Dorothy Daniels's rat-infested house, along with half of the 320 single-family homes in the "Carleton Park" subdivision in Central Islip, Long Island. Many were in severe disrepair. Aside from rodents gnawing through the drywall, other tenants lived with overflowing cesspools, crumbling foundations, broken windows, leaky pipes, and failing heat systems. These houses were no aging tenements though. The single-story ranches were only sixteen years old when Dorothy Daniels fended off rodents in 1969. Carleton Park was twenty miles east of Levittown, that famous suburb of 17,000 single-family homes mass-produced atop former potato fields. Like Levittown, developers constructed Carleton Park according to Federal Housing Administration (FHA) standards. The developers who built Ms. Daniels's rental originally applied for federal mortgage insurance, protecting the lender if the borrower defaulted. Qualified buyers only put down $290 and carried a $35-per-month mortgage to own the houses. The first occupants owned the house as members of Long Island's upwardly mobile working class.

But in the intervening years, Levittown and Carleton Park's trajectory diverged. In Levittown, homeowners sold to new generations of homeowners. In Carleton Park, property speculators spooked homeowners to sell and get out. They then transformed the single-family ranches into rentals, "rent-to-buy" schemes, or vacant tax write-offs. By the 1960s, James Northrop, a disgraced high school principal turned landlord, bought out the speculators and remaining homeowners. He then turned to the local welfare office for tenants. Northrop earned the nickname "Long Island's Slumlord." But he scoffed at the derision. After all, he became a millionaire. His profit derived not from property upkeep and rising values, but neglect and cramming as many people into the single-family homes as possible.[1]

Dorothy Daniels's life, and that of her neighbors and their landlord, are suburban stories. But they are not ones you're likely familiar with. No one thinks "oh, of course, the rats!" when recalling Levittown. America's largest single-family residential project after World War II, Levittown was famous for its order, its cleanliness, and its material abundance. It was a place where young families, cooped up in their parents' New York City apartments after World War II, bought homes with enormous yards, by global standards at least. The Levitt company included electric refrigerators and even a TV built right into the living room with every purchase. Fresh sidewalks, curbs, and asphalt were right out front, making it easy to walk to public pools, shopping centers, and schools. And thanks to the economic boom, these families filled their property with cars, lawnmowers, and vacuum cleaners. Levittowners were just one among the thousands moving out to "Long Island," the two counties east of the New York City border, a suburb larger than all but three American cities by 1960. It was also the country's richest urban area. This was not because millionaires lived there (though a few still did), but because modest families with white-collar careers in the city or local jobs in sleek suburban factories bought Levitt Cape Cods. More than anywhere else in the country, Long Island was the place where working-class Americans could enjoy living standards unparalleled in human history.

The rats remained in the city they left behind, so the story goes. Poor people, and Black families regardless of income, made do with jobs and homes among the aging tenements, public housing mega-blocks, empty factories, and denuded downtowns of America's declining cities. They couldn't avail themselves of the opportunities beyond the municipal boundary on Long Island. Exclusions barred them from the suburbs. Levittown builders Levitt and Sons, like many other developers, included racially restrictive covenants in all sales, prohibiting white buyers from reselling or renting to people of color. Realty agents turned away Black veterans at Levitt offices. Exclusionary zoning prohibited multifamily housing near Levittown. Suburban vigilantes did their best to block sales or rentals to Black families in the subdivision.[2] For the 70,000 Black suburbanites who found housing elsewhere on Long Island by 1960, real estate agents, developers, and property speculators steered the majority into just ten segregated places.[3] Unequal schools then enabled white suburbanites to pass educational advantage onto their children. The tragedy in the dominant narrative was access. Black and poor urbanites trapped rats in cities while upwardly mobile white families trimmed crabgrass in the suburbs.

Dorothy Daniels's life doesn't fit into this familiar narrative of post–World War II suburbia. Single-family zoning did not deprive her of a job—she was right there working in the suburbs. Racial covenants and racist real estate agents didn't preclude her from owning a home; low wages and a lack of credit did. And despite all the zoning laws, racist agents, and vigilant suburban homeowners policing their neighborhoods, her home was an FHA-standard single-family house nestled in Long Island's endless sea of Capes and cul-de-sacs. What distinguished Dorothy Daniels's life from the mass of suburbanites around her were the terms and conditions of her labor and housing. The typical suburbanite found security on Long Island; Daniels was exploited there. A true history of postwar American suburbia, one that accounts for Dorothy Daniels and 12 percent of Long Islanders, must consider the institutions responsible for suburban prosperity rather than access to suburbia.

This revised story begins with jobs. When Dorothy Daniels traveled in the van each morning, she passed homeowners who paid down their mortgages by welding airplanes, filing corporate paperwork, or keeping the lights on and toilets running in suburban homes. They made Long Island a broadly affluent place, and their jobs paid well thanks to robust federal intervention. Defense spending encouraged industrial growth on Long Island after 1940, propping up aerospace manufacturers such as Republic Aviation and Grumman, Long Island's largest employers. New Deal labor laws turned thousands of other jobs into the means to a good life.[4] Together, military contracts and labor protections lifted over 400,000 families into economic security. Workers then plowed their steady paychecks into their monthly mortgage and house projects, transforming income into new comforts, and over the long term, wealth.

In contrast, Dorothy's domestic service raised the living standards of others all while lowering her own. And she was hardly alone. Across Long Island, workers dormered out Cape Cods, mowed lawns, stocked department store shelves, cared for young and old, picked vegetables on truck farms, and sewed garments in suburban factories that underwrote local property taxes. These jobs made postwar suburbia's economic boom possible. But no laws mandated minimum wages, union recognition, or basic workplace protections to those stooped down in vegetable fields or scrubbing baby vomit out of a living room rug. From the 1940s through the early 1960s, scores of cashiers, nannies, landscapers, and construction laborers worked at the margin of employment and labor law. They earned too little to meet the benchmarks for homeownership, and sometimes too little to survive. All of these jobs lacked state protection in one way or another, perpetuating the old dynamic of work as a necessary means of survival, not the route to a decent life.

Federal policy also determined the deplorable housing conditions the Daniels family and others endured. The government's largest and most famous housing initiative, the FHA mortgage insurance program, shaped Long Island more than any other suburb after World War II.[5] There were few legal options for those considered mortgage ineligible. Carleton Park's slumlord James Northrop was one among many who exploited the FHA program to house the unqualified. In nearby Wyandanch, Black and white property speculators chopped up single-family homes into tiny "informal" multifamily apartments, units that failed to meet minimum building standards or land-use laws. In Roosevelt, a suburb just five miles from Levittown, down-on-their-luck homeowners repurposed dormered attics as rented rooms to cover their FHA monthly mortgage payments. And in New Cassel, a hamlet that included Levitt-built Cape Cods, owners partitioned garages into new bedrooms. All, in one way or another, skirted the building, zoning, and fire codes passed with single-family owner-occupation in mind. Thus, property speculators enabled poor people to live in postwar Long Island.

Both owner-occupied and rental units sat along leafy-green streets, near suburban schools and well-paying suburban jobs. But they produced radically divergent outcomes. Homeowners like those in Levittown built equity as they paid down their mortgage debt. Tenants living in Carleton Park, Wyandanch, Roosevelt, and New Cassel enriched their landlords in exchange for shelter. If tenants were lucky like the Daniels, they received rent subsidies; if not, high rents forced them to forgo food, clothing, or medical care. And while homeowners could count on a lengthy foreclosure process if things didn't go well, tenants had no such recourse. Federal homeownership subsidies, for those public officials and private lenders considered qualified, made suburban housing affordable and secure. The government's absence, save the threat of code enforcers condemning houses, reproduced conditions associated with cities, i.e., shelter that caused poverty, precarity, and illness.

Dorothy Daniels, and the roughly 200,000 Long Islanders in similar circumstances, are part of the postwar suburban story. Rats and evictions, unemployment and low wages, overcrowding and deindustrialization; these were suburban problems, not only urban ones. We have written them out of history because we have inherited a spatial narrative from the postwar period, premised on the idea that the great fault line in America fell between cities and suburbs. Housing segregation, exclusionary zoning, and suburbanizing jobs accumulated prosperity on one side of the municipal boundary. The prosperous left the poor behind, concentrated in the inner-city without jobs, tax dollars, or decent housing. This spatial narrative has shaped antipoverty policy since. Policymakers have aimed to relocate the urban poor or redistribute their burdens among suburbs, all so the poor could enjoy the "milk and honey" on the other side of the suburban wall. Bringing the poor back into suburban history compels us to rethink this narrative and policy proscription. The suburban poor help us consider the politics and institutions flowing through suburbs that produced both widespread prosperity and poverty *within* places like Long Island. And they help us reconsider the conceptual approach policymakers took toward solving it, as well as the alternative ideas suburban poverty reveals.

This book's exploration of poor people's lives in the richest, fastest-growing, and most segregated suburb in the United States challenges the traditional narrative in two ways. First, Long Island's history exposes how suburban prosperity depended on poverty. The federal government, principally through defense contracts and mortgage insurance, lifted a million people into material comfort. But so did low-wage workers who performed necessary labor in the suburbs, and property owners who carved out informal housing so the poor could live nearby. In other words, *exploitation* defined the divide in postwar Long Island. Suburbanites depended on low-wage labor for needs the state ignored, and some of those landowning suburbanites got rich from the dearth of affordable housing. The state didn't provide, and in some cases criminalized, such options.[6] Second, policymakers overlooked suburban poverty, believing Long Island was exceptionally affluent. Their policies centered on *exclusion*, the barriers preventing the poor from enjoying the prosperity locked in suburbia.[7] But these policies were informed by an ideology I call "suburban exceptionalism," which obscured poverty's root causes and foreclosed the possibility of solutions that could have helped people living in cities and suburbs alike. Suburban poverty matters for what it unmasks: both poverty's root causes, regardless of where one lived, and the folly of using the suburbs to solve it. The way we have understood postwar suburbs has narrowed our policy horizon and impoverished our language for even talking about poverty. This matters all the more today because suburbs are now the nation's poorest areas. The pages that follow offer a new narrative of America's "golden age," one that points us toward more effective solutions for ending poverty in the twenty-first century.

## Historicizing Suburban Poverty

Dorothy Daniels's struggle subverts the established story of suburbia because the narrative we have inherited from the postwar period rests on her absence. Through the long arc of history though, diversity—racial, social, and economic—defined suburbia. Historian Ken Jackson notes that prior to the nineteenth century, suburbs were filled with hardscrabble farmers, paupers, and enslaved people seeking freedom, among others cast out beyond city boundaries.[8] This definition increasingly applies to twenty-first century suburbs, where most of America's poor now live, part of the "Great Inversion" currently wooing the affluent back to the city and pushing everyone else to the fringe.[9] Scholars have even chipped away at the postwar tropes of America's prosperous golden age. They have unearthed forgotten stories of working-class people building their own suburban homes, Black pioneers who challenged racial segregation, Mexican American colonias engulfed by postwar suburbanization, Asian American ethno-burbs, and vast suburban regions riven with class divides.[10] Dorothy Daniels was part of a long tradition. And like her forebears and successors, her poverty was historically specific. The exploitation Daniels experienced reflected the limits of America's post–World War II welfare state.

Poverty itself is what philosopher and economist Mozaffar Qizilbash calls a "fuzzy" concept. While scholars broadly agree that lacking the basic needs of life defines one as "poor," they argue over what things are necessary and what causes people to lack those things.[11] The federal metric, a measure of "absolute poverty," or what the government considers the bare minimum needed for basic survival, put Long Island's poverty rate at a mere 6.8 percent in 1960 (figure A.1). Nassau, the largest of Long Island's two counties, had the nation's lowest poverty rate that year, beaten only by Los Alamos County, New Mexico, home to a few thousand engineers and scientists working on the former Manhattan Project site. That rate nonetheless translates into over 130,000 residents, the same number of poor people as lived in Boston, Buffalo, or Cincinnati at the time, and more than San Francisco or Milwaukee.[12] When considering needs beyond a full stomach and clothing on one's back, over one in nine Long Island families, roughly 200,000 people, earned less than half the median income in 1960 (table A.1). This is "relative poverty," the standard of measurement in wealthy democracies. Relative poverty is what experts consider the minimum set of resources necessary to participate in the customs, behaviors, relationships, and accepted roles of the larger community.[13] By another useful metric, about one in ten families earned too little to afford housing costs as of 1967, having to cut back on food, clothing, medicine, or other needs. They were "shelter poor" as Michael Stone defines it.[14]

While each measure offers insight into the causes and depths of suburban poverty, what they demonstrate is the contextual nature of poverty. In other words, the resources people need, how they are provisioned, and how people are deprived of them depends on time and place. Understanding the context means going beyond the ambiguous boundaries of what constitutes "poverty" to analyze how poor people relate to others. This means studying working-class people living near the thin line between "just getting by" and "not getting by at all." It also means including the people who depended on low wages to reduce prices for their basic needs in the story, as well as the landlords, employers, and wealthy estate owners who profited from poverty.[15] This capacious view of poverty, which changes depending on what need we are talking about and how society distributes it, permits us to examine the politics and institutions that create poverty, sustain it, and offer the potential to reduce it.[16]

No institution was more important to poverty—and prosperity—on postwar Long Island than the American welfare state. While we may think people make choices that lead to their own misfortune, or that inexorable labor market dynamics deprive them of a decent life, scholars such as David Brady prove that poverty is the political outcome of the welfare state. "Welfare" refers not only to social security, food stamps, and rental subsidies, but to the variety of ways a government supports the well-being of its citizenry. States can directly supply housing, income, and other basic needs. But more often states organize the markets that people depend on for survival and security. Minimum wage laws are an obvious example. Less obvious are the central bank interest rates that shape purchasing power, mortgage lending, and the number of jobs in the economy. Comparative research demonstrates that wealthy democracies differ in how they mediate or directly satisfy needs. This has a direct impact on poverty. Policymakers, through the ways they construct, augment, or dismantle parts of the welfare state, decide the magnitude of poverty, who is likely to fall into it, and how long they may remain there over the course of their lives.[17] Prior to the 1930s, the line between worker, unemployed person, and pauper was blurred. Once European and North American nations formed welfare states through macroeconomic policy, social insurance programs, and labor rights, they determined living standards. They also redefined poverty as welfare-state failure—unprotected forms of work, gaps in welfare coverage, or insufficient public domestic spending.[18]

Long Island epitomized what America's unique welfare state produced. Unlike in Europe, the United States subsidized the private sector, leaving private market actors in charge of provisioning housing, jobs, and healthcare, among other needs.[19] Long Island benefited from two massive federal subsidies in the post–World War II era: defense contracts and housing credit subsidies. Defense spending, while no public employment program, was nonetheless a job creation tool, responsible for 9 percent of all jobs in the nation and 16 percent of Long Island's jobs in the quarter century after 1945.[20] The FHA mortgage insurance model, which guaranteed loans in the event of foreclosure, financed two in five homes sold across the country between 1945 and 1958. Long Island was the nation's largest recipient of FHA insurance, as builders put up fifty single-family houses per day in Nassau and Suffolk during the 1950s.[21] In short, military Keynesianism and selective credit programs geared toward homeownership made Long Island a land of superlatives. In the postwar years, Long Island was the fastest-growing place east of the Mississippi.[22] Job growth quintupled the national rate, rivaling Southern California, Nevada, and Arizona.[23] Nassau became the most affluent American county with 100,000 or more people in 1960.[24] And Long Island had the cheapest single-family houses in the New York metropolitan area, despite its rich population.[25]

But postwar Long Island also reveals the failures of America's welfare state, and Dorothy Daniels's life is a window into understanding its limits. Defense contractors hired few women and proved a poor substitute for public employment programs because they depended on the vagaries of US foreign policy.[26] America's mortgage insurance guarantees were aimed at lenders and developers, not homeowners or tenants. The FHA and VA left thousands like Dorothy Daniels out of the housing market altogether and made Long Island a perennial frontrunner as the most segregated place in America.[27] The broader federal laws regulating work and housing did not include her either. The Fair Labor Standards Act (FLSA) did not cover her wages. The National Labor Relations Act (NLRA) did not protect her right to organize. And because the federal government did not supply other needs on Long Island and elsewhere—e.g., daycare, elder care, public housing, and public school fiscal support—exploitative employers and landlords filled the vacuum. Daniels and others like her were the exploited. Employers drove down wages to build cheap housing, offer daycare and cleaning services, or keep their textile sweatshops competitive in the suburbs. Property owners surreptitiously cobbled together rickety but expensive apartments from single-family houses the poor did not qualify to own. Together, they produced a poverty specific to the postwar era and plainly evident in suburbs like Long Island: the squeeze between high housing costs and low incomes.[28]

## The Disparities of Poverty

Dorothy Daniels lived in shoddy housing and worked a low-wage job because labor laws, public spending, and housing programs did not extend its benefits to her as a Black single mother. Her neighbors in Carleton Park were mostly Black or Puerto Rican. The other domestic workers sharing seats in the van that picked her up were likely Black women too. These facts were not unrelated; they were a product of the American welfare state as well. To repurpose a quote from historian Barbara Fields, the only check upon exploitation is the strength and effectiveness of safeguards against it.[29] Without state protections, employers, landlords, real estate developers, speculators, and regular suburbanites exploited already oppressed populations—southern African Americans, Puerto Rican migrants, and women—to reduce labor costs or enrich themselves with rental income. The outcome was disparities in poverty that mirrored other places and time periods in the nation. Moving to the suburbs did not shield one from exploitation. Only national policies, including antidiscrimination law, tight employment, and affordable housing programs could tip the power toward people like Dorothy Daniels.

In terms of jobs, employers took advantage of existing racial and gender hierarchies, filling low-wage jobs with an oppressed workforce in a region of otherwise high-paying work. Racism and sexism served them well, doing the ideological double-duty these social practices always do: giving employers captive laborers and reinforcing the hierarchy on Long Island so the people occupying these lowly positions came to be seen as belonging in them.[30] Long Island employers took advantage of racial divides across regional migration streams. They drew from the Jim Crow South to fill jobs in domestic service, farm work, and day labor with Black workers. Sexism operated along a slightly different axis, as employers tapped the intensive labor divide in suburban homes rather than the extensive migrant streams across states. Without publicly funded day care, employers took advantage of suburban women's dual role as caretakers and extra earners to cover suburbia's high living costs. Women filled inconsistent retail, textile mill, and other low-wage jobs, justified as extra spending income earned while the kids were in school. And while not all female laborers were poor, single motherhood, a divorce, or a husband's unemployment, illness, death, or desertion often led to poverty. All of this reinforced racial and gender disparities on postwar Long Island: in 1970, the first year of available data, only one in twenty white households lived under the federal "absolute" poverty line, but one in five Black, one in four single mother, and almost half of Black single mother households lacked enough income to survive by federal standards.[31]

Landlords exploited the welfare state's failure to house otherwise excluded people on Long Island too. As scholars have long noted, the FHA epitomized exclusion. Real estate interests wrote the bill that formed the FHA, inscribing their preferences for racial homogeneity (enforced through redlining and covenants) and for newly constructed, owner-occupied, single-family housing in exclusively zoned residential areas. Exclusion was an industry strategy to create value and guarantee profit. But as scholars of race and housing emphasize, *exploiting* the exclusionary housing market was lucrative too. Predatory practices like blockbusting (preying on racial fears to buy white houses on the cheap and flip them to Black buyers at inflated prices) and land installment contracts (where a buyer did not get legal title to the deed until the house was paid in full), or even special FHA programs designed for Black suburbanites were highly profitable.[32] All of these factors helped some 16,000 Black Long Islanders become homeowners by 1970, albeit in segregated places, at higher cost, and at significant profit to speculators. Exclusion was in the service of exploitation.

Similar dynamics opened up single-family houses to people like Dorothy Daniels. To best understand how, it is useful to consider how houses in Carleton Park's single-family subdivision—rented rather than owned, filled with multiple families rather than one—were *informal* housing units. Informality is a concept commonly associated with poor housing in the developing world: the favelas of Brazil, Dhaka's bastees, or the slums sheltering over 330 million people in sub-Saharan African cities. Shanty dwellings are a far cry from the neatly shingled Cape Cods of American suburbs. But informal housing is shelter that "fails to adhere to the established institutional rules or are denied their protection." And housing like this exists everywhere formal housing does not meet demand, including American suburbs. Recent scholarship reveals its ubiquity in places where single-family housing predominates such as Los Angeles and Texas.[33] Informal suburban housing repurposes the single-family house: refrigerators and stoves tucked into basements; improvised bedrooms in garages or attics; a self-built apartment in the backyard; multitudes of inhabitants stuffed into single-family houses otherwise indistinguishable from all the other houses on the block. But the purpose is the same. Informal housing resolves a need for shelter the state chooses not to satisfy within the formal regime. Studies estimated around one in every ten housing units were informal on Long Island.[34] And while not all inhabitants were poor, high costs immiserated, dilapidated housing harmed one's health, and eviction was a constant threat.

The shoddy attic apartment inside a suburban house, or the day laborer waiting on a suburban street corner are examples of the postwar welfare state's failures. Long Island was awash in federal contracts and credit guarantees, generating well-paying jobs and clean single-family houses. But legal protections covered only so many jobs, leaving thousands to satisfy suburban needs and wants outside basic labor and employment laws. Suburban housing policy left out anyone who was not white with means. Exploitation, in all its forms, filled the vacuum. Employers slashed prices with low-wage labor and took advantage of racial and gender hierarchies to fill those jobs. Landlords subverted the housing market's exclusionary mechanisms to shelter the poor in precarious conditions at high cost. If one wanted to reduce exploitation, they only needed to look at how well the American welfare state worked for Long Island's more fortunate working class. From that vantage point, tipping power further toward working-class people through comprehensive labor laws, jobs, and housing for all could have ended exploitation and poverty. But this required seeing the welfare state as the source of both Long Island's prosperity and its poverty.

## Why Suburban Poverty Matters

Though poverty was suburban and rooted in welfare-state failure, a public narrative has long obscured the connection. Historically, policymakers, politicians, and activists have rarely considered the challenges that Dorothy Daniels or others in her position faced. Instead, a discourse emerged in the postwar era that *depended* on ignoring the suburban poor, or at least the exploitation responsible for their poverty. Suburban exceptionalism took suburban prosperity as a given and contended exclusion from suburbs caused poverty, inequality, and related racial disparities. Most importantly, policymakers steeped in the ideology believed they could harness suburbia's alleged exceptional wealth for egalitarian ends. Developers, lenders, and local government officials crafted the myth of poverty-free suburbs when they designed exclusive subdivisions. The public imagined homogeneous, affluent, leafy-green hamlets as the suburban norm. And policymakers reified the idea when they devised antipoverty policies that understood poverty as rooted in places, concentrated in cities and absent from suburbs. But poverty was not a place-based problem concentrated in cities; employers and landlords exploited and impoverished people in suburbs too. Long Islanders did have to deal with poverty in their places, however, and policymakers failed them. Those adhering to suburban exceptionalism set the terms for political debate, drawing political divides along racial lines and foreclosing the potential for solutions that could help urban and suburban residents alike.

Because suburban exceptionalism informed what policymakers believed caused poverty and prosperity, it shaped how they constructed, maintained, or altered the welfare state. The United States was an outlier among postwar welfare states because debate occurred "within narrow limits bounded by the market."[35] Suburbs shaped the market-constrained discussion in three ways. First, adherents believed the suburbs were indeed exceptional in the American urban landscape. Aggregate statistics proved suburbs were affluent, socioeconomically homogeneous, filled with jobs, and free of poverty. The numbers also depicted cities as diverse, disproportionately poor, and bleeding jobs to the suburbs. Second, economists argued the market, rather than targeted public investments, determined suburban affluence. This grew out of the "neoclassical" economic consensus that synthesized Keynes's revolutionary insights about the virtues of public spending at the national level with the classical model of perfect markets at the local level. Prominent economists still believed supply and demand, including jobs and wages, leveled out in equilibrium if the government stimulated the economy on a macro scale. Suburbs exemplified the alleged virtues of aggregate growth.[36] Finally, suburban exclusion distorted market efficiency. Housing segregation, suburban job discrimination, restrictive zoning, hoarded tax revenues, and inadequate public transportation deprived poor people, Black Americans, and cities of the bounties stockpiled behind suburban barricades.

A history of poverty on Long Island helps explain why local and national figures came to embrace suburban exceptionalism. All of Long Island's superlatives—the richest, least poor, fastest growing, most segregated—gave people up and down the policy ladder ammunition to claim that suburbs could solve broad social problems. That was especially true because policymakers contrasted Long Island's positive attributes with nearby New York

City, America's largest, most diverse, and well-known ailing metropolis. From the suburban exceptionalist perspective, dismantling suburbia's exclusionary barriers could solve poverty. In the 1960s, Black and white homeowners on Long Island, inundated with informal housing conversion in their neighborhoods, insisted that the suburban poor be evenly distributed across white-exclusive suburbs. Local governments obliged with code enforcement and housing condemnation. Civil right activists demanded Long Island's defense manufacturers hire and promote fairly to reduce racial income disparities. Local officials of President Johnson's War on Poverty deployed training programs, public buses, and job fairs to absorb the poor into suburbia's purported prosperity. By the end of the decade, federal housing officials called on Long Island to take their "fair share" of New York's inner-city poor. They looked to build suburban public housing and disperse the urban poor into Long Island's employment-rich and tax-flush suburbs.

What policymakers thought was exceptional about Long Island—uniformly affluent, filled with opportunities, racially homogeneous—turned out to be false. Their varied efforts to harness suburbia's "exceptional" prosperity only exposed the exploitation beneath the wealth. When suburban activists challenged housing segregation they believed was behind informal housing, they exposed how segregation was only the means by which landlords and speculators built informal housing. The dearth of legal housing was the problem. When civil rights groups demanded fair hiring among defense manufacturers, they realized they needed stable jobs to make it a reality. But defense officials instead targeted Long Island for defense cuts because suburbia's "prosperity" could absorb the losses. When bureaucrats aimed to use Long Island's job market in the War on Poverty, their antipoverty programs uncovered the low-wage jobs that undergirded suburban affluence. And dispersing the urban poor into the suburbs ignored suburban inequality. Poor people already filled suburban neighborhoods. Public housing projects did little to stem housing informalization. And local property taxes had to fund services, placing the burden of poverty on those least able to pay. The same problems found in America's cities—inequality, exploitation, unemployment—stalked the suburbs on a smaller scale.

Suburban exceptionalism did more than ignore exploitation in the suburbs, however. Adherents of this ideology also foreclosed solutions to the exploitative mechanisms responsible for poverty in cities and suburbs alike. Social-democratic ideas bubbled up amidst the policy fights from Long Islanders themselves. Informal tenants demanded their right to stay in their suburban homes when they faced eviction. Planners considered public ownership of informal housing to reduce speculation. Defense workers aimed to convert warplane factories into mass-transit plants, and defense dollars into civilian funds for local public works. Local politicians responded to the War on Poverty's failures with free childcare and a public job guarantee for all suburban residents. Fights over suburban public housing revealed the need for legal housing conversions and rental vouchers, as well as federal, rather than local, funding for public schools. But the power players repeatedly set the terms of debate around exclusion, blaming intransigent employers, racist suburbanites, and local political officials for withholding suburbia's fruits from the poor. Federal officials canceled defense contracts rather than reimagining them. They denied money to a job guarantee program. And they encouraged political divides between suburbanites and policymakers, homeowners and tenants, Black and white when they cast suburbs as exceptionally racist, class-exclusive, and affluent. Those who subscribed to the ideology of suburban exceptionalism left the federal institutions responsible for unequal labor and housing markets off the hook.

Suburban exceptionalism still matters because we live with its consequences. Activists, policymakers, and politicians recognized suburban prosperity but ignored its federal foundations. Instead, they condemned the exclusionary barriers between cities and suburbs, but not the exploitation occurring within cities and suburbs. Most consequentially, they drew political fault lines between city and suburb, Black and white, homeowner and tenant. This suppressed the demands from suburbanites for things Americans across municipal boundaries needed: good jobs, safe housing, well-funded public schools. In a word, public goods to reduce, rather than rearrange, poverty. Putting the suburban poor into postwar history helps us to demystify an ideology which has done little to improve America's welfare state. Their experiences force us to reconsider the policy cul-de-sac we still find ourselves in, to both dispose of failed solutions and salvage policy tools from the flawed institutions that built suburban Long Island. These tools can address the social problems of the twenty-first century, especially now that suburban exceptionalism, premised on the city–suburb divide, no longer reflects suburbia's widely accepted diversity, poverty, and municipal challenges.

*

The following chapters align with the book's two overarching claims. The first half uses Long Island to show how suburban prosperity and poverty were outcomes of America's welfare state. The second half shifts to the discourse and policy proposals that obscured suburban poverty's welfare-state roots. The reason for the divide is simple: only by understanding why there was suburban poverty can we see the folly of privileging the exclusion *from* suburbs over exploitation *within* suburbs. Each chapter analyzes poverty from a different angle in order to illustrate the multiple ways people can be deprived of needs, and to show how definitions of poverty do as much to obscure as clarify the causes of deprivation. The book also follows characters across chapters, although it is not often possible to follow many people. Dorothy Daniels and so many of the suburban poor appear in the public record when a journalist interviewed them, when they testified in court, or when they staged a protest. Then they disappear from archival sources. Other kinds of characters appear throughout. They include the major defense contractors like Republic Aviation and Grumman, which dominated employment on Long Island. Suburban neighborhoods like the Carleton Park subdivision in Central Islip, or Wyandanch, New Cassel, and Roosevelt (figure A.2) serve as settings to see how poverty affected places. Homeowner civic associations in these places, such as the Progressive Civic Association of New Cassel (PCANC), also recur because they help us see how suburbanites wavered between blaming exclusion and exploitation as the main culprit of their suburban woes

The first chapter begins before World War II, when "poverty" was the norm across Long Island's working class. It then moves into wartime, when federal spending temporarily reduced poverty. Before 1940, a diverse cohort of low-wage workers serviced the industrial elite and affluent white-collar commuters who made Long Island one of the nation's most unequal places. But war changed all that. Unlimited labor demand and an avalanche of federal dollars had social-democratic effects. It pulled the suburban poor out of their service jobs, compelled the state to supply childcare, and forced the federal government to dismantle discriminatory hiring practices that excluded Black southerners from industrial employment. But it was an egalitarian moment, made possible by total war, not policy intended to end inequality.

Chapters 2 and 3 analyze what the American welfare state evolved into after the war. Using relative poverty as a measuring stick, chapter 2 proves how suburban prosperity depended on poverty. The forms federal spending took—Cold War defense contracts and federal mortgage insurance programs—offered unprecedented living standards for working-class Americans, but it left key social needs unmet. Private employers stepped in with day laborers, domestic workers, and sweatshop operatives toiling in taxpaying suburban factories. Employers used racial and gender hierarchies, inscribed in labor law and social policy, to disproportionately fill these jobs with southern Black migrants, women, and other marginal workers. The jobs paid too little to make it on Long Island, forcing disproportionately non-white and female Long Islanders into relative poverty.

Chapter 3 looks at shelter poverty, or housing costs that deprive people of other needs. The chapter argues this was a consequence of the FHA mortgage program and its failure to house all in the postwar period. Here I use property records to show how homeowners and speculative landlords took legal properties, converted them into informal housing units, and hid their activities from local authorities. I also use the four Long Island hamlets under study—Wyandanch and Central Islip in Suffolk County, Roosevelt and New Cassel in Nassau County (figure A.2)—to demonstrate how racial housing segregation enabled informalization on a large scale. The chapter reveals how the goal of securing shelter through homeownership failed not only the uncreditworthy, but also homeowners exposed to the gaps built into the racist and income-dependent mortgage system.

Beginning in chapter 3, the book shifts to how the ideology of suburban exceptionalism obscured the roots of poverty. This starts in chapter 3, which analyzes the politics surrounding informal housing. Using local records of civic association meetings and government agencies, the chapter shows how both Black and white homeowners decried housing segregation for concentrating the poor in their midst. They demanded local government redistribute the poor across Long Island. But they proved unable to address the poor's housing needs, goad local officials into enforcing housing laws, or challenge the power of landlords. Their efforts revealed how they misplaced their focus on housing segregation. Homeowner activists attacked the means and not the source of exploitation, the lack of affordable housing for all.

Chapter 4 explores how civil rights struggles for fair employment collided with major defense contract cancellations on Long Island in the 1960s. Defense officials defended the cuts on the grounds that Long Island's strong economy could absorb laid-off workers and withstand the job losses. But cuts forced civil rights activists to narrow their demands from fair hiring, to promotions, and finally to shielding Black workers from layoffs. Defense workers meanwhile tried to save their jobs, demanding federal contracts serve civilian, rather than military purposes. The cuts came anyway, revealing the weakness of the American welfare state in the suburbs. Jobs, already vulnerable to the vagaries of war, were sacrificed in the belief that the suburbs were prosperous without federal intervention. Ultimately, contract cancellations worsened inequality and blunted the efforts to improve the job prospects of Black suburbanites.

Chapters 5 and 6 address antipoverty measures that touched Long Island. Chapter 5 focuses on President Lyndon Johnson's War on Poverty. At the local level, the poverty war aligned with the premises of the national project: that poverty stemmed from isolation and a lack of skills necessary to compete in the affluent economy. Repeated policy failures on Long Island pushed local politicians further. By the late 1960s, Nassau County officials embraced a job guarantee program. But federal officials, wedded to the idea of suburbs as exceptionally prosperous, denied the program needed funding. Chapter 6 meanwhile investigates the emerging consensus of "concentrated" poverty in the late 1960s and early 1970s. Proponents who viewed poverty as a problem of place, that is people stuck in cities far from suburban jobs and public tax dollars, looked to disperse the poor into Long Island so suburbanites shouldered their "fair share" of poverty's burden. Their efforts proved the problem rested in federal institutions governing jobs and housing, not the ways segregation distributed resources. And they confronted Black and working-class homeowners, already burdened with poverty in their midst, high taxes for poorly funded schools, and property value instability, who thwarted the public housing proposals. It is the most direct example of suburban exceptionalism confronting the reality of suburban exploitation.

The final chapter follows the themes from the postwar years into the twenty-first century. It illustrates how contemporary suburban poverty originated in the postwar years, accelerating as labor laws have weakened, federal spending produces fewer jobs, and federal support for housing receded. Antipoverty politics and policy proposals are still strikingly similar to the postwar period too. Policymakers still focus on segregation over affordable housing, and how to keep prosperity going rather than creating the jobs Long Islanders need. The chapter makes the case that Long Island's history provides us a template to draw from in order to confront the looming challenges of the twenty-first century.

# 1

# The Future Detroit of the East

## *From Residential to Industrial Suburbia*

James Baxter was born in 1913, in Aiken, South Carolina, then known as the "Queen of Winter Resorts." America's industrial elite used Aiken as one of their many leisure colonies along the Eastern Seaboard, and they needed people to care for their vacation homes. James recalled that Aiken's jobs carried "prestige," even for the bellhops, waiters, or carriage boys, because you were "not digging a ditch, you were not plowing a mule. It was a very good way to make a good living and at least be decent." But James aspired to a better life. He left Aiken and struck out on his own when he turned fourteen, making his way to Long Island. The Burtons, a wealthy family who vacationed in Aiken but called Long Island's Gold Coast their main home, recruited him to care for their horses. James traveled north from South Carolina to Penn Station, then hopped on the Long Island Rail Road to Westbury. James found a place to stay in New Cassel, a tiny bit of unincorporated land just outside the formal boundaries to some of America's wealthiest suburban villages. Though James hoped to earn good money, his father passed away in 1928. After that, James wired most of his earnings to support his family in South Carolina. As he recalled years later, there was still enough to eat and sleep: "in those days, you did not need a lot of money."[1]

James Baxter's story reflected that of millions in the early twentieth century. He was among the one in six southern Black migrants who moved directly to northern and western suburbs during the first Great Migration.[2] And there he joined many foreign- and US-born white people likewise searching for work and housing in the sprawling suburbs of New York City. Collectively, they formed a suburban working class. But they did not fit the stereotype of early-twentieth-century suburbanites, those commuters living "residential parks," the bucolic subdivisions built around private leisure, family life, and union with nature.[3] Instead, the suburban working class labored in those subdivisions, its country clubs, nearby vacation spots, Gilded-Age estates, or the farms in between. They dug the foundations for Long Island's Tudor houses, laundered suburban sheets, served steak dinners, tended to estate gardens, and picked vegetables on suburban truck farms. They came to Long Island looking for work.

But Long Island's working class did not benefit from the bounties they produced. James Baxter survived on little. In his time, the line between working class and poor, or unemployed and employed was thin and blurry. Seasonal changes led to layoffs. Construction booms went bust. New migrants undercut wages. Employers further depressed pay by drawing lines between them, exploiting racial hierarchies to sort Italian, Polish, Irish, and African American suburbanites into occupational niches. This inflated the labor supply in particular job categories, reinforcing racial disparities between working-class people. Baxter was a horse groom, or "stable boy," for this reason: Black men rarely got jobs inside estates. But the suburban job market offered little upward mobility anyway. As he remembered, neighbors and friends "were working on estates . . . you had to either work for Hicks Nursery or on an estate or farm. And the coal yard. That was all."[4] In a suburban economy based on imported private wealth, where one earned a living mattered above all. Long Island's commuters frolicked in a suburban playground. Long Island's working class just got by there.

But poverty is always historically specific, and working-class suburbanites found a safety valve from deprivation in early-twentieth-century Long Island. Baxter's new hometown, New Cassel, was one such place. As the residential parks and Gilded-Age estates spread across Long Island, so too did the legal tools to keep them exclusive, including village incorporation, restrictive covenants, and land-use laws, not to mention the escalating prices that followed. But in an era without reliable or affordable roads, trains, or trollies, suburban workers needed housing near their jobs. Cramped apartments near railroad tracks or behind suburban downtowns offered one source, albeit at high cost and in dilapidated conditions. Unincorporated places like New Cassel offered another source: suburban refuges from the harsh vicissitudes of wage work, places where they could buy some property and supplement their meager incomes with vegetables, a renter, or self-built improvements.[5] These havens could keep working people out of poverty. They existed because middle-class suburbs hugged railroad stations, farmers sold off extra land to small-time developers, and the rich lobbied against infrastructure to preserve their pastoral landscapes. They left unincorporated areas like New Cassel untouched by residential park development.

Suburban poverty was time-specific, too. World War II completely transformed Long Island's service economy, offering the potential to radically redraw the divide between the suburban haves and have-nots. From 1940 to 1945, 2.6 billion federal dollars (roughly $37 billion as measured in 2021 dollars) flowed to Long Island, turning tiny recreation-oriented airplane shops into industrial behemoths, and farmland into factories abutting residential subdivisions.[6] A sudden need for 100,000 workers forced publicly subsidized employers to transform day laborers, butchers, chauffeurs, horse grooms, and maids into factory workers. The insatiable appetite for labor compelled federal and state officials to mandate fair employment, placing Black workers into the same factory jobs as European-descended Long Islanders. Labor demand also forced the state to cover childcare needs. The "arsenal of democracy," as President Roosevelt called America's war machine, felt like social democracy at the local level. Full employment nudged the state toward supplying social goods and guaranteeing universal access to decent work. The war pulled James Baxter into a "different type of job." His employer, A. G. Bostick, drove him to Grumman Aircraft Corporation, where he would weld airplanes until the end of the war. While he continued to feed Bostick's horses, "it got so that it was too much so I told them to get somebody else to do it."[7] Suburban industrialization, in other words, enabled him to quit the stable for higher pay and better hours.

Baxter's story, like the narrative that follows, demonstrates the local effects of what John Maynard Keynes called the "Grand Experiment:" the public spending spree unleashed by World War II. Defense dollars flooded the entire country, tilting power toward workers and doing more to close the nation's income gap than any other factor in the mid-twentieth century.[8] Long Island, arguably the nation's most unequal place, suddenly became egalitarian. As factories blossomed alongside railroad suburbs, estates, country clubs, and farms, industrial suburbia supplanted service suburbia. Employment opportunity shifted away from the private subdivisions of wealthy commuters due to the insatiable appetite for labor from state-subsidized military contractors. A tight labor market empowered the new drive to smash racial hierarchies and pull everyone into decent work. Full employment severed the ties between working for a living and poverty.

Long Island's mid-twentieth-century history is thus a case study of poverty's contingency, of how federal spending unleashed the potential to end it. But only the potential: military contracts left housing untouched, and total war caused a temporary wage hike, not a durable policy-led pay increase. Long Islanders looked to bend federal spending toward domestic and social needs, to place state-induced economic growth on a more permanent footing. But they had little power to do so. This is a story of possibility, of how Washington transformed America's wealthiest and most unequal suburb into a place where low wages and poverty might disappear.

## The Gold Coast and the *Sub*-urban Economy

The story begins in the early twentieth century because that's when Long Island as a suburb, an adjunct to New York City, first took shape. Private wealth flowed outward from Gotham, forming a suburban service economy with jobs in domestic work (then called domestic "service"), construction, estate maintenance, and farm labor. These jobs attracted locals, New York City transplants, European immigrants, and southern African Americans. Together they formed Long Island's working class. They labored in the suburbs, serving those who, aside from the farmers, only lived there. While they spared themselves the grueling and monotonous factory work in America's industrial cities, they nonetheless performed backbreaking tasks for suburban property owners. Farmers plucked laborers from the padrone system of Italian immigrants or Black migrant streams along the Atlantic Seaboard; estate managers imported experienced British domestic workers (then called "servants") for lavish parties; Polish gardeners tended the estate flora; Black workers only got part-time gigs cleaning the chimneys and stables. Employers took advantage of existing racial hierarchies elsewhere and reified race on Long Island. They divided workers by race, squeezed them for extra profit, and centered local discourse around race. But precarious work threatened all working-class Long Islanders with prolonged unemployment, low pay, and poverty. Their laboring lives reflected an economy where the suburban have-nots served the suburban haves.

One could see Long Island's working class by taking the same journey James Baxter did, buying a train ticket in New York City's Penn Station. Or perhaps doing what many middle-class suburbanites did on a brisk Sunday, driving along one of the delightful parkways planned by Long Island State Parks commissioner Robert Moses. After all, Long Island's suburban origins date back to the late nineteenth and early twentieth centuries, when new transportation networks and market demand drew the island into New York City's orbit. Long Island's political elites successfully preserved political independence from the city's municipal expansion in 1899 when the eastern part of Queens County broke off to form Nassau County. But the new county, and its eastern counterpart, Suffolk, had already become embedded in the burgeoning metropolitan economy. Like the urban fringes of Detroit, Philadelphia, Chicago, and Los Angeles, mass urbanization spilled beyond municipal borders at the turn of the century. Residential and industrial development pushed New York's perishable food supply beyond city limits to the benefit of Long Island farmers.[9] Robert Moses and Long Island Rail Road president Austin Corbin opened the island's sandy beaches, quiet harbors, rolling hills, and quaint woodlands to resort and suburban subdivision development. Collectively, they made Long Island into an appendage of New York City. Leisure retreats dotted Long Island's South Shore beaches, commuter suburbs hugged its rail lines, exclusive enclaves nestled along the North Shore inlets, and farms prospered in between.

An early-twentieth-century train from Penn Station would likely be filled with white-collar commuters and weekend vacationers, or an industrial titan riding to their Gold Coast mansion. The wealth commuters accrued in stocks or the income they earned in high-paying jobs encouraged a labor market in retail, the building trades, public works construction, domestic service, and agriculture. Nearly half of Long Island residents worked in these fields as of 1930, and they were the primary jobs available in Nassau and Suffolk Counties.[10] Because imported wealth from New York City or large landholdings produced Long Island's labor market, there was little vertical mobility. The well-to-do lived or leisured on Long Island but labored in the city. Those without means lived and labored on Long Island. The latter were a diverse lot. Native-born white people who descended from Long Island's early English and Dutch settlers left the ailing coastal and agricultural industries to try and earn more in the suburban economy. Foreign-born immigrants from abroad or New York City and African Americans making their way north during the Great Migration made the direct jump into suburban service or farm work. Not all immigrants labored in suburbia. German Americans often commuted to the city for example, using the suburb as a steppingstone to property ownership and middle-class status. But most, including some 9,000 Irish and Polish migrants, along with 13,000 Italian and southern Black migrants as of 1930, toiled as laborers on the estates, farms, and road projects across Long Island.

If you were anyone influential riding this early-twentieth-century commuter rail, your likely destination was a lavish party, an intimate soiree, or at least a day of gawking at Long Island's mansions. America's industrial elite shaped Long Island's labor market more than any other group. Long Island was arguably the country's most unequal place because it was the most gilded of the gold coasts ringing America's cities in the early twentieth century. Industrial titans constructed country estates in Pennsylvania's Montgomery County, Rhode Island's Newport, even New York's Westchester County, just north of the Bronx. But Long Island's Gold Coast outdid them all. Here,

Gilded-Age elites gobbled up property and took the reins of local public power, turning Long Island into a private playground of resorts, golf clubs, horse tracks, and ostentatious mansions.[11] Gotham's rich constructed nearly one thousand French châteaus, English castles, and Italian villas across Nassau and Suffolk Counties. By 1937, the region housed fourteen of America's twenty-five wealthiest families. On the South Shore, running from Nassau County's eastern border out to Montauk, sat the mansions of financier August Belmont, sugar refiner Henry Havemeyer, and railroad manager William K. Vanderbilt. On Long Island's North Shore, over six hundred estates stretched from the Queens border into Suffolk County in near-uninterrupted sequence, all at least fifty acres large. Immortalized in F. Scott Fitzgerald's *The Great Gatsby*, Long Island's Gold Coast included the Morgans, Hearsts, Sages, Astors, Woolworths, Guggenheims, Fricks, Goulds, and Fords. They mingled at seventy-one private clubs, golfed among the nation's greatest concentration of courses, and participated in every conceivable social activity—including dinner parties, fox hunts, polo matches, and automobile races along America's first private highway.[12]

The estates and private clubs formed an "estate economy." It was a collection of complex tasks to support the estate structures and rituals of elite life. Even a modest country house was a small business with ten or twenty employees tending the gardens, bedrooms, pantries, children, and horses, not to mention the occasional mason or florist. The largest estates employed hundreds. The two thousand–acre "Caumsett" estate of Chicago department store heir Marshall Field employed over four hundred people. They managed the dairy farm, stables, cottages, athletic facilities, power plant, yacht dock, and several houses. Caumsett had its own business office to organize the daily work routines and approve new building contracts and employee transportation, among other duties. Most estates were not as complex, but all relied on a stable workforce both within and beyond their grounds.[13]

Given the size and needed maintenance of Long Island's estates, working-class Long Islanders could depend on estate work for steady jobs. Some came with housing and utilities included. Ella Russell, daughter of southern Black migrants from North Carolina, grew up in a six-room cottage on the Hewlett family estate. Her father and mother took care of the household duties for a small salary, but free housing—and a small pigpen and garden—increased their living standards.[14] Similarly, Gold Coast real estate developer Lorenzo B. Smull hired Hubert Goode's parents to serve in his household, wiring money to the Goodes in Raleigh, North Carolina so they could move to Port Washington in 1917. They lived upstairs on Smull's estate. Hubert's father cooked for the Smulls while his mother was a housekeeper and nanny. Young Hubert and his sister helped around the house and yard.[15] But estate work had its drawbacks. Estate employees were at the whim of their employer, who owned their housing, slept nearby, and demanded they cater to every whim. As Hubert Goode remembered, "whoever's in charge tells you what they want you to do."[16]

Because estate work was deeply hierarchical and owners had total control, their biases determined who did what jobs. Domestic service was long considered degrading work, though one's status depended on their estate task. In-house caretaking and skilled construction labor was relatively prestigious; chauffeuring or horse grooming less so; at-will "live-out" (as opposed to "live-in") landscaping or laundry jobs were at the bottom. With a deep historical precedent to segment these occupations along racial and gender lines, and in an era when upper-class prejudices gained legitimacy as "race science," estate owners preferred certain ethnic groups for particular tasks over others. Their choices produced stark racial and gender hierarchies in opportunity, status, and pay within the estate economy, equivalent to widespread practices in the industrial working world.[17] Northern Europeans served as in-house butlers, chauffeurs, and housekeepers. Italian and Polish immigrants tended to the gardens and estate facades. Black workers labored along the periphery, with the horses or doing contract jobs when estates needed extra help. The wealthiest estate owners sometimes avoided immigrant and Black workers altogether. Utilities and railroad magnate John E. Aldred filled his "Ormston" fief with British workers to maintain the thirty-seven-room, fourteen-bath mansion, two gatehouses, double cottage, and small farm. Most, though, spared expenses with cheaper immigrant labor from eastern and southern Europe, and Black workers at the margins. Alec Sucilsky, a Polish immigrant and longtime employee on the Harry F. Guggenheim "Falaise" estate, recalled how Polish and Italian men labored on the huge ninety-acre estate, but the only "colored help" was "around the horses . . . they didn't live on the estate."[18]

On the train to a Gold Coast enclave like Glen Cove or Locust Valley, you would have passed a dozen stations, all with smaller but idyllic Tudors and Colonials lining streets along the tracks. These railroad suburbs served as another important source of jobs. Large estates played an outsized role in the economy, but estate jobs were few and far between. Most working-class Long Islanders cobbled together livelihoods serving the burgeoning suburban middle class or vacationing New York City residents. Suburban residential housing tracts sprouted up in the early twentieth century, hitting their peak during the 1920s speculative boom when Nassau was the nation's fastest-growing county. On a given Sunday, a *Brooklyn Eagle* subscriber could pull out an entire fifty page "Long Island Section" of the paper. It was really a series of real estate ads targeting the newspaper's mostly white-collar readers living in Brooklyn but longing for more land and social cachet. The section listed railroad costs and timetables, assuring white-collar readers they could still reach their jobs in downtown Brooklyn or Midtown Manhattan. Then it had full page spreads of Long Island's three-dozen residential parks, carefully designed streets and Tudor homes influenced by England's Garden City movement, often linked to country clubs, golf courses, pools, and waterways.[19]

Real estate developers sparked a construction and consumption revolution on Long Island, and they needed an army of diggers, masons, maids, and waiters to build it. They erected facsimiles of what large estate owners enjoyed: smaller country clubs, one-time landscaping projects, and houses that didn't require a small business enterprise to maintain. As such, they used cheaper and more flexible workers—day laborers, seasonal resort cooks, building contractors, live-out rather than live-in domestic workers. Facsimiles paid less and compelled suburban workers to constantly hustle for a living.

Live-in versus live-out domestic work exemplified the divide between estate and residential park jobs. A live-in domestic worker could conceivably depend on year-round work. Live-out domestic workers competed for daily gigs. This had its advantages, including some autonomy and choice in employers, hours, and days off. But earning enough depended on stringing enough jobs together, and the large 1920s suburban homes took a long time to clean. Vacuums and washing machines only elevated cleanliness standards, threatening the time and money advantages of live-out work altogether.[20] As one Long Island domestic worker complained in 1933, work was "drudgery," requiring "all day going, cooking and serving, cleaning, wax floor, wash windows inside and out, oftimes [*sic*] expected to wash walls, scrub porch," and in "winter attend [to the] furnace."[21] And domestic workers just as often took work home. Marjorie Biddle remembered how her neighbors "took in laundry . . . just for private people cause all these rich people had initials on their napkins and things."[22] Overall, while no comprehensive wage data exists, live-out domestic workers earned less than their estate counterparts. In the Roaring Twenties, monthly wages for live-in domestic workers ranged from $90 to $150. During the Depression, live-out domestic workers took home only $40 per month.[23]

Domestic work proved relatively stable, at least compared to the inconsistent jobs otherwise available. Outside domestic service, men especially wore many hats on estates, like chauffeur, butler, chimney sweeper, or maintenance worker.[24] Other times, they navigated between construction jobs during boom times and estate work when building slacked. Contractors segmented these jobs racially—builders tended to hire Italian or Polish laborers for housing construction, and Black workers to dig home or road foundations. Localized building booms produced a few months or even years of work, though new migrants undercut wages and reduced future employment prospects. In the Gold Coast City of Glen Cove, where some of the world's wealthiest people lived—including the Morgans, Pratts, and Phipps—contractors imported Polish and Italian immigrant labor in the early twentieth century. But in the 1920s, new contractors muscled their way into the business, recruiting Black southerners at lower wage rates. As locals lamented, the new workers bloated the local labor supply and aggravated racial division within the city. The Depression only further stoked animosity when unemployed laborers competed for dwindling estate jobs.[25]

Early-twentieth-century suburbia's job of last resort was visible from your train ride *between* the stations: backbreaking farm labor. Land speculation gobbled up Long Island's farms. Between 1875 and 1930, Nassau County farmland dropped from over 90,000 acres to 23,000 acres. But farmers nonetheless deployed new machines, fertilizers, and growing techniques to increase strawberry, cauliflower, cabbage, cucumber, pea, and potato yields. And although Long Island farmers couldn't underbid other chicken farmers on the East Coast, they transformed Long Island into the nation's premier duck producer. Farmers needed humans to harvest their crops and raise their fowl. Like their counterparts elsewhere in the Northeast, they tapped into the seasonal stream of Italian-born laborers that fanned outward from New York City in the early twentieth century. By the 1920s and 1930s, they recruited Black laborers who followed the year-round harvest rhythm from New England to Florida.[26]

Farm labor's seasonal nature attracted both regional migrants and locals in need of extra cash, a kind of early-twentieth-century Uber rideshare gig. The Nash family, who traveled from Virginia to eastern Long Island's Riverhead in 1926, straddled the agricultural and service economies, cutting potatoes and harvesting the spuds during the spring and summer, then cleaning houses during the winter.[27] Clarence Phillips, a Gold Coast cook, janitor, and estate gardener whose employment prospects dried up in the 1930s, switched to farm work. He moved seventy miles east from Port Washington, a Gold Coast estate town, to Mattituck, earning "3¢ a bushel for picked potatoes . . . workin' on a farm down in the eastern end of the island, on Sound Avenue."[28] Adeline Fischer, a young girl living out in Mattituck in the 1930s, recalls how she and her siblings picked potatoes and beans to help the family through the Depression.[29] Even in more suburbanized Nassau County, Italian immigrants relied on farm labor to survive. When the Mancuso family patriarch of Bethpage passed away in the early 1930s, the three Mancuso boys and their mother resorted to picking bushels of fruit and potatoes on nearby farms. Son Joseph Mancuso complained that the work "paid practically nothing!"[30]

On a train ride from Penn Station, you would not only have passed what made Long Island an iconic early-twentieth-century suburb—giant mansions, green country clubs, tidy Tudors in residential parks—but also those who made the suburbs possible. From the train window you could see domestic workers, ditchdiggers, farm laborers, and gardeners. They performed necessary labor, enabling those who derived their livelihood in New York City to enjoy the private property and social comforts available on Long Island. But the enterprises also depended on low wages. Seasonal rhythms of work, periodic influxes of new competitors, and economic downturns only intensified instability and low wages. Long Island's working class and "poor" were indistinguishable; the employed were virtual paupers who could only avoid real pauperization by moving to another job. Employers meanwhile further depressed wages by exploiting diverse migrant streams according to their own racist beliefs about which groups excelled in given jobs. They placed Black Long Islanders closer to the pauper side of the spectrum, a division that gave race its local salience.

## Finding a Place to Live

Low-wage workers may have surprised riders on the rail trip from Penn Station, but so would many of the houses you could see from the window. You might catch a glimpse of a massive multi-acre estate behind thick shrubs. Neat residential parks encircled suburban train stations. But tenements also hugged the tracks, something an urban rider would have recognized from Manhattan or any other industrial city. The train also whizzed by clapboard bungalows and self-built shacks erected on otherwise undeveloped land, resembling the "gap-toothed" urban fringe of the developing world.[31] Working-class Long Islanders inhabited the last two housing types prior to World War II. Tenements further impoverished working-class Long Islanders, but the small homes on the outskirts offered solace from the exhausting world of low-wage labor. The reach of suburban governance distinguished the two choices. Village incorporation spread like wildfire across Long Island in the early twentieth century. Village status protected residential suburbs as elite and middle-class enclaves but forced working-class people into expensive and dangerous living arrangements. But village boundaries reached only so far, leaving wide expanses open to small-time property ownership, self-building, and unregulated land uses. Poverty then was contextual: in the early twentieth century, whether suburban housing impoverished or stabilized one's life depended on its location.

Most working-class Long Islanders lived in suburban tenements, despite their appalling conditions. Tenements resolved a contradiction rooted in the regulated landscape of residential parks. Long hours and on-call work compelled workers to live near residential parks and millionaire estates. But developers and suburban residents deployed new legal tools to prohibit working-class housing. Any glance at the restrictive covenants on individual properties and residential parks reveals what Robert Fogelson calls "bourgeois nightmares": middle-class fears that, in one way or another, related to poverty. Laws and contracts sold Long Island's residential enclaves as "cleansed" of the poor and all the instability poverty entailed. There were prohibitions on the sale or lease to all but "Caucasians." Covenants restricted subdividing property and prohibited "undesirable" land uses.[32] In addition to using covenants to protect individual subdivisions, affluent Long Islanders also incorporated their suburbs as villages or cities. Incorporation served two purposes: to enclose the tax base and to regulate land use, building quality, and housing occupancy. Seventy-three incorporated villages formed across Long Island by 1930. Long Island led an incorporation frenzy that gripped suburban areas nationwide, from Chicago's DuPage County to Southern California. In all places, incorporation looked to preserve socioeconomic homogeneity, defending bucolic havens from urbanization and the poverty it entailed.[33]

Armed with new municipal powers, Long Island's villages passed codes to regulate both structures and land use. But given the intense time demands of service work and the high cost and inefficiency of suburban transportation before World War II, suburban workers had to find housing within a space that legally denied them shelter. Units that predated codes, or buildings that village inspectors quietly ignored served as two sources of housing. Property owners took advantage of the exclusionary mechanisms to exploit people in need of housing, leasing whatever space they could. Cots converted kitchens into makeshift bedrooms; outhouses served as restrooms for forty or more people. A 1934 housing survey of Bennington Park in Freeport Village revealed that of 213 dwellings, only fifty-five had sewer lines and only forty-two had gas stoves. Owners converted storefronts into apartments, as figure 1.1 shows, and residents of these "flats" drew water from a hydrant near the privy, relying on a single coal kitchen stove to heat multiple units.[34] In the Banks Avenue section of Rockville Centre, property owners converted former barns, morgues, cellars, and storefronts into dwelling spaces. Most incorporated villages had domestic enclaves, from "the Hill" in Hempstead to "Long Branch Road" in Glen Cove. In these districts, families survived without insulation

FIGURE 1.1. "Bennington Park." Rear view of building at 132 to 138 East Sunrise Highway, in the Village of Freeport. Courtesy of Freeport Historical Society and Museum, New York Heritage Digital Collections.

or water during the winter, and sewage overflowed into wells, threatening the health of those who drank from them.[35]

These units were not cheap, especially because workers were stuck near their jobs, producing isolated housing markets that were sometimes just miles apart. Average monthly rents ranged from $18 to $20 in Freeport's Bennington Park, while similar housing rented for $27 to $37 just six miles north in "the Hill" section of Hempstead Village. But domestic workers could not simply move from Hempstead to Freeport, a four-mile trek, unless they could find a new job in Freeport. And when the typical domestic worker earned only $40 per month on average, many had to rent their kitchens, or even beds, out to others despite the consequences to health and housing quality.[36] High costs translated to profits, however, encouraging longtime working-class suburbanites to exploit demand. Social workers noted that earlier migrations among foreign-born Europeans and their slightly better economic circumstances led to higher homeownership rates compared to Black residents. In Inwood, an unincorporated hamlet nestled among affluent incorporated villages in Nassau County's extreme southwest, former Italian homeowners in the swampy "Frog Hollow" neighborhood rented their housing to incoming

Black tenants. Southern Black migrants lived in most of the units, but they owned less than a quarter of the single-family homes in Frog Hollow. Overcrowding, meanwhile, further impoverished Black tenants while cesspools overflowed, flooding basements and producing open sewage pits.[37]

While more fortunate suburbanites decried the tenements near their residential parks, incorporated villages did little to improve the housing. Villages first adopted building codes in the 1920s to establish safety and structural standards, but they applied to new construction, not existing units. None adopted housing codes governing occupancy or the conduct of owners and tenants until after 1945.[38] These enclaves, largely sheltering domestic workers, only faced legal action when villages deemed units were in disrepair. Condemnation disrupted occupants' lives and didn't solve tenants' problems either. When Rockville Centre Village forced landlords in the Banks Avenue section to renovate, property owners either raised rents to offset the repairs or evicted tenants. The displaced moved into overcrowded units nearby. Glen Cove officials chose to ignore housing problems "to discourage colored families from coming to Glen Cove." The affluent near Inwood preferred the low-tax route of personal septic tanks to public sewer lines, despite the clear health benefits of sewers to Black residents in Frog Hollow.[39] Ultimately, homeowners, ensconced in their covenanted residential parks or estates, and local governments, with little power or money, tolerated and abetted the conditions. Only charities or housing reformers decried the dangers and advocated public housing. But public housing wasn't practical until federal intervention after the war.

Unincorporated land offered alternative spaces for cheap property ownership and self-building that could shield people from poverty.[40] Wide expanses of land sat beyond the villages hugging Long Island's rail stations and shorelines. One could not build just anywhere. Farms made up the majority of open space, New York State managed three massive mental hospitals, and there were still plenty of golf courses, hunting grounds, and polo fields scattered about for the wealthy to play. But with cheap land and little regulation, uneven development spread between farms, railroad depots, and speculative subdivisions. As Becky Nicolaides and Andrew Wiese eloquently document, this underdeveloped land along the urban fringe offered working-class people, Black and white, a chance to buy property, build their own homes, and supplement their meager incomes with small gardens or rental units.[41] Working-class property ownership occurred in two ways: failed middle-class speculative subdivisions and the rare entrepreneur targeting working-class Long Islanders. Three of the hamlets mentioned in the introduction, New

Cassel, Roosevelt, and Wyandanch, exemplified the working-class enclaves that shielded people from poverty in the early twentieth century.

New Cassel, the unincorporated hamlet where horse groom James Baxter lived, was one of these places. Existing records date to a small community of formerly enslaved people in the 1700s, though no doubt Native Americans preceded them. In the next century, farms proliferated, and speculators made a few attempts at suburban housing. One builder, looking to attract German immigrants, coined the hamlet's name. By the early twentieth century, incorporated villages and estates surrounded the unincorporated area. Old Westbury, one of the country's wealthiest places, was to the north. The railroad commuter hub Westbury Village was to the west. Farms in Hicksville bordered New Cassel's eastern edge. New Cassel was nestled amidst Long Island's major economic sectors. Some local elites, like William W. Cocks, child of old Long Island money and longtime politician, opened the area to homebuilding for Italian immigrants and southern Black migrants. He bought three hundred lots in New Cassel through tax defaults, claiming that his property investments were "more to help my tenants than myself," though his rentals and land sales earned him a pretty penny.[42] But here, working-class Long Islanders like James Baxter found relatively decent housing near all sorts of job opportunities. Baxter could walk north to Frank Burton's stables, and his later gigs with George Edward Kenton and A. G. Bostick were only a bit further east, in Jericho. His neighbors did live-out domestic work in Westbury and Old Westbury, performed farm work on Hicks Nursery, the florist of Long Island's millionaires, or found seasonal work on Hicksville potato farms.[43]

Speculators intended New Cassel to be an affordable enclave; builders didn't have the same plan for Roosevelt, an unincorporated area five miles south. At the turn of the twentieth century, property speculators eyed sparsely settled land north of Freeport, one of Long Island's bustling South Shore railroad suburbs. These entrepreneurs, including Arthur Whitehouse, Charles Edwards, and Edward Uhe, named the area after the popular Republican president. They also controlled every aspect of Roosevelt's early suburbanization. All three sat on the hamlet's board of trade, Roosevelt's utility company, and the school district board. They also had their own subdivided lots to sell. While they successfully constructed sidewalks, sewers, and power lines, Roosevelt remained isolated from commuting links to New York City.[44] In 1909, Uhe led an automobile protest to the Long Island Rail Road headquarters, demanding a new rail line for Roosevelt's fifty or so commuters. The effort failed, though a trolley line did eventually run through Roosevelt's main corridor, and Uhe's ads claimed that his empty plots "in a few years will be worth double present prices."[45] The dream didn't pan out, and Uhe's "Roosevelt Manor" subdivision, along with the dozen or so others in Roosevelt, periodically appeared on tax sale lists.[46] But this middle-class failure turned into working-class success. During the 1930s and 1940s, Irish, Italian, Slavic, Jewish, Portuguese, and African American suburbanites bought properties and homes. With domestic and construction jobs in nearby Freeport, Merrick, and Hempstead as well as a little land to raise chickens or plant a vegetable garden, Roosevelt epitomized the working-class suburb of the pre–World War II era.[47]

Further east in Suffolk County, the unincorporated area of Wyandanch reflected both deliberate efforts for working-class housing and failed middle-class subdivisions. Wyandanch sat on the far western edge of Suffolk County's Pine Barrens, and while the Long Island Rail Road ran through the area since 1842, the poor soil discouraged farmers from cultivating the land. The place didn't even have a uniform name until 1903. But Long Island's resort and estate economy absorbed Wyandanch. A few millionaires, including William K. Vanderbilt and investment banker Herman Baruch (brother of financier and public official Bernard Baruch), constructed estates north of Wyandanch, while local springs encouraged developers to build summer cottages for middle-class vacationers. Real estate speculators hoped for more. Property hustler William Geiger, a rags-to-riches German immigrant, advertised Wyandanch in the general-interest *National Magazine* as a better bet than the stock market. Geiger bought up a huge swath of land, subdivided the property into lots, and hoped to flip them to gullible investors.[48] The boom never happened, and Geiger sold four hundred acres to developer Harry Levey in 1930, who advertised the lots to working-class people.[49] Levey sold to Irish immigrant and Black families, who burned the oak and pine, dug cellars, and constructed their own homes. These residents, numbering only 647 as late as 1949, used Wyandanch's cheap land to supplement their meager incomes from nearby service and farm work. They were also known to scavenge for coal along the Long Island Rail Road tracks.[50]

Though not all could access Long Island's prewar safety valve—only 16 percent of Nassau's and 33 percent of Suffolk's Black residents owned their own homes by 1940—unincorporated areas did offer something in a place and era where low wages limited working-class buying power and the regulatory regime excluded all but the prosperous.[51] Both produced an intense contradiction between wages and housing prices. Working-class suburbanites resolved the contradiction by doubling up in hyper-concentrated village tenements or buying land where property speculation failed and developers targeted low-wage workers. This was sustainable because the tools and will to improve housing were weak and Long Island remained a residential suburb for a small cohort of well-to-do commuters.

## The Suburban Arsenal of Democracy

A train passenger in 1920 might assume Long Island's Beaux Arts mansions and residential parks were like Europe's 1,000-year-old medieval castles or burghs. But the homes had a remarkably short life. Elites lost fortunes in the 1929 stock market crash, ending the Gold Coast era. Residential park developers went bankrupt, middle-class homeowners faced foreclosure, and farm prices dropped to near zero. As it did elsewhere, poverty spiked for those dependent on Long Island's service economy. At the Depression's nadir in early 1933, a fifth of Nassau County workers applied for public emergency relief.[52] But tough times wouldn't last either. America's fledging "welfare" state—federal intervention in the markets people depend on for survival and security—transformed both Long Island and its working-class residents after 1940. Forged in the Depression, and put on overdrive amidst total war, federal spending produced a mass suburban aircraft industry that absorbed Long Island's service sector workers and farm laborers. Unlimited labor demand also strengthened efforts to challenge Long Island's racialized labor market. Put simply, the federal government tipped power toward ordinary Long Islanders, thereby reducing the exploitation responsible for both poverty and the racial disparities among the poor. Long Island then illustrates the radical potential of the state to reduce inequality, end poverty, and redistribute power. But Long Island's wartime transformation also epitomizes the federal approach's limits. War caused the brief respite from poverty, not deliberate state policy with social-democratic goals.

Like it did everywhere else in the country, large-scale federal intervention on Long Island started with the New Deal. And the New Deal's greatest impacts on Long Island, like those elsewhere, came during and after World War II. In the short term, FDR's programs seemed like a "holding operation" on Long Island, sustaining the service economy until the war brought recovery.[53] That is not to say the New Deal did not help working-class people. A 1933 survey of Nassau County families receiving work relief reveals that skilled tradesmen or unskilled workers made up nearly 80 percent of the county's relief workers. A third were foreign born and 7 percent were Black.[54] African Americans in particular depended on public jobs programs: in 1933, public relief programs employed almost 30 percent of Nassau County's Black men.[55] As Black domestic worker Beatrice Nixon recalled, "in Glen Cove, nearly everybody was on the WPA. That's the only work they could get." Her husband, after years of sporadic estate gigs, took Works Progress Administration (WPA) jobs "as long as the Depression lasted, until he could go out and get a job like he wanna, of his own."[56] But the work they performed shored up Long Island's service and leisure economy. Master Builder Robert Moses harnessed federal funding to complete his state parkway network leading to green spaces, an amenity for relatively affluent car owners. The WPA likewise constructed the famous Bethpage State Park golf course, a "public park" for those who could afford to play the sport. And Civil Works Administration workers laid nearly thirteen miles of drainpipes, 296 manholes, 1,300 feet of curb, and over 10,000 square feet of sidewalk between 1934 and 1935.[57] New schools, sewers, and parks poured more concrete for tourists and suburban homeowners when the economy would return to "normal."

But Long Island's estate economy held the seeds to a deeper revolution. Gold Coast elites experimented with early planes among their many leisure pursuits. They carved seven airfields out of Nassau County's Hempstead Plains, held internationally recognized tournaments, and even founded the Aviation Country Club in 1929, an airplane equivalent to the golf, polo, and tennis clubs nearby. Many of the major aviation breakthroughs, including the first transcontinental flight and Lindbergh's trip to Paris, started on Long Island. Gold Coast elites funded Long Island's infant aircraft industry, which remained small, boosted only by World War I defense contracts and the 1920s Lindbergh Boom.[58] It was a craft industry, done in job shops with a small number of skilled workers. These men (all men prior to World War II) designed handmade tools and parts drawn from their own expertise. They assembled parts for an order, moving from one component to another. New York City supplied the craft workers, including Polish, German, and Italian immigrants with backgrounds in Old World metal and woodworking trades.[59] Overall, few Long Islanders labored in aviation prior to World War II. In 1930, Nassau County had only four thousand manufacturing workers in any industry.

The federal government fundamentally changed this leisure-oriented industry when war broke out in Europe and Latin America in the late 1930s. To strengthen the nation's air defense and help allies, the War Department distributed contracts to Long Island firms. Grumman Aircraft Engineering Corporation, founded in 1929 by six men in a garage, won navy contracts. By 1936, the company expanded to a 120-acre site in Bethpage. In neighboring Farmingdale on the Nassau–Suffolk border, Russian expatriate Alexander de Seversky founded the Seversky Aircraft Corporation in 1931. With Army Air Corps contracts, he developed record-breaking military aircraft like the P-35. While the board ousted Seversky in 1938 and reincorporated as the Republic Aircraft Corporation, his early relationship with the army helped the company survive. Other firms, including the Brooklyn's Sperry Gyroscope Company and Fairchild's Ranger Aircraft Engineering Corporation in Farmingdale, powered through the Depression as developers of military instruments and engines.[60]

Early contracts remained small, and neither Grumman nor Republic's workforce exceeded one thousand people. But in May 1940, President Roosevelt requested 50,000 planes a year from American manufacturers. The federal government also reoriented the New Deal apparatus for public works investments and federal contracting to expand the nation's military capacity. The government chose the most expedient route to war mobilization, favoring the industrial heartland and preexisting manufacturers in relatively undeveloped places like Long Island.[61] Grumman and Republic received contracts worth over $2 billion, and federal agencies invested nearly $43 million in plant construction for both firms. With free federal industrial space and stable cost-plus contracts that socialized risk, they churned out thousands of planes, making Long Island the nation's sixth largest military contract recipient during the war. Republic was the Army Air Corps' second largest contractor, producing over 15,000 P-47 Thunderbolts, the first single-engine, single-seat pursuit aircraft.[62] Grumman built thousands of F4F Wildcats, F6F Hellcats, and TBF-1 Avengers for the navy. Around these airframe producers formed a network of subcontractors crafting instruments, flight equipment, and engines, including Sperry, the Ranger Engines division, and Liberty Aircraft Corporation. Long Island was leaving the nation's collection of suburban gold coasts and joining the emerging "gunbelt" of suburban arsenals stretching down the Atlantic Seaboard, across the southern US border, and up the Pacific coast.[63]

Federal investment transformed Long Island's airplane job shops into massive assembly-line plants over acres of former potato fields. They needed thousands of trained factory workers to design, manufacture, and assemble each plane's 100,000 parts. In sparsely settled Texas, rural Michigan, and Southern California, filling factory jobs involved massive migrations and coordinated actions between housing agencies, private builders, and government officials to build whole new cities. On Long Island, a workforce already existed, and several factors compelled firms to employ Long Islanders. Transportation from New York City was limited and difficult. When Grumman and Republic began tapping city residents after 1943, the Long Island Rail Road had to run special trains to their plants, and the trains never matched the shift changes.[64] Public agencies also set labor market boundaries. The navy wanted Grumman to only hire "bona fide residents of Nassau and Suffolk Counties," and a succession of federal agencies, eventually centralized under the War

Manpower Commission (WMC) in April 1942, calculated that Long Island's labor supply matched labor demand, encouraging firms to exhaust local applicants from local United States Employment Service (USES) offices.[65]

With only a small manufacturing employment base (the New York Department of Labor counted about 3,500 industrial workers), contractors had to turn farmers, fishermen, housewives, domestic workers, construction laborers, and high school students into riveters, welders, and assemblers. Local firms depended on federal help once again. The government established new industrial training courses and transformed New Deal–era WPA and National Youth Administration (NYA) offices into defense training programs.[66] Despite the heavy federal hand, firms still controlled who they hired and how they organized production, and racial beliefs about worker aptitudes predominated. Before Pearl Harbor, Grumman refused to hire any German- or Italian-born Americans, while Ranger Engines required citizenship papers dated before 1932. Proof of American birth was difficult for both European immigrants and southern Black migrants, as their births often went unrecorded. Republic, the largest employer in December 1940, demanded all employees be "white, full citizens, aged less than fifty."

When labor shortages hit in 1941 and 1942, employers reduced citizenship rules, and defense companies swiftly accepted European immigrants.[67] The companies hired women over time as well, who accounted for a third of Long Island's overall industrial workforce and reached nearly half in scientific instruments and chemical plants by 1945.[68] Barriers against Black workers did not recede, however. In 1940, Republic employed only one African American, a chauffeur, among the company's 2,400 workers. Republic's public relations director William L. Wilson claimed the company could do little to hire more Black Americans "because of objections from white workers in the plant if Negroes were employed," which would "interfere with efficient production on defense orders."[69]

Despite growing labor shortages, racist beliefs in differing work aptitudes, diligence, and intelligence prevailed. Dismantling the racial hierarchy required directly confronting discrimination. Luckily, a decade of labor-oriented civil rights activism built the foundation for such a movement, which culminated in A. Philip Randolph's famous March on Washington Movement in 1942. The march never happened because President Roosevelt agreed to Randolph's demands, enacting Executive Order 8802, which banned discrimination in the defense industry.[70] Local activist pressure in New York State forced Governor Herbert Lehman to form the Committee on Discrimination in Employment (COD). Together, the New York COD and federal Fair Employment Practices Committee (FEPC) monitored Long Island's defense firms for discriminatory practices. While historians contend these underfunded committees were toothless, their success depended on local labor supplies, office commitment, and firm cooperation.[71]

On Long Island, Black workers found a friend in Edward Lawson, who led the FEPC's local efforts as the committee bounced around different federal agencies during the war. In September 1941, Republic refused to hire William Hendricks, an experienced Black electrical engineer. Hendricks wrote to Lawson, who got him a job, making him Republic's first Black assembly-line worker.[72] It was an incomplete victory, however. Hendricks reported feeling ostracized "because it was unusual for a Black to be seen here," and felt discriminated by "a superior who possibly was afraid that I might aspire for his job." He managed several employees, but they fooled around "shooting oil from pressure cans, throwing towels knotted up at one another and tying cups of water to whirling machines." When Hendricks disciplined them, the company removed personnel from his charge until he managed only one worker. His supervisor justified the decision, saying "no matter how qualified a colored man was, still white men did not want to take the work from him."[73]

Hendricks wrote Edward Lawson again. His coworkers then escalated their harassment. Some believed he was a government spy. (Admittedly, he had been writing letters to government officials blaming "German" elements at Republic for workplace inefficiency.) Pranksters removed the screws and bolts from his chair. Hendricks recalled, "when I sat down, the chair fell apart and I found myself on the floor." Despite his stellar work record, the company transferred him to the methods engineering department and wrote him a reference letter to find work elsewhere. Republic claimed he was "unhappy on the job."[74] Lawson tried negotiating with Republic again, but management feared a hate strike. Lawson then threatened that if the company could not control their employees, "the Army representatives of the War Manpower Commission would see to it that no serious stoppage of work occurred because of the refusal of individuals to work with a Negro," and that "any employee who refuses to continue normal work because of his personal prejudices will be considered disloyal to the Government and not only will be subject to immediate dismissal, but may be prevented from obtaining employment in other industrial establishments engaged in war production."[75] Republic conceded, promoting Hendricks to senior operation sheet writer.

As a duly qualified engineer, Hendricks was an exception to the typical Black Long Islander. Most never even got their foot in the door because training schools screened birth certificates, literacy, and physical health. In this way, companies rejected Black workers while still claiming "nonracial" hiring practices. Domestic worker Myrtle Lebby experienced this firsthand.

A training school refused her because she recently worked in Washington, DC, and therefore failed the local residency requirement. The Freeport National Defense School dropped local resident Arthur Lindsay because a "confidential investigation of his residence, associates, and habits" deemed him unfit to work for the company, despite high marks and good rapport with his teacher.[76] The Freeport school's 425 enrollees in June 1942 had no Black students despite the fact that Freeport Village was one of Long Island's largest Black domestic enclaves.[77] Firms selectively claimed New Deal public programs graduated incompetent workers when Black students attended.[78] Here again, state antidiscrimination agencies played a key role. In this case, New York State's COD forced the Freeport school to reenroll rejected applicants, and by June 1943, the COD and FEPC required that all schools standardize their nonracial admissions criteria and submit to periodic investigations.[79]

After nearly two years, workers and government officials pried Long Island's defense industry open, and their antidiscrimination efforts converged with the unlimited labor demand by mid-war. Between the draft and the over 70,000 people working in defense-related manufacturing, the WMC considered Suffolk County "pretty well drained of applicants." By late 1944, the local USES office estimated there were only one thousand unemployed Long Islanders actively seeking work. Companies knocked on suburban doors to find a theoretical pool of four thousand housewives. They also reduced the regulatory hurdles for noncitizens and erased local residency requirements.[80] In this climate, the FEPC and COD functioned as referral agencies resolving the labor shortage. When five Black women did not receive jobs after graduating from a training school, the FEPC alerted Republic Aviation, who found them jobs as they opened.[81]

As Black Long Islanders got defense jobs, the early antidiscrimination battles diminished in importance. After a year of defending William Hendricks at Republic Aviation, the FEPC backed his dismissal in September 1943. They cited the fact that Republic had hired another Black worker in the tool room and 280 in total. Lawson, Hendrick's previous defender, believed Hendricks suffered from a "very pronounced persecution complex."[82] Hendricks was no longer the key to the FEPC's efforts in a tight labor market. The effects of the combined tight labor market and antidiscrimination enforcement is evident in recorded statistics (table 1.1). While the number of Black workers was relatively small, keep in mind that as late as October 1941, Grumman and Republic, 40 percent of all Long Island's defense jobs, hired a statistically insignificant sixteen Black workers. Three years later, those numbers exponentially jumped. Black workers made up nearly 900 of Grumman's 24,000 workers. At Liberty Aircraft Engines, they reached 5 percent of the workforce.[83] Overall,

TABLE 1.1. Non-white Persons Employed in Twenty-Two Firms among Selected Industries, Nassau and Suffolk Counties, 1942–44

| | *November 1942* | | | *November 1943* | | | *November 1944* | | |
|---|---|---|---|---|---|---|---|---|---|
| | *Total* | *Non-white* | *%* | *Total* | *Non-white* | *%* | *Total* | *Non-white* | *%* |
| **Manufacturing** | 45,276 | 447 | 1.0 | 66,724 | 1,935 | 2.9 | 58,028 | 2,089 | 3.6 |
| Chemical products | | | | 756 | 31 | 4.1 | 681 | 32 | 4.7 |
| Aircraft and parts | 33,473 | 297 | 0.9 | 49,355 | 1,530 | 3.1 | 40,353 | 1,372 | 3.4 |
| Instruments | 8,236 | 130 | 1.6 | 13,292 | 319 | 2.4 | 14,395 | 619 | 4.3 |
| Other | 2,308 | 20 | 0.9 | 833 | 5 | 0.6 | 1,000 | 8 | 0.8 |
| **Non-manufacturing** | 2,757 | 69 | 2.5 | 2,205 | 86 | 3.9 | 2,246 | 137 | 6.1 |
| Transport and utilities | 456 | 9 | 2.0 | 2,000 | 18 | 0.9 | 2,000 | 18 | 0.9 |
| **Total** | 48,033 | 516 | 1.1 | 68,929 | 2,021 | 2.9 | 60,274 | 2,226 | 3.7 |

*Source*: "Labor Market Development Report," June 1943, 59, box 6, folder 271, WC; "Labor Market Developments Report – New York Metropolitan Region," 4, no. 6 (October–November 1944): 37, Box 7, folder 319, WC.

by 1944, Black defense workers represented slightly less than a fifth of Long Island's 1940 Black labor force, compared to the quarter of the white labor force employed in defense manufacturing.[84]

Disparities still existed. Agricultural contractors in the non-manufacturing category kept using Black workers to pick potatoes and other vegetables (table 1.1). Even manufacturing work did not entail equal status on the job. Fairchild's Ranger Engine plant in Farmingdale, Long Island's most intransigent defense plant, employed only one Black woman on the shop floor. A male employee confided to the WMC that despite his industrial training, managers told him, "the only job for Negroes in the plant were those of porters or washers." Another male employee complained that he worked a burring machine but was stuck at a custodian's pay rate.[85] Ranger was the exception because once workers and corporate heads accepted Black employees on the factory floor, they climbed the corporate ladder. Republic categorized 57 percent of their 107 Black employees as skilled or semi-skilled in September 1943. Sperry Gyroscope's Long Island plant placed almost two-thirds of its Black workers in skilled or semi-skilled categories, and only four of the 717 Black employees labored in menial jobs.[86]

The federal plant investments, contracts, and fair hiring agencies offered a "sharp lesson in Keynesianism," to paraphrase economist Joan Robinson.[87]

War mobilization was by no means deliberate Keynesian policy, but Keynes himself noted that the war realized his theory's implications: federal defense spending broke the decade-long economic slump, redistributed income, reallocated resources, and ultimately achieved a more egalitarian society.[88] Keynes didn't say anything about America's hierarchical labor market, but the infinite labor demand gave the efforts to end racism their teeth. Fair employment, reducing discrimination in jobs, needed full employment, jobs available to all, to reduce exploitation at the root of poverty on Long Island. The radical transformation of Long Island's job landscape within a few short years severed the ties between working for a living and struggling for survival. But short-term war needs caused this change, not deliberate policy with long-term horizons.

## "Death in One Hand and Prosperity in the Other"

If you boarded a train from Penn Station in 1943, you would see a very different Long Island from the windows. First, there were new train lines and stations, destined for hulking factories rather than little railroad suburbs. The train would pass scores of machine shops abutting the tracks, churning out rudders, bolts, rubber belts, and leather seats. Your fellow passengers were not white-collar commuters on their way home, but blue-collar assemblers and machinists on their way to work. And these workers commuted in all directions, often just a few miles *within* Nassau and Suffolk Counties to their nearest defense plant. From the train window, you could also see children hurried into local day care centers. A 1943 train ride offered a glimpse into a place transformed by federal spending. Defense contracts pulled Long Island away from its dependence on New York City and into the federal government's orbit. It also compressed wages and empowered workers who no longer depended on the whims of the wealthy for their livelihood. But a Long Island Rail Road passenger would no doubt also notice other less egalitarian changes: a half-dozen workers pouring out of a single-family house near a train station; campers on dusty side-roads; undeveloped lots still fallow. This was what war spending looked like. So, while it felt and looked social democratic, it was a violent perversion of the ideals behind the WPA or the 1937 National Housing Act. Broad-based prosperity was contingent on war, and military production subsumed all other needs. It was what one local journalist later referred to as "death in one hand and prosperity in the other."[89]

When the federal government spent money, it created new jobs. There was nothing more revolutionary than this. It is hard to overstate the impact of these jobs, however temporary, on former service workers. As estate employee John Gregory recalled in an interview, prior to the war

> there was nothing but farm and estate. That's where most of the people worked. You didn't have the factories or all the developments you have today, you know. That's just started from World War II . . . in 1940 or so, when Grumman and different factories opened up, a lot of these men went. The younger fellows were drawn into services, like jobs with the town or the county, and the others went to Grumman and what not.[90]

Adeline Fischer, the young girl who picked potatoes in Mattituck during the Depression, remembers how her mother almost starved the family because she refused welfare during the '30s. Her father's job at Grumman was truly a "God send . . . the best time of our life because he had a steady paycheck and we had food on the table."[91] Few, though, felt the transformative effects as acutely as Joseph Mancuso, the Bethpage farm laborer whose backbreaking harvest work "paid practically nothing." In 1941, the federal government bought his family home so Grumman could expand. The Mancusos relocated a few blocks away. But thanks to federal spending, Joseph Mancuso found "work both in the winter and summer, full-time, with all the overtime we wanted in the airplane industry." He took a job at Kirkham Engineering in nearby Farmingdale building aircraft parts. Workers unionized the plant, and he noted how wages and working conditions improved. But his expectations rose too, as Mancuso complained how "other unions in other companies that were able to do a lot more."[92]

Imagine going from an intimate work environment where you might clean your employer's kitchen floor as they watch from the living room, or periodically bend down to dig up potatoes in the shadow of the farm owner, to entering a single-story plant stretched across hundreds of acres. There you labor above, below, and alongside hundreds of other workers as they assemble fighter-bombers, aircraft engines, or flight instruments. This would be the case for the former domestic workers and laborers entering Sperry Gyroscope's Lake Success Plant in Nassau County.[93] As Long Island's most progressive company, white male laborers worked alongside Black and female coworkers in nearly every sector of the plant, which an FEPC official described as stretching "out beyond the limit of vision." Here scientific instruments moved along a belt. Workers added various components and then covered the instrument with cellophane as it traveled to prevent dust particles from clogging the device. One employee was assigned to each machine, though they traded places to prevent boredom and broaden skills. It was a hot, noisy, and dirty factory (save the electronics production department, which was air conditioned and clean) with long hours, but the same was true of their former jobs, and those did not offer unionized industrial wages.[94]

Work life changed beyond the shop floor. At Sperry, cafeterias fed employees, a plant hospital offered medical care, and at lunchtime, "negro and white workers were playing games together" including horseshoes and volleyball. At Republic Aviation, workers held dance parties. At Grumman, employees cultivated a forty-acre farm, three nurseries watched their kids, and several sports programs offered needed respite, including over one hundred softball teams. Grumman was famously paternalistic, a tactic to ward off unions, though workers embraced the family culture.[95] And where subcontractors could not or would not offer corporate welfare programs, federal agencies stepped in. Congress passed the Community Facilities Act of 1940 (the Lanham Act), which funded over 3,000 childcare centers nationwide during the war. On Long Island, ten opened, feeding preschool children three meals and keeping older kids busy after school, all for $3 per week.[96]

While defense spending revolutionized work life, it did little to alter the housing arrangements working-class Long Islanders endured prior to the war. In less developed parts of the country where defense manufacturing blossomed—Los Angeles, Texas, Seattle—federal officials, defense companies, and real estate builders coordinated to build large-scale suburbs.[97] Builders hoped wartime spending might turn Long Island into "the future Detroit of the East," as real estate developer Frederick Leeston-Smith anticipated when he invested in land near Grumman's Bethpage plant.[98] The federal government included Long Island as one of the nation's 146 shelter-starved areas. But the Federal Housing Administration (FHA) earmarked money for only 1,200 dwelling units as of 1941. As a point of comparison, the FHA authorized 95,000 homes in Los Angeles between 1940 and 1942. By July 1942, State FHA director Thomas F. Greene authorized money to remodel Long Island's single-family homes for multifamily use near plants. By 1944, War Production Board deputy director John B. McTigue told builders at a Long Island Association for Commerce and Industry forum that construction wouldn't resume "until Germany is defeated, or a successful beachhead in Europe is established."[99]

Housing production dropped because Long Island already had units scattered across its two suburban counties. This differed from the West Coast or Deep South, where structures lagged far behind labor demand. But few workers could afford Long Island's existing housing stock, disappointing mass builders like Frederick Leeston-Smith, who decided to sell his tract to Grumman, a Detroit-esque conclusion to his property speculation that was perhaps a little more literal than he envisioned. Overall, housing starts plunged during the war, two-thirds lower than the already anemic Depression years.[100] In Nassau County, developers submitted just 168 plats for public approval during the war, less than the county registered during the 1930s (394), and a fraction of the plats submitted from 1945 to 1950 (781 total).[101] Developers built only a few affordable FHA-insured housing subdivisions near wartime manufacturing hubs: unincorporated land in South and East Farmingdale near Republic Aviation, a smattering of homes in Bethpage near Grumman, in Uniondale near Mitchel Air Force Base, around the Sperry plant on the Nassau–Queens border, and other dispersed factory areas along Suffolk's South Shore.[102]

Without new units, property owners exploited housing need by putting attics, basements, and spare beds onto the market. Farmingdale, a village resting between Republic Aviation and Grumman, was overrun with workers trying to secure even temporary housing. A 1941 survey noted that "most of the houses are rented even before they have been vacated." Homeowners capitalized on the limited housing stock, charging exorbitant rents "even for the shabbiest dwellings."[103] Many were roomers paying for a night's rest rather than an apartment. Adeline Fischer's father commuted sixty miles west each Monday, renting a room near Grumman in Bethpage before returning home to Mattituck for the weekend.[104] Federal and state agencies tried to relieve the congestion with new bus routes, rail services, and carpools as alternatives to new housing.[105] But the efforts had little impact, and like in big cities like Chicago and New York, or every urban area the federal government considered to have enough units, landlords jacked up rent prices. Only the Office of Price Administration's rent control regulations tempered rent inflation, which was rarely enforced on Long Island.[106]

Federal investment encouraged industrial dispersal into existing residential neighborhoods as another alternative to housing construction. With federal aid, Grumman opened five auxiliary plants in 1942, stretching from Port Washington on the North Shore to Amityville on the South Shore, so local employees could walk to work.[107] Republic and Sperry likewise opened multiple plants in Oyster Bay, Great Neck, and Lake Success. Subcontractors were even more decentralized, spread from former airfields in Valley Stream on the Queens–Nassau border to Greenport in eastern Long Island. Unlike the South's military bases, or the massive industrial Willow Run Bomber plant twenty-five miles outside of Detroit, industrialization came to the suburbs on Long Island. With scarce construction materials and rationing, federal officials chose to force Long Islanders into existing housing, repurposing residential suburbs for industry.

As the housing situation reveals, Long Island epitomized the potential, and limits, of state spending. Total war mobilization absorbed Long Island's working class into high-paying jobs that didn't exist a few years earlier. Tight employment raised wages and disintegrated the social divides of the service economy. Women worked alongside men; Black southerners ate in cafeterias seated next to European immigrants; former domestic workers learned how to operate press brakes. The government supplied day care centers to help working-class Long Islanders handle childcare they used to manage themselves. But the state ignored needs that did not contribute to the war. Workers continued to live in their tenements or self-built homes. If they had to relocate, chopped up single-family houses or trailers were their new options. Prosperity was a byproduct of war. The question was whether the egalitarian impulse could outlast the war and serve other needs.

## The Challenge of Peace

As the Allied powers racked up significant victories in 1944 and 1945, critical domestic questions came to the fore. Would the economy return to stagnation? Would Congress keep federal childcare centers open? Would the state support high employment and wages? In other words, could Americans enjoy a "peace dividend" as the government redirected defense spending to other social ends? Long Island's new industrial economy depended on war spending, making these questions more relevant. And it mattered most to Long Island's working class. Wages were higher, jobs came with benefits, seasonal layoffs disappeared, and mothers could work thanks to local day care centers. All was unimaginable before the war, and Long Islanders envisioned a suburb where such things might continue.

At the national level, Congress, policymakers, and public opinion polls debated the questions. On one hand, Congress shuttered key institutions that could harness state spending for social-democratic ends. The WPA ended in 1942. Congress disbanded the National Resources Planning Board, which in 1943 released a report to convert military facilities for civilian use and develop a public employment program. Congress also trimmed the federal day care budget, preparing its alleged redundance. On the other hand, the federal government became the nation's largest industrial property owner during the war, funded over 3,000 childcare centers, and expanded its planning powers to an unprecedented degree. Most importantly, the government had several tools to manage inflation, from the close relationship between the US Treasury and Federal Reserve, to the Office of Price Administration, which could regulate prices and wages. Economists were still debating what lessons to draw from the wartime boom. Prominent institutionalists pushed planning as the way forward. "Social" Keynesians advocated public investment and jobs.

"Commercial" Keynesians prioritized technocratic aggregate demand management. All jockeyed for dominance in academic and policymaking circles toward the end of the war.[108]

Most importantly, full employment was the most pressing issue in the Western world. After fifteen years of Depression and global war, the victors expanded or established social-democratic welfare states. Labor unions, government, and business would cooperate to support high employment, while the state prevented poverty in its various forms, including unemployment, high housing costs, low wages, disability, illness, and child-rearing. Sweden, under the Social Democratic Party, offered the most extensive and broadest coverage, but the programs were no less popular in nascent welfare states. Sir William Beveridge's famous 1942 report, which laid out a blueprint for the United Kingdom's welfare state, was a best seller there. And polls showed that over three-quarters of Americans wanted government to keep people employed, with over 40 percent wanting a new WPA or PWA.[109]

On Long Island, the same debate took place, illustrating just how radically Long Island's economy, and the expectations of its residents, changed. Eleven days after the US dropped its second atomic bomb on Nagasaki, Japan, the International Union of Electrical Workers (IUE) Local 450, which had organized the Sperry plant during the war, called an "emergency conference." Prior to the war, industrial unions were unheard of on Long Island, and organized labor barely existed in Long Island's service sector. Over three hundred workers, union representatives, bankers, business owners, and public officials gathered at the Garden City Hotel. The hotel was the centerpiece of the exclusive Garden City residential park, a palace for elite social gatherings during the Gold Coast era. Now, working-class Long Islanders used it for a meeting. Their guest of honor was Long Island's congressional representative, Leonard W. Hall. A lifelong Republican, Hall was the son of Theodore Roosevelt's coachman and grew up near "Sagamore Hill," Teddy's Gold Coast estate in Oyster Bay. His upbringing and political career rested on estate society. But here he was addressing blue-collar workers whose jobs did not exist when he went to Washington in 1938. Neither did the American Labor Party, the local National Negro Congress branch, or the labor unions attending the conference for that matter.[110]

IUE Local 450 representative George Rooney set the agenda, calmly laying out Long Island's "peculiar" unemployment problem: "we don't want to revert to conditions as they were before the war. Then there were only 3,000 persons in industry in both counties, while at the peak of the war effort, there were 70,000 with another 90,000 in the armed forces." Sperry president R. E. Gilmor followed, defining the challenge as "the problem of productivity: our production capacity is so great that we may have trouble deciding how to best distribute and use what we produce . . . the situation is unprecedented, and it calls for unprecedented attitudes." IUE Local 1217 representative Joseph Malfetta denounced the empty "faith and courage" speech of Sperry president Gilmor, demanding government jobs and security for veterans and "cast-off war workers." American Labor Party treasurer William Raben urged the business leaders and politicians to prevent Black workers from being "swept" back into their former status as domestic workers. National Negro Congress representative Thelma Dale concurred, contending that Black workers have "equal rights to a job and a living" and that society shouldn't let their recently learned skills atrophy. Finally, George Hauser, Liberty Aircraft Parts president, laid out a concrete idea: a cross-island transportation network.[111]

Their demands came to nothing though. Hall agreed the federal government should extend unemployment benefits, but he argued only the "free market" could create jobs, not the government. When he returned to Congress, he would debate a full-employment bill already shorn of any job creation powers in committee. Even liberals sided with Hall's claim that "free enterprise" should employ America's workforce, and they joined their more conservative colleagues to pass a feeble Employment Act with only vague guidelines for employment and inflation stability.[112] And despite pleas to save them, the Federal Works Agency only funded federal childcare centers through early 1946.

With federal largesse receding, Long Island's war boom quickly went bust. When federal day care funding disappeared, working mothers asked school districts to assume the cost, contending the centers should be "an essential part of peace-time life." But school board officials feared property tax hikes.[113] In 1945, the military canceled over 18,000 contracts, and fifty of the nation's sixty-six airframe plants ceased producing planes.[114] Republic Aviation ordered a ten-day shutdown, and employment dropped from its wartime high of 24,000 to 3,700. Sperry's workforce shrank from 30,000 to 5,000. Grumman dramatically dismissed everyone over a loudspeaker announcement, and only notified certain employees to report for work the next week.[115] Questions of "last hired, first fired" took a back seat to what looked like the industry's total collapse. For many, the American Labor Party's fear came true. James Baxter, that horse groom who had traveled from South Carolina eighteen years prior, returned to estate work after Grumman laid him and everyone else off. The war economy's end meant the poor paying, racially hierarchical, inconsistent service economy returned. Baxter tended horses for another eleven years until he secured a job as a groundskeeper for the Great Neck public school system in 1956.[116]

## Conclusion

The IUE's "emergency conference" attendees showed how swiftly Long Island's job market had changed. Since the early twentieth century, Long Island's working class had toiled in potato fields, reared other people's children, or dug ditches for basements and roads. They competed for jobs among employers who paid little and further depressed wages by sorting them into ascriptive hierarchies. The very places they built forced them into cramped apartments or self-built homes along the fringes. They lived in or near poverty. And then the war started. Nationwide, the war ended the Depression. But on Long Island, federal spending laid the foundation of a new suburbia, drawing workers into higher paying, more consistent industrial jobs. Total war produced full employment, which in turn strengthened fair employment efforts, as activists took advantage of unlimited labor demand to surmount the racial and gender divide pervading Long Island's service economy. But as scholars have long noted, the warfare state was no social-democratic extension of the New Deal. It was a violent perversion of the full-employment ideals first espoused in the 1934 Committee on Economic Security, the New Deal blueprint for American social democracy.[117] Jobs served destructive and conditional ends, not long-term domestic needs. On Long Island there was an explosion of jobs, but not of housing. A temporary reprieve from poverty, rather than an eradication.

Despite the limitations, the conference laid bare the new demands from industrial suburbia's beneficiaries. They imagined new possibilities for public spending. The only means to avoid a return to the low-paying, racist, and precarious service economy was to reorient federal spending toward domestic ends, to harness the productive capacity now laid across Long Island for projects they may benefit from. That their legislative representative, and Congress at large, left their demands unmet proved how fleeting the moment was to put Keynes's larger ideas into genuine practice. Public officials unleashed socialized investment during total war, with its resource scarcity and constrained consumption.[118] By war's end, the window to reorient investment closed, leaving Long Island with two foundations for its future. The first, the norm since its suburban origins, depended on poverty for its affluence. Federal investment offered an alternative egalitarian suburbia, with the potential to absorb the many into its fold. The question in 1945 was what suburbia would dominate, and this depended on what form federal spending might take, who it included, how suburbanites would satisfy their service needs, and how housing policy aligned with the two suburban trajectories. The answers to these questions shaped the degree, distribution, and risk factors of poverty.

# 2

# The Crabgrass Wasn't Always Greener

## *Poverty Amidst Suburban Plenty*

In 1966, Logan and Bessie Jackson finally made it. After eighteen years of marriage, five kids, and $2,800 saved, the Jackson family could move from Harlem to Long Island, thanks to Logan's new trucking job in Nassau County. As a Black family, they had few housing options, so they secured a mortgage for a small single-family house in New Cassel. This was same place James Baxter moved forty years earlier. Because of New Cassel's unincorporated status and earlier Black settlement, developers sold homes to non-white buyers. By the 1960s, builders filled in the empty lots with Capes, ranches, and split-levels. Collectively, they made New Cassel indistinguishable from the sprawling suburbs elsewhere on Long Island, which had tripled in population since 1940, approaching two million people.

For the Jacksons, the house was a move up, not just a move out, to the suburbs. James Baxter used New Cassel's housing stock as a shield against the vicissitudes of waged labor; the Jacksons viewed their home as a hard-earned achievement. In their former Harlem apartment, they kept their food in an icebox and shared a bathroom with all the neighbors on their floor. Now they owned a single-family house with a private bathroom, an electric refrigerator, and a yard for the kids. Bessie used to clean people's homes in Manhattan; with Logan's new job, she enjoyed tending to the house and kids. Even Logan was around more because his trucking employer was only a few miles away. Their little house in this unincorporated place, and their new lives on Long Island, reflected what suburbs offered after World War II: jobs that paid well enough to buy homes with yards of unprecedented size, available to otherwise working-class families.

But two years later, the Jacksons' dream collapsed. Logan contracted tuberculosis, a disease largely eradicated in the United States, though still afflicting people segregated in overcrowded urban housing.[1] He entered a sanatorium. Because his job didn't offer disability insurance, Bessie was left without any support. Black women didn't have many job opportunities in the suburbs, especially if they lacked a college degree. So, Bessie returned to cleaning people's homes, now across dispersed suburbia rather than dense Manhattan. Without a car, she depended on Nassau County's disconnected private bus system for her daily commute. Waiting at a bus stop while drivers passed by on their half-hour commutes, she rode twenty-five minutes to a Hempstead domestic employment agency. There, she received her daily address and returned to the tangle of bus routes for another thirty-minute ride. After scrubbing a kitchen floor and tidying up a house, she walked back to the stop, watching car commuters whiz by once again, each paying six times less for a quicker trip.[2]

She then arrived home, long after her five kids returned from school. Without affordable day care, Bessie left her oldest, aged sixteen, in charge of the other four children. On weekends, her eldest son watched his siblings all day. Sometimes he would hand over the responsibility to his younger sister while he caddied at the local golf course or hung out with friends. His antics gave Bessie agita, but so did the burdens of groceries, heating fuel, and mortgage bills. For a day's work Bessie received $12. Even if she worked every day of the year, her income would not put the family above what the federal government considered the "absolute" poverty threshold, i.e., the minimum needed to subsist in postwar America.[3]

The crabgrass was not much greener than Harlem's concrete. The Jacksons had achieved homeownership, the key marker of America's post–World War II living standard, when private builders, insured by the federal government, enabled the majority of the nation's households to become small property owners.[4] But there was another aspect to suburban life less discussed and studied, but no less important: a consistent income stream to cover monthly mortgage payments and property tax obligations. The federal government, first through New Deal labor and employment laws, and then through Cold War defense contracts, turned millions of jobs into a route to economic security. On Long Island, defense spending contributed to what historian Robert O. Self calls the "industrial garden," the virtuous cycle of money flowing from factories into mortgages, schools, and local merchants, lifting working-class people into suburban comfort.[5] Bessie's job didn't offer the same benefits. Domestic work resembled the low-pay and precarious jobs of the old suburban residential parks. Other sources of assistance were either unavailable or insufficient for a decent living standard. Logan's trucking job didn't include disability. Public day care didn't exist. Homeownership precluded Bessie from receiving welfare. The Jacksons had moved to the suburbs, but misfortune and low-wage jobs prevented them from enjoying its bounties.

While Bessie's job resembled that of her predecessors, the evolving American welfare state altered domestic work after 1945. The industrial gardens blossoming across Long Island severed the link between working and living at the precipice of poverty. Well-paying factory or office jobs, close to affordable single-family homes, lured working-class New Yorkers to the burbs. They and a new crop of white-collar commuters made Long Island the fastest-growing and most affluent place in America. But federal intervention secured a limited number of livelihoods and fulfilled only some of people's needs. Federal protections didn't cover jobs in domestic service, retail, farm labor, and the building trades. Washington did not adequately fund day care, affordable housing, and local schools. People like Bessie filled in the gaps.

Defense workers hired babysitters, cleaners, and landscapers to care for their kids, lawn, and kitchens while both spouses worked. Their modest wages bought them a single-family house, made possible by federal mortgage insurance and low-wage laborers reducing construction costs. The textile mill down the road subsidized their school tax base, but the mill owner only moved there because he could still profit from low-wage labor. Suburban consumers could shop at the unending strip malls since minimum wages kept food, clothing, and merchandise prices affordable. Defense contracts and FHA-insured mortgages sustained a prosperous suburban working-class on Long Island. But so did an estimated 110,000 people digging foundations, scrubbing floors, and hunched over sewing machines, around 16 percent of all Long Island working residents in 1960.

Exploitation filled the void for basic social needs the federal government did not fulfill. Long Islanders needed Bessie to make as little money as possible because their own material well-being depended on it. Small businesses gleaned their profits from low-wage occupations left out of New Deal labor laws. And employers filled these low-wage jobs by taking advantage of oppressed populations, including Black laborers from the Jim Crow South and women subordinated in the suburban household. They rationalized segmenting women and people of color as "natural" sorting given the presumed "aptitudes" and "scheduling needs" of these oppressed groups. Employers in turn produced a sharpened divide between working-class people who benefited from welfare-state protections and those who did not. Government intervention raised the basic standard of living on Long Island: the necessary car to get around; money for childcare, eldercare, and routine repairs; the detached federally insured single-family home filled with furniture and gadgets. But an estimated one in nine families on Long Island earned half or less than suburban median family income, unable to afford what they needed for suburban living (table A.1).

Despite unprecedented federal support underwriting Long Island's broad-based affluence, the suburban job market reproduced inequality *within* postwar suburbia. The postwar suburbs are typically depicted as places where factories attracted residents, subsidized the tax base, and enabled homeownership. Exclusionary barriers, including racist housing policy and restrictive zoning produced a "white wall" denying urban non-whites and poor people access. What the Jacksons and others reveal instead is that the poor were not left behind in the city; they were left out of the institutions that enabled suburban upward mobility. Postwar suburban prosperity, like its prewar counterpart, *depended* on poverty. And poverty was a political outcome, a consequence of welfare-state design. After the war, violent and market-friendly military Keynesianism eclipsed the New Deal's social-democratic vision. Congressional Republicans and Southern Democrats dismantled New Deal and wartime planning powers. Liberal Keynesian economists, committed to the Employment Act's "maximum employment" mandate, joined the upper echelons of policymaking. But they embraced market-oriented means to get there: tax cuts, interest rate tinkering, deficit spending regardless of content.[6] The Cold War military budget was what Michael Brenes calls a "marriage of convenience" between these groups.[7] And it was also convenient to have low-wage workers like Bessie Jackson fulfill the remaining social needs in suburbia.

Chapter 2 investigates the jobs that sustained the "industrial garden." It explores why Long Island produced both upward mobility and economic struggle, how many experienced low wages and unemployment, who predominated in low-wage jobs, and why. Long Island's economic and population boom may be a one-of-a-kind story, but the dynamics of both prosperity and poverty in Nassau and Suffolk Counties mirrored suburbs across the nation. Long Island epitomized the conclusions of President Lyndon Johnson's Task Force on Suburban Problems, the Great Society working group, which found that suburban labor markets were more unequal than America's central cities, which had a plethora of unskilled but better-paying jobs.[8] This translated into Nassau County having the nation's lowest poverty rate and highest median family income, with Suffolk close behind. But it also meant that roughly 11 percent of all Long Island families lived in relative poverty, with women, Black, and Puerto Rican suburbanites overrepresented among its ranks.

## The Seeds of Mass Suburbia

In 1947, the Long Island daily *Newsday* published an advertorial entitled "LI Shakes 'Boudoir' Complex." The "boudoir" referred to Long Island's prewar economy, symbolized by the separate and extravagant boudoir room for private "female" contemplation. World War II swept the boudoir away as "workers learned the advantages of local work, our civics learned that light industry does not mean dirt and smells and refuse, and our municipalities grew conscious of the value of industry's taxes." Growing Cold War hostilities had already reinvigorated defense manufacturing, and Long Island was fast becoming a "separate entity" from New York City, with "phenomenal growth in housing paced by a similar growth in light industry which is absorbing the labor thus furnished." Within a few short years, the suburb had gone from a haven for "boudoir" suburbanites laboring in the city and living in the suburbs, to one where average people both lived *and* labored in the suburbs. The tax burden likewise shifted from commuters and estate owners to a shared cost between industry and homeowners.[9]

*Newsday*, a newspaper with a vested interest in new subscribers, was celebrating the industrial garden, the geographic manifestation of the nation's largest welfare programs after World War II: federal defense contracts and mortgage insurance guarantees. While not all of America's industrial gardens rested on military spending, the fastest-growing suburbs did. Single-story factories and cul-de-sacs sprouted up across the gunbelt that encircled the country in a giant horseshoe, including some of the postwar period's fastest-growing places: the outskirts of Boston, Florida's "Space Coast," Huntsville, Dallas and Houston, all of California's major cities, and Seattle.[10] On Long Island, as elsewhere, defense spending offered working-class people a degree of unprecedented economic opportunity that aligned with federal housing programs. But defense contracts were a peculiar way to secure people's livelihoods. The Cold War budget was the most politically palatable form of federal spending, though the vagaries of war determined prosperity and private contractors distributed the jobs. Without total war mobilization, economic security proved elusive. Employers meanwhile favored white male workers in a loose job market, relegating women and people of color to less remunerated work. The industrial garden thus laid a new foundation of inequality atop the old. It gave some working-class Long Islanders a boost into material comfort while keeping others at the margins of security.

While defense spending is not something we associate with the welfare state, it served as a surrogate for welfare-state provisioning in the United States. Scholars have long studied the intimate links between warfare and welfare-state development across the industrialized world; even in the US, the 1944 GI Bill helped millions of veterans buy homes, earn college degrees, and start businesses.[11] But as European democracies expanded their domestic welfare states after World War II, Congress deconstructed America's key social-democratic tools. When Congress shuttered the Works Progress Administration (WPA) in 1943, and then neutered the Full Employment Act, the federal government's ability to directly create jobs died. When conservative legislators shut down the Office of Price Administration, they killed the inflation-fighting tool necessary to achieve full employment. Labor reforms, including the Taft-Hartley Acts and amendments to the Fair Labor Standards Act (FLSA), sapped the labor movement's vitality in the late 1940s. And once the National Resources Planning Board folded in 1943 and the Fed-Treasury Accord of 1951 divorced the Federal Reserve from its commitment to underwriting federal deficit spending, the federal government could no longer publicly plan or finance welfare-state expansion.[12] The postwar right-leaning Congress also thwarted President Truman's "Fair Deal" domestic agenda, including universal health care, large-scale public housing, and income supports for farmers.

The defense budget filled the void. As the Cold War intensified, Congress greenlit a military buildup through what Benjamin Fordham calls the "Cold War consensus" between 1949 and 1951. The consensus tied the Truman administration's foreign policy agenda to a variety of domestic interests, from Republicans and Southern Democrats willing to spend more on war than social welfare, to labor unions dependent on defense manufacturing jobs. The Council of Economic Advisers allayed the Truman administration's budget fears by extolling the economic benefits of military-led deficit spending. And the Defense Department functioned as a surrogate industrial planning agency, steering US production according to foreign policy goals and strategy. Industrial policy served to strengthen America's military might to outmatch the Soviets, but more broadly to rebuild global capitalism with the United States at the helm. They flooded the world with US dollars to encourage American military goods purchases, shore up allies, encourage technological innovation, and fill military bases with planes, guns, and missiles. The money concentrated in areas dependent on defense spending since World War II, reinforcing the ties between military budgets, local economic growth, and political support for Cold War outlays. Defense spending also smoothed the business cycle and relieved economic downturns. In short, defense was a planned industry, serving to meet the nation's geostrategic interests, stimulating local economies, and acting as a quasi-employment policy. And work, provided via defense spending, was the predominant form of federal fiscal intervention in Americans' lives, consuming more than 60 percent of the federal budget between 1945 and 1965.[13]

As part of the gunbelt, Long Island prospered from federal largesse. Washington committed to keep Grumman and Republic Aviation open in 1947 under recommendation from the Air Policy Commission. NSC-68, and then military action in Korea, solidified their businesses.[14] Federal contracts both boosted employment and further expanded the industrial real estate market. During the Korean War, federal officials excluded over $10 million worth of plant expansion from taxation on Long Island. Firms actively recruited workers from New York City, and the region led the state in manufacturing employment growth.[15] Republic Aviation's F-84 Thunderjet fighter-bomber, capable of air-to-air refueling and atomic weapons deployment, was a devastating asset to the US Air Force, destroying dams and flooding North Korea.[16] Republic produced over 7,000 F-84s and became the "workhorse of Korea," the world's biggest private jet producer and Long Island's largest employer in 1954 with over 29,000 workers.[17] Grumman's F9F Panther proved useful to the navy, and they built over 1,000 during the war, as Grumman's workforce reached 11,000 by 1953.[18] After the armistice, firms sustained their businesses with experimental weaponry contracts during the guided missiles boom and later the space boom following *Sputnik's* space orbit. Long Island's contracts slowed the New York metropolitan area's industrial losses: While New York City's consumer electronics industry migrated to the Midwest, firms developing military goods relocated to Long Island instead.[19]

Just as importantly, *Long Islanders* benefited from federal largesse. In all, defense-related industries—transportation equipment, scientific instruments, and electrical machinery—employed about one in four Long Islanders who did not commute to the city during the Korean War. While Long Island's economy diversified afterward (figure A.3), defense still accounted for one in every six jobs and half of all manufacturing employment in 1963.[20] Most importantly, these jobs enabled working-class prosperity. Despite intense contract competition, Republic and Grumman could nonetheless forecast capital equipment purchases, subcontracts, labor force needs, and profit margins once the Pentagon awarded contracts.[21] This planning ability, coupled with internal training programs and heavy state involvement, produced a high-wage industrial sector where workers could climb the occupational hierarchy. Unions helped too. The International Association of Machinists (IAM) organized Republic Aviation's workforce in 1950, winning Republic workers the nation's highest hourly industrial wages by 1954. The International Union of Electrical Workers (IUE) organized several of Long Island's electronics manufacturers, including Sperry and American Bosch Arma. By 1955, around

80 percent of Long Island's defense industry was unionized; Grumman remained the only non-unionized major plant, though they paid high wages and offered generous benefits as a bulwark against unions.[22]

Put simply, state intervention, in the form of labor rights and defense spending, coalesced to elevate a working class into suburban comfort. In 1959, a defense production worker earned a few dollars shy of $6,000 per year, about 70 percent of Nassau's and nearly 90 percent of Suffolk's median family income.[23] These jobs, and their pay, were the lynchpin to Long Island's mass suburbanization. Although scholars debate whether people follow factories to the suburbs or factories chase people to the burbs, the planned defense industry indeed "pulled" workers to the suburbs, as housing officials, manufacturers, and social scientists all noted at the time.[24] A 1951 housing survey found that a quarter of their sample size were defense workers, while over three-quarters of Nassau County mortgage borrowers earned the typical defense worker wage.[25] FHA officials reported that defense manufacturing wages buttressed the thin-margined but high-volume sub-$8,000 single-family housing market on Long Island. This was Levitt and Sons' Cape Cod price point, the prototype for mass suburbia.[26] The big manufacturers noticed how quickly their workforce suburbanized. In 1962, Sperry Gyroscope found that despite their main plant straddling Nassau and Queens, just 12 percent of their employees resided in the boroughs.[27] Republic likewise determined that of 12,681 employees, only 9 percent hailed from New York City, while over half (6,884) lived nearby in Oyster Bay, Hempstead, and Babylon.[28] Eighty percent of Grumman's workforce called Long Island home during the 1960s.[29] Levittown perhaps best illustrates industry-driven suburbanization, as the subdivision shifted from a primarily white-collar commuter suburb during the 1947 housing crunch to a majority blue-collar enclave fourteen years later.[30]

But when public spending filtered through private defense manufacturing, only certain working-class people got the jobs. Without a tight labor market, and because Congress did not extend the Fair Employment Practices Committee (FEPC), defense manufacturers and subcontractors hired European immigrants through social networks. They pulled New York City residents into the vast expanse of suburbia that served as the material foundation to a white "ethnic" racial identity in the postwar years. Long Island's new postwar suburbanites included Italian Americans, who replaced Germany as the single largest country of origin, Polish and Irish Americans (about 8 percent and 7 percent of the island's population, respectively), and over 400,000 European Jews.[31] No longer relegated to low-paying jobs, they now lived among the same people their predecessors worked for on Long Island.

The old story about returning veterans replacing women on the assembly line held true on Long Island. Defense employers practically cleansed the sector of female workers after the war, returning to a "neo-traditional" work culture on Long Island as elsewhere. Former defense worker Catherine O'Regan recalled that Grumman "removed *all* of the females from the shop . . . [and the] next day they were all replaced by men." As Stephen Patnode argues, Grumman developed an unwritten rule against women on the shop floor, recasting females as "assistants" for clerical and non-production positions, a practice replicated across Long Island's major firms. O'Regan was one among the few female employees retained, though her supervisor moved her off the shop floor, having her sort tools from a telephone rather than physically handling the tools herself. Women could not even enter the shop, relegated to personnel, accounting, and other clerical offices.[32]

Black suburbanites faced similar disadvantages. The state abandoned its pledge to protect Black employees' rights in defense manufacturing for almost two decades after the war, thus companies didn't hire them. The few Black workers held unskilled positions, a problem as the defense industry shed its unskilled jobs in the late 1950s and early 1960s. Black Long Islanders did not accept exclusion without protest; chapter 4 delves into the civil rights efforts to pry open Long Island's defense industry in detail. But they were marginalized across Long Island's industries. They held menial positions, or jobs threatened by automation among Long Island's primary metal, chemical, fabricated metal, and printing industries. Overall, because Long Island's manufacturing sector skewed toward defense, Black industrial job prospects were worse on Long Island compared to other suburbs in the postwar period.[33]

Defense spending was not the only stimulus to Long Island's postwar boom. In 1960, a third of Long Islanders commuted to New York City for work, and they earned about twice as much as local workers.[34] Their imported income, along with defense dollars, supported well-paid jobs servicing suburban needs, from education and law to banking and medicine. And these jobs offered women and Black suburbanites what defense did not. The public sector in particular paid well, thanks in part to the wage floor set by the defense industry and state labor laws. Between 1952 and 1965, public employment doubled as a growing army of sanitation workers, public works employees, police officers, teachers, and other civil servants served suburbanites. The public sector was vital to Black Long Islanders, who used government jobs to move up as they moved out to the burbs. Black workers were a third of the staff servicing 16,000 patients in Long Island's three massive state mental hospitals: Kings Park, Central Islip, and Pilgrim State, then the world's largest.[35] As public sector organizing took off in the 1960s and competition for suburban teachers heated up, education offered some of the best careers for suburban women.

Prosperous Black Long Islanders were a visible presence by the 1960s. Their suburbanization rate doubled that of white people during the decade, reaching roughly 5 percent of the bi-county population. They had jobs that financed homeownership and afforded at least one car, a washer machine, and a TV. They suffered through interminable traffic during their daily commutes, fretted over taxes, spent weekends fighting crabgrass, and entertained guests in their living rooms. Families like the Jacksons from this chapter's introduction briefly joined this cohort. Their neighbors, Carl and Lorraine Blackman, who lived a few blocks away, exemplified the new Black suburbanite. Both Carl and Lorraine graduated from college. Carl was an engineer at a Suffolk County defense contractor, while Lorraine taught prekindergarten classes in nearby Westbury. Both stressed education as the great equalizer, the means to "make the Negro a sharer of wealth with all and not just a producer of wealth for others" as Carl Blackman put it. And for both, the suburban home and job symbolized that they had "made" it, a variation of the "immigrant roots" narrative European-descended Long Islanders subscribed to, with the added caveat of breaking racial barriers.[36] The Blackmans represented the selective entrance of Black Long Islanders into the avenues of upward mobility.

Overall, Cold War spending, mediated by federal contractors, added a new layer to Long Island's suburban population. Defense workers, aided by government money, labor safeguards, and FHA mortgage insurance, moved next door to white-collar commuters, enjoying a living standard unparalleled in human history. Men who formerly worked low-wage suburban jobs, or labored and lived in the city, benefited most. A limited number of Black suburbanites and women entered high-wage sectors that served commuters, defense workers, or state needs on Long Island. But defense spending and imported commuter wealth generated only a limited number of well-paying jobs. Other needs had to be satisfied outside the scope of state intervention, and the employers preyed on the people cut out of Long Island's well-paid sectors to fulfill them.

## The Gardeners of Mass Suburbia

While federal programs planted the seeds of the "industrial garden," low-wage workers helped those gardens grow. Defense contracts and mortgage insurance programs flooded Long Island with jobs and cheap housing. But there were plenty of other basic things the state did not furnish or regulate. Suburbanites still needed help raising kids, caring for grandma, or cleaning up their homes and yards. Even with thirty-year fixed-rate mortgages, the costs of building and supporting a physical house put homeownership beyond many Long Islanders' means. Municipal services rested on local property taxes, which only added to expenses. And living standards depended on low food and consumer goods prices. The federal welfare state did not cover these needs, but low labor costs made them affordable to working-class suburbanites. The welfare state didn't protect the people who labored in them either, estimated to be around 110,000 Long Islanders as of 1960, about the same proportion as those laboring in defense factories.[37] Employers filled these jobs by exploiting the same hierarchies that made the prosperous suburban economy disproportionately white and male. They hired purportedly "flexible" suburban housewives or southern Black and Puerto Rican workers from the depressed South and Caribbean territory. Low-wage workers cultivated the industrial garden but did not earn enough to enjoy the fruits of their labor.

Low-wage work was partly a consequence of federal lawmakers relegating critical social needs to either states or individual Americans after World War II. Rather than extend federal day care funding, Congress ended the program in 1945. Legislators likewise did not pass the Maternal and Child Welfare Act of 1946, which included federal day care grants.[38] Federal mortgage programs only eased the burden of mortgage loans—they didn't subsidize construction or maintenance costs. Cooperative housing, which spreads maintenance costs among an entire housing development, was cut from the 1950 Housing Act. Without public support, private developers had to find ways to reduce costs.[39] And with little federal support for public education or municipal infrastructure, state and local governments, and by extension homeowners, picked up the tab.[40] The lack of federal support was tragic because only the federal government could spend with no other constraint than inflation to fund schools, build housing, support day care centers, underwrite infrastructure projects, or finance fighter jet programs, among other things.[41] By contrast, neither states, localities, businesses, nor households could create money. Local governments borrowed and operated with constrained budgets. On Long Island, as elsewhere, localities fiercely competed to attract tax-subsidizing industry; school districts weighed the fiscal burdens of subsuming day care into the property tax bill; parents chose whether to forgo dual incomes to raise young kids; and developers devised construction cost-cutting measures to match FHA-targeted income groups with FHA-standard housing.

But low-wage work was also the outcome of gaps in the federal system of labor relations. The three pillars of workplace democracy—the Social

Security Act (SSA), National Labor Relations Act (NLRA), and FLSA—established the framework by which Americans could secure a decent living. The SSA protected workers from bouts of unemployment and illness. The NLRA protected workers' right to collectively bargain. The FLSA set a national minimum wage, overtime rules, and empowered workers to negotiate industry-wide wages through "industry committees." But legislators omitted entire job categories when Congress first passed the acts in the 1930s. The original SSA and FLSA left almost half of the US workforce uncovered.[42] All three acts excluded domestic workers, agricultural workers, and casual laborers, due in part to the administrative difficulties of enforcing the laws in these informal job arrangements, and because agricultural lobbying groups fiercely opposed losing their low-wage labor force.[43] Exclusions were not set in stone, but amendments only slowly expanded coverage. The federal minimum wage did not include construction and retail workers until 1961, many service sector workers until 1966, or domestic and farm workers until the 1970s and 1980s. And even as coverage expanded, legal powers weakened. As legal scholar Kate Andrias argues, the FLSA originally set wages through industrial deliberation rather than legislative fiat. For the decade after 1938, committees of employers, unions, and workers hashed out wage rates across an entire industry. This was a wage-compressing social-democratic model popular in Europe. But it only lasted in the US until the late 1940s: the Taft-Hartley and Portal-to-Portal Acts reduced the FLSA's powers to a bare minimum wage floor.[44]

One state failure solved another. Jobs excluded from some or all of America's labor market interventions served critical needs on Long Island, as in other parts of the country. Put in the terms of comparative welfare-state scholarship, unprotected "outsiders" served the "insiders," i.e., those included within welfare-state security or provision.[45] Private employers used low wages to slash construction costs, provide needed services, and reduce tax burdens, all to increase the living standards of others. And they filled these jobs with oppressed populations, giving the welfare state divide stark racial and gender disparities, although plenty of white and male Long Islanders labored in poorly paid jobs too.

Long Island's low-wage job market began with the single-family house. As scholars have documented, the FHA shaped postwar suburbanization in two ways. First, the FHA standardized the long-term amortized mortgage. Second, the FHA popularized modest single-family housing forms, especially the basement-less, four-room, one-bath unit. These standards lowered the price and therefore access to housing, but it depended on private builders to lower costs. They had to find ways to profit within Long Island's expensive building codes, permits, and land prices. Pressuring local governments to revise codes was one means to lower costs. Squeezing labor and finding ways around unions was another.

Levitt and Sons, the famous developers of Long Island's Levittown, innovated the anti-union labor squeeze in postwar housing construction. While celebrated for introducing assembly-line techniques, the Levitts also reorganized how workers constructed houses. This innovation was no different from the way Chicago slaughterhouses simplified the tasks of butchers in the nineteenth century, or how Uber restructured the taxi industry in the twenty-first century. The Levitts outsourced housing construction to factories and then transported completed parts to building sites, but they also reorganized work routines, which proved just as consequential. They staunchly opposed unions and the subcontractor system that dominated homebuilding. They instead used a complex system of sixty superintendents who oversaw fifty-four subcontractors responsible for hiring, paying, and supervising the workers building Levitt's historic project. These subcontractors were such in name only. They were former Levitt employees, and their close relations allowed the Levitts to negotiate fees rather than accept competitive bids. Levitt and Sons paid fees based on completed houses, not work done, which in effect compelled laborers to work faster.[46]

Levitt and Sons' piecework incentive system received public praise and attracted productive workers willing to put in long hours for higher pay. Its brilliance also rested in exporting labor strife to subcontractors, who risked losing a contract if they conceded to labor demands. In this way, the Levitts did not face direct labor agitation. Instead, subcontractors bore the brunt of worker strife. In 1947 and 1948, sheathers attempted two strikes against their Levitt subcontractor Edward Bouffard, complaining of low pay and ten-hour days with only fifteen-minute lunch breaks. Bouffard threw his hands up, citing fixed costs and the profit losses from any pay increases. The sheathers returned to work without any gains. The AFL-affiliated Nassau–Suffolk Building and Construction Trades Council mounted a more consequential drive to organize Levitt's project in 1950. It was the opening gun to unionize "not only Levitt, but the whole Island" as trade council president John E. Long put it. With support from rival contractors who used union labor, the trades council picketed a model home and planned to have American Federation of Labor (AFL) workers walk off their worksites.[47]

The strike never came. Members of two locals, the Hoisting Engineers and Heavy Construction Workers Union, joined the picket. But "Big Bill" William DeKoning's Operating Engineers crossed the line. DeKoning was long considered Long Island's building trades "Czar," running the entire construction union front since 1933. His 1950 decision to cross the picket struck at the heart of the entire Levittown strike, forcing the Nassau–Suffolk Building and Construction Trades Council to oust him a month later. Turmoil then ensued as DeKoning "raided" the council, forcing union representatives to resign and join his budding rival organization, which crossed other picket lines.[48]

In 1953, DeKoning's arrest and conviction on ninety-two counts of extortion, coercion, and conspiracy revealed why DeKoning's members didn't strike. DeKoning had been running a racketeering scheme with 250 building contractors in Nassau and Suffolk Counties, affecting an estimated 40,000 homes. DeKoning and his Operating Engineers Local 138 promised no labor turmoil and "soft" union agreements if contractors paid $8 per concrete foundation into the union welfare fund. With this, a contractor could forgo a union supervisor, hire two union equipment operators for ten machines rather than one per machine, and underbid unionized contractors with little threat from organized labor. Contractors themselves filled leadership roles in DeKoning's union, acting as both employers and shop stewards. For example, Hendrickson Bros. president Arthur Hendrickson, head of Nassau County's largest public works contractor, sat across the negotiating table from his son Milton as they settled "union" stipulations with their own firm.[49]

The corruption charges made public what other members of the Nassau and Suffolk Construction Trades Council had long suspected—that DeKoning's back-door dealings eased Long Island's building activity and made the labor front on Levitt's massive project strangely quiet. The Nassau County district attorney questioned the Levitt firm, though their loose ties to subcontractors left Levitt and Sons untouched by the controversy. DeKoning's power lingered long after his prison sentence and eventual death in 1957 because his son assumed union operations.[50] With rank-and-file workers afraid to challenge DeKoning's power, subcontractors wielded immense power on Long Island, especially because developers preferred the flexibility of contracts to internal personnel.[51]

The history of Levittown, and of Long Island homebuilding, may have been different if not for labor leaders choosing corruption at a historic moment of union strength and an acute housing shortage. This was especially important for an inherently volatile and competitive industry covered by the NLRA but not the FLSA until 1961. Without comprehensive coverage, there was a wide gap between unionized and non-union pay and benefits. Nationwide, the building trades' "high wages" was a mirage. Construction workers rarely worked more than two-thirds of the year, facing an average unemployment rate twice that of other nonagricultural workers.

Relative labor weakness compelled construction laborers to fiercely compete for jobs and close union ranks rather than expand their membership, a detriment to less skilled or Black workers and the building trades writ large. This was true nationwide, especially so in New York City, where Gotham's 122 unions almost entirely excluded Black workers.[52] During Long Island's home-building frenzy, craftsmen like carpenters, painters, and masons hoarded jobs for themselves and their personal networks, letting in few new recruits. Of the 762 painters in Nassau County's Brotherhood of Painters, Decorators, and Paperhangers local union, only six were Black in 1963. The Bricklayer's local boasted a 10 percent Black membership. But Black unionized members rarely secured more than four hundred work hours per year. They averaged only eight hours per week, which excluded them from union benefits like health care and paid vacation time. White masons, meanwhile, managed between 1,200 and 1,400 hours.[53] The closed ranks further weakened union power because many laborers remained unorganized. Contractors could find cheaper labor, and workers could accept extra work outside union rules. This put downward pressure on wages.

Those who worked outside union protection and entitlements like unemployment insurance, social security, or health care lost the most. Scores of ditchdiggers, landscapers, and generalized laborers built and repaired Long Island's suburban homes. They struggled with the industry's seasonal nature, inconsistent work, and little labor organizing to improve conditions. State agencies did not record employment numbers, earnings, or turnover in these sectors, largely because few qualified for unemployment insurance. But a county report found that Black and Puerto Rican workers disproportionately did these kinds of jobs. They were almost completely non-unionized, laid off between six weeks and six months of the year, and earned wages that did not afford them the homes they built, not to mention the irony of Black workers building suburban subdivisions with racial covenants and mortgage exclusions.[54]

Long Island's housing industry was inherently volatile, and suburban day laborers filled out the workforce during busy seasons. Though associated with Latino workers seeking daily gigs on twenty-first century street corners, contingent day labor had a long history in cities and suburbs. In Detroit, the city's peripheral Eight Mile Road had a large "open air labor mart" where Black men waited with their tool bags for casual day jobs.[55] Long Island builders and contractors used similar casual workers in the nation's most affluent suburb. They needed extra hands to dig foundations, build out a second-story dormer, or transform a carport into an enclosed garage. Like the prewar period, Long Island contractors drew from migrant streams down South. On a particularly hot August day in 1966, a *Newsday* reporter sat among fifteen Black southern migrants waiting outside a suburban strip mall at 6 a.m. The day laborers could expect between $1.30 and $1.80 per hour, which in 1966 hovered slightly above the national minimum wage. But a day's pay depended on whether they secured work at all. On that day, two contractors drove by before a third finally stopped. Two laborers approached the vehicle, quietly bartered over wages, hopped in the truck, and took off for the day. Thirteen others on the corner got nothing. Some returned home; the rest hung out on the corner or entered the nearby tavern.[56] They, and the more fortunate unskilled laborers in the formal homebuilding industry, all served the same purpose: they lowered housing construction costs, so that developers could meet the $7,999 home price floor that FHA mortgage insurance still covered. Like in the prewar period, they built houses for others to live in.

Suburbanites needed help once they bought their single-family homes too. They turned to domestic service, the same labor their pre–World War II forebears depended on. While the estate era ended after 1945 as elite culture shifted from mansion dwellers to jet-setters, the domestic workforce grew on Long Island. In 1960, some 19,000 domestic workers labored in private households, about the same number of people working at Republic Aviation, Long Island's largest employer.[57] They were in demand for two reasons. For one, living standards rose during the suburban boom. Labor-saving appliances didn't save time, instead raising the bar for cleanliness, and parents filled children's days with all sorts of extracurricular activities.[58] For another, living costs also increased, compelling women to join the workforce without any public resources to rear children. Men may have returned from war, but women didn't return to the home. Economic growth slowed during the 1950s and two recessions rocked the nation, pushing working-class families to depend on women's wages to make ends meet.[59] Long Island's married female labor force participation only slightly trailed the national rate, all while hopes of public day care died with the war. Long Island moms fought to have local school districts assume day care center operations, framing childcare as a peacetime need as well. But school boards didn't want to burden taxpayers, especially as the number of schoolchildren swelled. Only charity sustained childcare centers reserved for fatherless veteran families.[60] Without other options, some turned to domestic workers.

Private household help was only a solution as long as it remained affordable to the postwar suburbanite. Exclusions from FLSA and NLRA protections kept domestic work cheap. Agencies also dipped further into the depressed southern economy as European household workers left the industry.[61] By 1960, Black workers filled 59 percent of Long Island's domestic service jobs, and it was still a female-dominated sector. In fact, more Black women labored in domestic service on Long Island than Black men in *all occupations combined*. This reflected both the concentration of Black women domestic work and Black men's dominance in the casual labor market, which went unrecorded in state labor market data and census records.[62]

To attract business, domestic service agencies adapted to postwar suburbia. Thirty-six domestic employment agencies formed in Nassau County after the war. They dressed up an old industry for the drive-in era. Agencies sported catchy names like Maid-o-Rama, Bon-Bon, and Gem Agency. They inundated newspaper classifieds, including those distributed in relatively modest blue-collar hamlets like Farmingdale, near Republic Aviation, or Bethpage, home to Grumman. They offered a diverse array of services, from live-in maids and mothers' helpers to a dayworker for weekly cleanings. The agencies promised the utmost convenience. Maid-o-Rama advertised "women by the day, delivered to and from your door." Others included free item giveaways with a domestic servant contract.[63]

Like prewar agencies, these were small-time operators. Some had storefronts and business addresses; others ran out of residential homes, like Ace Domestic Employment Agency of Hicksville, a husband-and-wife team. But they were nothing more than coordinating services. They recruited domestic workers in southern newspapers, and then lodged the arrivals for thirty days as per New York State law. During this time, they matched the recruits with households. Then they collected fees from contracted workers and employing households.[64]

Domestic workers were otherwise on their own. As Bessie Jackson's story in the chapter introduction reveals, they relied on a complex and often informal transportation network to reach their multiple jobs sprawled across suburbia. While agencies sometimes coordinated taxi services for a fee, domestic workers more often used Long Island's fragmented private bus system or illegal taxicabs. Henry Holley, born to North Carolina sharecroppers in 1939, ran one of those cab businesses, driving domestic workers across suburbia during his breaks at a Hempstead laundry factory.[65] Domestic workers needed their own childcare, which meant either leaving the kids with the eldest sibling (as Bessie did), cobbling together help from family and neighbors, or taking the kids to worksites. Bars frequented by domestic workers served important functions. They were hubs for women to network and find childcare, recruitment centers for households seeking help, and cabbie pickup and drop-off points.[66]

When *Newsday* wasn't running stories about the challenges of finding good help, reporters offered rare glimpses into the postwar suburban domestic work routine. In 1970, *Newsday* journalist Vanessa Mares went undercover as a domestic worker for the paper. She first entered an employment agency in

Hempstead where she met Mrs. Sims. At the age of twenty, Mrs. Sims moved from South Carolina to Hempstead, cleaning homes across Long Island. She got married and had kids, but without childcare options, she trucked her young children to work, at least until her son asked to eat dinner with her employer's family. "I stopped takin' them. No place for my children to be."

After leaving Mrs. Sims, the undercover journalist visited a local bar where live-ins and dayworkers danced and sought companions. There she met Murray, a one-man domestic agency run from his van, who promptly offered her a job. Murray picked her up early the next morning with three other young ladies ready for a day's work. They passed women walking dogs, children heading to day camps, and commuters on their way to work. Murray then dropped the undercover reporter off in Wantagh, a hamlet of Cape Cods along Levittown's southern border. A typical suburban scene played out: parents escorted a young child to a yellow station wagon labeled "Creative Kindergarten" parked in the driveway, a sailboat departed in the channel nearby, and the journalist was "delivered to the house with the same convenience that a London Broil had come from the market." She proceeded to clean the house, taking orders from a woman who alternated between talking on the phone and reprimanding a toddler. After scrubbing all the rooms, Murray picked her up at 4:45 p.m.[67]

Domestic service was important work in postwar suburbia. For stay-at-home housewives, hiring a domestic worker offered a brief respite from the constant chores. When another *Newsday* staff writer went undercover, her second employer was a pregnant mother no longer able to clean the home. Her husband picked up the slack after work, but things had gotten out of control without a full day's scrubbing.[68] Domestic workers played an even more important role for dual-earner households, like the Baeckers of North Babylon, residents of a blue-collar suburb in western Suffolk County. Both husband and wife worked into the evening to afford the mortgage for their postwar Cape Cod. They needed a nanny to care for their children, ages two and seven. They turned to an employment agency, who contracted with Mae Washington of Welch, West Virginia. Washington resorted to domestic service after the 1956 steel strike idled her husband in coal country and they exhausted their emergency funds.

The Baeckers needed Mae, and Mae needed the job. But a few of the Baeckers' neighbors felt threatened by Washington's arrival. Mae received anonymous calls at the Baecker home warning her that "we don't have and don't want any niggers in this area. Get out of Babylon if you want to live." Mae feared for her life. While the Baeckers tried to alleviate her concerns and neighbors rallied around in support of Mae, she returned South.

Washington's decision no doubt complicated her family's finances. By contrast, her departure only briefly inconvenienced the Baeckers because the employment agency recruited another southerner.[69] Like the builders constructing suburban houses, domestic workers offered respite, orderly homes, and enabled women to join the workforce. These were small but important means for families to afford suburban homeownership and its accompanying necessities. But the pay and precarity of gigs didn't offer the same to domestic workers.

"Hidden" low-wage jobs subsidized postwar Long Island's affluence too. After all, while FHA and GI loans made monthly housing payments cheaper than New York City rents, the sticker price concealed property tax burdens. Suburban municipal budgets ballooned as Long Island's tangled web of service provision collided with Long Island's booming population. Industry proved critical to relieving residential property taxes, as factories "paid their way" without adding children to schools or the elderly to welfare rolls. Public works projects, such as the Long Island Expressway, set the stage for industrial growth. Defense factories also encouraged an industrial real estate market. Planning boards carved out exclusive industrial zones to subsidize residential property taxes. Real estate attracted industrial firms to new single-story factories complete with copious floorspace, setback requirements, and parking, the ideal structure for the automobile age. These were known as "industrial parks," factories without the soot, congestion, or noise associated with urban industry. Long Island developer Abraham Shames allegedly invented the industrial park in 1956. He ushered in a rush of industrial park construction that by 1965 reached sixty-eight industrial parks across Long Island. The parks pulled factories to Long Island in search of larger, more flexible industrial space.[70]

Manufacturers did not move to Long Island to help their employees buy single-family homes. When a defense firm expanded, or a high-wage publishing, chemical, or fabricating factory relocated, there was a largely symbiotic relationship between the firm, tax base, and employed suburbanites (save the noise and polluted groundwater, soil, and air). But when apparel, textile, toy, and food companies moved from New York City, they sought lower property taxes, more factory space, and cheaper labor. Jobs in these sectors doubled from 6,800 to 14,700 between 1947 and 1965, and they paid $4 less per week than their counterparts in the city and $5 below the state average.[71] Like in New York City, these factories employed less than one hundred people, operated on thin profit margins, and had high turnover rates, periodic layoffs, and production gluts limiting hours. A Long Island food, apparel, or textile employer laid off between 10 percent and 20 percent of their workforce at least once a year; the norm was twice in apparel.[72] Despite NLRA and FLSA protections, the elimination of federal sectoral pay committees in 1949 limited the political tools available to improve wages. Unionization also proved difficult. The Nassau–Suffolk Congress of Industrial Organizations (CIO) Council estimated that organizers had reached only 10 percent of these workers, and the CIO did not even pursue these industries, hoping instead that defense worker organizing would trickle down.[73] These factories, while smaller than the massive defense employers, nonetheless subsidized suburban schools and services in places as diverse as the relatively affluent Jericho and Plainview, where family incomes surpassed the county median, to blue-collar suburbs like Hauppauge, Commack, and New Hyde Park, and even one of Long Island's poorest hamlets, Inwood.[74] They contributed to tax bases, relieving the burden on homeowners. But non-defense manufacturers didn't help their workers afford suburban living.

Like non-durable manufacturing, suburban retail establishments subsidized property tax bases while offering more consumer goods than suburbanites ever imagined. Prior to the war, retail hugged railroad stations. After World War II, urban retailers followed the moving vans across Long Island, initiating a process of commercial decentralization alongside industrial dispersal. The most famous example was Macy's 300,000-square-foot anchor store in the newly constructed Roosevelt Field shopping "mall" in 1956, part of a complex that became one of the nation's biggest. Long Island quickly emerged as the country's fourth largest retail market by 1964, and with it came retail jobs, which surpassed manufacturing as the highest source of employment that year.[75] Retail was a cutthroat industry, and the FLSA didn't cover retail workers until Congress slowly incorporated the sector between 1961 and 1974. Retailers used low wages and seasonal hiring rhythms to undercut one another.[76]

Retail offered jobs, rather than careers, for most. To ensure a low-wage labor force, both non-defense manufacturers and retailers targeted marginal populations. Retailers preferred teenagers for seasonal work. Long Island's apparel manufacturers relocated to Long Island but continued to employ Puerto Rican operatives as they had in the boroughs, a move that permitted factory upgrades without forgoing their cheap labor source.[77] Others took advantage of the dearth of day care options and after-school programs, recruiting from an inflated labor supply of women seeking "flexible" jobs before their second shift at home. Stores justified the low wages as "pin money," a term connoting allowances for personal spending, and offered consumer-oriented benefits like discounts or free items rather than health insurance or pensions.[78] Electronic component, toy, and textile manufacturers valued female employees because they could simply fire and rehire them from their suburban homes as labor needs waxed and waned.[79]

Long Island's most exploited workers didn't directly build or sustain suburbia at all, but instead labored on Long Island's shrinking but still profitable farms (figure 2.1). Although most farmers discovered that housing was their most valuable crop (in Nassau County, farmland declined from 32,000 to 5,500 acres between 1945 and 1964), farmers in eastern Suffolk County deployed new disease-resistant crop strains, fertilizers, equipment, and pesticides.[80] They helped make Suffolk County the nation's third largest potato producer and America's premier duck region. Wartime rationing boosted the duck market, and after the war, waterfowl rivaled poultry for America's favorite dinner bird. The Hollis Warner duck farm sat on 250 acres along the Peconic River in Riverhead, raising 500,000 fowl per year, more than any other farm in the country. They and seventy other Suffolk farmers used the latest technologies and organizational techniques to reach peak production of 7.5 million ducks in the late 1950s, thriving amidst postwar suburbanization. Where Nassau and western Suffolk County developed into an urban agglomeration of homes, factories, and retail centers, eastern Suffolk was a sparse cluster of commercial farming and small housing tracts.[81]

Automation and production line efficiencies only reduced labor costs so much. Farmers still needed a small army of farmworkers, who ranged from an estimated 5,300 in 1957 to 3,600 in 1966. With local jobs available elsewhere and suburbanization creeping in from the west, southern Black migrants and Puerto Rican laborers exclusively filled the farm labor jobs: Black laborers made up 88 percent of the workforce, Puerto Rican contract laborers the remainder.[82] Like their prewar counterparts, crew chiefs recruited Black workers in the South and trucked them north, and as filmmaker Morton Silverstein put it, crew chiefs "allocated their work, supervised their lives, and paid them at the end of the week."[83] Akin to the domestic employment agencies, the crew leader offered credit to cover transportation and food costs, and since most lived on site in makeshift camps, food, shelter, and other living expenses were deducted from wages.[84] Work was physically demanding. During harvest season, workers endured fifteen hours of backbreaking picking, sorting, and lifting per day. And because farm laborers could not legally bargain or demand the minimum wage, pay was low and working conditions difficult. A 1964 study found nearly a third of Long Island's migrant families survived on incomes below the federal poverty line for a four-person family, while those above the poverty threshold lived in relative poverty.[85]

Taken together, workers toiling in homes, in malls, in fields, on roofs, or with sewing machines accounted for at least one in six employed Long Islanders

FIGURE 2.1. Farmworkers harvest crops in front of newly constructed Levitt Cape Cods. Photograph by Art Green for cover of *Thousand Lanes: Levittown's Own Magazine* (November 1951). Courtesy of Levittown Public Library.

as of 1960. This is an underestimate: the New York State Labor Department did not keep track of casual laborers, domestic household help, or farmworkers.[86] And these low-wage jobs, unlike their better-paid counterparts, did not pay enough to support independent living on Long Island. If we take a defense production worker's wage as Long Island's living wage, we can see how welfare-state gaps encouraged depressed wages in sectors that served important functions on Long Island. Federal labor regulators used defense wages as their metric when intervening in local labor disputes. The FHA also used defense wages as the floor for federally insured mortgages. Their yearly wage of $6,000 in 1959 ($57,000 in 2021) also matched what the US Department of Labor considered a "modest but adequate" income for a four-person family in the New York City area.[87] Apparel workers, covered by FLSA and NLRA regulations, earned half that. Retailers paid on average around two-thirds of a defense worker's average weekly earnings, but those jobs rarely offered full-time year-round work. A domestic worker could expect to earn around a quarter of a defense worker's wage, assuming work was steady. An agricultural worker might make two-thirds that of a defense worker, assuming a good crop yield, steady earnings, and no migrant influx undercutting wages. And casual laborers could earn half that of a defense worker, if they secured a gig at all.[88]

Someone had to fill the jobs satisfying suburban needs. In the absence of labor protections for all, or public daycare, housing, and other services, private businesses did so, gleaning their profits from depressed wages. Subcontractors cut corners because they met little labor resistance. Footloose textile manufacturers hired "flexible" suburban working moms to keep wages low. Domestic and farm employers recruited help and farmworkers across the Eastern Seaboard. Ultimately, these jobs, a necessary part of the suburban economic fabric, hewed closer to the historical norm of labor exploitation rather than a means to a decent life. Those outside state protections, the less fortunate working class, served those inside welfare-state coverage, the more fortunate working class.

## The Limits to Mobility

The two preceding sections present a seeming conundrum, one that confounded policymakers in the 1960s, as we will see in chapter 5: unprecedented opportunity for working-class suburbanites on one hand, and over 100,000 workers in poorly paid jobs on the other. White men were concentrated in the former; Black, Puerto Rican, and female workers in the latter. While the welfare state produced the divide between high-paying and low-paying work, two related factors shaped the racial and gender disparities in Long Island's labor market. Unlike when "tight" employment and antidiscrimination law absorbed marginalized workers into well-paying work during World War II, neither strong state labor interventions nor tight labor markets defined the postwar boom. Without both, employers and suburbanites reinforced the racial and gendered hierarchies from the prewar period and other places in postwar Long Island.

Despite Long Island's booming economy, employment never tightened enough to tip power away from employers. Even in the late 1950s and early 1960s, when Long Island's economy was running hot, unemployment barely dipped below 4 percent (figure A.4). This was well above what economists consider "frictional" or "tight" unemployment rates of 3 percent or 2 percent, or when the rate derives from people voluntarily quitting rather than getting laid off. It was also well above social democracies in western Europe and Australia, which ran below 3 percent through the 1970s.[89] The scales weighed in employers' favor, who segmented Long Island's labor force into their preferred gender and racial niches. Employers also relied on screening criteria such as diplomas to identify "qualified" applicants. This put Black workers, disproportionately arriving from the South or educated in racist schools up North, at a disadvantage. During the wartime economy, tight employment and unskilled laborer demand was a boon to uneducated workers. After the war, diploma premiums returned. Government spending also favored credential-based jobs as federal and local public dollars poured into R&D and education. Even among Long Island's airframe producers, the shift to high tech favored technicians and skilled blue-collar workers, as chapter 4 details.[90] Beyond industry, Long Island's burgeoning white-collar sectors demanded high school and even college degrees, from office work and accounting to law and business. Essentially, Long Island exemplified what economist Charles Killingworth called the labor market "twist"—the decline in low-skilled labor demand coinciding with long-term growth in high-skill jobs.[91]

The education premium contributed to racial disparities in occupation. As late as 1960, half of all Long Islanders had completed high school, compared to a quarter of Black Long Islanders. By 1970, the Black graduation rate climbed to 42 percent as the overall rate hit two-thirds. Puerto Ricans were even less likely to have finished high school.[92] This was mostly because Black and Puerto Rican Long Islanders came from different places. While only one in ten Long Islanders arrived from outside the New York metropolitan area in 1960, one in three suburbanizing African Americans moved from other regions, mostly the South. Puerto Ricans often relocated to Long Island after brief sojourns in the city, if not directly from the island territory.[93]

Of course, southern Black migrants were not all poorly educated—as a number of scholars show, the second Great Migration included well-educated African Americans directly moving to America's affluent suburbs. But they did disproportionately receive inferior educations in the Jim Crow South.[94] Educational inequality aligns with the lopsided occupational distribution, and rising equality in the 1960s correlates to rising educational attainment. As late as 1959, Black Long Islanders remained tied to historically Black occupational categories (domestic, laborer, and operative). Newly arriving suburbanites in the 1960s, who were more likely to carry degrees, climbed up the occupational ladder into white-collar jobs. Just under 40 percent of all Black workers held white-collar and skilled blue-collar jobs in the 1970s, an identical proportion to suburban African Americans nationwide (table A.2).[95]

Tight employment alone wouldn't have redistributed people into higher-skill occupations. During World War II, the state trained people and compelled firms to hire non-white and female Long Islanders. After 1945, the state receded from those roles. As previously mentioned, the federal government loosely enforced fair hiring until civil rights activists forced their hand in the 1960s. Federal training and job referral programs either disappeared or weakened. The United States Employment Service (USES), a Depression-era public job recruitment program federalized during the war to funnel people into industrial work, was gutted afterward. Congress returned USES control to the states, turning USES branches into referral services for local private employers.[96] They left training to localities or private firms. As a result, state institutions often further segmented oppressed people into low-wage work rather than redistributing them into better-paying jobs.

Long Island's USES branches illustrate how state institutions satisfied private-employer prerogatives. In the Great Neck USES office (a Gold Coast neighborhood turned industrial suburb with Sperry Gyroscope as its anchor), authorities still sorted Black applicants into separate "active domestic files." After an AFSCME (American Federation of State, County, and Municipal Employees) union member complained of discrimination, an investigation found some 350 applicants in the file. Half had high school diplomas, and USES documents considered them qualified for non-domestic work. But the USES office placed them in "day worker" and "yardman" folders. Office employees claimed Black clients preferred day jobs, allegedly forgoing unemployment insurance, social security, and other provisions for the immediate benefit of casual work. But the files recorded clients' character traits like "drinker," "borrows money," and "submissive," not work preferences or skillsets.[97] The office treated domestic workers as a class apart in person as well, complete with a separate employment office telephone number, a caseworker assigned exclusively to them, and limited hours to call (3 p.m.–5 p.m.), all for job offers they received with only a single day's notice. An office employee exposed the discrimination behind these policies when he complained to the union, saying that a supervisor commanded he "either get those dark clouds jobs, or get them out of here," and was repeatedly pressured to deal with the "Mississippi car of seven, eight boogies in it . . . looking for day work jobs."[98]

Long Island schools also contributed to disparities. Long Island's own schools were deeply segregated, and curricular decisions within districts assumed differential student needs based on ascriptive categories. Officials placed Black students in remedial classes because they were seen as a "culturally deficient" group rather than individuals in need of help.[99] This affected Long Island's prewar Black youth in places like Freeport, where school officials proudly celebrated their Cleveland Avenue elementary school, "the only school of its kind in New York State, outside of Harlem, in that its enrollment is exclusively Negro, except for eight Italian children."[100] Officials considered the students "retarded," and devised remedial classes so students could reach high school. Only a few students entered Freeport High, though, so the segregated school failed even by its own standards. Postwar suburban districts assumed generalized racial difference as well. They consigned Black children to special education classes, segregating them for years thereafter. Protests forced reform, but districts like Roosevelt and Westbury (which included New Cassel) introduced "cultural deprivation" compensatory programs in the 1960s. The programs still segregated Black students, and Westbury schools assessed students within their track, stigmatizing Black children throughout their education.[101] Fewer Black Long Islanders completed high school, and workers without high school diplomas were less prepared for postwar jobs.

Without federal support for training programs, local vocational efforts proved inadequate. Prior to the war, local charities operated youth training programs, which prepared Black students for menial domestic and manual labor.[102] During the war, public schools never instituted industrial training; defense firms and the federal government filled the gap. The defense industry's training schools briefly reopened during the Korean War, but firms preferred internal training because New York was filled with qualified blue-collar workers.[103] As of 1955, only one Nassau County public school district (Sewanhaka) had a technical program. Similarly, only one of 102 Suffolk high schools developed agricultural training courses.[104] Nassau County opened a trades center in 1957, and by the mid-1960s, ten Nassau school districts offered vocational training in craft trades and technical work. Nine centers were in all-white schools. The single diverse district center enrolled only thirty-three students.[105]

This brief overview of Long Island's unequal schooling does not do justice to the subject, which demands its own book.[106] The point here is that the institutions responsible for instructing students, preparing future employees, and placing jobseekers did little to change who got which jobs. If anything, USES offices and high schools only further reified the racial and gender hierarchies in Long Island's labor market. Someone had to do the jobs the welfare state didn't protect. For the more fortunate working-class suburbanite, there was nothing odd about a Black laborer digging a home foundation, a Black housecleaner entering a suburban Cape Cod, women shuffling into a textile mill, or Puerto Rican farmworkers sorting spuds in a field.

## Progress and Poverty

Long Island's postwar industrial gardens produced suburban inequality. "Insiders," those privileged working-class suburbanites with federally subsidized or protected jobs earned more and enjoyed greater economic security than Long Island's "outsiders," working-class suburbanites lacking some or all rights enshrined in the NLRA, FLSA, and SSA. But were those laboring "outside" welfare-state protections "poor"? Teenagers took suburban retail jobs for gas money. Working suburban mothers often added to their husband's income so the family could install a fence, expand a second-story dormer, or build an outdoor patio. And Long Island's labor market couldn't improve disabled or elderly people's fortunes, a quarter of Long Island's federally designated "poor" in 1970.[107] But those who depended on these jobs *were* poor. Social scientists, government bureaucrats, and the American public might not have considered them so, but that's because of how they defined and measured poverty. Welfare-state failure left people ranging from Bessie Jackson to unemployed defense workers impoverished at some point in their lives.

Researchers developed the modern conception of "poverty," with its quantitative sophistication and state approval, alongside the postwar suburban boom. In the 1950s, critiques of American affluence, like James Galbraith's *Affluent Society* and David Potter's *People of Plenty*, obscured poverty. Commerce department reports on rising living standards buried it. And debates over juvenile delinquency and "depressed areas," talked around it. Behind the scenes, federal bureaucrats amassed research on poverty to justify expanding the US welfare apparatus. Economist Robert Lampman used the sophisticated budget thresholds published by the Bureau of Labor Statistics (BLS), which measured food, housing, heating, and taxes across different cities. Since the late nineteenth century, the BLS had been calculating these costs to determine a socially acceptable standard of living. But after 1946, the BLS switched to measuring a "Consumer Price Index," or what a basic market of goods cost. Lampman used the data to reconfigure a basic postwar living standard. Economist Mollie Orshansky, then working for the US Department of Agriculture (USDA), devised a different measure. She tripled the USDA's lowest food budget and compared the number with 1959 census income data. Social scientists, politicians, and even Orshansky herself condemned this absolute poverty threshold as too spartan. Federal officials nonetheless adopted the food-based absolute measure in the 1960s, in part because it offered an achievable benchmark for President Johnson's War on Poverty.[108]

Many scholars write about the federal poverty measure's origins. What matters for our purposes is that the official metric not only undercounted the poor but offered little insight into the welfare-state policies responsible for living standards. In robust European social democracies, government agencies measured how effectively their welfare states secured people's well-being rather than how many fell below a "poverty line." Most did not devise poverty measures until the twenty-first century.[109] The US poverty rate started from the opposite premise, measuring how many people lived on the edge, which policymakers then used to devise remedies. The federal poverty measure, gleaned from the US Census, also narrowed what researchers could interpret.

The federal poverty rate revealed where the poor lived, but not where they worked; how much they earned, but now how they earned it; the varying poverty levels of demographic groups, but little insight into what caused the disparities. This is not to say data alone could illuminate answers, but the measure lent itself to particular analyses. Census records enabled social scientists to analyze poverty across space, i.e., why the poor lived in some places and not others. Census demographic categories likewise encouraged researchers to study family breakdown, poverty "cultures," and delinquency.

The official federal poverty measure distorted suburban poverty in places like Long Island. Census records showed that Nassau was the country's wealthiest large county in 1960. With such broad-based wealth, Nassau County could also boast the nation's second lowest federal poverty rate (5.3 percent [figure A.1]). Suffolk County wasn't quite so wealthy; 10 percent survived under the federal threshold. But compared to Brooklyn, where nearly one in five people were poor, or Manhattan, with five times the poverty rate of Nassau County, Long Island indeed appeared poverty-free. Lopsided disparities aided non-economic interpretations. In 1970, there were four poor Black residents for every white Long Islander, a wider gap than the 3:1 national ratio (figure A.1). Furthermore, suburban residence was more meaningful for white New Yorkers than Black: the white poverty rate on Long Island was half that of the boroughs, but the Black poverty rate (19.9 percent) differed little from the Bronx (25.9 percent) or the New York metropolitan area generally (23.6 percent).[110] Puerto Rican suburbanites were also twice as likely to live in poverty as their white counterparts. And a quarter of white, as well as 45 percent of Black female-headed households survived below the federal threshold.

The census statistics obscured the exploitative dynamics responsible for Long Island's poverty and inequality. Suburban officials emphasized where poverty concentrated, decrying Long Island's "poverty pockets." Local discourse also revolved around disproportionate Black and female poverty, applying the popular "culture of poverty" arguments circulating the public and academic spheres. Long Island residents fretted over the "seedy" men who pursued "lonely and impressionable" southern Black domestic workers, only to abandon them and their children. Journalists denounced the latchkey kids learning the ropes of juvenile delinquency as their mothers worked all day, like Bessie Jackson's five children. Social workers studied suburban single mothers to understand why Nassau's welfare load ballooned in the early 1960s. The reports noted that over half of all mothers were domestic workers, clerical employees, or factory workers. But the authors chose race as their analytical frame, comparing the white Catholic teenage moms and

Black southern migrants. They assessed the differing cultural attitudes toward single motherhood rather than their meager incomes. Once the War on Poverty got underway, illiteracy and skill deficiencies "shocked" county bureaucrats, who then pushed education as an antipoverty program.[111]

Relative poverty measures offer a better proxy to understand the ties between work, living costs, and poverty in postwar Long Island. The primary jobs driving Long Island's high median incomes reflected local living costs, which included a car, a mortgage or rent, and fees for children's school and extracurricular activities, among other needs. Families earning half or less of Long Island's median family income ($4,250 in Nassau County, $3,398 in Suffolk in 1959) couldn't afford those things. The US Labor Department determined that $6,000 in 1959 ($57,000 in 2021) was a "modest but adequate" budget for a four-person family in the New York metropolitan area—enough to afford rent, utilities, food, and taxes. The department considered families "poor" if they earned below $4,000 ($38,000 in 2021).[112] They struggled to make car payments, keep the pantry stocked, afford medical bills, get the needed house repairs, or make sure the kids had school supplies. They were over one in nine Long Island families; for Black Long Island families the number was one in three (table A.1). And their incomes reflected the fact that they likely worked a low-wage job on Long Island or in the New York metropolitan area.

But suburban poverty, and conversely economic security, rested in public institutions, evident in the lived experience of individuals. The welfare state failed Bessie Jackson, the mother of five compelled to reenter the workforce after her husband caught tuberculosis. She reentered domestic work because Long Island lacked day care options, and her job opportunities existed thanks to low wages. The same childcare dearth forced her kids to watch one another after school. Without disability insurance, her husband couldn't support the family. And because welfare was means tested, social services denied her relief. Because Bessie owned a home, assets had to be drained first. Public childcare, minimum wage coverage, labor rights, disability, robust public transit, housing relief, or even a guaranteed income would have saved the Jacksons from poverty amidst their tragedy.

But we need not look at Long Island's low-wage workers to see how the welfare state failed. As scholars have long noted, poverty is a condition, not an attribute of the poor. People enter and exit poverty throughout their lives—by some estimates, most Americans will end up poor at some point.[113] Defense workers, fully included within America's militarized welfare state, nonetheless faced bouts of poverty. A rare social work survey reveals this. The "M" family, a social work pseudonym, lived in New York City, just like the Jacksons. When Republic Aviation hired Mr. M during the Korean War boom, he, his expectant wife, and their two sons moved into a Long Island rental. They saved $300 for a down payment on a $9,600 mortgage, briefly achieving material comfort. Then mass plant layoffs in 1957 forced the family onto welfare. Mr. M couldn't find commensurate work; he took a summer beach job for a fraction of the pay. His coworker, Mr. L, faced similar challenges. With his job at Republic and his wife's beauty shop job, they bought a VA-insured home. But the home was a shell, and they needed a freezer, car, fence, bedroom furniture, storm windows, and a finished attic for their children. Without paid maternity leave or day care, Mrs. L quit her beautician job in 1957 when she became pregnant. The family tried managing on Mr. L's income alone, but Republic Aviation's layoffs squashed those plans. Mr. L was unemployed for over thirteen months. Debts ballooned, and the family turned to welfare to make ends meet after Mr. L could only find low-paying jobs.[114]

## Conclusion

The anecdotes above illustrate the limits to Long Island's "industrial garden," and by extension, the US welfare state. The single-family residences and industrial jobs dispersed across Long Island's former potato fields and Gold Coast mansions was America's ersatz social democracy, manifest in concrete, cul-de-sacs, and crabgrass. Federally insured, long-term, fixed-rate mortgages underwrote the homes; defense contracts created the jobs. Workplace democracy's three stools—the NLRA, FLSA, and SSA—enabled workers to buy homes, afford home repairs, and pay their property taxes. But good jobs were finite, dominated by white men, and tied to an erratic industry where strategic and budgetary concerns overshadowed employment needs. Defense workers were exploited to meet Cold War objectives, and they, alongside white-collar commuters, exploited others to raise their kids, expand their houses, fund their schools, and buy cheap food. Legislators excluded workers in these low-wage occupations from the welfare state. Private employers, faced with volatile competitive dynamics, depressed wages and working conditions. They exploited existing racial and gender hierarchies, disproportionately miring women and southern Black migrants in low-wage work. At the bottom were the suburban poor, who cultivated the industrial garden but could not reap what they sowed. Exploitation built suburban Long Island, the exemplar of postwar affluence.

Put simply, suburban prosperity depended on poverty. Federal spending reproduced inequality on Long Island after World War II. But it didn't have to be that way. From the New Deal through Fair Deal, Democratic Party legislators, who elsewhere in Europe might have been called "social democrats," envisioned a less exploitative society. They put childcare, cooperative housing, fair hiring, public jobs, and democratically determined minimum wages on the legislative docket. But Republicans, along with conservative and even liberal Democrats, rolled back existing social-democratic institutions and blocked new laws in the 1940s. Long Island epitomized the best of what remained. Bending the state toward social democracy would extend the economic security and living standards some Long Islanders enjoyed to all. But that required seeing welfare-state failure as the culprit. As we will see in the next chapter, suburbanites were aware of poor people in their midst, but suburbia obscured the federal government's role in producing suburban poverty.

# 3

# Attics, Basements, and Sheds

## *Housing the Poor during the Suburban Boom*

Let's return to New Cassel, this time in 1947. It was the same place James Baxter settled two decades prior, and where Bessie Jackson bought property twenty years later. But in 1947, Levitt and Sons eyed the sleepy unincorporated hamlet to extend their patented mass-produced single-family subdivisions. "Levittown" was then nothing more than former potato fields and barren parcels strung together across three towns, two congressional districts, and several ill-defined rural places. 268 empty lots sat within New Cassel's boundaries. The lots were a still-born subdivision from the 1920s suburban speculative boom, bare since the Depression. Roads already crossed the parcels, and the local governing body, North Hempstead Town, had zoned the lots for exclusive single-family residential use.

The Levitts transformed the deserted lots into a Levittown subdivision. They named the streets after pleasant flora—Holly, Elderberry, and Juniper. Subcontractors built Cape Cods at the standard $7,000 price point. To ensure FHA mortgage insurance approval, the Levitts also attached covenants to the properties, in effect until 1970. Stipulations ranged from the mundane, like fence and sign prohibitions, to the more consequential, namely that single families inhabit the homes and that "no house shall be used or occupied except by members of the Caucasian race," unless they were domestic workers.[1] Though the Levitts built this property near New Cassel's diverse pre–World War II working-class inhabitants, the company absorbed this corner into postwar, white-dominated suburbia.

Surely Ellery and Patricia Mann presumed New Cassel was part of Long Island's mass suburban future when they bought 13 Dogwood Lane in 1947. Over the years, they added a garage with Levitt and Sons' approval, who adjusted the covenant. In 1951, they sold the house to former Bronx residents

Nelson and Margaret Jane Lewis, who turned the empty attic into a two-room second floor. In 1956, the Lewises moved further east to wealthier Syosset, selling to William and Evelyn Dooley. For the Dooleys, the move was not far, but no less transformative. They previously rented a multifamily house overlooking the train tracks in nearby Westbury. Now, they enjoyed their own two-story single-family house on a quiet street.[2] From 1947 through 1956, 13 Dogwood Lane exemplified the expandable starter home new suburbanites bought, built upon, and sold as they moved up the income ladder and across Long Island's endless subdivisions. Postwar suburbanization likewise transformed New Cassel. Before World War II, a diverse working class sheltered in the neighborhood to avoid suburbia's tenements. After the war, New Cassel became a place where a more fortunate white working class could improve their living standard thanks to the FHA-insured loans and developers like the Levitts.

But in 1963, a new owner turned the Dogwood Lane Cape into something neither the Levitts, zoning officials, nor former owners intended. That year the Dooleys sold the property to a young Black guidance counselor for double its 1947 price. Theoretically, the buyer violated the Levitts' racial covenant, although legally they could not enforce the ban anymore. The real estate agent also exploited the fact that Black homebuyers purchased houses nearby. Many flipped homes from white to Black ownership around 13 Dogwood Lane, a practice derisively known as "blockbusting." But the guidance counselor violated other laws. She turned the garage into a bedroom, breaking the Levitts' ban against using the garage as a living space. She also rented 13 Dogwood Lane to multiple occupants. A local directory listed two households residing at the address, neither matching the owner's name. This was against both the covenant and municipal zoning regulations barring multifamily units. But enforcing covenants required costly lawsuits, and the town couldn't impose land-use laws on an existing legal single-family structure. In a few short years, the Black guidance counselor converted 13 Dogwood Lane from a federally insured single-family starter home into a revenue-producing, multifamily rental.[3]

The Dogwood Lane Cape Cod was nothing more than a husk made of concrete, wood, and linoleum atop a grass lot. Laws, codes, covenants, and contracts determined who lived there, on what terms (owned outright, mortgaged, rented, etc.), what they could alter, and whether they could expect passive income, asset appreciation, or only higher rents over time. We rarely distinguish between the physical structure and the rules governing its ownership and use. In most instances, the two aligned. The problem, as the story goes, were the exclusions: the restrictive single-family residential zones, the racist mortgage practices, or the racial covenants prohibiting people of color from buying or renting in suburban subdivisions.

But people severed 13 Dogwood Lane from the rules. In doing so, they helped resolve Long Island's housing shortages. The blockbusting real estate agent challenged the boundaries of racial housing segregation for a tidy profit.[4] The Black counselor then subverted the institutional rules governing the single-family unit, repurposing the Cape Cod for multiple families. This is what scholars call *informal* housing. Both the agent and counselor created housing for those excluded from Long Island's predominant housing market: Black families, single moms, young couples, and poor people. And they did it through exploitation. The same house had different prices for Black versus white homebuyers. Informal housing was the sole choice for individuals who couldn't afford legal housing. Both options proved lucrative, especially in New Cassel. Real estate speculators, debt-saddled homeowners, and enterprising landlords all took advantage of New Cassel's racially bifurcated market and inconsistent regulatory enforcement to transform single-family units into multifamily rentals (tables A.3, A.4). Informal housing resolved Long Island's dearth of low-income shelter options, and property owners used segregation to produce them.

Many accepted the transgressions. The Levitts already made their money. Tenants got needed shelter. The welfare department called landlords when they needed to house a recipient. Local governments could forgo controversial public housing. But neighboring homeowners, both Black and white, objected. They faced declining property values, overcrowded schools, rising taxes, and destabilized neighborhoods. To them, housing segregation and lax code enforcement caused informal housing. Homeowner activists organized civic associations, insisted local governments pass "housing codes," and demanded welfare departments evenly distribute recipients across Long Island rather than concentrate them in places like New Cassel. It was a local variant of suburban exceptionalism, the idea that the suburbs were, or at least should be, poverty-free. And it was part of a broader ideology that political scientist Preston H. Smith calls "racial democracy" circulating among housing activists in the postwar period. These homeowners decried racial discrimination and segregation in housing, i.e., exclusion, while accepting the class inequality embedded in the housing market. People should be free to buy what they can afford, regardless of color.[5]

But homeowner activists only attacked the means landlords used to produce informal housing (racial housing segregation), not the dearth of legal housing options. While they compelled local governments, building departments, and civil rights groups to criminalize informal housing, their attacks mobilized informal tenants to defend their right to suburban housing. Informal tenants found allies in layers of government as well, namely welfare departments and the courts. What they in effect demanded was a social-democratic approach to housing, that people should have legal and decent housing regardless of their ability to pay. Only that could end the exploitation at the root of discrimination and informal housing conversion.[6]

The local battles between suburban homeowners and informal tenants revealed how weak suburban regulation was, how much public officials depended on informality, and how deeply private property owners controlled suburban housing provision. The federal government baked informal housing into national housing policy. Means-tested FHA mortgage insurance excluded a diverse cohort of Americans who needed shelter. Nationwide housing code adoption (through federal urban renewal legislation) turned existing ways people inhabited suburban homes into illegal uses of housing units. That these became the predominant federal housing tools was not foreordained. That same postwar political conflict that eclipsed the social-democratic impulse in labor crushed both public and cooperative housing programs too. Private actors, both adhering to and breaking federally determined rules, supplied most of the nation's housing stock.[7] Postwar liberalism abandoned an egalitarian solution to housing; exploitation filled the void.

What follows is a story of how houses like 13 Dogwood Lane came to be, and the suburban political battles they triggered. The Cape Cod was but one example of an unknown but ubiquitous part of postwar suburbia, a clandestine housing market for Long Islanders excluded from the single-family owner-occupied housing market after World War II. While landlords rarely appear in postwar suburban histories, they served a critical function. Suburban prosperity depended on low-wage workers, but those workers depended on landlords who surreptitiously subdivided garages, furnished sheds, and finished basements. Informal housing was not affordable, as the squeeze between low incomes and the high housing costs produced shelter poverty, forcing people to forgo other needs. The politics surrounding informal housing nonetheless obscured housing needs. Activists focused on poverty's concentration in certain suburbs, seeing poverty as a problem of place. But poverty was rooted in the dearth of affordable housing, and suburban places were ill-equipped to address it.

## Vacuums in Housing Finance

Informal housing was Long Island's low-income shelter solution for a simple reason: the federal government's selective credit policies did not meet the needs of suburbia's diverse populace. Just as defense spending willed industrial suburbia into existence, so too did the Treasury-backed mortgage lending "guarantees." Legislators paid defense contracts from the federal budget. The government chose to fund most of the nation's housing through FHA mortgage insurance, with the full faith of the US Treasury behind lenders. This gave banks the *capacity* to lend to otherwise ineligible families.[8] And banks did so. After World War II, FHA officials flooded Long Island with mortgage insurance to a degree unmatched elsewhere.[9] Single-family housing, exclusive residential zones, and white male–breadwinner families predominated. But the FHA's influence on Long Island severely constrained housing choices for young adults and the elderly, single moms, Black suburbanites excluded from the FHA program, and low-wage workers well below borrowing thresholds. Builders and private property owners resolved their housing needs by exploiting regulatory gaps.

With a fresh highway network, New York City's acute housing shortage, and the exploding industrial job market, Long Island was the perfect place for FHA-insured housing sales. After World War II, Nassau and Suffolk Counties accounted for 80 percent of all FHA-insured mortgages in the New York metropolitan region. By 1960, FHA-insured mortgages covered a third of all Nassau County units. The average Long Island property was the FHA-standard 854-square-foot house on a 6,000-square-foot plot.[10] Nassau and Suffolk builders favored FHA-approved single-family dwellings. Between 1951 and 1961, both counties issued over 266,000 single-family permits. By comparison, the counties issued only 19,000 multifamily permits, a category encompassing two-family homes, cooperatives, and large apartment complexes.[11] And in 1947, the year before *Shelley v. Kraemer* declared racial covenants unconstitutional, racially restrictive covenants covered 47 percent of Nassau County subdivisions.[12] Planners extended plumbing, electrical, fire, building and zoning codes to Long Island's unincorporated areas, anticipating FHA-style subdivisions. Thanks to federal housing programs and local planning boards, Long Island became the quintessential postwar suburb.

Of course, the FHA and other related programs, like VA mortgage insurance, were not public housing programs. Instead, they socialized private lending. Banks still had to screen borrowers, and "creditworthiness" determined whether one could encumber long-term mortgage debt. Ultimately, credit is about whether a lender can trust someone to repay debt. It is, at its core, a subjective measure. Because the federal government shouldered the risk, the FHA devised credit eligibility guidelines. Most infamously, the FHA adopted the real estate industry's entrenched biases, draped in scientific language, attributing differential property values to racial groups. This severely constrained Black home buying while folding European-descended Americans into an entitled "white" category. FHA officials likewise considered women as household members rather than individuals, excluding their income from eligibility calculations. And as political scientist Chloe Thurston finds, lenders subjectively determined ostensibly "objective" criteria like income as well. Before federal mortgage insurance, lenders generally used high down payments as the hedge against risk. After the FHA popularized the low down payment, long-term amortized loan, lenders used other metrics to judge creditworthiness. They scrutinized a borrower's job, their future earning potential, employment stability, and even their morality, like whether they drank or treated their wife well. The FHA also encouraged developers and planners to adopt property value-preserving zoning laws and restrictive covenants. This assured lenders they would be repaid and reduced the foreclosure risks the government assumed under the FHA.[13]

Exclusions effectively locked many Long Islanders out of the insured mortgage market. Only 6 percent of Long Island's FHA loans covered the 60,000 households earning half or less than Long Island's median family income.[14] Real estate agents steered Black homebuyers, regardless of income, away from white subdivisions and toward rare FHA-approved "open housing" developments. Lenders meanwhile pushed Black borrowers into the uninsured mortgage market. And even for otherwise eligible white working-class Long Islanders, land-use policy often raised housing prices beyond their means.

But builders found ways around Long Island's land-use, building, and lending restrictions. Some wielded significant power to alter zoning or building codes, like when Levitt and Sons goaded the Town of Hempstead to remove their basement mandate. Most though exploited Long Island's balkanized political jurisdictions: two counties, two cities, thirteen towns, ninety-two villages, 135 school districts, 126 fire districts, and 477 special districts.[15] Incorporated villages passed comprehensive codes, but unincorporated towns only slowly adopted them. Zoning ordinances predated World War II in all thirteen of Long Island's unincorporated towns, but only one town regulated buildings.[16] Enforcement proved tricky too. FHA or VA inspectors approved projects based on model homes, while a town's building department sometimes granted occupancy certificates to blueprints.[17] And Long Island FHA inspectors colluded with local builders to such a degree that federal courts convicted a few for bribery and extortion.[18]

Developers used legally ambiguous unincorporated places to house people barred from regulated and FHA-creditworthy suburbia. In these spaces, they could cut corners and reduce prices below Levitt and Sons' rock-bottom $6,999. Dozens of complaints reveal the consequences. In a 1952 congressional hearing, disgruntled homeowners complained Long Island builders secured FHA approval for boilers in model units before switching to cheaper and faulty heating systems in actual houses. In western Suffolk County, builders exploited the 1950 National Housing Act amendments, intended to insure "low- and moderate-income" housing in the US South and West, where "practically all you have to do is sheet-rock and put a door on the bathroom." Heavy rains flooded FHA-insured homes because builders didn't grade yards. Other units lacked electrical grid hookups. Alabama Congressman Albert Rains, who wrote the 1950 amendments, admitted he had never intended the low standards for Long Island. But Suffolk builder Lawrence Ingoglia testified that he was the first to use the program, offering $4,999 suburban single-family homes. "These people received exactly what they paid for," Ingoglia retorted.[19]

These subdivisions were "suburban," but a poor facsimile of Levittown's functional Cape Cods and clean curvilinear streets. The rock-bottom home prices did offer homeownership and wealth-building opportunities for otherwise excluded families, however. With a little extra sweat equity and a few town hall protests, homes and subdivisions could get the amenities found elsewhere on Long Island. Just as importantly, these spaces offered rare instances for Black homeownership and racially integrated neighborhoods in an otherwise segregated housing landscape. Cheap subdivisions were not the only places Black homeowners or the mortgage ineligible lived. But loosely regulated spaces supplied larger concentrations of new postwar housing outside the race- and class-exclusive suburban landscape.

While developers found ways to build cheaper single-family units, their projects further reduced rental options, especially for families. Rent control only applied to apartments constructed before 1947. Developers preferred erecting efficiency and one-bedroom apartments after the war, which accounted for two-thirds of all multifamily units.[20] Long Island's poorest packed into old domestic enclaves. Where a homeowning suburbanite enjoyed a garage, electric stove, and maybe even a washer or TV included in their home purchase, domestic enclave residents crammed into decrepit buildings without central heating, hot water, indoor toilets, or bathtubs.[21] Otherwise, they moved out to Long Island's East End (figure 3.1). There towns lacked zoning regulations, encouraging farmers, including Riverhead's duck magnate Hollis Warner, to enter the low-income housing market. Warner sold two models. The first was a five hundred-square-foot unit with gas stove, refrigerator, kerosene gas heater, and hand pump. The second was a free standing eighty-one-square-foot single-room apartment with refrigerator. None had bathrooms; Warner erected outhouses behind the units. Though fifty miles or

FIGURE 3.1. Migrant housing on Suffolk's East End, 1951. © Eve Arnold/Magnum Photos.

more from suburban jobs, long-distance commuters moved in. A Warner homeowner named Mary commuted to her Roslyn domestic job sixty miles west. Another tenant hitched rides to landscape Nassau County yards fifty miles away.[22]

But even domestic enclaves and rural shacks didn't survive postwar suburbanization. Local planners and politicians harnessed federal money to "renew" these enclaves. As one journalist remarked, domestic enclaves were "destined for redevelopment," a euphemism for what historian Andrew Wiese rightly calls *suburban* renewal, clearing out affordable housing, and the poor, for middle-income units or tax revenue-generating commercial property.[23] Though most plans included public housing, by 1965, local authorities erected only 658 family units, a negligible fraction of the 37,000 units needed.[24] Among Long Island's fifteen urban renewal projects, developers replaced seven hundred substandard dwellings with only 303 new apartments.[25]

By the 1960s, the affordable housing squeeze intensified. Developers preferred "luxury" apartments, the state further deregulated rents, planners reduced maximum zoning densities, and construction generally slowed. This produced an interesting paradox. Despite Long Island's high median family incomes, Nassau and Suffolk had New York's most affordable single-family homes. The Nassau Planning Commission attributed low prices to "large-scale development and lower costs of construction." In contrast, Nassau and Suffolk Counties topped the metropolitan list for highest median rents.[26] High housing costs led to what Michael Stone calls "shelter poverty." Available data suggests one in ten Long Island families, 60,000 in total, could not afford the median four-room rent lest they cut back on basic needs as the Bureau of Labor Statistics (BLS) defined them. This included haircuts, medical visits, or low-cost grocery items like potatoes, beans, and cereal. Housing segregation forced Black tenants, who paid 10 percent more than white tenants for the same unit, into greater shelter poverty. One in four Black Long Island families could not make rent without sacrificing some need. On Long Island, the squeeze between high housing costs and low incomes caused poverty.[27]

The severe rental shortage, combined with acute housing demand, encouraged suburban informal housing. By informality, I mean what the state considered illegitimate construction and occupancy. Rented basements, garages, attics, and sheds violated plumbing, building, electrical, fire, and zoning codes, or as we will see below, newly devised housing codes passed amidst the informal housing boom. Measuring their extent is difficult given informality's clandestine nature.[28] The Nassau County Assessment Department offers one estimate. They conducted a two-family structure census across Nassau's three unincorporated towns in 1970. The count included 55 percent of all Long Island housing (over 380,000 units). In these towns, building departments permitted only 40 percent of the census-recorded two-family units; the other 60 percent were multiple families occupying single-family houses. This means unpermitted two-family units accounted for one in every twenty Hempstead, North Hempstead, and Oyster Bay housing units.[29]

The number understates housing informality's extent because property owners no doubt hid their tenants from census enumerators. It also captures all types of informal renters, from newlyweds saving for a down payment to college students living off campus or a retiree downsizing from a full house. To understand how informality housed the poor, we must examine hamlets where mass informality occurred. Below we take a deep dive into places like

New Cassel, where predatory lenders, fly-by-night developers, blockbusting real estate agents, and debt-burdened homeowners encouraged rapid turnover and foreclosures, encouraging the conversion of owner-occupied homes into multifamily rentals. It also means identifying "poor" suburban residents. I use "home relief recipients" as a proxy, beneficiaries of a state welfare program administered by county governments, similar to the federal government's later Section 8 rental voucher program.

## Embedding Informal Housing

13 Dogwood Lane's conversion from Levitt single-family Cape to informal multifamily dwelling was a mundane suburban act. The owner likely blasted a new doorway to the garage or partitioned the front ingress into separate entryways. It was a project completed with tools and materials readily available at the local hardware shop and lumber yard. But property owners replicated informalization across New Cassel and similar places, including Roosevelt in Nassau County, and Wyandanch and Central Islip in Suffolk County (figure A.2). Because Long Island's housing market and zoning policy aligned with FHA guidelines, these loosely regulated unincorporated places served the mortgage ineligible and uncreditworthy well. Here developers put up cheap and shoddy housing conducive to rapid turnover. Speculators preyed on homeowners burdened with predatory mortgage financing, precarious jobs, or racist fears of Black neighbors next door. Homeowners with onerous mortgages also felt compelled to informalize their own housing. These dynamics, and the actors behind them, embedded informal housing within these places. Speculators turned structures built with FHA guidelines into informal units. Collectively they transformed single-family hamlets into distinct places that straddled the line between formal homeowner-oriented suburbs and informal tenant enclaves.

We begin in Central Islip, the Suffolk County hamlet where Dorothy Daniels lived, first described in the book's introduction. This is because Central Islip is a clear example of how the cheapest FHA-insured housing units were ripe for informalization. Central Islip's suburban history began in 1889 when New York State opened a 994-acre "farm" for Manhattan's mentally ill, which eventually turned into the Central Islip State Hospital. After World War II, patient numbers peaked, and veteran builders George B. Rabinor and Milton Spear secured FHA-financing to construct a 300-unit single-family subdivision in the hospital's shadow in 1953. Called Carleton Park, the subdivision catered to hospital attendants and others at their pay scale. The houses hewed to minimum FHA standards, with basement-less concrete foundations, four rooms, and six hundred square feet of living space on 8,000-square-foot plots. To cut heating equipment costs, the builders installed large metal floor grates that blasted hot air from the floor. They advertised it as "central air," though the inefficient vents burned children's limbs. Their efforts reduced prices to $5,990, a thousand less than Levittown. They advertised Carleton Park to the modest worker, people earning as little as $55 a week, three-quarters of the county median family income. With only $290 down and $35 a month, owners could build equity all while Rabinor and Spear counted on FHA-insured profit.[30] The homes quickly filled, mostly with white families and a few Black and Puerto Rican buyers.

While a success for Rabinor and Spear, Carleton Park's shoddy construction encouraged early buyers to escape. Mid-1950s hospital layoffs forced others into foreclosure and panicked sales. Speculators then plundered the subdivision. As early as 1956, George J. Trost, a "cash for homes" speculator, bought several Carleton Park properties, folding them into a holding company in 1960. His actions were not transformative because he resold the insured mortgages, ostensibly preserving owner-occupation.[31] But others had different ideas. In 1954, Richard Merkel purchased 40 Beech Street. Four years later, he sold the house to Harry and Patricia Carroll in a conventional transaction. All seemed normal, but in 1960, the home's status changed. That year, the Carrolls transferred the property and their $7,000 outstanding mortgage to Louis J. Modica, a prominent developer and then president of the Suffolk County Real Estate Board.[32]

Modica, a failed chicken farmer turned local real estate tycoon, dabbled in all sorts of housing markets across Long Island. He exploited the National Housing Act's 1950 amendments to construct shoddy four-room homes at rock-bottom prices in western Suffolk County, where cesspools flooded and building inspectors refused to grant occupancy certificates. He moved families into the FHA-insured housing anyway, much to their chagrin.[33] He also bought foreclosed properties or offered cash buyouts and then dumped the homes back onto the market with "lease-to-purchase plans." These were a variation of the land installment contract. Depending on the lease terms, tenants paid rent until they reached a down-payment threshold to obtain ownership. Under some contracts, occupants may not secure the deed until they completely paid off the property mortgage. One missed payment could forfeit all the equity the "buyer" had built over time. It was an old practice that long predated the FHA-insured mortgage; even Jurgis Rudkus, the main character of Upton Sinclair's 1906 *The Jungle*, had one that bankrupted the family and left them homeless.[34] Installment contracts didn't disappear after the FHA program. Modica, who under his name or his mortgagee and building companies, owned at least thirteen Carleton Park houses in the early 1960s, illustrating that Carleton Park had slipped to the unregulated speculative side of the housing market.[35]

It is unclear when the federal government no longer extended mortgage insurance, or "redlined" Carleton Park. Homeowners secured FHA loans as late as 1958, but by 1960, the transformation was underway. As original resident Frank Russo put it, "suddenly it was like the other end of a boom town . . . people lost jobs and their homes were bought up by real estate operators and other people just up and left. Everything just fell apart." Homeowners could no longer refinance insured mortgages or sell to FHA-qualified buyers; they instead accepted between $50 and $300 cash rather than the equity they had accumulated over the preceding years.[36] In 1962 and 1963, the South Shore Mortgagee Corporation, National Mortgagee Corporation, Repurchase Corporation of America, and Jaro Homes, Inc. came to own over forty Carleton Park homes. These holding companies accumulated properties and debt from former owner-occupiers, Louis Modica's and George Trost's previous holdings, and other speculators. They offered "lease-to-purchase" or "rent-to-buy" land contracts, or they sought tenants for traditional rental agreements.[37] Their investments bore little fruit, though. By March 1965, an estimated seventy homes remained vacant, a quarter of Carleton Park, including some twenty-eight FHA and VA foreclosures. Vandals broke windows and people abandoned cars in the area. Then came James Northrop.[38]

In his former life, James Northrop was a school principal, but he lost that job in 1954 after school board investigations revealed he assaulted thirty-five students. The state supreme court reinstated him the same year, but a physical altercation with protesting parents, which had Northrop allegedly chasing a father down a suburban street with a rake, forced him out once and for all. According to his first wife, the ordeal drove him "to become the first millionaire in his family." Thanks to a small inheritance, Northrop entered the Wild West of Long Island rentals. At first, he leased homes to teachers and other professionals. By 1965, Northrop plunged into Carleton Park. With a deep portfolio of properties as collateral, Northrop secured a $75,000 bank loan. On a single August day, Northrop paid between $500 and $7,000 cash for thirty National and South Shore Mortgagee Corporation houses.[39] In the following months, Northrop financed the purchase of VA foreclosures with purchase-money mortgages, offering cash down and negotiating a payment plan with the VA for the remaining debt. He also pressured remaining homeowners out of their properties, like Roberto and Rose Vega of 38 O'Kane Street.[40] In total, Northrop owned sixty-five properties in Carleton Park by December 1965.

From the very beginning, property owners found ways to balance risk and profit. Builders Rabinor and Spear skimped on building materials and left the risk to the FHA and VA. Trost, Modica, and the mortgagee companies held onto the properties and exported the risk to the mortgagors through various exploitative financing instruments. Northrop chose a different path, accepting "home relief" payments from Long Island's most destitute rather than the unpredictable market of contract loans. Enshrined in New York State's 1938 Constitution, state welfare law required both Nassau and Suffolk Counties to shelter struggling residents. Albany covered between 40 percent and 100 percent of rental costs while counties and cities had broad discretion over what housing they offered welfare recipients.[41] Without public housing, Nassau's and Suffolk's welfare departments left the homeless to find their own private accommodations. The department only determined rental ceilings and performed safety inspections. Home relief was nonetheless a lifeline to Long Island's poor, and also a guaranteed income stream for property owners who capitalized on the tight rental market to price-gouge the state.

Northrop actively pursued welfare recipients, particularly those of color. Suffolk's welfare department had difficulty helping Black welfare recipients because as Mae Sloane, Suffolk's family care director admitted, they "just cannot find better housing" for "certain groups for which it is difficult."[42] Over a quarter of non-white welfare recipients lived in single rooms within deteriorating or dilapidated housing units, and 13 percent lacked heat or kitchens and baths.[43] Northrop offered fully equipped single-family homes, and he cultivated a personal relationship with welfare officials. Suffolk's welfare housing inspector Alice Shaw admitted, "I have a feeling of trust with Mr. Northrop . . . if he does have a house available, I'm sure it will be in good shape when he puts someone in it. There are few landlords who have a multiple number of houses that you can work that way with."[44] The trust paid well. At the standard $135 a month, Northrop pulled in at least twice the monthly mortgage payments per property, assuming he limited each home to a single family. With stable passive income streams, Northrop acquired more Carleton Park houses thereafter.

In seven years, speculators created housing for the poor in Carleton Park. They transferred FHA-insured housing to the unregulated market, which Northrop then purchased and guaranteed himself a tidy profit via state welfare payments. But Carleton Park was an anomaly, a perfect storm that completely turned the single-family subdivision into a de facto rental project. The other three hamlets were more emblematic of suburban low-income housing production. Each remained single-family-homeowner-dominated suburbs through 1970, with poverty "pockets" or dispersed informal units.

We turn next to Wyandanch, only nine miles west of Central Islip. Before 1940, Black and European immigrants built their own suburban homes and scavenged for coal along Wyandanch's railroad tracks. With preexisting racial diversity and low-income homeownership, Wyandanch was an ideal space for non-white housing subdivisions after the war. In 1949, Taca Home Builders Incorporated constructed Carver Park, an "open" FHA-insured housing development around the Levitt standard $6,990 mark. Other developers followed, and in total, builders made some four hundred homes available for Black buyers. Like Central Islip's Carleton Park, advertisers promoted the area's affordability, where earnings as low as $60 per week qualified one for an FHA-insured mortgage. And like Carleton Park, Wyandanch was situated within the unincorporated Town of Babylon, where the local building department issued occupancy certificates for "practically a shell" as a real estate attorney joked.[45]

Speculators exploited Wyandanch's non-white housing market, its small self-built shacks, and its tiny resort cottages scattered throughout the Pine Barren scrub. Samuel Crowe, a prominent funeral home operator and Black Democratic political activist from Jamaica, Queens, bought three properties, including 23 Lake Place. William and Charlotte Crosby first purchased 23 Lake Place in 1961 thanks to an uninsured mortgage with Republic Investor's Corporation. But they moved out within a year, transferring the deed and $13,000 mortgage to Crowe through a "purchase-money" mortgage arrangement. Crowe privately worked out payments with Republic Investor's Corporation and rented the house to welfare recipients. The two-story, single-family unit quickly fell into disrepair, as pipes leaked, the toilet sprayed water all over the bathroom, and rainwater trickled down through the walls. The water traveled into the basement, slowly corroding the furnace until it broke down altogether in 1972, forcing Mary Gordon, her three grown children, and a grandchild to rely on a space heater and open oven to keep warm.[46]

The same occurred elsewhere in Wyandanch. In 1956, Walmark Realty sold modest ranches and Cape Cods a mile south of Crowe's 23 Lake Place property. *Amsterdam News* advertised the tiny subdivision, an obvious ploy to profit from the constrained Black housing market. But the purchaser of 199 Parkway Boulevard, Milton Farnum of Jamaica, Queens, had other plans. In 1957, Farnum and his wife took out an $8,000 conventional mortgage for the house. But the Farnums may never have lived there, because by the mid-1960s, Farnum and nearby Wyandanch resident Justers L. Cobbs were joint absentee owners. They transformed it into a multifamily rental and passive income source. By the early 1970s, Farnum and Cobbs folded 199 Parkway Boulevard into their Arbee Holding Company for tax purposes, and Cobbs even used the house as collateral for a car loan.[47] Beyond postwar subdivisions, white owners of the old summer cottages, never intended nor legally sanctioned for year-round use, rented out their vacation bungalows to two, three, and four families all year round as Wyandanch's resort appeal faded.[48]

Unlike Wyandanch, which sat at postwar suburbanization's eastern edge, New Cassel was right in the middle. This is why Levitt and Sons expanded their subdivision into New Cassel in 1947, and others quickly followed, though few matched the Levittown's infrastructure. Developers of nearby "Hicksbury Homes" eschewed paved streets or curbs, despite promising such things.[49] They got away with it because the Town of North Hempstead granted variances and proved slow to enforce building codes in the unincorporated area. Between 1940 and 1960, New Cassel's housing stock blossomed from five hundred to over two thousand single-family homes. The unincorporated place offered the fifth most affordable single-family houses in Nassau County out of ninety-four hamlets. With earlier Black settlers, Black families bought homes, many of whom had "less financial means than 'middle class' may imply . . . [and] strapped themselves to buy their homes, often necessitating full-time employment of wives and mothers in order to meet expenses." Over half of white residents labored in factories or blue-collar craft jobs, while Black residents worked as operatives, clerical staff, and domestic help, though Black professionals and clerical staff joined them.[50]

FHA-approved subdivisions did not erase New Cassel's historic role as a domestic and day laborer haven. The 13 Dogwood Lane informal conversion (mentioned in the chapter introduction) was but one example of the changes afoot in New Cassel's Levitt homes. Just next door, at 17 Dogwood Lane, three owner-occupiers bought and sold the house with conventional insured mortgages. But in 1958, buyer Robert F. Snyder resorted to a predatory "purchase-money mortgage," an uninsured home financing mechanism where lenders could demand the mortgage in full any time they wanted. Now ineligible for federal mortgage insurance, "purchase-money mortgages" became the vehicle for both subsequent property owners to buy the house. By 1965, a local reference directory confirms a tenant lived in the Cape Cod, not the owner, and a local survey identified that the tenant paid their rent via state home relief.[51]

All told, discrepancies between deed names, reference directory lists, and a local welfare survey suggest that non-owners and home relief recipients occupied a third of New Cassel's Levitt-built Cape Cods by the late 1960s. Figure 3.2 offers a snapshot into the various informal housing arrangements in New Cassel's "Levittown." Conventional owner-occupiers shared suburban blocks with a diverse cohort of neighbors: owners on home relief; welfare

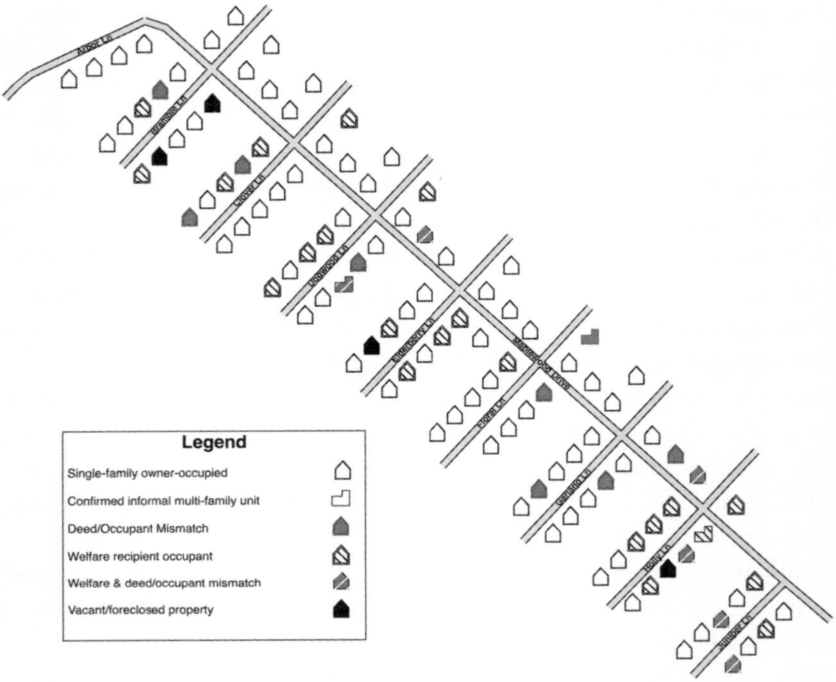


FIGURE 3.2. Housing occupancy among Levitt and Sons' Maplewood Drive subdivision in New Cassel circa late 1960s.

*Sources*: Section 11, Block 11, Lots 21–33, Block 112, Lots 830–877, Block 117, Lots 52–837, Block 118, Lots 27–182, Block 173, Lots 124–134, Block 329, Lots 327–372, NCLR; *Cole's Metropolitan Householders Directory, Nassau 1971*, 121, 213, 267, 290, 325, 360, 450, 497, 591; Organization for Social and Technical Innovation, et al., *Poverty in Spread City*, fig. 17C.

tenants; renters paying market rates; and landlords splitting garages, dormered second floors, or back rooms into informal apartments. By the 1960s, locals referred to the subdivision as "Maplewood Drive," no longer associated with Levittown.

Figure 3.2 also reveals the distinction between New Cassel and Carleton Park. Informal housing didn't dominate Maplewood Drive's Cape Cods. Code-breaking multifamily rentals sat alongside regular owner-occupied houses, law-abiding absentee landlords, homeowners-cum-landlords, and hard-on-their luck "home relief" owner-occupiers. And unlike in Carleton Park, small-time landlords or desperate homeowners drove informality. It reflects homeownership's precarity in New Cassel and the survival value of rentals. As one local civic association activist described the process:

> Here were, in many cases, hard pressed non-whites, running to get away from slums and ghettoes. . . . They came. Taxes skyrocketed and their income was not commensurate. The children grew up and moved on their own and the homeowner takes in roomers at $20, $25 a week. Suddenly, the first hint of crabgrass suburbs, absentee landlords and all.[52]

Just to the south, Roosevelt demonstrates how real estate blockbusting enabled informal housing. The unincorporated hamlet in the Town of Hempstead never quite reached Edward Uhe's railroad suburb dreams in the early twentieth century. Instead, it became a haven for Black and European immigrant homeowners. After 1945, developers constructed all-white subdivisions in the hamlet's undeveloped north and west, including Hausch Manor and the Baldwin Woods subdivision along the western border. Black buyers meanwhile purchased homes in the "Black" section south of Washington Avenue. Roosevelt developers built the cheapest single-family housing in Nassau County outside of white-exclusive Levittown and Bellmore. But not all Black buyers could access FHA mortgage insurance. They instead relied on predatory risky financial instruments. Precarity, exploitative mortgages, a weak tax base, and acute demand for limited housing stock among arriving Black suburbanites made Roosevelt a national exemplar of "blockbusting." Real estate agents exploited white homeowners' racial anxieties to buy their properties at lower prices, and then resold them to Black homebuyers at higher prices. They flipped the one-square mile place from majority white to majority Black within ten years (table A.3).[53]

Alongside the high-profile blockbusters were heterogeneous property owners exploiting Roosevelt's tumultuous market to house low-income informal tenants. Hardship encouraged some informal conversion. In 1958, John and Louise Griffon bought a brand-new Cape Cod at 44 Cumberland Avenue. As a war veteran, John qualified for a VA-insured mortgage, and in 1964, the Griffons took out a second mortgage for a new roof. But the next year, Valley Stream National Bank foreclosed on the property, leaving it in the hands of Veterans Affairs. The VA held the deed for nine years afterward, though whoever managed the property rented it out because *Cole's Reference Directory* lists a tenant.[54] Other struggling homeowners entered the landlord business themselves. In 1960, George and Ethel Wormley bought a brand-new one thousand-square-foot ranch at 22 Elizabeth Street with a $13,200 mortgage. But the Wormleys struggled to make ends meet. They took out a second mortgage in 1963, and around the same time, rented to at least one welfare recipient. Unfortunately, the extra money proved inadequate, and in 1965, the bank foreclosed on the house, recording six unidentified "tenants" living in the house on the tax lien.[55]

For every small-time struggling homeowner, two or three bigger players added to Roosevelt's informal rental stock. Insurance agent Stanley Phillips was a white Roosevelt resident of 62 Mansfield Avenue, a property he bought in 1953 with a $9,250 mortgage, just $58.53 per month in principal and interest. He and his wife raised eight children there, and the kids outgrew the eight hundred-square-foot house, so Phillips moved out of Roosevelt. But rather than sell the Mansfield Avenue property, Phillips added a two-car garage and a 128-square-foot shed. Then he rented to welfare recipients. With five rooms and three additional "living" spaces carved out of the shed and garage, Phillips made at least $300 a month, five times his monthly mortgage obligation. Phillips cultivated a close relationship with his tenants, giving them rides to doctor's appointments, lending them money, and helping them navigate the welfare bureaucracy. The favors no doubt gave Philips altruistic satisfaction. But those relationships, and the public money flowing into his bank account, encouraged him to invest in two other nearby Roosevelt properties: 96 East Clinton Street in 1967 and 21 Rose Avenue in 1968. Like his first multifamily apartment "complex," he spliced 21 Rose Avenue, fitting four families into a nine hundred-square-foot house, with another tenant crammed into the backyard garage.[56]

All these property owners—Stanley Phillips in Roosevelt, Justers Cobbs in Wyandanch, James Northrop in Carleton Park, and New Cassel's down-on-their-luck homeowners—produced a kind of housing that had a long history in urban America. Like Chicago's bulging "Black belt," Harlem's "kitchenettes," or the bathrooms converted to bedrooms in Baltimore, each exploited the racist and means-tested housing programs that artificially constrained housing choices for Long Island's excluded residents. But this happened in postwar America's most affluent place, often in units constructed for the upwardly mobile working class. The federal programs supporting those units never intended to serve everyone who needed housing; neither did local building standards and established lending practices. Speculators, developers, and homeowners ignored the building standards, secured alternative financing, or secretly converted single-family homes for those left out, the poor especially. The problem was how to best address informal housing's many consequences, from threats to health, housing quality, and property values, to the perceived ideal of suburbia.

## Enforcing Codes

On a technical level, the rental units in unincorporated hamlets were not "informal" in the early 1960s. Shed dwellings were no doubt an aluminum equivalent of the makeshift shanties encircling cities in the global south. 13 Dogwood Lane's second-story apartment? Not so much. "Informal" housing though is less about the structure than the regulations imposed on them. And as late as 1963, no Long Island unincorporated town codified proper forms of occupancy. But as property owners carved out apartments in these hamlets, neighboring homeowners fought back. These homeowners, both Black and white, formed civic associations, and they identified the agents exploiting housing segregation—blockbusting real estate agents, speculative landlords, welfare caseworkers—as the source of neighborhood problems. Contending that these unscrupulous actors threatened racially integrated suburbs, civic associations compelled town and county authorities to define the boundaries between legal and illegal housing uses. But their efforts were a local variant of suburban exceptionalism, the idea that the suburbs should, or even could, be free of the poor. They wanted the housing market, and municipal housing regulation, to treat them as it did white-exclusive suburbs. They wanted the right to exclude, embedded in land-use law and building codes, extended to everyone, not only privileged white people. This was the "racial-democratic" approach popular among housing activists across US cities.[57] Their efforts brought civic associations and local governments into direct conflict with poor tenants. Informal renters likewise looked to the state to defend their stake in these hamlets, including the courts who defended their legal rights and welfare offices with vested interests in preserving an informal housing market. The outcome of these battles ultimately determined what these suburbs would become.

Multifamily rentals in single-family units were not "informal" in the 1950s because Long Island's regulatory regime focused on structures rather than occupancy. While all unincorporated towns had plumbing, building, electrical, fire, and zoning codes, towns applied the regulation during construction or purchase. Aside from New York City, few municipalities in the US passed "housing codes," which regulated how people lived in housing after initial construction. New York's were on the books since 1867. Chicago did not pass a systematic housing code until 1956. Most other cities, towns, or villages only passed housing ordinances in the 1950s and 1960s. In other words, Long Island's unincorporated towns were not outliers. And federal prodding was the reason most passed housing codes. This was the other way federal officials restricted housing options for people otherwise excluded from the means-tested FHA programs: the Urban Renewal Act of 1954 required any locality that accepted federal funding to adopt local housing codes.[58] The idea was to prevent housing dilapidation and slums, especially after cities bulldozed housing stock and redeveloped them. And undoubtedly housing codes could improve living conditions. But when aligned with FHA-standard single-family owner-occupancy, they had the effect of turning the varied ways suburbanites inhabited their homes into civil violations.

Housing codes were not the sole means to regulate how people used homes, but other enforcement mechanisms were weak. Tax assessors periodically checked homes to capture more tax revenue from structural improvements. But they could be fooled. Roosevelt landlord Stanley Phillip's tax assessment card for 62 Mansfield Avenue illustrates how he convinced (or bribed) inspectors to write that the garage was a "children's play area" and not one of his five apartments. Debate in the 1950s revolved around structures, not occupancy, as local planners fretted over low construction standards. By the 1960s, however, occupancy took center stage as the building boom subsided, the rental housing squeeze intensified, and thousands fretted over the biggest investment of their lives. Multifamily occupancy raised the likelihood of neighborhood redlining, encouraged blockbusting, and strained the fiscal and physical integrity of each hamlet's overcrowded housing stock and schools. Some homeowners believed suburban homeownership should bestow middle-class status, deliver decent municipal services with low property taxes, and secure an appreciating asset. They in turn formed a contingent homeowner class who mobilized against informal housing as a perceived threat to property and neighborhood. These homeowners included white people of modest means who cast their homes as symbols of upward mobility, along with Black homebuyers who interpreted their purchases with the added significance of breaching housing segregation. Both were determined to protect their hard-won property.[59] They led the charge against informal housing.

The "civic association" was the institutional vehicle these homeowners used to advance their interests. Town governments recognized these private organizations as quasi-official "representatives" of their respective hamlets.[60] When mobilized homeowners stuffed town officials' mailboxes, crammed town hall meetings, or picketed constructed sites, local politicians listened. The challenge was organizing homeowners as a united constituency. How each civic association framed property value protection and how they attracted membership depended on two factors: each hamlet's institutional context, and the appeal of ascriptive categories.

Race played a particularly important, and complex, political role in Long Island's integrated hamlets. In New Cassel for example, the Black-dominated Progressive Civic Association of New Cassel (PCANC) infused their homeowner concerns with demands for racial equity. PCANC's leadership had close ties to the hamlet's National Association for the Advancement of Colored People (NAACP) branch, and the civic association challenged multiple attempts to rezone parts of New Cassel for industrial parks as a "sinister form of slavery."[61] Elsewhere, local contexts produced different coalitions and rationales. In Central Islip, the rash of vacancies compelled Black and white homeowners to assemble the Carleton Park Civic Association. They focused on material inequities without appeals to race: unpaved roads, missing street signs, broken streetlights, and rapid housing turnover.[62] In Roosevelt, disparate civic associations reflected the segregated housing market within the hamlet, but rapid blockbusting compelled these civic associations to form the "United Organizations of Roosevelt," an umbrella organization that cast their civic efforts as a means to preserve racial integration, a 60:40 white–Black ratio according to the organization's leader Morton Decker.[63]

The most interesting civic endeavors developed in Wyandanch, largely because a contingent cross-racial civic coalition coalesced around the eccentric longtime resident Hermann Griem. Affectionately referred to as "The Little Nemesis of Town Hall" and "Hermann the Griem," the five-foot two-inch German immigrant was a mainstay among civic associations in western Suffolk County. He dominated public discourse to such a degree that the Town of Babylon limited town hall meeting comments to twenty-minutes just to silence him. He was "not color blind" as one Black Wyandanch leader remarked. He was once arrested as the lone picketer against a Congress of Racial Equality (CORE) demonstration to integrate the Wyandanch Fire Department. But he nonetheless included Black Wyandanch civic associations into his umbrella civic association, the Joint Council of Civic and Taxpayer Associations, and when interests aligned, like closing sandpits surrounding Wyandanch or stopping proposed industrial zones, Black civic members joined forces with Griem.[64]

Despite varying contexts, these civic associations shared a similar approach to their perceived problems. Parity was the goal, measured in brick-and-mortar improvements white-exclusive suburbs took for granted. They pressured town officials, and the miles of asphalt, electrical wiring, and drainpipes marked success. These civic associations applied their strategies to multifamily housing conversion. They interpreted informal housing as another inequity imposed on *them*, poverty concentrating in *their* hamlets to the detriment of property values, taxes, municipal services, and neighborhood quality. But unlike streetlamps and sidewalks that towns had long furnished, regulating occupancy required new laws and novel enforcement strategies, or at least creative ways to apply existing codes. Civic associations did find allies in town government to pursue their ends. But attacking informal housing confronted private property owners, forbade the living arrangements of people with few choices, and challenged state authorities dependent on the informal housing market to house recipients.

Of all the civic efforts against informality, the Carleton Park Civic Association faced a nearly insurmountable task: fighting absentee landlords, holding companies, and bank-owned foreclosures. By 1964, Carleton Park residents attacked the landlords and holding companies responsible for housing degradation. They called upon on the Town of Islip, their most local governing body, to pass housing codes regulating occupancy of single-family housing. In December, the civic association organized a protest march to town hall. Mrs. Paul Mirabella, Carleton Park resident since 1955, attacked the town board members for the hamlet's troubles: "I blame town hall. They've done nothing. This problem is here and they can't get away from it." The civic association insisted Supervisor Thomas Harwood raze burned-out houses. Harwood responded that "you just can't go in there and tear down a home just like that." Residents also demanded the county welfare department stop concentrating recipients into Carleton Park. Suffolk's welfare commissioner Richard DiNapoli countered that recipients found their own housing and that "there seems to be a feeling that just because people are on welfare they've been sold into bondage and can be moved from place to place."[65]

Within a week, the Town of Islip responded. First, the town enforced existing building codes in a highly publicized "crackdown," enforcement actions well beyond the building department's routine inspections. Despite lacking the power to regulate occupancy, nine building inspectors swept 270 homes, noting building code violations from the curb, and when needed, asked permission to enter homes. Unsurprisingly, they discovered overflowing cesspools, unsafe walls, broken windows, and chimneys built for gas but emitting oil-based smoke. But code enforcers were not police officers. Building violations could only prod property owners into compliance. Inspectors marked only three of the fifty-two abandoned homes for demolition, itself a lengthy court process.[66] The town board also passed a housing ordinance, which regulated housing occupancy and required licensing of all rentals. In a packed board meeting, Carleton Park residents were overjoyed. One resident, allegedly in tears, proclaimed, "this is the miracle I have been waiting for." Only landlords opposed the laws.[67]

The new ordinance nonetheless proved disappointing. The Carleton Park Civic Association returned to town hall in April 1965. Association president James Smith identified the source of Carleton Park's troubles: seventy vacant homes, fifty-four owned by the four mortgagee companies, the rest sitting empty under VA or FHA ownership. He then cited 151 county health department violations in occupied units to illustrate the town's continued negligence. Town Supervisor Harwood responded that that the town could not do anything about the property owners: they could only compel owners to comply with laws, not bring speculators to justice as homeowners wanted. Within four months, James Northrop began his buying spree in Carleton Park, ending the civic association's hopes to preserve the subdivision as a place for "low-cost" homeowners.[68]

Carleton Park's civic efforts illustrate housing code enforcement's limits, but it was nonetheless a more effective approach than existing building codes. In Wyandanch, the local governing body, the Town of Babylon, did not pass a housing ordinance until the 1970s. This limited Hermann Griem's civic association to laborious and ineffective tactics. Griem scanned legal notices for signs that property owners converted homes to rentals, and then flooded town hall meetings to appeal. In 1966, Griem's civic stopped a single-family conversion on 16th Street. The owners had already dormered the upstairs to make room for more occupants, and in a rare instance, followed the legal process to convert the property's land-use status. Griem's Community Association feared the outcome, not whether the unit was legal or not. As Griem stated, "if [the apartment] cannot be rented, welfare will take it over." Their appeal succeeded but prove futile. For every home they stopped, others turned over to the informal market. They were playing whack-a-mole, and they were losing. Griem and Wyandanch civics demanded strong health and building code enforcement across the neighborhood. While important for improving living conditions, this would only legitimate informal rentals.[69]

In Nassau County, Roosevelt and New Cassel civic associations proved more effective. They cast their efforts as moralistic fights against racial segregation, and they compelled public authorities to creatively criminalize multifamily housing. PCANC and Roosevelt civic associations went beyond town powers, attacking the collaborative relationship between speculators who converted single-family homes and the county welfare departments abetting the process. It was a tactic that directly addressed a source of both informalization and blockbusting. First, removing rental demand would reduce the incentive to speculate and subdivide. Second, welfare recipients were disproportionately non-white, feeding into white flight and threatening the struggle for racial integration.

The shift first occurred in New Cassel, as PCANC and local NAACP branch members surprised the Nassau County Board of Supervisors in late November 1966. They accused the county welfare department of "dumping" Black recipients into New Cassel and helping to "blockbust" the Levitt-built Maplewood Drive section from white to Black. As Olivia Hollis, a teacher, mother of three, PCANC and NAACP member, exclaimed, "the welfare department is the real blockbuster." Nassau County welfare commissioner Joseph Barbaro denied any wrongdoing. He cited data proving that of New Cassel's 315 welfare cases, caseworkers moved only thirty-two into the hamlet. The rest applied for welfare after they arrived. His defense obscured how recipients found housing and obtained welfare. Landlords first converted single-family houses, poor people then found the units, and finally, landlords helped tenants apply for relief, with occasional help from a welfare caseworker.[70]

In Roosevelt, however, the outsized efforts of Morton Decker's umbrella civic association, the United Organizations of Roosevelt, prompted both the Town of Hempstead and Nassau County to take deliberate action. In 1967, Decker demanded that the county appoint a full-time coordinator to stop blockbusting, or else he would nationally publicize the county's welfare dumping.[71] As a hedge against Nassau County, the United Organizations of Roosevelt also called upon the Town of Hempstead to enforce its recently passed housing code. Hempstead's code enforcement started only a year before, in 1966, when the town hired Matthew Russo as building commissioner. A City College and Brooklyn Law School graduate, Russo was no ordinary town machine appointment, envisioning his responsibilities "not only to areas of public construction but to public safety, planning, and beautification."[72] When the United Organizations of Roosevelt approached the town, they found a sympathetic ally in Matthew Russo. A little more than a month after the United Organizations of Roosevelt met with the county, Russo gathered ten inspectors and a gaggle of reporters for a Roosevelt "housecleaning" drive on June 29, 1967. They inspected 118 houses, handing out fifteen summonses and forty-one violations.

Russo, Decker, and the United Organizations of Roosevelt considered the crackdown a success, but the housecleaning drive revealed people on the other side of the violations. In one stop at 16 Valentine Avenue, Russo entered a two-family house with two reporters, two photographers, two inspectors, and a public relations official. They walked in and snapped a photo of Beatrice Desvignes in her nightgown. Desvignes was a former domestic worker and ordained minister. She had moved from New Orleans to Roosevelt with her husband and eleven children in 1964 but was recently widowed. Russo barged in "to make sure this place is maintained properly," contending that "this is for your own benefit." Mrs. Desvignes didn't agree: "overcrowded, overcrowded, that's all I can hear. Every week it's inspectors, inspectors. I have eleven children and thirty grandchildren, and they come to visit me. Everyone they see around don't live here." Her absentee landlord, Ira Mitlin, defended her, saying "the only crime of this family is that they're poor and prolific." Morton Decker meanwhile supported Russo, stating he had "the expressed mandate of the citizens of Roosevelt." Without Russo's efforts, "there is no hope for the rehabilitation of welfare recipients and the fight against slumlords."[73]

The June 1967 crackdown and tenant response foreshadowed the battle to come. On July 6, 1967, the United Organization of Roosevelt met with Nassau

County executive Eugene Nickerson to prevent Roosevelt "from becoming a ghetto." By the end of the meeting, County Executive Nickerson proposed a full-time county coordinator stationed in Roosevelt. The coordinator would both prohibit the county social services (previously the welfare) department from authorizing welfare rentals in Roosevelt and stop real estate agents from moving recipients into Roosevelt. The step pleased United Organizations of Roosevelt chair Morton Decker. But Hempstead buildings commissioner Matthew Russo contended it was "full of nothing" because the plan did not halt "the disintegration of neighborhoods by welfare recipients who crowd several families into single-family homes." Russo asked the social services department to withhold rent money from existing recipients as a stick to improve housing conditions. Social Services Commissioner Joseph Barbaro agreed and also promised to report housing violations back to Russo.[74]

By July 1967, both the town and county launched a coordinated front against welfare recipients in Roosevelt. Russo forwarded reports of forty-three houses directly to the county social services, who then withheld welfare checks until the landlords fixed the violations. Russo also contacted the New York State Office of Rent Administration to impose rent control on multi-family dwellings, hoping that the reduced rental income would disincentivize informal housing.[75] Roosevelt's county coordinator helped to steer recipients away and relay housing code violations to the building department. Between July 1967 and March 1968, social services only moved one family into Roosevelt, an administrative error because welfare officials authorized the security deposit before realizing the location. The department did not prevent existing residents from applying for welfare, though. Roosevelt's caseload still grew 4 percent between July and December 1967 to 489 cases. It was nonetheless a fraction of the 15 percent countywide growth.[76]

Nassau County's efforts extended beyond Roosevelt to New Cassel and Long Beach, each with powerful anti-welfare civic activism. The policy pleased homeowner activists. But it put the social services department in a bind because places like Roosevelt and New Cassel had been safety valves in the low-income housing squeeze. With these hamlets off limits, Nassau County turned to renting entire motels, an "emergency" measure that became a permanent feature of both counties' welfare departments. Nassau's motel population climbed to over three hundred families by the early 1970s, and motel room costs fluctuated between $500 and $1,000 a family per month, over two to four times the median rent in 1970. In today's dollars, this would be $3,700 to $7,400 a month, luxury rent in San Francisco or Manhattan's glass towers. But these rooms lacked basic amenities like stoves, refrigerators, or laundry machines. And guaranteed checks from the welfare department discouraged maintenance. Cesspools quickly overflowed, vermin infested the rooms, and heating systems stopped working. Deplorable living conditions surpassed what building inspectors flagged among single-family homes. Motel owners were the new slumlords in what became small poverty colonies, while tenants became their prisoners.[77]

Welfare recipients challenged the county's refusal to let them into Roosevelt. Caroline and Cain Badger, Black welfare recipients and parents of two toddlers, lived separately because they could not find housing approved by the social services department. Cain resided in a single-room apartment, while his wife lived in an overcrowded single bedroom in her mother's home with their two young children. In January 1968, the Badgers found a two-bedroom unit in Roosevelt for $145 a month, under the department's rental ceiling. The apartment would finally reunite the family. But the appointed county coordinator denied them because they could not place "a welfare recipient into the Roosevelt area from another town." Diane Greggs, another recipient, encountered the same obstacle. She shared a single-bedroom apartment with her four young children but found a three-bedroom unit for $165 a month in Roosevelt. The social services department nonetheless refused to authorize a security deposit or inspect the home, and the rental sat empty as Diane Greggs juggled five people in a single bedroom.[78]

Tenants organized to counter the joint civic–local state actions against them. Amidst the War on Poverty and national welfare protests in the 1960s, twenty-two welfare advocacy organizations formed on Long Island. Two umbrella foundations united them: the Nassau Welfare Tenants Coordinating Committee and Suffolk's People for Adequate Welfare, both affiliates to the National Welfare Rights Organization.[79] Empowered though the Nassau Welfare Tenants Committee, the Badger and Greggs families sued the Nassau Social Services Department on May 2, 1968. The lawsuit claimed the department violated the fourteenth amendment, denying them the freedom to choose where they wished to live because of their race, their poverty, and their need for public assistance. In effect, the Badgers and Diane Greggs demanded a right to live in Roosevelt, which until then was prerogative of organized Roosevelt homeowners, building inspectors, and the county.[80] The social services department sided with homeowners, privileging their definition of the suburb and enforcing policy in their interest. The department responded that they would continue the policy because it referred to all recipients without respect to race, color, or creed.[81]

Despite their defense, the social services department dropped their policy effective July 30, 1968, thirteen months after first instituting the recipient ban. The department settled with the complainants and promised uniform

FIGURE 3.3. Building commissioner Matthew Russo (*left*) delivers summonses to Stanley Phillips (*right*).

*Source*: "Building Aide, Landlord Skirmish over Housing," *Newsday*, March 18, 1969, 13. Courtesy of PARS International Corp.

treatment of all rental requests "regardless of the community in which the housing unit is located, including the Roosevelt community," a return to the earlier open market policy.[82] By then, the United Organizations of Roosevelt had collapsed after Morton Decker fell ill. Hempstead town building commissioner Matthew Russo likewise hit his limits by 1969. Two years of detective work led him to Stanley Phillips, the owner of three Roosevelt informal housing complexes stuffed into single-family homes. Russo readied seven summonses carrying $250 in fines or fifteen days behind bars. With three aides and a public relations official in tow, Russo personally issued the papers (figure 3.3). Phillips claimed the action was politically motivated. When Russo countered that the properties enriched Phillips, Stanley retorted he reinvested most of the profit back into the homes. Phillips only grew angry as Russo handed over the papers, shouting, "you say these rooms are unsafe, you're saying I should put these people out on the street now. How do you intend to take care of these people? Give me your address and I'll drive them over so they can stay at your house tonight." Russo awkwardly responded, "you're oversimplifying things, Stanley." Whether Phillips ended up paying the fines is unclear, but within six months he sold the property to Herbert Mahler, a prolific slumlord who bought the house and its mortgage debt as part of his own small welfare rental empire.[83]

By 1970, homeowner activism had done little to stop housing informalization. Housing code adoption was no panacea. Code enforcement proved a legal, administrative, and logistical nightmare, from the difficulties of identifying offenses and overlapping public agencies, to the time-consuming legal trials and the burden such activities placed on tenants. Enforcement came in spurts, brief responses to homeowner demands weighed against the interests of welfare departments responsible for housing the poor and the legal rights of tenants.[84] Ultimately, latent and occasional code enforcement could not stop a practice linked to widespread predatory lending, blockbusting, and shoddy construction in these places. Homeowner dreams that their suburbs could be exceptional in the American urban landscape, a refuge from the social problems plaguing cities in the postwar period, proved illusory. The suburban poor had to live somewhere; housing segregation offered the means to shelter them.

## Confronting Exploitation

Informal housing spread widely across Long Island, but in Roosevelt, New Cassel, Wyandanch, and Central Islip, informality became "embedded," meaning informal tenants reached a critical mass and came out of the shadows. They organized into tenant councils, compelling homeowners and the state to recognize their needs by the late 1960s and early 1970s.[85] Tenant councils refocused the debate toward the exploitation preventing them from having legal, safe, and affordable shelter. Homeowner activists still demanded they enjoy the same class homogeneity other suburbanites could expect elsewhere on Long Island. But tenants demanded a social-democratic right to the suburbs, that they have good housing regardless of ability to pay. That demand did alter how some homeowner activists approached the problem of informal housing.[86] Each hamlet's particular histories, including the scale of speculators and the prerogatives of civic associations and tenants' committees, shaped how the politics played out. But the battles nonetheless revealed both homeowner and tenant powerlessness compared to the clandestine landlords and real estate speculators operating in these hamlets. Without state protections for all Long Islanders, private actors filled the vacuum, hurting homeowners and tenants alike.

There is no comprehensive local data to measure informal housing density in the postwar period. But imperfect proxies suggest informal housing became embedded in these hamlets. While overcrowding eased across Long Island during the 1960s, it intensified in New Cassel and Roosevelt, reaching at least twice the bi-county rate across all four hamlets by 1970. Renters grew at four times Long Island's overall rate in New Cassel and Roosevelt despite relatively little change in total housing units (table A.3). Welfare recipient concentration also suggests embeddedness; 3 percent of Long Island's population lived in the four hamlets, while 10 percent of the bi-county welfare beneficiaries did (table 3.1).[87] Not every welfare household occupied "informal" units, but they were part of the process that converted owner-occupied housing into informal units.

In Roosevelt, the class-specific racial integration movement collapsed as real estate blockbusters bought up white-owned homes and resold to Black buyers. They turned Roosevelt into a majority-minority suburb with a turbulent housing market ripe for informalization. *Newsday* ran a highly publicized

TABLE 3.1. Home Relief Caseload in Four Case Study Hamlets, 1966

| | *Est. Caseload*[1] | *Total Households* | % |
|---|---|---|---|
| Central Islip | 323 | 8,925 | 3.6 |
| New Cassel[2] | 550 | 2,173 | 8.4 |
| Roosevelt | 404 | 3,865 | 10.5 |
| Wyandanch | 300 | 3,711 | 8.1 |
| **Nassau–Suffolk** | 15,967 | 696,643 | 2.3 |

*Source*: Raymond & May Associates, *Residential Market Analysis Progress Report Part IV*, 11, 22; Manson et al., *IPUMS*, database.

[1] Residential data extrapolated from Raymond & May Associates' 851 randomly selected cases in November 1966 for their study of welfare recipient housing on Long Island.

[2] The Nassau County Social Services Department did not distinguish between Westbury Village and New Cassel. This is the proportion of home relief caseloads across both places. It presumes an even distribution and is likely underestimated.

*Note*: "Home relief" refers to any "relief in the home" programs administered by each county, including federal programs, like Old Age Assistance and Aid to Families with Dependent Children (AFDC), and state programs like rental subsidies. These numbers understate the "persons" on welfare in each hamlet. A 1971 report reveals that 17.9% of Roosevelt's population and 10.8% of New Cassel's 1970 population received welfare in some form. No comparable data exists for Suffolk. See "Nassau Lists Welfare Cases," *Newsday*, February 23, 1971, 24.

report on Roosevelt's troubles in August 1968 entitled "The Making of a Black Ghetto." Peppered with representative biographies of Roosevelt's "fractured" constituencies—the white homeowner, their Black counterpart, the welfare recipient, the high school dropout—the article hinged on a thesis that Roosevelt's failed integration was rooted in "faltering communication and . . . the gaps that are splitting races, classes, and generations." But white homeowner and United Organizations of Roosevelt member Mike Carter attacked the reporter's thesis in a letter to the editor. Carter contended that the article sensationalized the alleged miscommunication while barely addressing what Carter believed were Roosevelt's structural problems: "real estate blockbusting, slumlords, the preponderance of welfare in one community when it should be spread out—regardless of color."[88] Though Carter expressed his desire to stay in Roosevelt, he moved to another Long Island suburb in 1969. Writing in *Newsday* again, Mike's wife Frances Carter said:

> The situation in Roosevelt has nothing to do with integration. Whites and blacks had a wonderful dialogue and we had made many sincere friends. We wanted desperately for Roosevelt to be the first truly integrated community in the United States. We envisioned having books written about us that would go down in history. The county deprived us of that pleasure. Integration can and eventually will work. This is a *class* problem and not a *race* problem. [89] [emphasis in original]

The Carters were closer to the mark than *Newsday*, aware of the material imperatives driving blockbusting. Their response nonetheless revealed the political limits of their class-specific integration vision, premised on parity with all-white suburbs. To them, only discrimination was the problem, not the dearth of decent, affordable housing.

Once the homeowner integration movement collapsed, a new cross-class strategy developed among Roosevelt's now Black-dominated civic leadership. In 1969, Utopia Civic Association's William Alston and Hausch Manor Civic Association's Dorothy Gardner joined with Lois Desvignes, daughter of harassed tenant Beatrice Desvignes and chair of the Roosevelt Welfare Tenant's Association, to form the Coalition for Communities in Crisis. The group asked Nassau County to construct public housing and reduce informal housing demand. The coalition inverted the United Organization's request to redistribute welfare recipients across Nassau County by promoting affordable housing development in the county's welfare-dependent hamlets. It was a sign of hope that ultimately rested on New York State to empower counties to build housing, a threat to the town and city planners who controlled building and land use across the state.[90]

Political silence illustrated housing informality's embeddedness as much as action. In New Cassel, North Hempstead Town planned another crackdown in August 1969. By then, informal housing residents organized their own welfare tenants association. Tenants gained support from the local War on Poverty community action program and a radicalized CORE branch. Local CORE chair Harold Russell protested the crackdown, asking whether the town would "find decent places to live" for evicted tenants. Tenants also found allies among homeowner activists, namely Edward Hunter, PCANC member and former NAACP branch chair. He feared the crackdown would "displace people. If they are without homes, then it is not helping them." Though locals lodged the housing violation complaints, when code enforcers walked through New Cassel, an estimated 40 percent of residents refused to let inspectors in. Assistant inspector Charles Milo complained, "you ring one doorbell after another, and if they're home, they're suspicious. Sometimes they make threats." Because housing codes did little to stem informal housing all while threatening eviction, homeowners grew weary of code enforcement, while tenants chose to suffer with a broken stove or flooded basement. It was still better than a welfare motel.[91]

Increased political activity among tenants did not produce cross-class coalitions everywhere, however. In Wyandanch, Herman Griem started a secession campaign for the northern part of the hamlet. He achieved that dream in 1974, when he carved out a new hamlet called Wheatley Heights. Wyandanch residents fought over informal housing's tax burdens through the school district. Meanwhile, speculators and landlords continued to convert single-family housing, especially because the Town of Babylon, the most local governing body, did not pass housing ordinances. On a cold night in December 1972, a fire broke out in 199 Parkway Boulevard, the single-family house where absentee landlords Justers Cobbs and Milton Farnum crammed four families. The gas heater exploded, and the fire proved so intense that firefighters had to cut through the front wall with an electric saw. When Wyandanch Fire Department deputy chief Jack Miller entered the house, he fell through the floor into the basement. Fellow firefighters rescued him and most of the inhabitants. But they could not revive unconscious thirty-six-year-old Elizabeth Branch, nor could they find a moaning girl through the maze of rooms. The desperate cry was eight-year-old Felicia Mills, trapped in a front bedroom. As firefighters climbed around furniture to find her, Felicia choked to death on the smoke. They pulled her lifeless body from the house just as her mother returned from the grocery store.[92]

Tenant organizing was no magic bullet either, because like homeowner activism, it proved no match against the speculators who dominated property markets. This was clear in Carleton Park, where half of all single-family units housed welfare recipients by 1969. In the early morning, small white vans snaked around Carleton Park picking up domestic workers like Dorothy Daniels from the book's introduction. The welfare checks went to James Northrop, who owned half of Carleton Park's houses by then. The homes, and others in Suffolk County, made Northrop a millionaire. It was his lifelong dream, or at least his life goal after losing his high school principal job. The Town of Islip pursued Northrop through a $1.7 million Department of Housing and Urban Development (HUD) grant to beautify the hamlet, offer low-interest loans to remaining homeowners for property improvements, and most importantly, fund more stringent code enforcement. 150 tenants also formed the Central Islip Tenants Council in late 1969, chaired by Roberta Benton, a mother of seven who lived in an unheated Northrop-owned Carleton Park house. Benton's goal was to amass code violation complaints and organize a rent strike if Northrop did not fix them.[93]

The council did not wait long to act because violations turned deadly. On January 9, 1970, Laurene Peters, tenant of a Northrop-owned four-room house at 22 Oak Street, put her fifteen-month-old down for an afternoon nap. A few hours later, she discovered her baby's lifeless body. Medical examiners first presumed sudden infant death syndrome killed the baby, but further examination determined carbon monoxide poisoned the child. They traced the problem to a missing piece of the furnace's exhaust pipe. The baby's death galvanized Central Islip Tenants Council members to protest at the Fifth District Court in Bay Shore. Northrop was there to defend his eviction of another Carleton Park tenant, Patricia Colon, for her personal rent strike against housing violations.

The council managed to delay Colon's eviction, but they failed to build a broader rent strike. Council member James Woodbury remarked, "a lot of people are being intimidated by Northrop . . . he acts like the guiding savior, saying if I don't rent to them, where else would they go?" Tenants had good reason to fear him. Besides Northrop's rental units, "welfare" motels were the only other choice in the area, and Northrop owned the nearest one. Even if one were to check themselves into the Central Islip State Psychiatric Center due to Northrop-induced mental duress, the hospital would likely release them to a Northrop-owned welfare motel. There was no escape.

With his stranglehold on the local rental market, Northrop could mock his opposition. When the tenant's council threatened rent strikes, Northrop withheld heat, a tactic that forced the Islip Town to jail Northrop for ten days. The state supreme court ordered his release within three hours, and like a villain holding Gotham City hostage, Northrop penned a letter informing the

Suffolk County welfare commissioner that he was raising all monthly rents $15 to offset the legal fees he incurred from town "harassment."[94] When tenants complained to public officials, Northrop simply evicted them, as he did to Pedra Perez, who met with her local county legislator Michael Grant about the rats living in her one-bedroom apartment. Northrop openly admitted, like the Riddler or Joker, that he had evicted her because she talked:

> I want to see what big-mouth Mike Grant can do. I want to see if this guy, who's always shooting off his mouth, can find her a place to live like I can. That's right. I've looked for a reason to evict her, just so we could see if Mr. Grant could do better than me. He's a big-shot legislator, but I just know he won't do anything for her.[95]

The HUD grant eventually arrived, but Northrop demanded $2 million to repair his own properties, which the town refused to pay, leaving the bulk of money reserved for streets, new sidewalks, and freshly seeded lawns. As one resident bitterly remarked, the HUD grant laid "pretty sidewalks so we don't have to walk in the mud now. And the streets are beautiful, but what happened to all that money they said they had to fix up the people's houses?"[96]

## Conclusion

Northrop was the most unethical of Long Island's slumlords, a character who reveled in the power and negative media attention he wielded. But he astutely understood his own role, and that of many other landlords: "I'm not the cause of slums, I am just one effect of slums." He was right. Whether the landlord was the villainous James Northrop, the charitable Stanley Phillips, or a homeowner not far removed from their tenants in terms of income, occupation, or employment, they were all just resolving Long Island's housing market failures.

The federal government unleashed an unprecedented building boom across postwar America's urban fringe, evident above all on Long Island. But exclusionary mechanisms, built into FHA mortgage insurance and municipal codes, restricted who could live in the homes. Private actors ignored and subverted the exclusionary regulations to house Long Island's excluded. Fly-by-night developers skirted building standards and found loosely regulated land to construct subdivisions for homeowners barely eligible for federally insured mortgages. Predatory lenders enabled Black homebuyers denied insured mortgages to get their piece of the American dream. Property owners secretly turned single-family homes into informal rentals, altering the very purpose of the single-family units spread across Long Island. Speculators profited.

But tenants suffered shelter poverty and threats to their physical well-being. Informal housing's burdens reverberated upward, contributing to wider inequalities, including racial disparities in property wealth, declining housing stock, and strained schools between white-exclusive and diverse suburbs on Long Island.

The exclusionary mechanisms undergirding suburban Long Island also obfuscated effective solutions. Black and white homeowners in Roosevelt, New Cassel, Carleton Park, and Wyandanch reached for exclusionary tools, aiming to end the exploitation rooted in segregation. But they fought the means by which speculators concentrated informal housing within their neighborhoods. They overlooked the source of demand for partitioned garages and subdivided basements: the scarcity of decent and legal housing for everyone on Long Island. The civic association's efforts to impose law-and-order standards only highlighted informal housing's necessity. The tenant struggles exposed the power large property owners wielded over homeowners and the poor alike.

In a suburb that represented the apex of what America's golden age offered regular citizens—a single-family house, two cars, a front lawn—one could see the federal government's failure to provision a basic need. Rather than mass housing programs that could outstrip demand with decent and affordable units (like Sweden's social-democratic Million Programme), postwar federal housing policy preferred the means-tested FHA loan program and housing code enforcement to defend the integrity of FHA-standard homes. They left millions unhoused in the legal market. It was not for want of trying—public housing competed with private mortgage insurance for America's dominant housing policy in the 1930s and 1940s. President Truman famously promised a "decent home and suitable living environment for every American family" in the Housing Act of 1949. Members of Congress pursued both public and cooperative housing schemes to achieve it. But the same legislative coalition that dismantled other parts of America's social democracy—business-friendly Democrats and Republicans—gutted the Housing Act's social-democratic impulses.[97] Few understood the problem in these terms. Local activists, steeped in a liberal racial-democratic approach to urban problems, instead decried racial discrimination in the market. They fought to disperse, rather than dispel shelter poverty.[98] But federal policy, and the local political battles, forced the poor to depend on the landlords, speculators, and the welfare offices constructing the shadow housing market.

This is not to blame homeowners or welfare tenants for the outcome. Each drew on the familiar vocabularies in the postwar era about property rights and racial justice, deploying the limited tools available at the local level.

Instead, we should reconsider the idea of suburbs as shielded from poverty. Local land-use tools and slick marketing advertised suburbs as places filled with economically secure families living on tree-lined streets without a factory or apartment building in sight. Homeowners imbibed the ideal, believing they lived in an historically exceptional space. When confronted with the reality of poverty, homeowner activists argued the suburbs should be free of the poor, that public officials should redistribute the poor so as not to disproportionately burden them and not others. Homeowners were at least aware of the contradiction between what suburbs represented in the American urban landscape and who actually lived there. As we will see, policymakers, with more potent tools to alter the structure of the job or housing markets, still believed the suburbs were exceptional urban spaces.

# 4

# Fair without Full Employment

## *The Limits of Equal Opportunity*

On February 3, 1968, Grumman Aerospace Corporation sponsored a recruitment drive in Wyandanch, Long Island. This was the same place where working-class suburbanites built their own houses before World War II, where developers constructed "Carver Park" for Black homebuyers after the war, and where Herman "The Griem" surveilled single-family homes for informal conversions. By 1968, the unincorporated hamlet had switched from majority white to majority Black. By then Griem had also lost his battle with informal housing, as Wyandanch became one of Long Island's poorest neighborhoods (table A.3). This is why Grumman chose to hire in Wyandanch on a cold winter weekend. The company was by then Long Island's largest employer, a defense firm that secured the coveted NASA Lunar Module (LM) contract. But record profits and jobs attracted controversy. The Long Island branch of the Congress of Racial Equality (CORE) had been publicizing Grumman's paltry non-white employment numbers for almost three years. CORE's fiery leader Lincoln Lynch declared that he was willing to "take any action necessary to bring about full employment of Negroes," and Grumman was, unsurprisingly, CORE's "first shot" in their war against job discrimination.[1] By targeting Black applicants in Wyandanch, Grumman hoped to counter CORE's negative publicity.

What Grumman didn't expect was the turnout. They had sent one interviewer to the job fair but called in three more to manage the overflow. Applicants snaked around the building, waiting up to three hours for jobs as machinists, assemblers, riveters, fiberglass processors, clerks, and typists. The resumes surprised interviewers. Many had experience. Others could easily slide into unskilled production lines. And still others qualified for Grumman's training programs. Richard McGriff, one of the interviewees, had actually hitchhiked to Grumman's main plant the week before for a job interview. He was unemployed for over a year and willing to "take anything." His wife, Almeda, joined him at the recruiting drive because as Richard admitted, "it takes two jobs to make it today. I can't stand that welfare." All told, Grumman conducted 207 interviews. They hired thirty-five applicants on the spot and put another seventy-four on a waiting list. It was by all accounts a success, especially for Grumman's public image. As a newspaper reporter concluded, "the name of Grumman apparently enchanted the applicants."[2]

The applicants were less enamored with Grumman than with the defense contracts propping up the company's high pay and generous benefits. For nearly three decades, federal defense spending offered a route to working-class security on Long Island, accounting for one in every six jobs and serving as the income floor for mortgage eligibility.[3] Federal officials also barred discrimination in defense production, i.e., enforcing "fair" employment, long before other industries. With good jobs and a history of federal intervention, it is unsurprising that CORE chose Grumman as its opening bid to end Long Island's racial disparities in jobs, incomes, and poverty. But a long queue with Black applicants competing for a few spots was not a means to achieving "full employment of Negroes" or anyone for that matter. That activists demanded *fair* employment in a labor market without *full* employment—where everyone who wanted a job could find one—severely weakened CORE's hand. Without a tight job market, Lynch's desire to close the "gap between Negroes and whites in terms of family income" would prove elusive.

That CORE had to fight for "full employment of Negroes" on such diminished terrain is a story that began over twenty years before Wyandanch's job fair. Full employment had been a goal of American policymakers since at least the Great Depression. John Maynard Keynes offered the template for using federal spending to achieve it. Unconstrained demand for labor during World War II made it a reality. And the tight job market showed how full employment could absorb marginalized workers. At the end of the war, full employment remained the central objective of policymakers and politicians alike. The debate was over the best way to deliver jobs to all. As stated in chapter 1, everyone—from Long Islanders, to liberal Congressmen, to DC planners, and even to President Franklin Roosevelt—envisioned a "social Keynesian" route to full employment: federal investment in domestic public goods married to long-term strategic economic planning for the purpose of creating jobs and raising living standards. What Americans got instead was the "military Keynesian" route to full employment: public investment in arms as the most politically expedient means of stimulating growth and job creation. As Michael Brenes argues, communism's ideological threat justified the massive defense budget and therefore the jobs, economic development, and prosperity that came with it.[4] Defense spending was responsible for an average of six million jobs per year between 1946 and 1970, or one in eleven US jobs.[5] It accounted for roughly a tenth of the nation's gross domestic product, and the majority of the nation's scientists and engineers devoted their efforts to defense. Military Keynesianism was the narrow political landscape on which unions, defense workers, civil rights groups, and congressional representatives fought for publicly subsidized jobs in the 1940s and 1950s.

By early 1960s, just as civil rights groups secured stronger fair employment mandates in the defense industry, policymakers carved a new path to full employment: "commercial Keynesianism." Commercial Keynesianism favored fine-tuned interest and tax rate adjustments to manage business cycles and economic growth, with private enterprise, not the government, supplying the actual jobs. In this formulation, public spending was an inefficiency, a cost Congress should keep as low as possible.[6] By the 1960s, commercial Keynesians put military Keynesianism on the chopping block. With allegedly exceptional affluence and high employment, suburbs like Long Island were places that could absorb spending cuts. Commercial Keynesian advisers to President John F. Kennedy and the Defense Department pushed contract cancellations because they thought Long Island could bear it. But defense cuts sparked a revived case for social Keynesianism among Long Island workers, their unions, employers, political representatives, and neighbors. They fought not only to sustain contract flows, but to re-envision public spending beyond the narrow confines of national security. Contracts didn't have to feed the military; they could instead relieve air pollution, congested roads, or slum conditions. Workers looked to harness the government's unique ability to reformulate society for egalitarian purposes, with benefits extending well beyond defense employees. This was social Keynesianism. But Congress ignored their demands. By 1965, the Defense Department shuttered Long Island's largest employer, Republic Aviation, even as President Lyndon Johnson strengthened fair employment mandates.

The desperate jobseekers at the Wyandanch recruitment fair were on those long queues in 1968 because of who won—and lost—the political battle over the scale and goals of public spending on Long Island. Although few talked in such terms, locals recognized the role of federal spending in sustaining working-class livelihoods, but not the necessity of defense contracts per se. Federal-level economic advisers, Defense Department bureaucrats, and presidential administrations did not see the need for public spending at all. They were enthralled by Long Island's apparent prosperity—or with suburban exceptionalism, the idea that the suburbs were private market success stories, unaffected by public job subsidies and immune to cutbacks. When federal bureaucrats won, civil rights activists lost the tight labor market that had so powerfully fueled the high point of fair employment during World War II. Contract cancellations also reduced the number of good jobs available generally, lowering routes to a decent living in suburbia. Social Keynesianism's defeat on Long Island had national, even global implications. The 1960s was a pivotal moment to transform defense cuts into a "peace dividend," reorienting money away from war and toward civilian, domestic needs. It was another moment, like 1945, to fulfill Keynes's vision of public spending's civilizing, poverty-eradicating potential. Instead, public dollars went to burn villages and jungle in Southeast Asia.

This chapter tells two interwoven stories: federal spending's fate on Long Island and the civil rights demand that defense employers fairly employ Black Long Islanders. Although these stories are often treated separately, they are inextricably tied to one another. Without the broadest swath of workers having bargaining power in the labor market, employers could racially segment workers and replicate existing disparities in jobs and income. Fair employment alone addresses only the exclusionary barriers, leaving the labor market "loose" and empowering employers to divide workers racially, depressing wages further. The defense spending connection also extends to poverty. The "guns versus butter" trade-off, or whether a nation devotes its finite resources to national security or civilian needs, posed poverty and militarization against one another. But military spending was a means of supplying butter, or securing people's well-being, though a destructive, inefficient, and insecure way to do it. Long Islanders looked to reorient defense spending toward social welfare—public transit, environmental conservation, and public works. As international research shows, spending on butter is better for everyone except those who make guns, doing more to tighten the labor market, enhance economic productivity, raise living standards, and ultimately lower poverty.[7]

## Long Island and the Shifting Priorities of Defense Spending

Long Island politics and civil rights activity revolved around defense because the aircraft, and later aerospace, industry played an outsized role in Long Island's postwar prosperity. Military Keynesianism directly stimulated the region. Unlike during World War II, the absence of effective fair employment policy meant Cold War stimulus disproportionately helped white over Black New Yorkers, making it a target for civil rights groups. But the defense contracting system, the closest the United States came to industrial policy after 1945, proved a poor substitute for comprehensive industrial planning and stable working-class jobs, despite the possibilities embedded in its physical and fiscal capacity. Though one in ten American workers depended on defense spending for their livelihoods, employment played a subordinate role in defense planning decisions. Military Keynesianism was no coherent program, but the theoretical edifice legitimizing the permanent arms economy waging the Cold War. Vested interests—workers, labor leaders, and congressional representatives—had to satisfy domestic needs like jobs and local economic development through the defense budget. And through the 1950s, they failed to steer military spending toward social ends. This meant the defense sector was an insecure source of work, complicating efforts to reduce discrimination in the industry.

Defense as a quasi-jobs program reached its postwar zenith as fair employment fell to its nadir in the 1950s. When New Deal veteran Leon Keyserling assumed chair of the recently created Council of Economic Advisers (CEA) in 1949, he aimed to achieve full employment. Without the National Resources Planning Board (NRPB) or other social Keynesian tools to achieve it, however, Keyserling chose the defense budget to reach the same end. He warded off concerns about inflation and the "guns or butter" tradeoffs emanating from the Federal Budget Bureau by affirming the power of guns *and* butter. For Keyserling, spending, even for unproductive war material, could jumpstart growth at home and sustain high employment. The Korean War vindicated his views, and military Keynesianism became an entrenched means of financing full employment after the war.[8]

Fair employment mandates did not follow this spending boost. Despite Truman's aim to make the World War II Fair Employment Practices Commission (FEPC) permanent after the war, conservatives replaced the FEPC with the Government Contract Compliance Committee (GCCC) during the Korean War. Unlike the FEPC, Truman's GCCC could only advise contractors, and it achieved little. States like New York preserved their wartime antidiscrimination agencies, but even here the impact was limited. The New York State legislature empowered its State Commission Against Discrimination (SCAD) with powers to enforce non-discrimination law, but the commissioners chose "conciliation and persuasion" rather than the penal tools at their disposal.[9] In 1953 for example, SCAD investigated a Long Island defense plant that refused to hire any Black workers in its nine-hundred-person workforce. Here SCAD negotiated with the employer and conducted follow-up interviews, judging thirty-two new employees, 2 percent of the firm, a success. Overall, SCAD rarely targeted Long Island firms. From 1945 to 1960, SCAD received fifteen complaints against Republic Aviation: eleven from

African Americans, two from Jewish workers, and one Protestant employee, all dismissed "without probable cause."[10]

With only weak enforcement tools to challenge firms, Long Island's employers returned to a "neo-traditional" white male-dominated work culture, as discussed in chapter 2. By 1959, Black workers were 3.8 percent of the workforce among Long Island's five largest defense employers, or 1,974 employees of over 50,000 workers. Among Long Island's subcontractors, Black employment was even lower. Of 1,400 Reeves Instrument employees, thirty-five were Black, and Potter Instruments Company in Plainview employed five Black workers of 267 total employees. Despite the growing number of Black Long Islanders in both absolute and proportional terms during the 1950s, fewer Black than white workers relied on defense for their suburban livelihoods.[11] This aligned with generally low Black participation nationwide. Black aircraft employment at Nassau and Suffolk firms was 3.6 percent. This was below the country's most "diverse" aircraft employers, like those in Los Angeles and Ohio where the proportion reached 4 percent, but well above Massachusetts, where only one in every hundred workers were Black. Black employment was low even though many defense plants existed near large Black urban neighborhoods.[12]

Even for those lucky defense workers, security proved elusive after the Korean War boom. Bureaucrats and politicians weighed the employment effects of defense spending against military branch needs, foreign policy strategy, and the federal budget. While Congress, labor unions, military strategists, presidential administrations, and defense contractors all had vested interests in preserving the national security state, their power to shape the budget, and their stakes in defense spending, fundamentally differed. Those at the helm of America's war chest, namely the Defense Department, conceived of contracting as a strategic tool, not as a job creator. President Eisenhower, balancing pressures from the Defense Department, the CEA, budget officials, Congress, the public, and global contingencies, prioritized the defense budget as a means of countering the Soviet threat, not producing jobs domestically.[13] The military branches, meanwhile, doled out contracts to firms that could best meet their strategic needs, not to those with the best employment practices. Manufacturing firms, operating at the whim of larger bureaucratic decisions, worried about profit and efficiency. They hired as few people as possible.

It was the least powerful interests—Congress, labor unions, and workers—who were most concerned with the jobs defense spending created. Congressional representatives were obligated to procure jobs for their constituents. But without a political movement that championed civilian jobs programs, both parties leaned on the perennially reauthorized defense budget, the most expedient means of producing jobs. Debates in the Senate and House amounted to where and how the money was spent, not whether the nation's vast wealth should be spent on military goods. Organized labor, and by extension workers themselves, were the most visionary interests tied to military Keynesianism. With their fortunes deeply implicated in the warfare state, labor leaders sought to nudge military budget items toward social, domestic ends.[14]

The most powerful interests determined workers' fortunes. Following the Korean armistice, the Defense Department and military branches determined the nature of defense spending in three ways. First, the Defense Department made contracts more flexible by shortening orders to a monthly rather than a long-term structure. The Defense Department also shifted military procurement away from planes and tanks toward experimental weaponry as the United States committed itself to the escalating arms race with the USSR. The technological shift occurred in two bouts: first in "guided missiles" in the early 1950s, and then the related "space boom" that followed NASA's 1959 founding, an entirely new funding source for what was now the "aerospace" industry. Finally, the navy, air force, and army favored southern and western contractors over the industrial northeast. The technological and regional shifts jeopardized established aircraft manufacturers in places like Long Island. They made former airframe production facilities obsolete, pushed companies to hire a more skilled technical workforce, and exposed firms to competition from the electronics industry and regional rivals.[15]

Those dependent on defense contracts could only respond to these shifts. Long Island's two airframe producers, Republic and Grumman, jostled for new contracts. During the guided missiles race, Republic opened a dedicated missile plant in 1954, while Grumman expanded to electronic surveillance aircraft and a variety of smaller military goods. Both competed with Long Island's electronics manufacturers, including missile developer American Bosch Arma and instrument producer Sperry Gyroscope. During the space boom, Republic and Grumman's fortunes reversed. Republic Aviation had been the largest employer on the island through the 1950s, investing over $700,000 into space research, including the multimillion-dollar Paul Moore Research and Development Center in 1958. Nevertheless, the company lost a key contract for the Apollo spaceship. In contrast, NASA awarded Grumman the Apollo LM contract in 1962. From here, Grumman moved to the center of the space race, building twelve LMs as NASA's second largest contractor. By 1964, Grumman employed one out of every seven Long Islanders in manufacturing, becoming Long Island's largest employer.[16]

Contract competition within Long Island proved less consequential than the general spending tilt toward the South and West. West Coast companies like North American, Lockheed, and Martin adapted well to the guided missiles boom. Overall, New York's defense contract share fell from 13 percent to 10 percent between 1952 and 1962, while California's rose from 11 percent to 19 percent during the same period.[17] This was not because firms relocated from one region to another, but because firms lost contracts in one place to competitors procuring new contracts elsewhere. Stiff competition resulted. In 1959, Long Island's Fairchild Engine Division, formerly Ranger Engines, closed after the Airforce canceled their J-83 engine in favor of Lynn, Massachusetts-based General Electric's J-85 engine, leaving 2,600 workers unemployed.[18]

Workers and residents pressured their congressional representatives to confront regional inequality and job losses. But members of Congress operated within the boundaries of military Keynesianism, fighting to save contracts or win new ones for Long Island. After Long Island's industrial boom, politicians mindful of defense contracts, and often amenable to labor, replaced the old Gold Coast–aligned generation. In New York's First Congressional District, Democrat Ernest Greenwood, a Truman's Fair Dealer, defeated Groton and Harvard-educated Republican W. Kingsland Macy in 1950. Two years later, Stuyvesant Wainwright, derided as a "New Deal" Republican, beat Greenwood. Both allied with defense labor leaders when contracts were threatened. And Wainwright lost reelection to Democrat Otis G. Pike in 1960, who famously pestered JFK into sustaining a Republic jet contract. As Kennedy wryly noted, "I've heard from the Congressman." Even Leonard Hall's Second Congressional District replacement, conservative Republican Steven Derounian (a Barry Goldwater supporter in 1964), decried contract cancellations and fought for new ones. And New York's Senators, liberal Republicans Jacob Javits and Kenneth Keating, always responded to any threatened contracts throughout the state. None though, whether Democrat or Republican, House or Senate member, questioned using defense to create jobs. Politics revolved around who got what piece of the pie.[19]

The same narrow political conflict, focused on the distribution of contracts, emerged when organized labor pushed political representatives to act in the 1950s. Toward the end of the Korean War, President Truman, under pressure from Senator Hubert Humphrey and union leaders, enacted Defense Manpower Policy #4, an order to funnel defense spending to "surplus labor areas" with unemployment over 6 percent. Though the Defense Department opposed the policy as "inefficient," to labor and local politicians, the policy could serve as a violent alternative to social spending. Unfortunately, it was seldom used during the war, and it became moribund afterward despite efforts to revitalize it during the 1954 recession. But as regional inequality intensified, so did calls for redistributing defense contracts. With Long Island firms facing cuts in 1957 and 1958, the American Federation of Labor and Congress of Industrial Organizations (AFL-CIO) lobbied on their behalf. They demanded Defense Secretary Charles Erwin Wilson reverse his short-term procurement policy.[20] Meanwhile, New York Senators Jacob Javits and Kenneth Keating, along with every New York House member, introduced the Armed Services Competitive Procurement Act in 1959. The bill would ensure the Defense Department evenly distribute contracts among small businesses, areas with "labor surpluses," and most importantly, different geographic areas in the country, especially eligible contractors in defense-starved regions. As the bill argued:

> The security of the nation requires that its economy, and the economy of each section of the country, be maintained at a level which can support its programs for defense and sustain the private economic system, and that procurements by agencies under this chapter have a meaningful effect upon the Nation's economic health.[21]

This was a call for jobs couched in the language of national security. The bill did not pass, and Defense Department procurement policy director G. C. Bannerman testified that New York must "present new ideas if it expects more contracts."[22]

Overall, efforts to steer spending for domestic purposes lost to the military budget's national security interests. Long Island's defense contractors responded by investing in "brain-power" to remain competitive. Republic's white-collar proportion doubled from 9 percent to 18 percent between 1954 and 1959. Grumman hired physicists, medical researchers, hydrodynamicists, and all sorts of engineers. Nearly 7,000 skilled specialists worked on the Apollo contract, a project where production resembled a handmade cottage industry. About one-third of Grumman's entire workforce focused on the company's space projects in the 1960s.[23] While defense jobs did not decline in absolute numbers, skill requirements rose, and production workers competed with well-educated and younger engineers entering the field. Bob Schmidt, who began as a riveter at Grumman in 1941, watched as the industry

> got so high tech that you couldn't slump along as a high school graduate only, a tech school graduate, and really hope to get anywhere, because it got to be so that you'd have to be practically an engineer like the guys that work on the cars today. The airplanes got so complicated.[24]

These changes led to simultaneous layoffs alongside R&D investment and engineer hiring, reducing unskilled jobs while skilled jobs proliferated. This was especially true in the 1957 defense cutbacks, when Republic Aviation laid off 7,000 workers. The unskilled unemployed reentered the workforce as cab drivers, gas station attendants, construction workers, or retail employees, jobs that paid 10 percent less on average per year with fewer hours of work available.[25]

Production workers could hold onto defense jobs if they climbed the company ladder through promotions and training. In an industry that required all sorts of new and sometimes arcane skills to solve cutting-edge problems, firms designed internally coordinated training programs. Sperry paid tuition for those taking industrial technology courses, and the company subsidized a comprehensive professional engineering program to upgrade engineers for the space age. Unions like the Engineers Association of Arma (EAA) offered funds for college classes and even sponsored lectures on new equipment. Grumman developed the most comprehensive training programs, educating most of their employees in the late 1950s and early 1960s. Grumman even formed a Corporate Training Development Department responsible for all employee training across the company's divisions.[26] These training programs, whether union or corporate subsidized, were central to promoting workers within a firm since seniority did not prepare them for more technical work.

Any fair employment demand had to contend with hiring, promotions, training, and recruitment. After all, Black Long Islanders held jobs most threatened by the industry's trajectory. By 1961, Republic Aviation improved its fair hiring practices, though few Black workers held supervisory, professional, technical, or clerical positions; most were operatives, namely assemblers and fabricators (see table 4.1).[27] Grumman's distribution was similar. Of 605 Black employees, only fifty-nine held clerical, supervisory, professional, or technical positions, compared to the 242 who labored as operatives.[28] These numbers were even more skewed at electronics firms: Reeves Instrument had three Black workers in white-collar or technical jobs, while the remaining thirty were blue collar, and Fairchild Stratos in Bay Shore had no Black workers in any of its white-collar or technical ranks.[29] Overall, among nine major defense manufacturers in 1959, white workers were evenly distributed across high and low-skill work, but 88 percent of people of color held blue-collar production jobs.[30]

Educational levels partly explain the racial divide, but with training programs and promotional opportunities available, the issue was not simply schooling. Black workers pointed to bias as a potential source for the industry's

TABLE 4.1. Racial Composition of Republic Aviation, by Job Category, 1961

| | *All Workers* | *Non-white* | *Percent (%)* |
|---|---|---|---|
| Officials and supervisors | 1,816 | 17 | 0.9 |
| Professional and administrative | 2,374 | 47 | 2.0 |
| Sales | 23 | 0 | 0 |
| Technicians | 505 | 9 | 1.8 |
| Office and clerical | 2,278 | 22 | 1.0 |
| Craftsmen | 2,893 | 127 | 4.4 |
| Operatives | 5,342 | 655 | 12.3 |
| Service workers | 281 | 41 | 14.6 |
| Laborers | 31 | 3 | 9.7 |
| **Total** | 15,543 | 921 | 5.9 |

*Source*: Republic Aviation Occupational Distribution by Race Report, November 15, 1961, Box 31, folder C-4-1-538, Complaint Files, 1961–65, PCE.

racial disparity. Republic employee Norman Baskin claimed, "negroes in production jobs are often passed over for promotion to white-collar jobs in preference to white employees."[31] Such discrimination amidst industrial shifts toward high-tech weaponry threatened to decimate the industry's paltry Black workforce. President Eisenhower's Government Contract Committee (GCC), a successor to Truman's agency, proved powerless to reverse these trends. The committee collected racial data but did not mandate that defense firms even record their own numbers until the late 1950s. GCC officers had to enter factories and count heads to figure out the number of "very dark-skinned persons who may have some Negroid ancestry."[32]

John F. Kennedy's 1960 presidential victory opened new avenues to challenge Long Island's discriminatory industry. On March 6, 1961, JFK abolished Eisenhower's GCC and formed the President's Committee on Equal Employment Opportunity (PCEEO). The PCEEO went beyond antidiscrimination to a loose kind of affirmative action, demanding federal employers, contractors, and unions hire and promote people of color. The committee required compliance reports during the contract process, and accepted "complex group complaint situations," shifting from individual complaints to statistically based inquiries. Within its first year, the PCEEO received more complaints than the GCC during Eisenhower's entire eight years in office.[33] Dozens came from Long Island. Not since World War II could civil rights activists trust a willing federal agency to compel fair employment. The only question was how their interests aligned with the Defense Department's plans for Long Island's industry under JFK's helm.

## Fair Hiring and the Lost Peace Dividend

On one hand, the early 1960s was an opportune time to address racial inequality in Long Island's largest industry. The civil rights movement reached national prominence, the PCEEO had some teeth to challenge job discrimination, and Long Island's NAACP and CORE branches challenged local school and housing segregation. On the other hand, Long Island's defense industry was reeling from contract losses to the South and West, while production workers faced declining job prospects amidst the missile and space race. This hit Long Island's largest employer, Republic Aviation, particularly hard. The company had nothing to replace its almost completed F-105D Thunderchief jet contract. Stirred into all of this was an emerging commercial Keynesian approach to the defense budget emanating from the CEA. JFK, the Defense Department, and CEA chair Walter Heller aimed to trim military fat to make way for a massive economy-boosting tax cut. Long Island, judged affluent, was caught in Heller's crosshairs. With military Keynesianism on the chopping block, Long Island defense workers, their unions, and congressional representatives obligated to represent them, reconsidered social Keynesian alternatives. Workers demanded publicly subsidized jobs untethered from the warfare state. Members of Congress drew up the legislation to make it happen, to exploit a peace dividend to benefit the domestic economy rather than the war machine. The battle between federal bureaucrats and local defense workers would determine how working-class Long Islanders would secure their livelihoods in suburbia. It also shaped what kinds of discrimination civil rights activists fought against, and what kinds of Black workers they fought to employ.

Long Island's first major fair employment fight started shortly after the PCEEO's founding in 1961, and originated in the NAACP's national office, not any local organization like Long Island CORE. The tumult engulfing Republic Aviation also formed the contours of the NAACP fight. In November, NAACP labor secretary Herbert Hill excoriated the aerospace industry's "wide pattern of racial discrimination." Hill chose to first file a group complaint against Long Island's Republic Aviation. But job cuts, concentrated in blue-collar production, immediately forced Hill to direct the NAACP's efforts toward promotional bias, alleging that Republic favored white over Black "lower grade production workers" even when white candidates were less qualified, and that "many Negroes at Republic would be much further along than they are if color were not involved in many promotions."[34] With jobs on the line, getting Black workers into more secure positions, thereby saving them from layoffs, would at least secure Republic's existing Black workforce.

Hill's PCEEO complaint consisted of collecting sixty-two allegations from Republic's Black mechanics, riveters, assemblers, punch-press operators, and electricians. Most signed premade forms agreeing that Republic denied Black workers promotions because the "person was a Negro."[35] A few wrote extra details, revealing the complex nature of discrimination within the industry. One complainant was Randolph Ford, a former army air force engine mechanic who hoped to parlay his experience into a mechanic job at Republic. Despite his experience, he watched fellow white air force colleagues become Republic mechanics while the company considered him unqualified. Ford reluctantly accepted a stock clerk job, and though he excelled and broke few rules at the plant (aside from the prohibition against posted flyers inside workstations), managers promoted white clerks to supervisory positions over him.[36]

John Diggs likewise experienced promotion discrimination that ultimately cost him a job in 1961. Diggs assembled plane fuselages since 1958, though he contended the "assembler" classification was meaningless because he and others did a variety of jobs, including assembling, drilling, and installing rivets on plane skins. In July 1960, Diggs wanted his assembler rank changed, though management denied the request. A few months later, Republic laid him and eighteen other workers off during a company-wide reduction-in-force. But Diggs was the only employee who never received a call back. The company offered jobs to seven laid-off white workers elsewhere at the plant because Republic considered them "qualified," thus saving them from unemployment. Diggs filed a grievance, but Republic refused because reports said he had "poor work performance." He denied this, contending that his "slow" productivity was due to overwork with too few tools, part of the multitasking that occurred on the shop floor. Republic did not reclassify him, placing him in the rehire queue as per union rules.[37]

In both cases, the PCEEO dismissed the bias allegations because they lacked documented evidence, though their investigation revealed pervasive favoritism, sometimes along racial lines. Lawyer Simpson, International Association of Machinists (IAM) union steward, admitted that "by making a job offer to some favorite employee whom they did not wish to lay off," the company discriminated "against any other more qualified employee subject to lay-off."[38] This favoritism, like that in John Diggs and Randolph Ford's cases, promoted some workers, often white, to "safe" classifications and saved them from layoffs. Black and unconnected white workers, if unable to climb into these more secure positions, faced job loss. Promotions and reclassifications mattered because of Republic's looming contract losses, and the NAACP suit was a microcosm of the bigger battle to altogether save jobs at Republic.

JFK campaigned on military Keynesian solutions to the 1958 recession, proposing to resurrect "surplus labor area" defense contracting under "Operation Booster." Once in office, he switched gears and looked to trim the defense budget, choosing Ford Motors president Robert Strange McNamara as his defense secretary.[39] McNamara brought his business acumen to the job, planning wide-ranging cutbacks, including base closings, government-owned plant auctions, and shedding the government of nearly all internal production capacity. McNamara also addressed the defense contract system. He enforced the Department of Defense Reorganization Act of 1958, which gave the defense secretary control over weapons acquisitions formerly managed by the military branches. Overall, McNamara brought his private-sector acumen to the Defense Department, hiring systems analysts, introducing the Planning, Programming, and Budgeting System to the Pentagon, and creating an Office of Systems Analysis, among other changes.[40] The goal was to cut costs *and* improve military capability through increased efficiencies, because buying weapon systems for the entire military could reduce costs without sacrificing security. Weighing what system to buy depended on its function in the overall national security strategy, or as McNamara put it, asking whether each weapon system adds "something significant to our national security."[41]

The institutional changes, coupled with a "try before you buy" policy, introduced new market mechanisms to the contract process. It was a fundamental transformation in the industry's structure that forced all contractors to compete with one another. Aircraft contracts were ripe for reshuffling, as the navy, army, and air force each had their own jet fighters from distinct contractors. In 1961, McNamara compelled the navy and air force to jointly develop a new multipurpose fighter, known as the Tactical Fighter Experimental (TFX) program. Estimated to save $1 billion, the announcement threw all aircraft contractors into panic, especially Republic and Grumman, whose cozy, dependent relationship with the air force and navy respectively kept each firm running. Now, ten companies competed for the largest—and only—aircraft contract in the 1960s. On January 24, 1962, Boeing and General Dynamics–Grumman won the final eight-week runoff, though Grumman was the subcontractor, with most work done at General Dynamics in Fort Worth, Texas.[42] McNamara left the other manufacturers hanging. Because Republic Aviation depended on federal contracts for their entire business, the firm, and its 13,000-person workforce, was in trouble. With the end of the F-105 Thunderchief contract, and having lost space contracts and the TFX, Republic made its first post-McNamara "reductions-in-force" in February 1962 (figure 4.1). The company estimated 8,000 to 9,000 pink slips in the next two years, not including 8,000 local subcontractor job losses.[43]

McNamara's defense reshuffling paralleled an emerging reinterpretation

FIGURE 4.1. F-105D Thunderchiefs rolling off Republic Aviation assembly line in Farmingdale, early 1960s. Courtesy of National Air and Space Museum Archives, Smithsonian Institution.

of military Keynesianism's benefits and costs. In the 1950s, CEA chair Leon Keyserling, persuaded Truman and Eisenhower that there was little harm in budget deficits for the sake of constructing humanity's most powerful military machine. Afterward, the economics profession began moving away from such contentions. Some argued defense spending was economically inefficient, exemplified in Charles J. Hitch and Roland N. McKean's 1960 book, *The Economics of Defense in the Nuclear Age*. But economists and scientists such as Kenneth Boulding, Gerard Piel, Leslie Fishman, Emile Benoit, and Seymour Melman amassed research that not only proved the military budget's inefficiency, but also espoused the positive potential of conversion. They disagreed on the implications. Renowned science writer Gerard Piel was most akin to Keyserling. He attributed America's postwar prosperity to the war economy, though he noted how America's application of Keynesian theory would have scandalized Keynes. Piel advocated reallocating funds toward public works. Emile Benoit and Kenneth Boulding made similar points, admitting that the country could afford whatever it politically wanted, so disarmament offered a once-in-a-lifetime moment to exploit the defense industry's unique skills to solve human needs. Leslie Fishman and Seymour Melman were, by contrast, skeptical of defense spending's economic benefits. Fishman argued military spending crowded out private investment. Melman spent his career showing how the massive defense budget hurt American industrial competitiveness.[44] Collectively they made a strong case for widespread disarmament, grounding their opposition to war in the language of economics, long the means to legitimize moral commitments. But they advocated contrary solutions: Piel, Benoit, and Boulding recalled earlier social Keynesian public investments as a better use of federal money, while Melman and Fishman defended the superiority of private enterprise.[45]

In one sense, their debates remained academic because Kennedy was a Cold Warrior with little interest in disarmament. But the research resonated with Kennedy's CEA chair Walter Heller. Unlike Keyserling, Heller was a leading proponent of what scholars call the commercial brand of Keynesianism. He fused Keynes's teachings with orthodox or classical views on prices and the inflationary potential of full employment. Heller promoted policies that privileged aggregate demand, deploying tax cuts and credits as countercyclical policy in lieu of targeted planning. The government would tinker with monetary policy and taxes, but private businesses would do the employing, investing, and pricing. Workers and consumers would adjust: adopting new skills, buying new, cheaper products, and bringing everything back to equilibrium. Public investment through industrial policy or public jobs programs was less efficient than letting the market adjust. Above all, fiscal spending could spark inflation.[46]

As Heller pushed Kennedy to cut taxes, he likewise saw McNamara's defense cuts as a partial offset to predicted revenue losses. On July 10, 1963, Heller organized an informal disarmament committee to investigate the economic impact of cutbacks, and neoclassical economist Leslie Fishman was a member. After JFK's assassination, President Lyndon Johnson made the committee permanent, adding that the Committee on the Economic Impact of Defense and Disarmament would aid governments, private industry, and labor on ways to "minimize potential disturbances which may arise from changes in the level and pattern of defense outlays."[47] In the next two years, Heller's committee (later an agency) published reports concluding defense cuts would have no major impacts on jobs or growth, even complete disarmament. These findings coincided with the eventual passage of the 1964 tax cuts. Vigorous economic growth in 1963 and 1964, occurring alongside reduced proportional defense spending, marked the first time since World War II that unemployment fell during defense reductions. This confirmed Heller's economic approach.[48]

The new commercial Keynesian approach to the defense budget alarmed workers, unions, and politicians. When Defense Secretary McNamara imperiled

Republic Aviation's future, Long Islanders decried the looming collapse. But local vested interests reached for divergent solutions to the projected job losses. Almost all congressional representatives resorted to military Keynesianism, i.e., more defense contracts for Long Island firms. In 1962, the bipartisan New York State congressional delegation, which included every Long Island Congressman, pushed to avert layoffs. They failed, aside from Otis Pike pestering JFK into forestalling the expiring F-105 contract for a year.[49] Pike also tried to resurrect the contract distribution debate. When he asked Air Force Secretary Eugene M. Zuckert, "how are you going to keep the airframe industry competitive when one by one the companies are going out of business, and where Bell is gone, Curtiss-Wright is gone, and Republic is apparently going?" Zuckert replied, "what happens to the industry after that I can't say. There certainly is going to be need for some consolidation."[50] Zuckert's response illustrated the new approach: the competitive pressures of the defense market would determine a company's survival, a person's job, and a region's economic health.

But Long Island defense workers had their own ideas. They first bubbled up when workers struck in April 1962 in response to Republic's threatened 13,000 layoffs. In the strike, Republic employees demanded bread-and-butter needs like higher supplemental unemployment benefits and increased severance packages. After eighty days, Kennedy invoked Taft-Hartley to force negotiations. The union won, but jobs were still on the line.[51] After the strike, workers, their families, and other Long Islanders sent over 50,000 letters to Washington demanding more contracts. The general local response revealed that they did not merely want more defense contracts; they believed the government should sustain their jobs and hire them for peaceful ends. It was a social Keynesian solution, distinct from both defense and private market dependence for their livelihoods.

*Newsday* editors established the basic argument: "even before World War II, the government has encouraged Republic and similar defense plants to expand to the point where all of them represent a crucially important source of employment. . . . [The federal government] has a responsibility to these people that extends beyond emergency help."[52] Justin Ostro, president of Republic Aviation's IAM union Lodge 1987, similarly contended that "many of the men who will be laid off in the next month . . . came out to work in the defense industry for the Government and it's up to the Government to look out for these workers now."[53] Workers thought in the same terms, as one laid-off Republic employee demanded the government "use the billions of dollars they are wasting trying to reach the moon" to keep workers like him employed.[54] On its face it seemed ironic, because Republic thrived off space contracts. But space contracts did not help production workers. For them, their union leaders, families, community members, and local journalists, federal spending was still necessary to preserve employment, though defense contracts were not.

Once Republic laid off the final round of a total 13,600 employees in 1963, workers and their representatives considered explicitly social Keynesian policy proposals to keep federal money flowing to Long Island. The Suffolk County government, faced with a 7.1 percent unemployment rate, applied for "depressed area" funding under the 1961 Area Redevelopment Act. But Suffolk's proximity to New York City prevented them from qualifying.[55] The Long Island Federation of Labor, the regional AFL-CIO umbrella, organized Island-wide emergency meetings to figure out domestic alternatives to defense. They drew up mass-transit projects for the car-dependent congested suburb, a bridge spanning the Long Island Sound to Connecticut, efforts to reduce air pollution choking the New York metropolitan area, and air traffic control innovations to increase New York's airport capacity. The Long Island Federation also reached out to California's state AFL-CIO, themselves facing defense cutbacks. Together, the AFL-CIO pushed for a "national peace policy" at their 1964 Conference on Full Employment to convert military factories toward job-producing civilian ends. They were trying to turn defense cuts into a "peace dividend" opportunity.[56]

Workers and labor leaders also persuaded their federal political representatives into sponsoring social Keynesian legislation on Capitol Hill. In 1963, Congresspeople representing defense-heavy areas introduced three separate bills related to "defense conversion," or reallocating dollars devoted to the military toward domestic ends. Two had Long Island–related sponsorship. The first was New York Senator Jacob Javits's Joint Resolution 105. It was not strictly a defense conversion bill, calling instead for a Presidential Commission on Automation. But Javits contended that defense cuts had the same effect as a new machine or outsourced factory. The resolution hearings were filled with conversion ideas including urban renewal, mass transit, affordable housing, and clean energy. And defense contractors were some of the most forceful conversion proponents. Republic Aviation vice president John Stacks spoke on the Senate floor about the folly of defense and space spending, contending that "we in effect are indulging in a scientific and technological luxury that eventually could have ill effect in that it directs talent away from broad applications for specific projects." He argued the federal government should directly plan and invest in civic improvements. Pennsylvania Senator Joseph Clark called Stack's ideas "almost socialistic." Stacks replied "yes, unfortunately."[57]

Long Island labor leaders threw more weight behind South Dakota Senator George McGovern's competing bill in October 1963. Unlike Javits's generalized automation commission, Senator McGovern wanted to establish a National Economic Conversion Commission. The public body was tasked with planning peacetime production, including private and public projects ideas, state and local agency coordination, and civilian project proposals from defense contractors. Long Island Federation of Labor leaders went down to DC in February 1964 to drum up political support for the McGovern bill. They met with President Lyndon Johnson, who only promised a pilot program through his Disarmament Agency.[58] They also asked Long Island congressional representative Seymour Halpern to sponsor a House companion bill. The next month, Halpern announced on the House floor that the government must "right what it wrought," helping defense contractors and workers shift to civilian work. As Halpern said, "there are vast unmet domestic needs. The opportunity of channeling resultant savings into the more meaningful and beneficial sectors of the economy will go unheeded . . . unless the Nation is willing to plan ahead."[59]

In May 1964, the Senate held hearings on McGovern's conversion plans. The battle between social and commercial Keynesians came to Capitol Hill. George McGovern exemplified the views of politicians, unions, contractors, and workers when he contended that the "Federal Government has a clear obligation to those companies, communities, and individuals that have become dependent on our defense budget," and that "we have the opportunity now to apply a greater proportion of our national wealth and the talents of our people to solving some of the social and economic ills that still exist in this land of plenty." On the other side was CEA chair Walter Heller, his US Arms Control and Disarmament Agency, and the Defense Department, who asserted the supremacy of the private market. In the Defense Department's words, "it is very clear that the ability of communities and industries to adapt to shifts in defense spending depends much more heavily on the general health and general level of demand of the economy rather than on any special programs or planning that might be undertaken."[60]

The Gulf of Tonkin Resolution in August, authorizing the Vietnam War, nixed the prospects of defense cuts. But Republic Aviation still faced collapse, and Long Islanders took out their frustrations at the polls. Two Republican House members lost their seats to Democratic upstarts. Herbert Tenzer ran on a pro-labor platform, promising more defense contracts and conversion support, defeating Frank Becker. Democrat Lester Wolff beat Republican Steve Derounian with similar claims. Long Islanders also pressured New York Senate candidate Robert F. Kennedy to help Republic. To secure votes before election day, RFK promised that Labor Secretary Willard Wirtz and Defense Secretary Robert McNamara would visit Long Island. RFK claimed they would answer "where are we going to get the jobs?"[61] Once elected, Long Island labor leaders made one last push for peacetime conversion in December 1964. Meeting in the Garden City Hotel, the same site defense workers convened at the end of World War II, the Long Island Federation of Labor pitched local domestic projects that could benefit the suburb rather than the war effort. To representatives-elect Tenzer and Wolff, along with incumbents Republican James Grover and Democrat Otis Pike, they unveiled proposals for two bridges across the Long Island Sound, new schools, and a new airport, among other projects.[62]

Despite the support, the social Keynesian policy moment died in 1965. President Johnson's promise to help Long Island amounted to a report entitled the "Transferability of Defense Job Skills to Non-Defense Occupations." The report committed the government to "research and placement, retraining, and relocation," but not to creating new jobs. The Labor and Defense departments, meanwhile, jointly sponsored a relocation project through the Manpower Development and Training Act, encouraging former Republic employees to work for Douglas Aircraft Company in Long Beach, California.[63] These efforts enticed a few to relocate. They also created jobs in the federal bureaucracy. But they produced no jobs on Long Island. The new Congressman Lester Wolff resorted to military Keynesianism once in office, giving a dozen colleagues from two House committees (the Science and Astronautics Committee and the Armed Services Committee) a Republic Aviation factory tour. He hoped to drum up some new contracts.[64]

RFK fulfilled his campaign promise in October 1965 when Secretary McNamara landed to tour Long Island's defense plants. By this point, Maryland-based Fairchild Hiller bought Republic's carcass, transforming it into a subcontractor with a lean and R&D-oriented workforce around 3,700. Less than one-fifth of Fairchild Republic's workers engaged in production compared to 80 percent of Republic's former workforce. For the first time in recorded history, Long Island's unemployment rate exceeded the nation's (figure A.4). Here the three Keynesian approaches to growth and jobs confronted one another. Local politicians, desperate for a way to boost industrial jobs, voiced their desire for more military Keynesianism. They expected McNamara to forecast future defense spending. Union officials hoped for social Keynesianism, pressing McNamara to convert the local defense economy toward consumer production.[65] Instead, McNamara resorted to commercial Keynesianism, using his visit to inform Long Island that the defense boom was over. Though he discussed two potential contracts for Fairchild Republic and Grumman, he reminded workers that new contracts did not mean more jobs, and that Grumman's success depended on the company's ability to keep costs down. McNamara scolded Long Island's government, business, industry, and education leaders for relying on military Keynesianism, because "the defense industry is a highly erratic industry and you should not try to build an economy on it." When asked whether Long Island's high wages penalized the area, McNamara denied it, though added "if you are there isn't anything I can do about it."[66]

Essentially, McNamara informed these workers that the federal government was no longer committed to employing them, and what happened to these plants, workers, and Long Island was not the state's responsibility. Contracts still flowed to Nassau and Suffolk, though the funds depended on how well firms competed in the marketplace. His demand that defense firms and politicians shift to a non-defense economy without aid ignored the industry's structure. Defense manufacturers could not simply transition into private consumer production. They had little commercial marketing knowledge and no experience producing low-cost items in high volumes. They were an outgrowth of the warfare state, committed to satisfying their one customer with high-quality products made from over 10,000 parts. Helping defense workers enter the private economy emphasized worker skill deficiencies rather than the jobs available. But skills were not the problem because most production workers were light assembly operators working in gigantic job shops. The problem was the lack of factories on Long Island to hire them and offer similar pay.[67]

How does the plight of mostly white male blue-collar workers relate to poverty? On the surface, their problems were distinct from the challenges Long Island's domestic workers confronted in the suburban labor market. But workers' post-layoff experiences illustrate how poorly compensated and insecure work led to hardship. Unemployed Republic workers couldn't make rent or pay their mortgage, struggled to afford food, and had trouble filling the car with gas or covering bus fare. In other words, poverty. Professional workers had little trouble finding new similarly paying jobs, but only 5 percent of employees held bachelor's degrees. Blue-collar production workers—the assemblers, fabricators, and mechanics—were unemployed for an average of five months. When they returned to Long Island's labor market, they earned about half of their industrial wage. Republic Aviation was *the* high-wage mass employer in postwar Long Island: prior to layoffs, under 1 percent earned below Long Island's relative poverty cutoff. After layoffs, 43 percent earned wages below the relative poverty threshold. Former Republic workers likewise could not meet the lower budget threshold set by the Bureau of Labor Statistics (BLS), meaning they could not afford housing costs without cutting back on other needs. Unsurprisingly, they expressed discontent with their new lives. One Republic worker feared the "possible loss of my home if I do not find employment soon." Another claimed that "the local sweat shops take advantage of the situation and offer you a salary which it is impossible to live on . . . when most of them offer $2 an hour or less it is impossible for a family man to survive on such an insult."[68]

These workers now entered Long Island's "diversified" industrial economy that paid well below the wages needed to afford suburban living. But it did not have to be that way. Local Long Islanders, their union officials, political representatives, and even senators like George McGovern had an alternative dream: to repurpose federal spending for civilian and domestic purposes, saving their jobs while fulfilling Keynes's vision of public investment's poverty-eradicating potential. Defense workers were no radicals; they fought to save their jobs. Neither were their union officials or McGovern for that matter. But each nonetheless recognized mass prosperity's foundation in federal spending. The people in charge of federal purse strings—Defense Secretary McNamara, CEA chair Walter Heller, and Congress, among others—disputed the need for federal dollars to support Long Island's workforce. They instead believed suburbs like Long Island were exceptional, prosperous in spite of targeted spending, exemplary of what the private market produced (with a little fine tuning to monetary policy and taxes). These commercial Keynesians won. The others lost. The Vietnam War killed McGovern's conversion plan. The F-105 Thunderchief, the last jet Republic workers built, killed most of the 52,000 Vietnamese civilians who perished during Operation Rolling Thunder's first three years. Low-wage suburban sweatshop jobs crushed Republic Aviation workers' suburban dreams.[69]

Republic's collapse mattered for the NAACP's fair employment fight too. It emerged amidst the company's death throes and the industry's march toward technical employment. The disruption forced the NAACP to switch from fair hiring, to promotions, to saving Black workers from layoffs. The PCEEO challenged the NAACP's case, but it was all for naught because the jobs evaporated altogether. Here, then, the critical link between fair and full employment was apparent. What pulled Long Island's Black "servant class" into industrial work during World War II were fair employment mandates mixed with a tight labor market. In the 1960s, the federal government recommitted itself to antidiscrimination, but the Defense Department divorced federal spending from its job creating potential on Long Island. Pursuing fair employment without tight labor markets would have markedly different outcomes for Long Island's racial disparities.

## CORE versus Grumman

Long Island's other major civil rights organization, CORE, launched its first attack against the defense industry in August 1965, just two months before Defense Secretary McNamara made his inauspicious visit to Republic Aviation. CORE chose Republic's competitor Grumman for obvious reasons. Unlike Republic, Grumman's workforce had more than doubled from 1961 to 1965 thanks to NASA contracts, making the company Long Island's largest employer.[70] And despite Grumman's claims that it was "unique in its achievement in the field of human relations," the company's Black workforce grew from only 1.1 percent to 3.6 percent between 1962 and 1965.[71] Compared to Republic, Grumman was indeed a perfect target, especially when President Lyndon Johnson strengthened the federal fair employment apparatus. But defense was an even less secure job market than before the McNamara-induced "efficiencies." Fair employment without corresponding full employment, or enough labor market tightness to absorb all Long Islanders, would do little to improve the job prospects of Long Island's underemployed Black working class. Even if CORE could get more Black workers hired at Grumman, the labor market would remain loose, encouraging exploitation and leaving the racial income gap and disproportionate Black poverty untouched.

Long Island CORE, and its chair, Lincoln Lynch, took a different approach than the NAACP four years earlier. Rather than file complaints with the government, Lynch brought fifteen demands straight to Grumman in August 1965. They focused on placing local Black workers across Grumman's occupational structure. CORE demanded that Grumman recruit Black workers from local suburbs, give preference to Black Grummanites in training programs, and form an employee-elected minority grievance panel. Lynch first asked Grumman to voluntarily acquiesce, though he threatened to include federal officials if necessary.[72] Grumman balked at the proposal, believing CORE's social demands jeopardized Grumman's ability to hire the best engineers and scientists in the competitive space age. Grumman personnel manager P. E. Viemeister also took offense to CORE's publicity-gathering campaign that used Grumman as a "symbol" to "bend over backwards to compensate for past discrimination."[73] Despite Grumman's harsh rebuttal, they only resisted three demands: the employee-elected grievance panel, employee notifications of all new job openings, and CORE's review of their detailed implementation plans.[74]

For two months both sides refused to budge, and on November 1, Lynch called off further talks. He was "tired of agreements in principle which mean nothing in fact." Management, meanwhile, concluded that the company "can fulfill its obligations to all its employees and to the US Government . . . or it can follow the dictates of Long Island CORE. It cannot do both."[75] Though Lynch threatened protest, the pickets never came. Lynch admitted in April 1966 that "the exciting times of the demonstrations, while not over, are diminishing." Lynch himself left Long Island CORE that same month to become the organization's associate national director under Floyd McKissick.[76]

CORE's agitation temporarily disappeared, but federal fair employment policy came to mirror CORE's compensatory quota demands. In 1966, President Lyndon Johnson replaced the PCEEO with the Office of Federal Contract Compliance (OFCC). This agency, embedded in the Labor Department, had direct control over the contract purse and required affirmative action hiring policies *prior* to contract awards. Construction protests in 1966 and 1967, meanwhile, expanded affirmative action mandates to include numerical goals for non-white hiring, timelines, and fair occupational distributions. By 1968, the OFCC forced companies to include affirmative action plans as part of the bidding process.[77]

When mixed with McNamara's intensified contractor competition, affirmative action goaded recalcitrant companies like Grumman into action. The threat of losing contracts compelled Grumman to sponsor the Wyandanch recruitment drive mentioned in the chapter introduction. They also encouraged Black workers to enroll in training courses, who made up between 20 percent and 30 percent of all graduates between October 1967 and August 1968. Last, Grumman president Lew Evans formed the Open-Door Advisory Council (ODAC), a corporate-controlled grievance council with both Black and white employee representatives to manage discrimination charges and ensure equality in promotions and transfers.[78] Threats to Grumman's profits forced the company to satisfy CORE's earlier demands. The efforts paid off: Black employees reached 4 percent of Grumman's workforce by 1968.

Unfortunately, sustaining the gains amidst intense contract competition proved difficult. In 1967, Grumman had over 37,000 employees on its payroll, a company record. By year's end, their NASA contract and F-111B contract troubles forced the company to lay off eight hundred workers in 1968. This is why Grumman offered so few jobs at its Wyandanch recruitment fair. Saving Black workers' jobs once again came to the fore. In January 1968, CORE, the Suffolk County Human Rights Commission, Black Grumman employees Bob Caupain and Bill Paige, and other activists met with Black Grummanites to discuss ways of improving their job prospects. Together they formed Big Brother, an organization chaired by Bob Caupain to promote training programs among Black Grummanites and inform prospective employees of new jobs. Though Grumman refused to recognize them, Big Brother became a de facto "Black" representative organization. Bob Caupain met management on several occasions, negotiating forty-seven supervisory positions for minority members as well as a Black personnel director in December 1968. With five hundred members, one-third of Grumman's minority workforce, Big Brother formed what was essentially a Black labor union, and when Grumman did not address their demands, Big Brother broke off talks and turned to Long Island CORE.[79]

Unlike CORE's initial 1965 attempt, the civil rights group now had a substantial number of complaints to justify their protest, and the OFCC could cancel Grumman's recently won navy VFX jet fighter contract (eventually the F-14) if they failed to meet the affirmative action mandates. On March 24, 1969, Big Brother and CORE held a press conference in Hempstead. They alleged that Grumman had made "no real move to place blacks into decision-making jobs, or any positions of real power." They contended Black workers mostly held food service and janitorial jobs (half of these positions were minority-filled), few were foremen or managers (around fifty), and that Black Grummanites received different promotions, salaries, and raises from white workers. CORE demanded that the OFCC, Labor, and Defense departments review Grumman's hiring and promotional practices before granting the VFX contract. On April 1, 1969, the OFCC agreed to launch an investigation into discriminatory labor practices.[80]

Holding the VFX contract hostage provoked a hostile response from the local public. Suffolk labor commissioner Lou Tempera warned that CORE's attack posed "a threat to the corporation's position as Long Island's largest employer." Long Island CORE president Lamar Cox denounced Tempera as an "irresponsible bigot . . . an enemy of the black people" for defending the company, while Tempera reiterated how deeply canceled contracts would hurt Long Island's economy.[81] Grumman chose to wait until the federal investigation unfolded because their future rested in the OFCC's hands, which had yet to cancel any contracts due to racial discrimination. On April 14, 1969, the New York Regional Office of the Defense Supply Agency found no overt bias, though admitted there was "room for improvement." The company responded with an updated affirmative action policy and laid the groundwork for the Opportunity Development Department (ODD). The ODD took over and expanded ODAC's former roles. The ODD ran a promotion review board, organized job fairs for non-white workers, recruited qualified Black employees for supervisory jobs, and monitored the company's affirmative action policy. Essentially, the ODD was an internal bureaucracy, managing racial problems in-house to ensure contract compliance.[82] It addressed promotions above all, adding a layer of safeguards to avoid bad press and lost contracts.

The OFCC review and Grumman's new ODD did little to satisfy CORE or Big Brother. CORE sued again, this time targeting not only Grumman, but the Labor and Defense departments as well as the OFCC for violating the 1964 Civil Rights Act. It was an unprecedented lawsuit because no one had charged the federal government for failing to enforce contract compliance. CORE wanted to compel the government to "stop being hypocritical by passing laws that it has no intention of enforcing."[83] To CORE, defense firms discriminated across the industry, and Grumman's solutions only adjusted the promotion and hiring process to ensure non-discrimination and fair job advertising. The suit, which indicted all involved parties, intended to force firms to absorb Black workers from local labor markets and include them across the occupational ladder, a solution to two decades of exclusion.

While CORE prepared its lawsuit, Big Brother grappled with looming layoffs. The agreement reached between Grumman and compliance officers, including the new affirmative action policy and the ODD, did not address the disparate effects of layoffs, particularly when half of Grumman's 1968 pink slips, 329 in total, hit blue-collar workers. VFX production would not start until 1970, and the company announced it would dismiss another 3,500 workers over the course of 1969 as the LM program ended. Grumman president E. Clinton Towl admitted that production workers would disproportionately face layoffs.[84] Big Brother claimed that Grumman laid off two hundred Black workers, or between 17 percent and 20 percent of the total layoffs, even though Grumman would dismiss only 10 percent of the total workforce. While company officials challenged the data, stating that 164 of those minority members left the company for reasons other than layoffs, Grumman's Black proportion was nonetheless shrinking despite major breakthroughs in the company's racial employment policy.[85] An abrupt reversal of jobs revealed why fair employment mandates needed corresponding jobs to meet them. It was a social policy that worked when labor markets were tight; less so when the jobs were scarce and workers abundant.

Grumman's new affirmative action policy and the dedicated ODD could check discrimination in hiring and promotions but could only promise "color-blind" layoffs. Big Brother then threatened to shut down the company, and chair Bob Caupain promised to fight "even if it means bloodshed."[86] In July 1969, Big Brother and CORE laid out seventeen demands to Grumman, including company recognition of Martin Luther King Jr.'s birthday, hiring a Black vice president, and "extensive training to allow Negroes and 'exploited' whites to advance."[87] When the company ignored the demands and fired twenty-three Black workers as it hired thirty white skilled workers in late July, Big Brother staged a strike on August 4, two weeks after Grumman's

LM reached the Moon. Sixty protested outside the personnel building. They held signs reading "Blacks work for nothing—no respect, no money, no advancement," "How the hell can you get seniority when you are laid off?" and "Sweeper, Janitorial, Cafeteria: that's as far as you go Black Boy." Caupain wanted seniority waived in layoffs until more Black workers held skilled jobs. When prodded about how the company would select which white Grumman employees to lay off in lieu of Black workers, Caupain responded, "I don't have time to worry about whites. I'm worrying about black people."[88]

Big Brother's racial promotions-based approach generated only modest support, primarily because they challenged only one aspect of a broader layoff affecting Black and white workers. White employees still dominated the redundancies, and discrimination in hiring and promotion hurt Black employees at the bottom of the hierarchy, doing little to skilled workers and not inducing them to join. Big Brother staged a walkout and ten-mile march from Bethpage to Garden City to coincide with the nationwide "Black Monday" protests at construction sites on September 29, 1969. The walkout attracted five people at the Bethpage plant. By the time the march reached its endpoint in Garden City ten miles west, around eighty protestors joined, including current Grumman and former Republic Aviation employees.[89] The race-based strike, in combining both the problem of layoffs and discrimination, united few to its cause.

CORE's lawsuit likewise failed. The case, initially deliberated in US district court in 1970 and appealed in 1972, found Grumman innocent. Since Black Grummanites and CORE requested a general government inquiry into hiring practices, the plaintiffs had not exhausted all avenues to address discrimination claims through Executive Order 11246 or Title VII. Therefore, they could not to sue administrative bodies they had not contacted in the first place.[90] After over twenty years of weak fair employment committees, a labyrinthine network developed to formalize relations between employers and non-white workers. Long Island CORE and Big Brother continued to use publicity-gathering tactics, including the high-profile lawsuit, but fair employment mandates had returned. For CORE, though, fair employment meant something different in the new defense market. Grumman responded to federal and activist pressures, growing their Black proportion to 5 percent of their total workforce by 1971, half of whom worked as technicians, professionals, managers, or skilled craft workers.[91] To reach this number, though, the ODD ran vigorous recruitment drives for skilled Black workers, a national pool that all defense companies competed for. Grumman directly recruited from southern Black colleges to fill its racial quota, including Morgan

State, Howard University, and Bennett College, among others.[92] Through outside recruitment, Grumman could satisfy federal mandates while also hiring skilled workers for their new computer data system and space projects. Grumman followed federal regulations, Black representation improved, but Black Long Islanders, and the mass of Black workers, saw little benefit.

All of this occurred as Long Island's defense sector lost 23,000 jobs between 1969 and 1971, a fifth of the entire workforce.[93] Even the Black gains in proportional terms hid the fact that Grumman employed fewer Black workers by 1971 than it did two years prior. Like 1965, the racial protests occurred as local politicians, defense employers, and union representatives scrambled to assemble a "conversion to a peacetime economy" plan. The Long Island Federation of Labor established a "Save-A-Job" Committee with a specific conversion program. This included tax incentives for aerospace plants to fight pollution, explore the deep oceans, and build public transit. They also recommended a bridge spanning the Long Island Sound, a new airport for the metro region, and a Long Island Rail Road modernization program. Most importantly, the federation demanded a contract process that reflected local labor pools and needs rather than favoring the lowest bidders. Local politicians like Democratic state senate candidate Karen Burstein ran on a full-employment platform, contending that "the investment in the future requires our acceptance of the idea that the government must play as significant a role in waging peace as it does in waging war." The national conversation mirrored Long Island's local level concerns, with critiques of the military-industrial complex circulating the media. Senator George McGovern relaunched his defense conversion efforts, which became part of his 1972 presidential election platform.[94] But like the calls for social Keynesian policies from five years earlier, legislation did not follow. Instead, fair employment mandates would operate in a much looser labor market, with more workers competing for dwindling numbers of decent-paying jobs.

## Conclusion

Few things better illustrate fair employment's limits than the contrast between Grumman's two recruitment drives in the late 1960s. In 1968, they held the Wyandanch job fair for underemployed Black workers in an impoverished suburban hamlet. At the same time, they vigorously pursued highly skilled Black workers straight from southern colleges. Black professionals were headhunted; Black production workers waited on long lines in what amounted to a hiring lottery. This was not what CORE chair Lincoln Lynch or NAACP labor secretary Herbert Hill intended when they first demanded jobs and promotions for Black Long Islanders. They aimed to use the nation's best-paid industrial sector to close Long Island's "gap between Negroes and whites in terms of family income," as Lynch put it. But without enough jobs to lift everyone into decent wages, the income gap remained. This is not to indict CORE or the NAACP's strategies. Both organizations were committed to economic security for people of color through good jobs. It was a central plank of the 1963 March on Washington for Jobs and Freedom, the 1966 Freedom Budget for All Americans, even the Black Panther Party's Ten-Point Platform.[95] Long Island workers envisioned a path for actually getting to full employment—repurposing defense factories for domestic purposes to sustain jobs and stimulate local economies. They wanted to turn from military to social Keynesianism, public investments that put jobs and social needs at the center of planning.

As this chapter makes clear, it did not happen. Defense Secretary McNamara introduced market discipline to the defense economy, and public spending lost legitimacy among CEA economists. They collectively asserted market solutions for both the defense industry and those who lost defense jobs. In their calculation, affluent places like Long Island were exceptional from the rest of the nation and could absorb publicly subsidized job losses. They didn't understand, or chose to forsake, the importance of federal spending to working-class suburban prosperity. There was no market equivalent to publicly subsidized defense jobs. Long Island's poor already labored in low-wage private-sector jobs. When thousands of working-class Long Islanders, Black and white, lost aerospace jobs, they entered the competition for low-wage work. Labor market "looseness" only further encouraged racial division. Low-wage employers still held power to discriminate, even as Long Island's core industries abided by fair employment mandates. Without full employment, racial disparities persisted alongside fair employment.

Defense contracts may seem distant from poverty, but as the primary federal job creation tool in the postwar period, the US military budget was intimately tied to domestic economic security. Welfare states had many routes to ensure decent lives for their citizens after World War II. During the New Deal, welfare-state planners chose a job-centric path, "placing primary emphasis on employment" instead of "social insurance as an all-sufficient program for economic security," as FDR's seminal Committee on Economic Security Report phrased it.[96] Military spending proved a poor substitute for reducing people's market dependence for their well-being, even on Long Island, where defense dollars concentrated. The alternative that emerged in the 1960s, tax cuts and aggregate growth measures, was no substitute at all. But when policymakers believed that the private market—rather than targeted public spending—produced Long Island, they crafted policies that imagined the suburbs could solve poverty, rather than considering the federal programs that made Long Island prosperous in the first place. These ideas, premised on suburban exceptionalism, are what we explore next.

# 5

# The Suburban War on Poverty

In May 1968, Edwin Dove walked into New Cassel's community action program (CAP). It was one of a thousand CAPs established across the US by President Johnson's Office of Equal Opportunity (OEO). CAPs were the frontlines of the War on Poverty, set up to empower the poor by directly funneling federal funds to non-profits assisting in various programs of self-help. New Cassel's CAP established a job counseling office and Dove was their ideal client: a forty-six-year-old Black man from the neighborhood who had held dozens of jobs during his life but was unemployed and living near poverty. During the Depression, he supported his widowed mother and four siblings on the Works Progress Administration (WPA) payroll. After serving in World War II, he moved from job to job. He worked in a nursing home managing their ballpoint-pen manufacturing business. Then he moved boxes in a pharmaceutical warehouse until the company laid him off. He complained that he always earned "low salaries for dead-end positions," and quit his most recent job in the hopes of finding something better. That brought him to New Cassel's CAP.

Demac Manufacturing Corporation was looking for people like Edwin Dove too. The company scored a $240,000 military contract to produce chaff, strips of aluminum foil and glass used to jam enemy radar. The Vietnam War called for a lot of chaff. Making it wasn't a technical ordeal: workers stuffed fiberglass and aluminum shreds into small containers. But Demac had trouble filling their positions. Their one-story factory, across the street from suburban Cape Cods, was just five miles east of New Cassel in nearby Hicksville. The company approached New Cassel's CAP for referrals, which needed jobs to offer anyone who walked in. Demac Manufacturing had plenty.

But Dove didn't show much interest. Since he began with the CAP a month prior, he went on almost three interviews per day. Most employers just filed his application away. Others only hired trainees, "a good way for someone to get cheap labor," he thought. The jobs he actually got rarely turned out to be worthwhile. An employer down the block from Demac offered him $2.25 per hour, but the bus cost $2.40. Demac didn't have much luck with other jobless CAP walk-ins either. The company tried emulating Grumman, which had sponsored the job fair at the Wyandanch CAP two months earlier. But in contrast to Grumman's long lines of applicants discussed in the previous chapter, few people attended Demac's Wyandanch fair. Despite offering bus transportation between Wyandanch and their plant, Demac only hired eight people from its recruitment drive, not enough to sustain the route. "I wanted it to work," lamented Wyandanch's CAP director, Chester Davis. The event disappointed Demac's technical director, Walter Madey, too. So did the low turnout in New Cassel and other Long Island CAPs. But Dove wasn't let down. He didn't want the job anyway.[1]

Unfilled factory jobs, idle people not taking them. The fact puzzled antipoverty activists, corporate executives, and local reporters alike. *Newsday* framed it as a conundrum, "the uncommon nature of Long Island's unemployment problem: despite thousands of job openings, jobless people still cannot find suitable work."[2] The Long Island daily echoed how national pundits and politicians framed poverty in 1963. The deprived were the "invisible poor," part of the "other America," isolated in poverty "pockets," stuck in a "paradox of poverty in the midst of plenty."[3] After the 1964 Economic Opportunity Act sailed through Congress, philanthropists, neighborhood organizers, scholars, and other local antipoverty activists devised programs to bridge the gap between the poor and the affluent. Most dealt in skill-upgrading, job referrals, and better transportation links between poverty "pockets" and worksites. Despite the efforts on Long Island, wealthy by any measure, the poor didn't bite.

From Edwin Dove's perspective, there was no paradox. The Demac Manufacturing job paid $1.70 per hour in 1968 ($13.70 in 2021), well above the national minimum wage, but also well below what people needed to make rent, pay bills, and afford transportation on Long Island. By contrast, people waited hours for Grumman's jobs because the defense firm offered pay in the $2.00–$2.50 ($16.20–$20.25) range. New Cassel CAP aide John Gilliard remarked that "when I say to the people I've got a job for them for $1.70 an hour, they look at me like I'm crazy. Some of them figure they can go out on the street and hustle or write numbers and make a better living." Dove held out little hope that CAP could improve his prospects: "I came up in a hard time, I lived in a jungle.

But it's funny, people then seemed to have more respect for each other because everybody was doing bad. Today people have their own separate societies."[4] The poor, and the people who assumed responsibility for helping them escape poverty, recognized that low wages perpetuated their condition no matter how many opportunities private employers brought to CAP doorsteps.

Edwin Dove's experience wasn't supposed to happen. Lyndon Johnson's Economic Opportunity Act built directly on the 1964 Revenue Act. The Revenue Act was a new commercial Keynesian tactic to stimulate the economy via tax cuts, premised on the idea that employers would invest the savings and create more private-sector jobs. It was a liberal approach to full employment, harnessing state power at the macro level to steer investment but depending on the market to naturally produce the jobs. Johnson and his economists built the War on Poverty on this foundation, expecting that poverty would "disappear" in ten years, and declaring they had "mastered" the boom-and-bust cycle soon after the economy took off. The war was likewise steeped in liberal theories about how disempowerment, individual skill deficiencies, and opportunity deprivation caused poverty.[5] And suburbs were the geographic manifestation of this postwar economic conceit. The suburbs were the exceptional places where affluence concentrated and where a new bus route, a hiring drive, or a vocational program was all that was needed for the poor to succeed. If federal programs, mediated through local CAPs, could penetrate the exclusionary walls blocking the poor from the plentiful suburban jobs around them, poverty could be eradicated.

Dove's experience was supposed to be especially unlikely on Long Island because few places better exemplified suburban exceptionalism. Nassau and Suffolk checked all the boxes for a place with "poverty amidst plenty." The two counties had lower poverty rates than 99 percent of America's over 3,000 counties. Nassau was in the 99th percentile for economic growth, while Suffolk trailed close behind.[6] Suburban public officials enthusiastically supported Johnson's domestic program, particularly Long Island's new county executives, filled by two Democrats in otherwise Republican-dominated counties. Both reaped the political benefits of supporting Johnson's poverty war. And both wanted to reduce their high welfare burdens, which amounted to a third of each county's total budget, funded through the inefficient, regressive, and generally despised property tax.[7] Suffolk's county executive H. Lee Dennison celebrated the War on Poverty's potential to "build a better foundation for a more stable and equitable future general economy." Nassau's county executive Eugene Nickerson went further, contending that the fate of Johnson's project rested on Nassau County because "if the richest county in the world, with the help of the richest state and nation in the world, can't effectively eliminate its pockets of poverty in this affluent age, then the poor are truly justified in their fatalistic desperation."[8] Material plenty abounded across Long Island. All the poor needed was a little help in reaching it.

By working in War on Poverty programs, however, local officials learned that Dove's experience was typical. County executives, human rights commissions, labor departments, and CAPs all devised imaginative programs within the ideological confines of the national War on Poverty. Their efforts waged the war on several fronts. Antipoverty activists empowered the suburban poor through CAPs. County labor departments replaced migrant farm laborers with local workers. Federal and local officials trained the un- and underemployed for suburban jobs. Human rights commissions offered comprehensive referral services. And federal grants literally bused the poor to industrial parks. But rather than ending poverty, these experiments exposed the flaws in how national policymakers understood poverty's causes. Amidst suburban prosperity, CAPs couldn't organize or mobilize the poor. County labor officials could not attract local Long Islanders to pick potatoes. Referral centers could only locate minimum wage work because employers refused to raise wages despite supposedly "tight" labor markets. Buses dropped the unemployed off in industrial parks with jobs that paid little more than domestic worker gigs. Postwar affluence turned out to be an obstacle, not the path to ending poverty and inequality. Officials learned through their efforts what low-wage suburban workers had already known: suburban prosperity depended on poverty. Employers exploited low-wage workers to satisfy suburban needs. By the late 1960s, local officials considered a radical alternative to existing federal programs: a job guarantee, i.e., offering work to anyone who wanted it, to provide needed suburban services in child and elder care, recreation, and public works. In effect, decommodifying labor.

This chapter follows the War on Poverty as it unfurled across Long Island. It covers efforts to mobilize the poor in Long Island's "poverty pockets," replace migrant farmworkers with locals, set up bus routes between poor neighborhoods and industrial parks, match the unemployed with local jobs, and finally, devise a countywide job guarantee in Nassau County. In each case, officials realized the problem was exploitation, not exclusion from prosperity. The poor didn't need a few more skills, knowledge of jobs, or help getting to work. They needed better pay, more power in their working lives, and new ways to satisfy suburban needs. Long Island was ill-equipped to end poverty. The idea that suburbs were exceptional in the urban landscape turned out to be an ideology, suburban exceptional*ism*. Local officials peeled away that myth, revealing America's wealthiest suburb as a laboratory for *understanding* poverty's roots, rather than a place to end it.

## Community Action in a Centerless City

Edwin Dove walked into a CAP office because "community action" was the War on Poverty's signature program. Community action was a sociological theory of poverty, drawn from juvenile delinquency programs and cultural studies of poverty scholarship. It funneled resources to poor "communities" through local CAP offices and mobilized poor people so they could improve their own conditions. Initially, community action proved vague enough to please left and centrist liberals alike: radical organizers viewed CAPs as a vehicle to organize the poor as a political class, while liberals imagined CAPs could socialize the poor for mainstream society.[9] Both sides imagined the poor inhabited distinct "communities," concentrated into places where they could be mobilized. The government's chosen official poverty statistic, Mollie Orshansky's food-budget poverty measure, added statistical heft to their claims because the measure used census data, illuminating where the poor lived. But when CAPs came to Long Island, activists had trouble identifying concentrated poverty in dispersed suburbia. They had even more trouble organizing people when residents opposed labeling neighborhoods or themselves as "poor." Long Island's CAPs did find success. But suburban poverty's sprawling nature, and the poor's dispersal among wealthier people blunted what they could accomplish.

CAP funding arrived only months after the Economic Opportunity Act passed, but figuring out where to establish Long Island's CAPs proved tricky. The federal conception of "community" developed from inner-city social work research, not small poverty enclaves or poverty households spread across suburbs.[10] The federal government also relied on the census-determined poverty measure to determine where poverty pockets might be. Neither proved conducive to finding suburban poverty. In December 1964, both Nassau and Suffolk formed countywide umbrella organizations, the Nassau County Economic Opportunity Commission (Nassau EOC) and the Economic Opportunity Commission of Suffolk, Inc. (EOC Suffolk). The county EOCs collectively identified twenty-two "poverty pockets," evenly distributed between Nassau and Suffolk. Some places were obvious, like Wyandanch or Roosevelt, because the Census recorded high rates of federal poverty (table A.3) compared to Long Island as a whole. Hicksville, a hamlet that included Levitt-built Cape Cods, had its share of struggling families and elderly poor, also got a CAP. But other places with similar numbers, like Farmingdale, home to Republic Aviation, didn't get a CAP.[11] CAPs were not the most effective vehicle for aiding a dispersed poor across an affluent suburban landscape. Furthermore, there were no organic poor "communities" ready to run a CAP in "poverty pockets." By 1967, only six of the twenty-two planned CAPs were operational. It took nearly four years to set up all twenty-two.

When activists went out to organize people in Long Island's "poverty pockets," they discovered few viewed their neighborhoods as poor. TRI-CAP activists, which covered Westbury, New Cassel, and Carle Place, went door to door to figure out the area's most pressing problems. They instead met people who claimed poverty didn't exist in New Cassel. Central Islip organizers found residents were "ashamed of being classified" with Carleton Park even when they lived within its borders. In Roosevelt, CAP aides confronted homeowners trying to shutter the local CAP because they "do not want the label on their town that reveals the fact that there is poverty in Roosevelt."[12] In Long Beach, CAP organizer Hugh Wilson, the eventual founder of the Nassau Welfare Tenants Committee, noted that the suburban seaside city's white poor population, while friendly to CAP activists, never visited the CAP office or joined a CAP activity. As Wilson found, "whites stayed in the shadows" across Long Island. White apprehension made it difficult to organize most of Long Island's poor and to form CAPs in all-white Hicksville or Levittown.[13]

Once organized, Long Island's CAPs delivered useful services and resources to the suburban poor. CAPs functioned like this across the country, and it was no different on Long Island.[14] Head Start, for example, educated pre-kindergarteners year round across all twelve of Suffolk's CAPs. Suffolk's after-school programs attracted an estimated 1,000 children per week. In Nassau County's Five Towns area, Project ABC tackled child and adult illiteracy, while Project Reach Out created summer employment for teenagers. All ten of Nassau's CAPs ran day care centers, serving 350 children. They made all the difference. Coat factory employee Dorothy Harris admitted, "I don't know what I'd do without it." Nassau County was also a health care desert for the poor; only four doctors and one dentist accepted the newly created Medicaid insurance program. Long Beach's CAP organized caravans for hospital, doctor, and dental visits. Port Washington's CAP directly supplied medical services themselves.[15] CAPs also fed the hungry through the Commodities Distribution Program, an outgrowth of the Federal Surplus Food program that Nassau County first instituted in 1962. By the late 1960s, CAP organizers started thirty co-ops across Nassau to distribute non-commodified foods, a cashless supplement to the food stamp program. They doubled participation to over 174,000 people by 1968, 14 percent of the county's total population, distributing 4.6 million pounds of meat, butter, beans, and evaporated milk each month.[16]

Beyond social services, CAP employees fostered political organizing among Long Island's poor. Nationwide, grassroots activists used CAPs as a platform for radical and civil rights-oriented politics, a means to empower the poor, demand resources, and confront entrenched urban political machines, among other objectives.[17] On Long Island, this happened on a small scale. The CAP networks organized the informal housing tenant committees detailed in chapter 3, for example. The Nassau Welfare Tenants' Committee was founded by Long Beach CAP veteran Hugh Wilson, and the Nassau County Law Services Committee, Inc. had a presence in nine Nassau CAPs. Both sued Nassau County for prohibiting welfare recipients from living in Roosevelt. Through May 1969, the law services committee accepted nearly 6,000 cases ranging from family issues to housing, welfare, and jobs. CAP workers directly referred people to the law services committee, and welfare activists spoke of law service attorneys as "our lawyers." With legal support, the Nassau Welfare Tenants' Committee viewed welfare entitlements as rights and openly protested for adequate housing, higher welfare thresholds, and better treatment. CAPs made Long Island's welfare rights movement possible, embedding legal representatives in suburban hamlets and among the activists organizing suburbia's poorest.[18]

Long Island's CAPs reflected the promise and pitfalls of community action. On one hand, the poor were hard to organize, limiting their political voice. The difficulties pushed Suffolk EOC executive director Dean Harrison, who had prior experience in Newark, to quit after only four months on the job. He was "wearied by the sprawling nature of poverty in this suburban-rural county." Nassau EOC director Adrian Cabral was similarly exhausted by the organizing efforts that felt "like bailing out the ocean with a spoon."[19] But at the same time, OEO funding and community organizers improved the health of those previously isolated from Long Island's health care system, enabled working mothers to labor full-time, educated young children, decommodified food, and gave the poor tools to demand decent housing and sufficient income. Modest steps perhaps, but Congress never funded or supported community action to do more.

## The War on Imported Poverty

The actions of Long Island's CAPs differed little from their activities elsewhere in the nation. But Long Island's poverty problems were not one-size-fits-all. This was clearest on Suffolk County's East End. Each year, 3,600 migrant laborers arrived for harvest season, three-quarters of the county's entire agricultural workforce. They were a vestige of Long Island's preindustrial past, part of the seasonal-labor stream that still stretched across the Eastern Seaboard. As stated in chapter 2, they remained a necessary part of Suffolk's still viable agricultural sector despite creeping suburbanization from the west. But they were also a drain on the county's home relief program, responsible for Suffolk's higher poverty rates compared to Nassau County, and by the 1960s, a national scandal for the county government.

In 1960, Edward R. Murrow's CBS special *Harvest of Shame*, followed by congressional hearings the next year, exposed the harsh working routines, low pay, and appalling living conditions farm laborers faced while staying in Suffolk. This put the newly elected Suffolk County executive H. Lee Dennison, the first to hold the position, in a bind. With suburbanization marching eastward, Suffolk's polluting duck farms were almost extinct. But the large industrial farmers that ruled Suffolk's agricultural sector were an important political constituency on the East End. They needed low-wage workers to keep their farms running. Dennison chose to pursue the crew chiefs who recruited southern migrants, what he called the "questionable employment agencies . . . specializing in bringing in any kind of labor into the county at a price."[20] After the congressional hearing, Dennison established a task force to devise solutions. By 1965, Dennison launched what amounted to a war on *imported* poverty. He intended to replace migrants with local workers, a sharp turn from Long Island's long-standing dependence on low-wage imported labor. But would Long Islanders take these jobs?

County Executive Dennison believed he could not reduce Suffolk's poverty and the attendant public burden without addressing the migrant labor system itself. Welfare, police, fire, and health care budgets, not to mention the environment, all suffered so commercial farmers could exploit Black southern migrants and Puerto Rican laborers. Removing the migrants and replacing them with local workers would lower the county's unemployment rate. As he stated, "it may be time to start picking up some of our own potatoes, to initiate what might well be called useful and honest local home rule for a change."[21] With local seasonal workers, the county could invest in slum clearance, improve work conditions, and lower welfare costs, all while preventing new migrant streams from encouraging future slums. It was a bold plan, though other agencies had alternatives. Two War on Poverty CAPs looked instead to Suffolk's suburbanizing future, starting programs that could prepare southern migrants and seasonal workers for nonagricultural jobs. The Suffolk County Human Relations Commission, meanwhile, advocated for labor laws and union recognition to structure work relations in the field. These three approaches—using local labor, preparing migrants for suburban jobs, and regulating work conditions—offered radically different solutions to imported labor on Suffolk's East End, predicting divergent futures for Suffolk's agricultural economy.

Dennison's local labor plan was really a compromise between the farmers' needs and the county's desire to lower costs. The plan assumed manual farm laborers would be necessary in the foreseeable future but that the county could replace migrants with a local workforce. But farm labor was the lowest of low-wage jobs. Dennison claimed enough year-round labor existed in the county, particularly on the welfare rolls and in unemployment offices. His labor department could not find these local farmworkers. Suffolk's jobless made at least as much on unemployment insurance or welfare as they would harvesting potatoes. The county could only find twenty-four welfare recipients on the East End who could do the work, along with 657 welfare recipients countywide. The labor department concluded that "with the present low wages in existence in the agricultural industry, most local residents are looking toward employment in the areas of Suffolk where the wages are higher, the employment more stable, and the benefits greater."[22]

County officials debated the plan for two years until a space heater set an eight-room barracks ablaze, asphyxiating three of the fourteen people sleeping in the Bridgehampton camp on January 14, 1968. This high-profile fire coincided with a local public television documentary that aired in February, Morton Silverstein's *What Harvest for the Reaper*, a spiritual sequel to Murrow's 1960 film that followed one crew chief's migrant gang from their homes in Arkansas to their temp jobs in Cutchogue, Long Island.[23] Following the fire, the Suffolk County Board of Supervisors established a Seasonal Farm Labor Commission, a nine-person body of government officials, Long Island Agricultural Marketing Association members (a representative body of farmers), and church officials on January 22, 1968. Following the film's debut, Dennison demanded the commission solve the migrant problem because it had become "a matter of national advertising that I don't really care for." The administration reoffered local labor once again, though knowing farmers could not afford to pay higher wages lest they "force them out of business." County labor commissioner Lou Tempera laid out a "wage-subsidy plan" to support the agricultural industry's national competitiveness and attract local workers. The county would assure packers received the prevailing \$2.00 area wage and that field workers earned at least \$1.75 per hour. Tempera estimated a \$2.7 million annual operating cost to subsidize the wages of 3,890 shed workers and farmhands.[24]

The Seasonal Farm Labor Commission criticized the plan and Dennison's intentions. Even Tempera's calculations intended to prove local labor's high costs, and he was only willing to implement a test pilot. Farmers liked the idea of a local and stable workforce but knew they could not attract local workers to stoop labor, calling Dennison's plan "unrealistic." The wage-subsidy plan also altered the labor structure from piecework to hourly wages, made farmers wards of the state, and was so costly and controversial it could not endure long-term political challenges.[25] Farmers also disputed Dennison's contention that these migrants burdened the county. A 1967 welfare study found that only 9 percent of Suffolk's welfare cases resided in the county for less than two years. By contrast, over two-thirds lived in the county for five years or longer. For the 431 short-term (i.e., less than six months) migrants who applied for assistance in 1967, New York State reimbursed the county for all costs. The commission also found that the police rarely arrested migrants and private charity or the state absorbed most health care costs.[26] The commission ended its investigations in May 1968, shutting down the local labor idea and blaming Dennison for perpetuating the migrant system with his threats to "phase-out" migrants rather than improving housing, a proper function of government.[27]

If Dennison's plan looked to sustain the system with local labor, CAP programs took the opposite approach. CAP activists wanted to pull migrants away from the farm system and prepare them for Long Island's suburban economy. This would force farmers to mechanize and end the migrant labor system altogether. Two CAPs formed with alternatives to farm labor: Community Action Southold Town (CAST) and the Seasonal Employees in Agriculture (SEA). While all CAPs offered conventional War on Poverty services, SEA and CAST devised locally oriented initiatives. CAST set up a short-lived fish industry training program, designed to revive the dying fishing industry and help seasonal workers supplement their income beyond the planting and harvest seasons. They trained twenty men at a time in marine safety, navigation, wire splicing, and fish preservation.[28] SEA started a self-help housing program. With funding from the Federal Farm Housing Administration, enrollees received a low-interest mortgage they could repay in "sweat equity." Former migrants would develop applicable skills for the suburban economy as they built their own affordable home. SEA contended that these skills were necessary because "farms in Suffolk County are giving way to housing developments and those that remain find mechanization the answer to the greater efficiency and production demanded by rising real estate values." Within a year of its founding, the program had a woodworking plant, cooperative furniture repair shop, credit union, grocery store, and day care center. Self-help housing worker James Smith built everything from the kitchen cabinets and furniture to the roof for his $17,000 home. He planned to open a construction company with the skills he and his eight co-builders had gained.[29]

Cultivating construction skills was a promising alternative to the migrant system, especially as the East End began feeling the effects of an expanding building boom of luxury homes in the Hamptons. Unfortunately, these programs were expensive to run, and migrants didn't take advantage of them. The Self-Help Housing program included only twenty families in its first year, while CAST trained a similar number.[30] Robert Tormey of SEA admitted that despite having over 1,600 people enrolled in training and job placement programs, the migrant system made retention impossible. Tormey discovered that no matter when they scheduled a program, "no one can show up because they aren't finished work yet . . . they would have more time to learn if they didn't work. But they don't want welfare. They want to work."[31] Seasonal migrants were too dependent on the migrant system, and permanent residency far from home and family didn't attract them. Overall, farm laborers did not take the alternative jobs CAPs offered. Of 115 migrants SEA placed in 1966, only ten still held their jobs three years later. The CAPs waged a war to induce mechanization by removing southern migrants from the agricultural workforce, but farmers would not end the system if they could still access a steady supply of laborers.[32]

Between Dennison's unpopular war on imported poverty and the meager CAP skill development programs, local antipoverty measures proved inadequate. This was painfully obvious to Reverend Arthur C. Bryant, pastor of St. Peter's Lutheran Church in Greenport and vice-chair of the Suffolk County Human Relations Commission. Bryant was one of the first to demand a Suffolk County Seasonal Labor Commission in late 1967 to eliminate the migrant farm labor system. When Dennison offered the wage subsidy, Bryant condemned it as perpetuating the system. He argued crew chiefs would only suppress pay, destroying the subsidy's intended livable wage. Bryant also contended that the CAPs did not promote worker autonomy, and "only occasionally do we find ways to help a man escape from the industry." As Bryant noted, literacy, while a personal and social good, does not guarantee a job. Bryant and the Suffolk Human Relations Commission wanted farmworkers to unionize and New York State to extend minimum wage protections. He canvased to update the 1937 New York State Labor Relations Act and coordinated with the United Automobile Workers union to fund an organizing drive. Cesar Chavez's United Farm Workers Organizing Committee planned an Island-wide strike during the 1969 harvest season. But the union and the strike never happened.[33]

Collective action may have been the only means to improve the system, but as Cindy Hahamovitch argues, labor supply determined everything in the farmworker system. New immigrants could undermine unionization, improved housing, innovative health codes, or wage policies.[34] Labor organizing would have little impact if farmers could import an interstate workforce to depress wages and working conditions. This was true on the national level as well. President Johnson's labor secretary Willard Wirtz pursued the same migrant replacement strategy as Suffolk County executive H. Lee Dennison in the mid-1960s. The only difference was scale: Wirtz confronted an international stream of guestworkers and used his position to stop the visa program that enabled commercial farmers to import Mexican and Caribbean help during harvest season. He faced such vociferous opposition that he eventually rescinded the ban on farmers using guestworkers to harvest crops in the US South and West. Despite strike threats and increased wage disputes in the late 1960s, employers simply repatriated troublesome guestworkers and hired willing replacements to avoid labor strife.[35]

The key to altering this system lay west in the rapid suburbanization process making its way toward Suffolk's East End. Planners looked forward to urban development, and Dennison celebrated the end of "those goddam duck farms occupying priceless waterfront."[36] Speculators gobbled up farms for housing subdivisions, and Suffolk lost over 53,000 farmland acres between 1958 and 1972. Perversely, this transformation perpetuated the migrant system. When developers offered $3,000 an acre for empty land, $10,000 an acre after a nearby land purchase, and nearly $20,000 an acre after houses went up next door, farmers continued using migrants while awaiting more lucrative offers. Why indebt oneself to buy an expensive machine when there were still plenty of workers willing to pick the spuds themselves? As Reverend Bryant himself said, "every farmer knows that the time is not too far off when the most valuable crop he can grow will be houses."[37] This meant living and working conditions worsened for a smaller number of migrants as the number of farms dwindled.

Suffolk County saved the remaining farms in the 1970s as part of an open-space planning initiative designed as a bulwark against "sprawl," preserving Suffolk's "rural" past, and a means to recharge the county's groundwater aquifers. These farms continued to use migrant workers, now increasingly originating from Puerto Rico, but jobs disappeared for the thousands of local seasonal workers. The old migrant system that exploited Black workers died out, though over time, a new labor stream exploited Latino workers. Nonetheless, Dennison could claim victory against the war on migrant poverty as the East End suburbanized. But the migrants who stayed—i.e., ex-migrants—joined the ranks of Long Island's impoverished working class. The CAP drive to train the poor for construction jobs looked to the region's suburban future, though the programs were too small to have a broad impact.[38] Winning Suffolk's war against poverty would be fought in its western half, where county government and activists looked to incorporate the poor into the affluent mainstream rather than regulate a stagnating low-wage farm labor system.

## Busing the Poor to Prosperity's Doorstep

Demac Manufacturing, the Long Island-based chaff producer, didn't only offer job opportunities at Long Island's CAPs. In their desperate attempt to find workers, the company also planned bus routes between "poor" neighborhoods and Demac's suburban industrial plant. Demac executives were trying to rectify what policymakers considered a major suburban barrier to better jobs: transportation. Industrial jobs remained vacant, and the unemployed remained isolated from them so long as the private automobile was the only way to get around Long Island. Demac Manufacturing was one among a dozen companies pushing for public transit options on Long Island. By the late 1960s, federal antipoverty funding constructed a web of bus routes aimed at reducing the most direct exclusionary barrier: space. Of all the War on Poverty–era programs, Long Island's federal bus program best exemplified the "poverty amidst plenty" paradox framing. This front of the War on Poverty was a war on immobility, based on the premise that the obstacle to a better job was getting to it.

The War on Poverty bus program originated in an unrelated piece of legislation, the 1964 Urban Mass Transportation Act. It set aside almost $400 million for mass-transit projects in cities and states across the country. But the next year, people rioted in the Watts neighborhood of southern Los Angeles, the most violent postwar urban rebellion yet. Unlike other cities gripped by urban unrest, Watts was a suburb in a car-dependent, low-density city. California governor Pat Brown convened a commission, chaired by former CIA director, John McCone, to investigate the riot's causes. The McCone Commission Report, as the media called it, cited Labor Department research that found inadequate transportation deprived poor residents of job opportunities. President Johnson's Task Force on Suburban Problems, the suburban working group of Johnson's Great Society, concurred. Charles M. Haar, the assistant secretary of Metropolitan Development in the Department of Housing and Urban Development (HUD), and chair of Johnson's Task Force on Suburban Problems, believed suburban public transportation programs could be a "strategic weapon in the anti-poverty campaign." In 1967, HUD began rolling out suburban pilot programs. Watts got money. So did Long Island through a Tri-State Transportation Commission grant to test "the effect of improved public transportation to employment centers which are not located in central business districts."[39]

Long Island was indeed a haven for automobiles. Over three-fourths of all workers commuted by car, nearly everyone aside from the rail commuters going to Brooklyn and Manhattan. A car opened access to shimmering office buildings and clean industrial parks constructed along Long Island's highways and state roads. Those without a car depended on Long Island's bus system, divided among twenty-one ailing private companies running infrequent services and offering no intercompany transfers. A resident of Manhasset's Spinney Hill domestic enclave would have to ride three buses for ninety minutes to reach Roosevelt Field, a major shopping and job hub, all for $1.10 in bus fare. In a car, the ten-mile trip clocked in at fifteen minutes and about 32¢ worth of gasoline. Otherwise, carless workers depended on taxis, informal commuting arrangements, or long walks. In an automobile-dependent region, a car opened a whole new world of job opportunity, while living without one constrained one's reliability on the job, the distance one could travel for work, the jobs one could take, and even one's knowledge of jobs available.[40]

Undoubtedly people would benefit from physical mobility, but would access to suburban industrial parks lead to upward mobility? The Tri-State Transportation Commission first planned three bus routes from Hempstead, Massapequa, and Hicksville. They all converged on the Plainview Engineer's Hill Industrial Park, a complex straddling the Nassau–Suffolk border along the Long Island Expressway in 1967. The Massapequa route served an auto-dependent hamlet, while the Hicksville route linked a commuter railroad to the industrial park. Hempstead tied one of Long Island's target poverty areas to the park, and program coordinators hoped to decrease the village's high jobless rate. The commission added more routes over the next two years. They connected the Bay Shore domestic enclave and low-income subdivisions in Central Islip (home to Carleton Park) and Brentwood to three clustered Suffolk Industrial Parks: Perez, Cardinal, and Vanderbilt—then the nation's largest suburban industrial park—as well as the Pilgrim State Hospital—the world's largest psychiatric center. Eleven routes tied poor hamlets to smaller employment centers through June 1969, completing the bus program's antipoverty agenda, with service from Nassau and Suffolk CAPs in Glen Cove; Rockville Centre; Long Beach; Wyandanch; North Amityville; Inwood; Central Islip; Oyster Bay; and even Jamaica, Queens to employment, educational, and health care centers across Long Island (figure 5.1).[41]

Local officials hailed the new bus system. But a close analysis of the industrial parks reveals that the buses overcame the spatial divide between "poverty pockets" and jobs, but not the wage divide that pervaded Long Island's postwar suburban economy. The Hicksville Industrial Park, Engineer's Hill in Plainview, the Cardinal and Vanderbilt Industrial Parks in Hauppauge, and the Perez–Raddock Industrial Park near Commack, had grown to employ over 11,000 people. The parks had a mix of jobs that reflected both entrenched wage inequality and the rising occupational divide accelerating since the late

1950s. Sixty percent of jobs fell into three heavily defense-oriented categories. White men tended to hold these skilled production or professional and technical occupations. There were airframe and parts subcontractors, including semiconductor maker Amperex of Hicksville and electro-optic producer Quantronix Corporation in Hauppauge. Non-electrical machinery firms were defense subcontractors too, like Zarkin Machines Corporation, a subsidiary of Curtiss-Wright, with their technician-heavy staff. The remaining 30 percent of jobs were mostly low-productivity, low-wage industries. Ninety percent of them moved from New York City to reduce costs, including that of labor. These included fabricated metals, apparel, toys, sporting goods, and textile manufacturers, offering weekly wages competitive with low-wage service work.

Put simply, the buses dumped riders into a job market with wages people could find anywhere on Long Island. As a study of these jobs put it, "primary wage earners in these categories will find it difficult to survive in high-cost Long Island while earning the minimum wage."[42] A 1968 Polytechnic Institute of Brooklyn Survey confirmed that the 1,057 unskilled job openings in three of the four industrial complexes (Plainview, Hauppauge, and Hicksville), offered wages ranging from $1.97 to $2.06 per hour. While 30¢ above the 1968 federal and state minimum wage, a full-time year-round job, assuming no seasonal layoffs, placed a worker 30 percent below the relative poverty threshold in both counties. A 1968 Nassau County poverty study revealed that a single earner with three kids would need to earn $2.20 per hour for the bus commute to favorably compare to welfare or a walkable job.[43] Lacking a car wasn't the primary obstacle. It was low pay, and exploitation behind it, that stopped workers from availing themselves of Long Island's plentiful "opportunities."

Employers had the most to gain from the public subsidy for their low-wage workforce, though the bus program's benefits depended on exactly how employers exploited the labor market. The same 1968 Polytechnic survey canvassed 2,700 business establishments, discovering both support and opposition for a myriad of reasons. Disapproving employers revealed their preference for a captive labor force plucked from the racial and gender-segmented market. One employer feared that if the bus program widened the labor market, he would lose his locally recruited female workforce to other employers. Another similarly claimed the buses drained the local labor pool and forced him to raise wages 6¢ per hour. Proponents meanwhile cited the benefits of reduced absenteeism and lateness among existing employees. The most vocal supporters, like L. Bieler, whose company manufactured gutters, vents, and downspouts in the Cardinal Industrial Park, offered some of the lowest-paying and least stable jobs among industrial park firms. Consequently, he had a "serious problem" getting people to work. He had moved the business from Queens into a 155,000-square-foot plant and installed labor-saving equipment, but still needed about two hundred seasonal workers during peak production between May and November.[44] Unsurprisingly, a bus program would drive more low-wage workers to his plant.

Overall, the bus routes were not an effective antipoverty program. The entry-level jobs offered little above what people might find in their local neighborhood, not to mention the added potential burdens of extended commuting time, day care needs, and lost job networks. While bus use for work purposes accounted for 72 percent of all riders in 1969, and a third found their jobs through the bus system, these workers did not originate from poor enclaves.[45] Because the routes only breached the geographic and not labor market barriers, few poor workers made the trip. As Nassau EOC manpower coordinator Richard Ford lamented, low-income workers would not make the $1.10 roundtrip bus ride to work for $1.50 to $2.00 an hour. "They can get that kind of poverty pay in their own neighborhoods." He was right. Hempstead Village, an EOC determined "poverty pocket," had nearly double the number of unskilled openings of any other hamlet, and offered an average hourly rate of $2.13, second only to Glen Cove's industrial park, also near one of Nassau's poverty enclaves.[46]

Distance was not the barrier to getting out of poverty. The Tri-State Transportation Commission concluded as much when they ended fifteen of the twenty-two routes in 1970 (figure 5.1). Within a year of the program's establishment, Tri-State Transportation Commission executive director Douglas Carroll Jr. admitted, "I doubt if [the bus program] is making any improvement in the unemployment problem." By 1970, the commission's final report revealed that despite claims transportation "handcuffed" the poor, deeper problems—from day care and health care on the supply side to low pay on the demand side—prohibited or discouraged workers from using the bus program. They were not simply "ready and able to work if they could solve only their transportation problems," as the commission originally claimed. Furthermore, the program, like community action, rested on the false belief of "concentrated poverty" in the suburbs. But only a quarter of Long Island's poor lived in the poverty pockets (though a much larger percentage of Long Island's minority poor resided there). Dispersed poverty, when combined with dispersed industrial parks, made the "traditional, large-vehicle, fixed-route, scheduled bus transport unfeasible both in terms of service and economy for many areas." The commission concluded that "if the jobs pay decent wages, people will invariably find a way to get to work" and "will purchase an automobile as soon as possible, thus eliminating the need to ride the buses."[47]

The bus program attempted the most direct means of improving employment prospects: literally driving people to job centers. The project revealed,

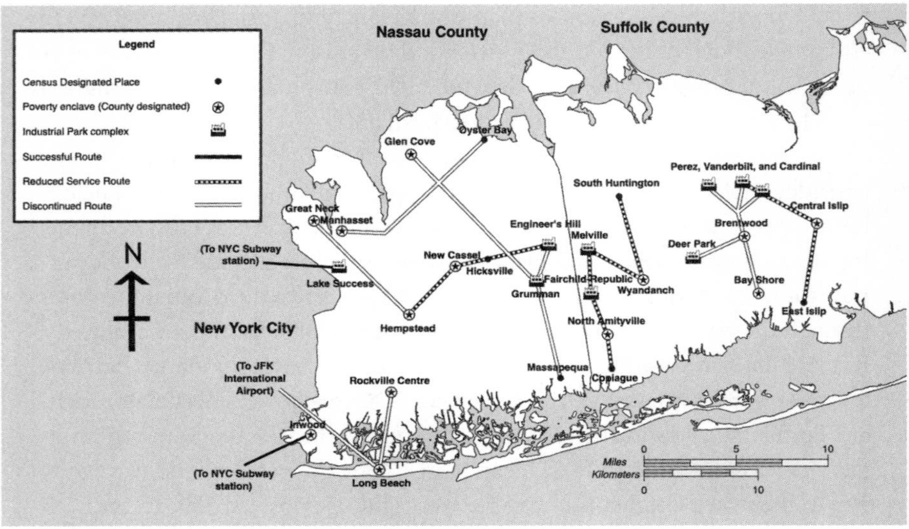


FIGURE 5.1. Tri-State Transportation Commission antipoverty bus routes across Long Island. Made with Mapdiva Ortelius 2.

though, the more formidable obstacle: the proliferation of low-wage jobs on Long Island. Since at least the early twentieth century, Long Island's prosperity depended on low-wage jobs. Buses couldn't change that. For those unable to afford a car, hopping on antipoverty buses was a risk. Was it worth disrupting childcare arrangements, forgoing local job networks, and throwing out their existing work–life balance all for jobs that didn't necessarily pay any better or prove more reliable than what they could find locally? Many chose not to take the chance because low-wage jobs, even if they were more accessible, did not reduce the likelihood of poverty. No antipoverty measure proved more idealistic than the bus program; the initiative, from Washington to the local CAPs, assumed Long Island's affluence and its ability to absorb all if only they had mobility. Shuttles that traversed space and opened the ghettoes to the bounties of suburbia could reduce poverty. But shaping the commutation links between labor supply and demand proved a losing battle. The poor needed secure living-wage jobs, not buses to get there.

## Matching Jobs with the Jobless

When Edwin Dove walked into New Cassel's counseling office in 1968, he was just looking for a job. But the CAP offered more than just referrals. They had interview workshops, job training courses, day care options, and programs to help people kick drug and alcohol addiction. This was how the War on Poverty's architects imagined CAPs would work. If the bus program treated suburban poverty through the lens of place, poverty as a problem of people was the most popular interpretation at the national and local level. The idea derived from two beliefs. First, the American economy was prosperous and adequate work with good wages existed. Second, an individual's education, generalized skills, and personal habits determined their wages. Long Island, the postwar poster child of prosperity, was exactly the kind of place that could easily absorb the poor into the mainstream. With a little skill development, a deeper knowledge of the local job market, and a few hiring pledges from local employers, poverty could be solved on Long Island, making it an example for the nation. But this war on deficiencies confronted the same low wages in the bus program, revealing how institutions and politics, rather than productivity, determined wages.

Poverty as individual failing has a long history in the US and across the Western world.[48] After World War II, two academic concepts coalesced to add analytical heft to individualized ideas about poverty. One was "human capital," a microeconomic theory contending an individual's education, health, and generalized "skills" determined their labor productivity that market wages then rewarded. The theory neatly explained the gap between the poor and the mainstream in a prosperous economy, an outcome of their own deficiencies or "disadvantages." The second was the culture of poverty thesis, popularized by anthropologist Oscar Lewis, which purported that behavioral and psychological traits prevented the poor from escaping poverty.[49] Both theories aligned with commercial Keynesian economics. The government could adjust interest and tax rates, tinkering with the economy at its commanding heights. At the local level, the "invisible hand" still allocated resources efficiently. If people weren't seeing their well-being rise in a booming economy, something was wrong with them. Politicians, academics, even American businesses threw their support behind War on Poverty job training initiatives because these concepts did little to challenge their power.[50]

As an exceptionally rich area, Long Island was the ideal laboratory to test this supply-side theory for reducing poverty. Long Island's local governments devised several initiatives, modeled on these ideas and funded with federal dollars, to boost employment outcomes. CAPs operated OEO-funded programs, and during the aerospace industry's early '60s upheaval, Nassau County executive Eugene Nickerson utilized the Manpower Development and Training Act (MDTA) to train and place defense workers. But locals often complained that the programs targeted the skilled rather than the needy and lacked the funding or organizational capacity to reduce unemployment and poverty. To combat this, the Nassau and Suffolk's human relations commissions designed their own programs that specifically targeted Long Island's disproportionately Black working poor. The Nassau County Human Rights Commission established the Job Development Center (henceforth Nassau JDC) early in 1964. The Nassau Human Rights Commission devoted over half its county-funded budget to the Nassau JDC. The center focused on Long Island's Black un- and underemployed, who made up 85 percent of the JDC's clients. The Suffolk County Human Relations Commission turned to federal funding for its Job Counseling and Development Program (hereafter Suffolk JCDP) too. Operating out of Suffolk's ten CAPs, the Suffolk JCDP aimed to "improve [the poor's] aspirations and self-confidence, and place them in gainful and satisfying employment." Like the Nassau program, the Suffolk JCDP focused on aiding the county's Black unemployed.[51]

Both human relations commissions positioned themselves as the vanguard of Long Island's War on Poverty. Their training and placement efforts linked human capital and culture of poverty theories together. Intake interviews determined an applicant's "employability" based not only on whether they had "outmoded or unusable" skills, but whether the applicant needed counseling, rehabilitation, or even a means to regain their sense of self. Applicants "have lost faith in themselves and have resigned in apathy" according to a Suffolk JCDP report.[52] The fact that both the Nassau JDC and Suffolk JCDP targeted Black Long Islanders with rehabilitative services reflected the racist assumptions undergirding job training and referral programs. Unemployed defense workers were out of work because Long Island manufacturers lost contracts and closed. By contrast, program officials called jobless domestic or construction laborers the "hard-core" unemployed. They allegedly needed self-improvement and help finding jobs to reenter the workforce.

Regardless of how they approached applicants, job training and placement programs depended on employers accepting people from their programs. The Nassau JDC publicly begged corporations to help because "if every Long Island employer could create just one opening, or fill that vacant job *now*, we shall have broken through on this issue."[53] The Suffolk JCDP directly contacted employers, surveying seventy-five of Long Island's largest firms to gauge their job openings and commitment to hiring from their programs. Two-thirds responded and offered an estimated 2,500 jobs, 1,749 of which employers considered "unskilled." Immediate openings tended toward service work: Grumman had 110 jobs in food service and maintenance, the VA offered housekeeping and laundry jobs, while 152 of the 185 jobs at two large hospitals were for orderlies, porters, housekeepers, or food service workers.

Manufacturing jobs otherwise predominated, including work as assemblers, packers, or general factory operatives.[54]

The programs found people jobs, but not ones that necessarily lifted people out of poverty. The Nassau JDC placed over 7,200 people from 1964 through 1968.[55] The Suffolk JCDP measured its ratio of applicants to placements, and 43 percent of clients, or 3,517 people, got jobs from August 1966 through 1968.[56] Together they placed over 10,000 people, and this doesn't include the other Long Island programs, like the Nassau CAPs, which in 1967 alone secured around 1,300 jobs, or the local MDTA office, which placed another 1,700 people by October 1968.[57] The data nonetheless provides little detail about the applicants, the jobs they actually procured, or the length of time workers remained employed. A single month survey of 102 job placements in Nassau County's CAPs claims that only twenty-eight jobs paid "poverty-level" wages. But fifty-six of the "above poverty" jobs in retail, health care, and maintenance services barely crossed the threshold.[58] A 1968 Suffolk JCDP report had job openings for security guards, orderlies, paint sprayers, pressers, and drill press operators. Wages averaged $1.94 ($15.86 in 2021) per hour, though thirty-four of the eighty-four advertised jobs offered training and raises that reached $2.53 ($20.69 in 2021) per hour in six months. It was a mixed bag. Full-time work earning the average wage ($1.94) still placed a family under the federal poverty line. Even if a breadwinner received raises to $2.53 per hour, they couldn't reach Long Island's relative poverty threshold.[59]

Qualitative evidence from employers is more damning. In a 1968 OEO-funded survey of one hundred Nassau County companies, eighty-three reported chronic labor shortages. This had more to do with the kind of worker employers wanted and the pay they offered rather than a tight labor market. As the survey noted, "there is a genuine shortage of skilled workers, but not of unskilled." The labor market was loose at the bottom, so employers could shun job referral programs. In fact, only twelve of the hundred surveyed companies used Long Island's programs. Employers complained of low-skills and "poor worker attitudes." But few sought to solve the problem by raising wages above $2.00 an hour. As the survey concluded, "low wages is the major cause of the difficulty in filling low and unskilled positions." They cited Grumman as rarely having trouble finding workers to fill any jobs. Generally, employers complained of high turnover in unskilled positions and a "labor shortage" in the sense that they could not find the kind of worker who would take and keep a sub-$2.00 an hour job. They wanted, and in some cases needed, docile workers willing to accept poverty wages to sustain their businesses. A higher minimum wage would have no doubt attracted workers, but employers were unwilling or unable to match that. They depended on poverty to service suburban needs or remain competitive in high-cost Long Island.

Even for "unskilled" jobs, Long Island's employers expected certain elusive "skills," complicating training course design. The MDTA's local efforts enrolled 3,472 people from 1965 through October 1968 in thirty-seven different occupational training courses. Some prepared workers for Long Island's growth fields. Secretarial work, drafting, nursing, stenography, and machine operation accounted for 40 percent of all enrollees. The MDTA was able to place over half of trainees in these fields into jobs. Another 30 percent of enrollees entered courses that did not match well. For auto mechanics, repair technicians, service station workers, or restaurant employees, either pay was too low, the labor market too saturated, or the training program too poorly designed to prepare prospective workers. Only a third ended up employed in the field, while another third were unemployed at the end of their training and the remaining 28 percent never completed the course.[60]

Forecasting appropriate "skills" was only part of the problem. When employers talked of "skills," they only applied its conventional definition (one's education and job-oriented training) to skilled positions, where high wages encouraged self-investment that complemented new technology in the workplace. For low-wage work, "skills" meant behavioral norms: showing up on time, staying with a company long term, accepting pay and work conditions, etc. It was an expectation tinged with biases. Verbalizing a racialized culture of poverty thesis, Albert D'Andrea, personnel manager of Oxford Filing Supply Company in Garden City, contended that industry had to acclimate their workforce to function "with these people," a challenge given the "high standards of the current labor force." Employers could hold such views because the jobs programs did little to alter their hiring practices, and if anything, squeezed more workers into the bottom of job hierarchy, supplying firms a bigger pool of low-wage labor.[61]

By 1968, job training and placement officials began voicing their concerns over the poverty-level wages Long Island employers offered their applicants. Long Island's *Newsday* put it best: "The jobs are there. The civic committees are there. The government programs are there . . . but the hard core remains unemployed . . . the chief reason given for lack of response to some help-wanted signs is simply a lack of persons interested in such work at a minimum wage." The conclusion echoed what frustrated the poor and the program coordinators. Richard Ford, manpower director of the Nassau EOC, found that $2.00 per hour tended to be the lowest threshold poor applicants accepted. If "some businessmen think there are lots of mythical characters called 'hard-core unemployed' running around looking for jobs for $1.60 or $1.70 an hour . . . they are sadly mistaken."[62]

Local public officials began calling out employers too. Nassau Human Rights Commission head Farrell Jones condemned the out-of-touch job qualifications as "unrealistic." It was an excuse to keep wages low and bar low-income minority workers from the affluent workforce. He cited World War II, when Long Island industry "took men and women of every type and every mentality—and they turned them into productive workers. That's the key word—productive. These people can produce, but industry has to give something to get something; it must train and offer opportunities." The rest of the county administration agreed. Thomas F. Greene, Nassau's Department of Commerce and Industry chair, called the cries of business leaders "nonsense . . . the people are there, and they want to work—but they also want to be treated like human beings." Nassau executive Nickerson condemned the minimum wage jobs offered to program recipients since they "can't get people off welfare or out of poverty . . . especially if the job isn't the beginning of something more." He declared business must do more than "create low-paying, dead-end jobs which again appears to be all they are now willing to do." Even Nickerson's Republican opponent, Hempstead town supervisor Francis T. Purcell, argued that the minimum wage did not make ends meet in high-cost Long Island, and private employers along with government must "upgrade these wages" to match the publicly trained workforce.[63]

Local officials came to recognize that low wages were the source of poverty, not the individual. But counties and towns couldn't legislate higher wages without the state legislature, and raising the federal minimum wage was the one 1960s antipoverty measure business lobbyists opposed at all costs.[64] Unable to augment the demand side of the labor market, county officials doubled down on their supply-side and job-canvassing efforts in 1968. Nickerson wrote an appeal in Nassau's official business newsletter, *Commerce and Industry News*, declaring that "we must invoke a new spirit of cooperation between private enterprise and public programs," and that while government must play a key role, so too must business, because

> in far too many instances, industry allots jobs and often fails to fill them. And a minimum wage is not sufficient for a family to subsist in the New York metropolitan area. So when we talk about creating jobs, or of assisting the disadvantaged, let's act realistically—and responsibly . . . those few extra cents an hour, and the opportunity for advancement, foster self-respect, improve abilities, and make it possible for an employee to absorb the expenses of working.[65]

Nickerson then instituted his own supply-side changes. First, he founded a County Department of Manpower to collect data about employment needs of industry so that "local training programs better fit the disadvantaged for the jobs that exist."[66] He then streamlined the county antipoverty efforts into a "Cooperative Center" program in March 1968. The co-op center was a single-stop social service center to tackle any obstacle to employment, including county-operated day care options, a car service, health clinics, skills training, and income support. Residents no longer navigated the multitude of employment and welfare services across the county. They instead met with one counselor who coordinated all the support services needed as the client searched for employment. The idea was to "to remedy the conditions which prevent men and women from enjoying the dignity and material benefits of employment." For Nickerson, co-op centers would remove all "barriers to a better life," whether family obligations, poverty, health problems, or emotional issues.[67]

The Suffolk JCDP set up a similar program, where a coordinator helped an applicant with supportive services and then referred the applicant to an employer. After getting a job, the JCDP remained in contact with both the applicant and the employer to assure the transition remained smooth. Unlike the Nassau program, the Suffolk JCDP focused on living wages and actively pursued employers who could either offer $2.00 ($16.40 in 2021) per hour or upward mobility within the firm.[68] To do this, the JCDP utilized the US Labor Department–funded On-the-Job Training program, where median wages started at $1.98 an hour, though training offered promotions to high-skilled positions with an average of $2.10 (some jobs scaled up to $4.50). The JCDP also aggressively pursued employers, meeting company executives, trade union leaders, and public employers to design clear routes toward high-wage employment. The Suffolk JCDP pushed the Suffolk-based Inter Chemical Company to furnish buses between CAPs and their factory. They also compelled Suffolk's building trades unions to broaden their apprenticeship program to include JCDP clients. And they got the Suffolk County police department to design adult education courses for their civil service exams.[69]

The super-heated efforts to improve job outcomes had some measurable impacts. Between January and April 1969, eight CAPs across Suffolk County placed 493 people into jobs. One in ten were welfare recipients, 80 percent were Black or Puerto Rican, while over three-quarters had been unemployed. Most importantly, their average pay jumped from $1.64 to $2.31 ($17.75 in 2021) per hour after placement, closer to a subsistence living, especially if they used the Suffolk JCDP's day care, transportation, or income support. But the Suffolk JCDP nonetheless confronted the same limited commitment from employers. High-tech companies, like Linear Electronics Laboratory, developer of communications equipment for the Apollo Missions, responded to the Suffolk JCDP inquiries that "our requirements always lie in a somewhat technical area and you have had very little success in matching candidates to our job openings." Lambda Electronics Corporation likewise suggested that the Suffolk JCDP should visit the job sites before referring their unemployed to the company. Even firms who hired the program's prospective employees, like Fairchild Republic, could not place these workers into skilled or semi-skilled positions, leaving them in low-wage service jobs.[70]

By 1969, the efforts to "match" Long Island's poor with jobs revealed that "poverty amidst plenty" was no "paradox" at all. There was nothing exceptional about Long Island's economy; businesses and consumers depended on low wages for their goods and services, like anywhere else in the nation. Boot camp efforts to reshape the poor and rely on private employers to hire them confronted suburban labor market exploitation. Black workers were disproportionately poor not because they were culturally deprived or skill deficient. That was the rationale devised to explain their degraded position. They were there because employers wielded labor market power to discriminate. No matter how much the programs trained their clients and removed the obstacles to taking full-time employment, employers responded by demanding more of their low-wage workers from the programs. Day care, transportation, or training courses made workers more available for jobs but did nothing toward making those wages rise. The programs rarely placed workers in a different track of the labor market, limiting the potential for wage gains. The unemployed and poor saw the programs for what they offered: horizontal, not vertical mobility. And while the Suffolk JCDP's aggressive efforts did secure higher pay, it required large budgets to train workers, heavy goading for firms to even consider a labor force beyond their established networks, and the possibility of raises or promotions in a constantly changing economic climate. It was inherently limited and did little to turn Long Island into a national exemplar of poverty eradication.

## Guaranteed Employment

By the late 1960s, the national conversation aligned with what Long Island officials discovered through their own efforts, and what unemployed worker Edwin Dove knew all along: the private labor market was not a source of economic security. The state had to do more than train, place, and offer temporary support. Since the War on Poverty's outset, a group of federal officials, primarily in the Labor Department, opposed the emphasis on training, rehabilitation, and empowerment. They instead wanted the government to directly employ people to end poverty, which would cut right through the private-sector low-wage job market. Instead of minimum wages deciding what workers earned, the government could set the floor by offering jobs to anyone who wanted to work. As stated in the previous chapter, the civil rights movement, labor movement, and Black Power radicals advocated for public jobs. Gallup found that three-fourths of Americans wanted the government to employ people who couldn't find work in the private market. Senators tried revising the Economic Opportunity Act in 1967 and 1968 to include public jobs. Even Democratic presidential candidate Eugene McCarthy added direct job creation to his 1968 campaign platform.[71] Removing the need to rely on the private market for one's livelihood, with all its exploitation, was in the air. But it was still theoretical, a dream stuck in a senator's bill draft, scrawled on a march banner, or shouted at a campaign rally.

Luckily, Long Island policymakers did not have to wait for Congress. In August 1968, Nassau County executive Nickerson drew up a countywide jobs program to simply create jobs as a way around the problems plaguing the job training and placement programs. Nickerson needed money to create the jobs, however. After Richard Nixon entered the White House in 1969, many feared he would gut the War on Poverty's institutional apparatus. Nixon indeed slashed parts of the OEO, but he nonetheless kept the office alive to "serve as a laboratory for experimental programs," appointing Donald Rumsfeld (the same Rumsfeld later in charge of the Iraq and Afghanistan invasions) to head the agency and assess local initiatives.[72] The OEO's new purpose gave Nickerson the means to fund a "guaranteed employment program."

To develop a direct job creation program in affluent suburbia, Nickerson turned to a new academic concept known as "New Careers." First devised by sociologist Frank Riessman and educator Arthur Pearl in 1963, New Careers claimed that millions of entry-level positions could be created in the automation-proof human services field. The jobs required no prior training while offering long-term career advancement. They could do this if private enterprise and public institutions implemented a Fordist-scheme of de-skilling professional positions. Aides, inspectors, or general assistants could perform the daily tasks of doctors, teachers, social workers, and other professionals—from feeding schoolchildren to clerical work or recording patients' vital statistics. These jobs, requiring little to no formal training, provided on-the-job experience, and with built-in credentialing, could lead to promotions and pay raises. A teacher's aide could become a tutor, then a teacher, or a home health aide could move onto a nursing or social work credential program. For the state, this eliminated both welfare relief and the costly "secondary educational system" of training programs. For workers, New Careers ended the dead-end nature of low-wage jobs. Professionals also benefited, since they could handle the more complex aspects of their job and meet the rapidly expanding needs in health care, education, and social services.[73]

New Careers was a flexible concept, steeped in both contemporary assumptions about the poor's cultural deficiencies and demands for direct public job creation. It found congressional support from Senator Robert F. Kennedy, who secured $70 million for New Careers in the 1966 Economic Opportunity Act amendments. Beyond federal legislation, Frank Riessman founded the New Careers Development Center at New York University to push municipal governments, hospitals, and unions to implement career ladders, credentialing, and outreach to the unemployed. School districts in Minneapolis, Oakland, and New York City implemented New Careers–oriented paraprofessional programs.[74] But Riessman and Pearl believed New Careers had even broader implications. They saw it as an alternative to reviving manufacturing, an antipoverty means of embracing the service-oriented future. Riessman even went as far as contending that New Careers could empower the service working class through hybrid union–professional associations linked to the New Careers concept.[75]

Nassau County executive Eugene Nickerson was more interested in New Careers' practical uses rather than its radical potential. But he took the concept a step further because unlike most grants-oriented New Careers projects that left the jobs to the private or nonprofit sector, Nickerson's program would create new public jobs. In June 1969, Nickerson reoriented his Office of Manpower Development, headed by labor economist and former textile labor organizer Elwood Taub, into a job creation department. In cooperation with Frank Riessman's New Careers Development Corporation, Nickerson filed for an OEO grant to design "the nation's first guaranteed employment program." The program proposal evolved from the county's cooperative centers. New applicants could receive immediate support services (day care, income assistance, Medicaid, etc.) while the office found them a job. The manpower office sought cooperative private employers who would design career ladders, but if they could not find a private-sector job, the government served as the employer of last resort. The job guarantee was the major innovation, so that "any individual who is willing to work ought to be able to work." Manpower office director Elwood Taub contended the program would complete the unfulfilled mandate of the Employment Act of 1946 to assure full employment through the government. And in a suburban county with high-cost human services, these jobs were not "make-work," but necessary public tasks in health care, education, nutrition, childcare, and consumer affairs, among others.[76]

The Nickerson administration contended that the job guarantee would solve many of Nassau's poverty problems, above all the soaring welfare costs strangling local government. Aside from a 3 percent sales tax, property taxes were the only form of county revenue and had reached "confiscatory" limits, according to the administration. The program would reduce the welfare rolls by a fifth and turn the recipients into "taxpayers" with career prospects and higher incomes in the future. It would allow the county to meet service demands, particularly for Long Island's elderly, and draw from the poor already laboring in domestic services. Nickerson also understood the political value of replacing the welfare system with guaranteed jobs. His program would reassure taxpayers their "hard-earned dollars are not perpetuating someone's laziness," instead going toward a valued public service. Furthermore, public service employment fit squarely within Nickerson's county-level reforms, as an efficient means both to provide services and to improve the health and welfare of county residents.

But the Nickerson administration's support for guaranteed employment also reflected a broader realization: that the suburban economy had its share of low-wage jobs that mired people in poverty. Long Island was no panacea for inequality. A War on Poverty, whether suburban or otherwise, needed interventions in both the supply and demand side of the labor market. The guaranteed employment proposal recognized that "there are persons who are unemployed or underemployed who cannot be placed in the private economy." Despite relative full employment, there were those who "do not show up in the very low insured unemployment statistic published and revised monthly," and instead in other data, from welfare loads to poverty surveys.[77] Direct job creation was necessary to reach full employment, absorbing people at the low end of the labor market, thereby empowering low-wage workers and ending private employers' ability to exploit, rooted in the surplus of labor available.

The guaranteed employment proposal found a receptive audience in Nassau County. Nickerson promoted the program for all county residents and not only for the poor, contending that the county could publicly employ recently laid-off defense workers and returning Vietnam veterans. At a public hearing on October 14, 1969, antipoverty activists and residents expressed overwhelming support for the idea in a five-hour session. Emma Morning, Nassau Welfare Tenants Coordinating Committee chair, endorsed the program because "it's about time that people realize that everybody on welfare isn't there because they are lazy and shiftless." *Newsday* journalist Martin L. Gross, normally an anti-government pundit, praised the plan as a step toward removing citizens from the "generation-to-generation dole," and likened it to New Deal work relief programs. Even critics, like Conservative Party candidate for North Hempstead supervisor Robert J. Valli, considered the program commendable, though he believed the "innumerable" want ads in newspapers could employ people without a public program.[78]

The program's success nonetheless hinged on federal funding, the only level of government that could employ on any scale. After an initial $37,000 OEO research grant, Nickerson finally submitted a full plan to the OEO in late 1969. County manpower director Elwood Taub admitted that it was "an expensive program" and that while it would ultimately pay for itself, "society must first make the investment."[79] It turned out society, or at least the bureaucratic representation of society known as Donald Rumsfeld, was unwilling to invest. His OEO demanded a narrower pilot project, and Nassau responded with a pared down proposal covering only 450 volunteers. In April 1970, the OEO rejected even that, claiming the pilot project could not generate data for "expanded implementation," because from a national perspective, Nassau County's poverty problems were less severe than most areas, and "a program that is successful in reducing poverty in Nassau would not be necessarily successful elsewhere." Later that spring, the county received a much smaller $400,000 grant to restructure their civil service system and place 120 residents into paraprofessional and blue-collar career ladders.[80] County Executive Eugene Nickerson then limped through his final year in office. He failed to mount a third run for state governor, faced corruption allegations, and continued to run up the county debt. In Suffolk, Dennison became embroiled in a court battle after firing the Suffolk County Human Relations Commission chair George Pettengill in 1969 for favoring "low-income ghetto groups" before retiring two years later. In both counties, Republicans captured the executive office, paving the way for less expansive efforts at reducing poverty.[81]

## Conclusion

Edwin Dove's failed job search, and Demac Manufacturing's failed hiring drive in the New Cassel CAP office in 1968, reveal the limits of liberalism's rare experiment to eradicate poverty in America's most affluent place. Statistically, the number of Long Island families living under the federal poverty line declined from 36,000 in 1966 to just over 25,000 by 1970, even as the overall population grew. This was mostly a consequence of the Great Society's welfare expansions, clear from Nassau and Suffolk's recipient growth that outpaced all jurisdictions in the New York metropolitan area and pushed Nassau

County into its first deficits in the late 1960s.[82] At the "grassroots" level, CAPs played an immeasurable liberatory role. Long Island's CAP's provided day care, rides to health services, and free food. More critically, they empowered the poor, giving them a collective voice to demand basic needs like housing, social services, and access to jobs in a place dominated by homeowners often hostile to their very presence.[83] But welfare expansion and community empowerment were not the only tools deployed to end poverty. Policymakers also cut taxes to spark economic growth and designed training programs to prepare the poor for a jobs boom unleashed by tax cuts. Suburbs like Long Island were where this would work best. By 1970, it was clear that these tools had not worked as intended. Military contractors like Demac Manufacturing didn't have the jobs to end poverty, and the New Cassel CAPs could not deliver what Edwin Dove needed. That their efforts found little success in the place where, by the logic of the War on Poverty's architects, they were most likely to win, is a damning indictment of this antipoverty approach.

In this way, Long Island's antipoverty efforts exemplify the "lost opportunity" of the War on Poverty, rooted in the dissonance between what federal officials believed caused deprivation and what was actually responsible for material hardship.[84] Lyndon Johnson's War on Poverty and Great Society was the high-water mark of American liberalism. But politicians and policymakers didn't dust off the agenda of the New Deal or Fair Deal. Instead, they embraced a platform for the supposed "affluent age," with suburbia, the geographical manifestation of prosperity, as the place where tax cuts and training programs could combine to end poverty. Long Island had all the right ingredients—broadly distributed high median incomes, low unemployment, and rapid job growth. The goal was to extend that general prosperity down to Long Island's poorest. But aggregate data obscured what undergirded suburban poverty. Through local attempts to train the poor, bus them to job sites, and subsidize their wages in a repeat of the Speenhamland system, officials repeatedly came up against the plethora of low-wage jobs across Long Island. Their frustrations exposed suburbia's celebrated prosperity as an ideology, suburban exceptionalism, a flawed framework for understanding what caused inequality in an affluent suburb.

This did not mean locals resigned to fatalism. By 1970, County Executive Eugene Nickerson developed a job guarantee program, recognizing the need to intervene on the demand side of the labor market. Although he harkened back to the ideas circulating policymaking circles in the 1930s and 1940s, he also drew from the obvious source of public jobs via military Keynesianism that long buttressed employment on Long Island. He merely looked to reorient public job creation toward the labor market's bottom rather than the middle. A job guarantee would have restricted employers' ability to exploit low-wage workers and therefore reduce poverty along with the racial disparities that accompanied loose labor markets. That the federal government left it unfunded illustrated how suburban exceptionalism remained hegemonic in liberal antipoverty policymaking.

# 6

# Shouldering Their "Fair Share"

## *Why the Suburbs Could Not Resolve the "Urban Crisis"*

In February 1970, the US Department of Housing and Urban Development (HUD) selected New Cassel for a federal housing program called "Turnkey III."[1] Private builders used public financing to construct single-family homes and handed the keys to local government. Local housing authorities then found qualified low-income tenants who paid their monthly rent toward home equity, and eventually, full homeownership.[2] HUD planned just five prefabricated single-family houses scattered across New Cassel, fulfilling their recent Open Communities plan to build suburban housing for inner-city residents.[3] Turnkey III was low-income housing for the suburban age: private, homeowner-oriented, harmonized with surrounding subdivisions, and dispersed in the sprawling expanse beyond city borders. For the Town of North Hempstead, New Cassel's local governing body, Turnkey III could add some decent, legal, and affordable units to a place in desperate need of such homes.

But the Progressive Civic Association of New Cassel (PCANC) strongly opposed the project. The Black organization drew on their long-standing history with informal housing. Members feared the five homes' high prices (about 4 percent higher than the hamlet's median housing value) would burden the low-income occupants. PCANC chair Fred Meeks contended that homes like this, "although designed as a single-family, often serve two families and more, and in many instances has proven quite adaptable to rooming house operation." Fellow PCANC member Olivia Hollis warned there were "no safeguards to assure that the people who are moved into the houses will eventually buy them."[4] She united the Westbury NAACP and other civics under the "Save our Community Now" committee. They successfully pressured town officials to reject the HUD project by summer.

Outcry ensued, and each side labeled the other racist. Project supporters, such as the town's housing authority chair Edward Hunter, a PCANC member, called his colleagues "Oreos . . . Black on the outside but white inside." Lorenzo Merritt, vice-chair of the Long Island Congress of Racial Equality (CORE) said, "I am ashamed and embarrassed today by the latent racism from among my own people." Dr. Harold Russell, CORE member and local radio show host, called PCANC "Negro-class racists . . . attempting to stop Black people from gaining their share of housing."[5] Project opponents retorted that town officials were the real racists. Olivia Hollis accused the town of further corralling the poor into an "already segregated community with a wealth of social problems." PCANC chair Fred Meeks believed HUD targeted New Cassel because "it is normally expected that the black community accept what can be considered as the accommodating, or compromise type of measures with the pretense that these are in [our] best interest."[6]

On its surface, New Cassel's low-income housing battle appears as a classic "not-in-my-backyard" (NIMBY) conflict that journalists and scholars contend have driven housing project obstruction for decades. Turnkey III proponents surely read it as such. They claimed class interests trumped racial solidarity and that Black homeowners imbibed the exclusionary rationales that white residents usually deployed against potential non-white neighbors. But Turnkey III, and the underlying principles behind it, framed the problem as one between well-meaning bureaucrats and obstinate privileged homeowners. HUD established the battle lines between proponents and opponents. In their view, low-income suburban housing could give poor people access to suburban jobs, schools, and better homes. Suburban exclusion was the obstacle. But obscured in the NIMBY protests from project opponents and the racialized political appeals was a debate over whether exclusion or exploitation was at the root of poverty and its social ills. Proponents believed New Cassel could resolve metropolitan America's housing crisis. Opponents believed crisis already stalked New Cassel, and more units would only exacerbate problems.

The HUD project, and its ensuing demise, only briefly convulsed New Cassel. But it was emblematic of the new antipoverty approach touching Long Island and other parts of the nation. Turnkey III was one among a dozen housing programs that followed the explosive conclusions of the National Advisory Commission on Civil Disorders, better known as the Kerner Report. Assembled by President Johnson to interpret the wave of mid-1960s urban rebellions, the Kerner Report's scathing thesis reverberated across the country: the nation was divided into "two societies, one black, and one white—separate and unequal . . . one, largely Negro and poor, located in the central cities; the other, predominantly white and affluent, located in the suburbs and in outlying areas."[7]

The Kerner Report extended a thesis that informed two decades of suburban activism against housing exclusion, placing exclusionary barriers at the center of America's social ills. Activists and social scientists contended suburbs could resolve inequality if federal, state, and local governments dismantled exclusionary barriers. Suburban jobs, schools, and housing could reduce poverty. Advocates devised housing projects to "disperse" the urban poor or have suburbanites shoulder their "fair share" of responsibility for poverty. They were two sides of the same coin. According to this metropolitan-wide framework, exclusion either prevented the poor from having the right address (creating a "spatial mismatch") or living near the right neighbors (the wealthy, whose incomes served as the foundation of robust public goods).[8] Municipal boundaries deprived the poor of suburban exceptionalism. A locational fix would eliminate the income and housing deprivation.

The New Cassel conflict reveals how suburban exceptionalism informed both poverty dispersal and suburban fair-share proposals. Like the War on Poverty and Title VII, policymakers and activists took suburban prosperity for granted, framed Black poverty as a distinct problem of discrimination, and overlooked social-democratic solutions.[9] They went further than the War on Poverty, claiming not only that suburbs could end poverty within their borders, but that it could solve urban poverty as well. Reality proved their faith was misguided. Dispersal plans exposed how poverty was not place based: the city–suburb divide didn't matter because employers impoverished people on Long Island, too. And fair-share projects uncovered the ways the city–suburb divide *did* matter, because poverty already divided and segregated suburban neighborhoods on Long Island. PCANC opposed low-income housing because the project did not address, for example, speculators impoverishing the suburb. Others decried Long Island's regressive and balkanized property tax system, which placed poverty's burden on small subsets of suburbanites, who were often the least able to pay.

But most consequential was the fact that policymakers pushing poverty dispersal and fair-share programs set up counterproductive political fault lines. For policymakers, cities were poor and the victims of segregation. Suburbs were wealthy and benefited from segregation. Policymakers appealed to social responsibility and decried suburban opponents' racism. Suburbanites responded with both "color-blind" defenses of suburban exclusion and "color-conscious" appeals to victimhood, citing their experience with informal housing and racial segregation.[10] Ultimately, these fights obscured suburban needs like good jobs, aid to public schools, decent housing, and an end to real estate speculation. Suburbanites needed the same solutions as their urban counterparts; namely, policies that addressed exploitation. Political conflicts between policymakers and homeowners, public housing authorities and civic associations, and fair-share activists and overburdened taxpayers deflected attention from the non-geographic source of the problem. It also obfuscated the state's role in producing inequality in the first place. Most importantly, the outcomes satisfied neither policymakers, suburban homeowners, nor the poor. When PCANC defeated the Turnkey III proposal, the problems New Cassel shared with other suburbs and cities remained.

This chapter returns to subjects and themes from earlier chapters—Long Island's unequal labor market, informal housing, welfare motels, and poverty's public costs—demonstrating how policies rooted in suburban exceptionalism failed to help people in cities and suburbs in the late 1960s and early 1970s. It does so via case studies across Long Island. First, we cover an ambitious NAACP lawsuit to break down exclusionary zoning and disperse New York City's poor into the all-white Town of Oyster Bay. Then we examine two fair-share proposals in depth—a public housing project in Oyster Bay and a public housing complex in the racially integrated hamlet of Uniondale that aimed to end the welfare motel system. Both illustrate why distributing poor people "fairly" in Long Island's balkanized and regressive property tax structure was impossible. Finally, we return to Wyandanch, where a state-driven public housing project did not address the hamlet's long-standing speculative activity and informal housing. The project galvanized well-known characters like civic association activist Herman "The Griem" to stop the project, much like what occurred in New Cassel. These case studies reveal, in one way or another, that the basic assumption undergirding the Kerner Report and suburban exceptionalism—that suburbs hold the key to ending poverty and inequality—was flawed and inimical to political coalition-building.

## Crafting the City–Suburb Divide

The 1968 Kerner Report did not invent the Black/white, city/suburb, poor/affluent trope. The dualist framework didn't inform the report's central policy proposals, which included public job creation, a universal basic income, and six million public housing units.[11] The report didn't even advocate poverty "dispersal" over "enriching" cities through public investment in America's largest cities.[12] But the report publicized an otherwise small corner of civil rights activism and academic research during an amenable political moment. For decades, civil rights groups had been challenging exclusionary zoning, racial covenants, and urban renewal. For their part, academics studied the growing divide between cities and suburbs in jobs, education, and housing stock. In 1968, rooting social problems in the segregated metropolis struck a chord. The War on Poverty disappointed, riots rocked cities, and the civil rights movement stalled. If suburbs were thriving and cities ailing, giving the excluded access could remedy the imbalance. The antidote to urban poverty was in the suburbs.

Detailing the long history of civil rights struggles against suburban exclusion is beyond this book's scope, but policymaking to end the city–suburb divide has a briefer history. It first reached the national stage in 1961, when the Commission on Civil Rights popularized the term "white noose."[13] Harvard economist John F. Kain added statistical heft with his "spatial mismatch" hypothesis. The theory purported that racial housing segregation and suburban job dispersal led to higher rates of Black urban joblessness and poverty. Kain's work circulated during both the McCone Commission Report in 1965 (a response to the Watts, Los Angeles rebellion) and Kerner Report three years later.[14] His conclusions invigorated the long-standing struggle against housing segregation. Kain surmised that breaking down suburban barriers—whether zoning laws, school district boundaries, or municipal borders generally—not only addressed deep racial injustices in residential and school choice, but could work toward mitigating unemployment and poverty, the "urban crisis" writ large.

Besides Kain's "spatial mismatch" case studies, fellow economist Anthony Downs, whose attacks on zoning policy culminated in his widely praised 1973 book *Opening Up the Suburbs*, served on Lyndon Johnson's 1967 National Commission on Urban Problems. He was also one of the Kerner Report's influential consultants. Though Downs cautioned against a politically unfeasible "dispersal strategy," the report's final drafters edited out his concerns.[15] Roger B. Noll, senior Council of Economic Advisers (CEA) staff economist, contributed suburban dispersal research to Johnson's Task Force on Suburban Problems in 1967. His chapter, entitled "Central City: Suburban Employment Distribution," exemplified the most rationalist interpretation of the city–suburb divide, proving that jobs were moving to the suburbs across thirty metro areas and people should therefore follow for the sake of economic efficiency.[16]

These ideas spread beyond academic conferences and federal offices. The National Commission on Discrimination in Housing conducted research into the "relationship between access to housing and job opportunities" and warned that housing segregation forced Black workers into a dilemma "previously experienced by no other group in the history of this nation: denial of the opportunity to live in areas reasonably proximate to available jobs."[17] The

Regional Plan Association published their own findings in 1969, illustrating the "widening 'geographic gap' between the location of unskilled jobs and the location of housing for people who hold (or could hold) these jobs."[18] Entirely new think tanks formed to advocate poverty dispersal, including the Westchester-based Suburban Action Institute (SAI). Established by Paul Davidoff, the father of advocacy planning, and lawyer Neil Gold, SAI's six-person team formed a research and legal team for "clientless" poor and non-white urban residents to secure "locational choice" for all.[19] Like the others, SAI was committed to ending discriminatory housing barriers that "help create the poverty and ugliness of the slums." In SAI's logic, suburbanites should take social responsibility "by opening up their land, job markets, and tax resources."[20]

Collectively, these scholars and policy institutes defined urban poverty as a problem rooted in the city–suburb divide. All used three statistical categories: the racial demographics of cities and suburbs, high Black versus low white unemployment rates, and finally, long-term suburban job growth versus urban decline.[21] Their data proved reinvesting in cities, or even expanding commuter links between cities and suburbs, had only marginal benefits. Instead, building affordable housing, which required rezoning single-family suburban districts for multifamily housing complexes, could give the inner-city poor a shot at suburban jobs. Anthony Downs put it most succinctly: "the only way to establish the required linkages is to provide suburban housing opportunities near new job openings."[22] Publicly funded or privately financed multifamily suburban housing would shorten the *distance* between people and jobs. For these researchers, labor market barriers were rooted in the housing market. With suburban housing, the poor could escape "poor places" for the "right places," improving their job prospects, educational outcomes, and well-being.

This metropolitan approach to poverty, while embryonic, informed the strategies of local and national housing agencies. In 1969, HUD secretary George Romney launched a nationwide attack on housing segregation, fearing that the nation itself could not survive with "a run-down, festering black core, surrounded by a well-to-do, indifferent white ring." Romney's HUD designed the Open Communities program to "provide an opportunity for individuals to live within a reasonable distance of their job and daily activities by increasing housing options for low-income and minority families" in the suburbs. "To solve problems of the 'real city,'" Romney contended, "only metropolitan-wide solutions will do." In New York State, Governor Nelson Rockefeller empowered his new Urban Development Corporation (UDC) to override local zoning ordinances statewide. The UDC, under the command of planner Edward Logue, had unprecedented powers to construct low- and middle-income units in the suburbs. Logue believed that New York's urban problems could only be solved "within the wider metropolitan context." Even local agencies promoted expansionist ideas. On Long Island, the Civil Rights Coordinating Council of Suffolk County formed the Suffolk County Development Corporation in 1969 to build public or publicly assisted housing on a countywide basis. The goal was to free "black and other minorities from the deteriorating ghetto housing in which they had been locked by a combination of discrimination, poverty and powerlessness." The corporation associated inadequate suburban housing with "unemployment, inferior education, inadequate transportation for access to jobs and the debilitating effects of successive generations of welfare dependency."[23]

## Dispersing the Poor into the Lily-White Suburb

Long Island epitomized the kind of suburb strangling its core city. According to aggregate statistics, Long Island was exceptionally affluent, overwhelmingly white, bulging with jobs, and covered in a dense web of land-use restrictions. Suburban commuters left New York City each day, America's most diverse and poorest city, which was bleeding jobs and tax dollars while housing fell into disrepair. If exclusion deprived people of opportunity, here was the metropolis where it happened. "Dispersalists," those looking to end the spatial mismatch between people in one place and jobs in another, unsurprisingly looked to Long Island as a place to strike down exclusionary zoning. But their efforts revealed that poverty was not place based. Over the suburban wall, well-paying jobs were in decline, while low-wage work was on the rise. The city–suburb divide mattered far less than the federal spending programs, wage laws, and regional manufacturing losses shaping the New York metropolitan area.

The first poverty dispersal plan to touch Long Island came not from a public agency, but from the venerable NAACP. Spatial mismatch theory offered a more expansive view of housing segregation's costs. It tied racial disparities in homeownership, wealth, and urban versus suburban residence to the most pressing contemporary urban problems confronting the nation's cities. No organization had as much invested in the fight against housing segregation than the NAACP, whose housing lawsuits reached back to *Buchanan v. Warley* in 1917. Despite court victories, class-based zoning remained enshrined in law since *Euclid v. Ambler* in 1926, and the 1968 Fair Housing Act, along with hundreds of state and local laws, did little to alter the racially divided metropolis. Selective enforcement was partly to blame, but so too was the overtly class-exclusive deployment of zoning, obscured in professional planning jargon.[24] Spatial mismatch offered the new angle to challenge zoning's class-exclusive framing, since denying housing to low-income people in effect nullified equal employment opportunity, and by extension, the equal protection clause of the Fourteenth Amendment. They needed a zoning authority to sue, and the nearly all-white Town of Oyster Bay, Long Island, was the perfect defendant.

*Fair Housing Development Fund Corp. v. Burke*, the NAACP's zoning lawsuit against the Town of Oyster Bay, began as an effort to prevent displacement of existing suburban residents. It was an early example of tying old-standing battles for fair, quality, affordable housing to the new expansionist understanding of metropolitan inequality.[25] In 1968, James Davis, Glen Cove NAACP branch president and longtime activist, turned his attention to an urban renewal project next door in Oyster Bay. The Town demolished an old domestic worker enclave for a public housing project in the late 1950s. But the cleanup efforts displaced tenants: between 1959 and 1969, Oyster Bay Hamlet, part of the bigger Town of Oyster Bay, lost 40 percent of its Black population. Davis's investigations found that residents both desired to stay in Oyster Bay and could afford to remain, but they confronted local bias in renting and buying homes. As Davis concluded, "there's definitely a case of real discrimination here. I feel that the people here would like to see every Black person out of the community."[26]

Martin Luther King Jr.'s assassination in 1968 opened the local issue to broader attention. In October, Davis asked the Town of Oyster Bay to pass an open housing ordinance, which hundreds of municipalities approved in the wake of King's death.[27] The town, for its part, broke ground on their public housing project and named it after King. But the town did little beyond the symbolic act. Oyster Bay restricted occupancy to town residents with at least two years residency and favored locals in the project's immediate vicinity. Demand was so high that area outsiders couldn't get in; locals occupied all but two of the forty-eight family units. Evident need for affordable units compelled Davis, also the NAACP's state housing chair, to try a novel alternative. In 1969, Davis established a nonprofit housing firm, the Fair Housing Development Fund Corporation. The nonprofit could apply for federal housing loans and build moderate- and low-income apartments. As the first NAACP-sponsored housing project, Davis hoped to meet local moderate- and low-income housing demand in and around Oyster Bay. But privately constructed multifamily housing required a zoning variance from the town's zoning authority, a critical tool that empowered zoning boards to permit or deny whatever they wanted. In 1969, the town declined Davis's open housing ordinance proposal, while the zoning board sat on the variance request.[28]

The denial came at an opportune time for the NAACP's national office. With racial discrimination outlawed in schools, employment, and housing, suburbia was the "next frontier of the civil rights movement" because restrictive zoning effectively nullified all those laws. Spatial mismatch added the needed heft to this argument. Land restrictions not only raised housing prices near good schools, but near good jobs as well, depriving Black families of equal employment opportunity. Oyster Bay then "presented such outstanding examples of abuse of zoning that we had a beautiful case to serve as a prototype" as NAACP executive Roy Wilkins declared.[29]

From the metropolitan framing, Oyster Bay was indeed perfect. Located just twelve miles from the New York City border, the town enforced strict zoning laws that prohibited multi-unit construction. They even erased the Levitt-sized small plot category altogether in the 1950s. Already home to Grumman, Oyster Bay also vigorously lured firms. From 1963 to 1969, over half of Nassau County's job growth occurred within the town's borders, largely in industrial fields including electronic components, machinery, aircraft parts, and plastics. Last, despite growing suburban diversity, Oyster Bay's 333,000 residents were 99.2 percent white as of 1970, and half of the town's 2,700 Black residents lived in three segregated hamlets: domestic enclaves Oyster Bay and Locust Valley, and the integrated postwar suburb of East Massapequa.[30] The town's whiteness, when combined with its economic boom, exemplified the city–suburb divide. Oyster Bay was a white fortress, using zoning to block people of color from both housing *and* job opportunity.

In 1969, the NAACP's national office greatly expanded James Davis's local housing fight as their first test against exclusionary zoning. They hired Paul Davidoff's SAI as consultants, merging SAI's data expertise with the NAACP's "organized pressure from the people who are being done in."[31] NAACP national housing director William Morris then ordered the town to permit multifamily dwellings and affordable single-family homes on a fifth of its vacant residential land, or face legal action. According to SAI estimates, the rezoning proposal would add about 18,000 people to the town's population (an increase of 5 percent) and would raise property taxes by 2.3 percent. This was no longer an effort to house the suburban poor, but a means to solving inequality writ large. As Morris contended, "the resources for solving the cities' problems lie in the suburbs," with its well-funded schools, high-paying jobs, and more robust tax bases.[32]

The NAACP and SAI's conflation of race and class, that disparate poverty emanated from racial discrimination embedded in exclusionary zoning, gave them the legal case to invalidate zoning for violating the fourteenth amendment. Employing race in this way framed their opponent's response. Newly elected Oyster Bay town supervisor John Burke promised to defend "home rule" against the NAACP's suit, claiming that "Oyster Bay doesn't have any fences around it." Residents meanwhile conflated race and class to defend their material interests. The NAACP and SAI sponsored meetings across Oyster Bay. They encountered residents concerned that taxes would rise while public service quality would diminish, and that affordable housing would spread the "decay" occurring in city centers. As one resident proclaimed, "nobody wants a Negro project to spring up on the land they've cherished. We moved to this area because of the way it is." The town conducted its own poll in 1970, sending a questionnaire to over 62,000 households. Over 20,000 responded, and 95 percent opposed the NAACP. James Davis responded that the poll "doesn't mean anything to us. We're going ahead with our plans."[33]

Davis was right because the NAACP did not have to win over the public, only the courts. But opponents also questioned the NAACP's logic, particularly the alleged transformative power of dispersing New York's poor to the suburbs. The outgoing Oyster Bay town supervisor, Michael Petito, argued that the NAACP was "making a serious mistake playing with 50,000 human beings, moving them from a ghetto in New York to another ghetto in Oyster Bay." Petito exaggerated the numbers, but he also doubted whether a spatial move would improve their lives. The Oyster Bay Conservative Party likewise condemned the NAACP's proposal as a project of activists who "have apparently despaired of eliminating city slums, and who now propose to transplant them to Oyster Bay . . . without providing anything of value for the slum dwellers themselves." Local resident and city planning student Jerry Katz elaborated on these criticisms. For the residents to benefit, jobs would be necessary, but Katz doubted whether the local job market could employ thousands of new residents. Without jobs, poor residents would be worse off in suburbia, far from public transportation and social services. As Katz argued, the project increased costs to local and future residents without doing much for the relocated.[34]

After a year, the town finally denied the variance, and the NAACP commenced *Fair Housing Development Fund Corp. v. Burke* on March 24, 1971, in the US Eastern District Court. The ambitious class action suit accused Oyster Bay town supervisor John W. Burke, the town board, and the town housing authority of supporting a land-use policy that discriminated in three ways. First, zoning policy segregated existing non-white residents. Second, zoning excluded people of color and other disadvantaged low-income citizens from living in Oyster Bay. And finally, those same zoning laws excluded non-white and low-income workers from jobs they could otherwise attain. Therefore, zoning effectively nullified equal housing and employment laws. Since the courts allowed local zoning powers only if land-use policy promoted the "general welfare," Oyster Bay's codes were unconstitutional. The NAACP demanded the town set aside land for new dwelling units that "meet the needs of the Plaintiffs and the members of the classes they represent."[35]

The NAACP assembled a diverse group of plaintiffs to represent the affected New Yorkers. Six were Black town residents occupying "substandard" dwellings, including a county-subsidized motel room, a shack on a golf course, and a variety of dilapidated apartments. Among them was Francine Grier, a young mother of four living in a single room and sharing a bed in her grandmother's house. She could not find local rentals under the Nassau Social Services Department rental threshold. Another plaintiff, Edward Underwood, worked for Grumman but could not find suitable housing within the town, living instead in New Cassel. Finally, the suit also included an unemployed Bronx man who did not take a job in Oyster Bay because he was denied housing.[36] Since the NAACP sought a broad court decree rather than redressing narrow plaintiff grievances, they had to amass census data, housing statistics, job figures, and expert testimony to convince the court that land-use policy, while not explicitly biased, was in effect discriminatory because it had disparate impacts on housing choice and job opportunity.[37]

The NAACP faced formidable obstacles to their claims. The defense refuted the first by contending that income, rather than race, accounted for restricted housing choice among Oyster Bay's non-white and poor residents. This line of defense, that pure market forces and lawful efforts to stabilize property values caused economic segregation, was woven into the logic of "property rights" and land-use policy since the early twentieth century. As *Fair Housing Development Fund Corp. v. Burke* got underway, the Supreme Court upheld "color-blind" bans on low-income housing in *James v. Valtierra* (1971). The judge took a narrow reading of the Fourteenth Amendment's equal protection clause that thwarted struggles against economic displacement.[38] The NAACP used Grumman's Black workforce to demonstrate zoning's impact on housing choice for local workers. Only thirty-one of 1,100 Black employees lived within Oyster Bay's town border, while nearly a fifth commuted from New York City. By contrast, only 4 percent of white workers drove from the boroughs; the rest lived on Long Island. This disparity cut across occupational lines.[39]

Housing segregation was clear, but zoning's role less so. Edward Underwood, the plaintiff's representative Grumman employee, lived in New Cassel, one and a half miles west of Oyster Bay's town border. The defense questioned whether Underwood faced undue hardship because he could not live within the town. From New Cassel, he made an eight-mile trek to work each day, which took twenty-five minutes. His commute, while originating outside the town's borders, was shorter than trips from nearly half of Oyster Bay's neighborhoods. As Underwood's commute revealed, the town's borders were porous, and zoning did not burden out-of-town workers. This was true for Black Grummanites living in North Amityville, Wyandanch, and New Cassel, all less than ten miles from the Grumman plant in Bethpage, and for over half of Grumman's white workforce in Suffolk County. The defense, meanwhile, challenged the claim that zoning played a pivotal role in the town's housing segregation. Edward Underwood admitted that "because I'm black and if I go to the bank, they're not going to loan me the money to buy a house."[40] Depositions revealed a myriad of private discriminatory practices, from racial steering to real estate agent prejudice.[41] With zoning's economic exclusion on firm legal ground, the defense could absolve the town of responsibility for racist practices across Oyster Bay.

The claim that Oyster Bay excluded the urban poor from its vibrant job market was the case's most crucial point. It fundamentally challenged segregation's legal basis, which courts previously upheld. The plaintiffs leaned on reports from the Regional Plan Association, the National Commission against Discrimination in Housing, and SAI's own research. They amassed reams of data from the 1950s and 1960s, substantiating the fact that industry relocated from cities to suburbs, and that between 1963 and 1969, the Town of Oyster Bay enjoyed factory growth. They then projected the data forward to prove job growth would continue, using Regional Plan Association estimates to 1985 and their own appraisal of future plant expansion based on vacant industrial land in Oyster Bay.[42] For the plaintiffs, the town's very growth necessitated a diverse workforce via affordable housing. Restrictive land use contradicted zoning's "general welfare" purpose for poor town residents, local employers, and the town's own tax base.

But the plaintiff's contention rested on the city–suburb divide and the idea that spatial mobility could translate into upward mobility. This glossed over the deep inequality embedded into the suburban labor market. It also ignored the suburban poor, themselves mired in the low rungs of the suburban economic hierarchy. New poor arrivals would do little but intensify competition among low-wage workers and depress wages, as earlier chapters show. They also glossed over the economic dynamics Long Island shared with the metropolitan area. Low-wage service jobs grew faster than any other sector in the early 1970s, and Long Island lost manufacturing jobs. As figure 6.1 illustrates, machines and the South and West took New York's factories, not the suburbs, which despite small gains along the outer ring, collectively shed over 29,000 jobs. Academics and journalists focused on the economic decline

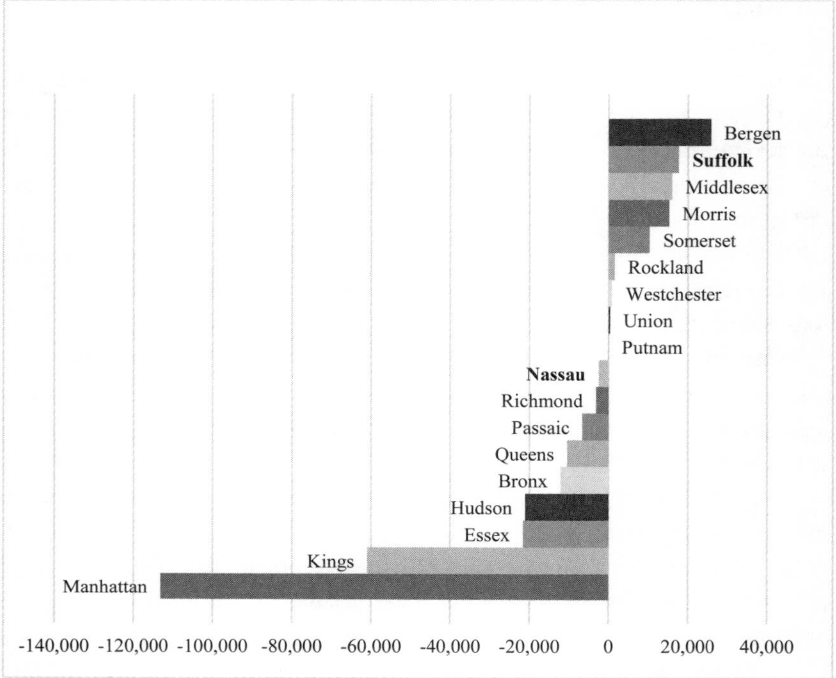


FIGURE 6.1. Net change in manufacturing employment, 1964–74, New York–New Jersey metropolitan area. *Source*: Pearl M. Kamer, *Nassau-Suffolk's Changing Manufacturing Base: A Case Study of a Suburban Labor Market* (Hauppauge, NY: Nassau-Suffolk Regional Planning Board, 1977), 19.

in central cities versus the new economic role of suburbs, but manufacturing was not a suburban growth sector.[43]

Local contexts determined why the New York metropolitan area lost factory jobs. For Nassau and Suffolk, it was the steep decline in defense spending. Oyster Bay's own Grumman, the fortunate recipients of the F-14 contract, contended with inflation eating away the "fixed-price" contract, forcing the company to adopt then-innovative corporate tactics like buying competitors, diversifying into the commercial market, and outsourcing routine production work to cheaper locales in the South.[44] Long Island's broader pain could be felt in Roosevelt Field, the former airfield turned megamall and home to defense contractors Reeves Instrument and American Bosch Arma. In the early 1960s, three-quarters of its land was zoned for industrial use. By the 1970s, however, industry accounted for less than half of Roosevelt Field's land use and only forty-seven of 542 businesses. Vacant factories became retail outlets, and office complexes sprouted from industrially zoned land. Finance, insurance, and service firms employed five thousand workers in the area. Retail accounted for another quarter of Roosevelt Field's twenty thousand jobs, the new source of "job opportunities for unskilled and semi-skilled people" as a local land-use study noted. Roosevelt Field, a planned industrial center that once housed guided missile and computer parts manufacturers, was now a regional center for furniture depots, clothing stores, and life insurance branch offices.[45]

Though Long Island weathered the recession, the suburb was not the panacea to the urban crisis. In response to the NAACP case, Nassau–Suffolk Regional Planning Board Chief Economist Pearl Kamer contended neither "Nassau or even Suffolk can provide substantial numbers of blue-collar jobs for central city residents whose blue-collar jobs have moved elsewhere."[46] The belief that the suburbs could improve employment outcomes rested on a faith in the market's overall affluence. It conversely de-emphasized other factors. This included the institutions producing and destroying jobs in cities and suburbs; the biases and exploitation segmenting people of color, women, and other discriminated people into low-wage work; and the possibility of improving housing, public resources, and job opportunities within cities themselves. And though their data matched suburban industrial growth by 1985, this was a feature of Cold War contingencies, namely President Reagan's early 1980s defense buildup, not inexorable market forces redistributing jobs. Like the War on Poverty, the city–suburb framework castigated one wrong (exclusionary zoning that left people in need of housing without affordable legal options) while leaving another (jobs policy) off the hook. The problem in the spatial mismatch formulation was housing supply in the right places, rather than demand for people's labor at a living wage.

These critiques appeared in the case's interrogatory when the defense repeatedly inquired about the supposed jobs in the town. The NAACP provided no concrete data that blue-collar demand existed within Oyster Bay, and according to the town attorneys, the NAACP "merely state the conclusion that there are job opportunities in Oyster Bay."[47] The defense, meanwhile, cited a 1971 HUD report, which found "no reason to believe that employment will expand . . . salaries are on the decline and unemployment is on the increase."[48] The defense then questioned each plaintiff about the local economy. Grummanite Edward Underwood agreed that his employer shed jobs in the early 1970s and that industry was contracting in the area.[49] When they asked Fair Housing Development Corporation chair and Glen Cove NAACP member William Joseph where they amassed their job data, he admitted it was from a 1965 Nassau County Planning Commission report. Defense Attorney Albert Bader then inquired about employment growth after 1969, to which Joseph replied, "we are in unusual times right now. We are in a recession. And I think that has affected the whole structure, the whole picture."[50]

The defense attorneys employed their questioning for instrumental ends. But they revealed the complex relationship between space and jobs, because where one lived mattered less for getting a good job than institutions and policy. The critique, in combination with the setbacks against the plaintiff's other claims, forced the NAACP to regroup and change strategy. The judge in the case had ruled as much during the initial court proceedings in 1971, suggesting the NAACP narrow their class action from the three groups (residents, non-resident workers, and non-residents in need of local jobs) to one. The plaintiffs returned to the court in March 1973 with a changed argument: that the Town of Oyster Bay should house some 34,000 new residents to match the racial demographics of New York City. This was necessary because

> the Town of Oyster Bay has a duty to provide housing for some of the black economically disadvantaged persons who currently live in the ghettoes of New York. Considering the fact that the New York City Housing Authority operates approximately 154,000 units of public housing, it seems reasonable to suggest that Oyster Bay build 10,000 units by 1985 as its fair share of public housing needs of the New York Metropolitan Region.[51]

The case still rested on the city–suburb framing, though the NAACP flipped the purpose of dismantling it. Rather than using the suburbs to solve poverty, the suburbs should now share the burden of urban poverty. Oyster Bay's own poor, or the suburban poor generally, did not fit. By the time the case reached a hearing in 1974, the original plaintiffs had largely forgotten about the suit. Of the five local plaintiffs, only the former golf course shack tenant qualified for Oyster Bay's housing project. Grumman laborer Edward Underwood still commuted from New Cassel, pausing his housing search because "I don't have the kind of money that they're asking." The other three locals managed in the tight rental market. Francine Grier, the young mother with four kids, could only move between Oyster Bay and Glen Cove's worst housing because of welfare rental ceilings.[52] The weakened case limped on for another two years before the NAACP withdrew the suit in October 1975.

The NAACP's withdrawal was strategic. Other exclusionary zoning lawsuits held more promise. *James v. Valtierra*, a similar case launched by welfare recipients against low-income housing restrictions in California, hoped to achieve similar ends. But the US Supreme Court upheld the exclusions. A recently settled case in Rochester, New York, in 1974 also destroyed the NAACP's class action strategy when the court limited petitioners to those "personally . . . injured." And since the Town of Oyster Bay applied for further HUD housing funds, both parties admitted land-use controls were "color blind," and variances could be resubmitted, the plaintiffs had little chance of winning.[53] Conversely, the NAACP had more success in New Jersey. There the state supreme court handed down the momentous *Mount Laurel* decision, itself originating as a local demand for affordable housing among displaced Black and poor residents. In 1975, the court required that New Jersey townships build affordable housing to meet current and future regional needs. *Mount Laurel* nonetheless exemplified a missed chance for affordable housing because the metropolitan view did not conceive of the suburban poor's existence. The plaintiffs instead tried to subsume their needs into a metropolitan framework to solve the "urban crisis" in its broadest terms. As Aaron Cavin illustrates in his work on the people behind California's *James v. Valtierra* lawsuit, the city–suburb binary and emphasis on desegregation obscured the poor suburban women who were fighting displacement in California's suburbanizing Bay Area.[54]

## The Uneven Burdens of Suburban Poverty

The city–suburb divide was not as important as dispersalists contended. But the city–suburb divide did matter in another regard, namely whether suburbs could manage poverty's fiscal burdens. Poverty dispersal was one solution to the spatial gap between where poor people lived and where alleged opportunities existed. Fair share was another. It was a policy ideal concerned with the public resources hoarded within suburbs, namely robust property tax bases with industrial and commercial firms. Cities had people in need, while suburbs had money to help them. Rather than siting more public housing in deprived cities, fair-share advocates argued suburbanites should shoulder some responsibility, accepting poor people they could support. Fair share made sense in the aggregate, but in reality, suburban public resources were unequally apportioned. The regressive property tax, when combined with balkanized tax jurisdictions in a segregated suburban landscape, meant that some suburbanites had more resources than others. This was especially true on Long Island, where the average Nassau County homeowner paid taxes to sixteen different public authorities.[55] Fair share depended on where it was targeted and who had to bear it.

Long Island epitomized fair share's rhetorical power and empirical fragility in the 1970s. It was broadly affluent, but also diverse, segregated, and unequal. Aggregate statistics still put Long Island near the top of America's metropolitan areas. But this obscured the suburbanites living off low-wage jobs or living within hamlets where predatory mortgages and informal housing proliferated. With Long Island's intensely balkanized tax system, where tiny areas bore the costs of educating and sustaining municipal services for their neighbors, public housing placement affected a few suburbanites, not the many. This mattered even more in the 1970s, when stagnating incomes and inflation imposed larger tax burdens on lower-income hamlets for their schools, sewers, and other amenities.

Property taxes, an already contentious issue linked to residents' pocketbooks and local service quality, rose and became more regressive in the 1970s. For one, assessment practices did not adhere to a property's "market value" on Long Island. In Suffolk, each of the ten unincorporated towns had different assessment practices and did not reassess properties on a yearly basis. Islip Town calculated assessments based on five-year-old market values, for example. The Town of Babylon forewent market values entirely, using 1954 construction costs as their standard. Nassau County likewise assessed based on 1938 construction costs minus depreciation. Using construction standards as the measure, two Cape Cods with completely different market values might have an equivalent *assessed* value for tax purposes. In other words, two identically built Capes, one in the tony suburb of Manhasset, and the other in struggling Roosevelt, may very well pay the same taxes for qualitatively different services. And residents with very different incomes would have to pay that same tax.[56]

Long Island's tiny taxing districts further compounded the problem. The burden of funding a school, police force, or sewer system depended on the property within a jurisdiction's "borders," usually the outcome of a larger governmental unit's land-use decisions. Towns and villages competed to attract taxpaying industrial and commercial companies all while trying to prohibit tax-exempt public buildings and multifamily dwellings within their borders. The outcome was a complex quilt of inequality, detailed in Michael Glass's masterful dissertation.[57] In districts like Roosevelt and Levittown for example, single-family homeowners shouldered over 80 percent and 90 percent of public school costs, respectively. Conversely, Bethpage residents milked Grumman for every tax dollar they could, and homeowners shouldered less than two-thirds of school costs. Wealthy Manhasset residents further enriched themselves with a diverse tax base of homes and stores.[58]

Basically, uneven assessments forced lower-income homeowners to pay higher taxes compared to their home's market value, while balkanized tax districts placed public service costs on these homeowners alone (save state funding) unless their district captured business property windfalls. These inequities, when combined with stagnating incomes and inflation, unleashed the property tax's regressivity. As table 6.1 shows, the tax rate for each one thousand dollars of assessed valuation was highest in neighborhoods where family earned less than the county median. Now, this does not mean that

TABLE 6.1. Total Tax Burden[1] of Selected Nassau County Communities, 1970–71

| | *Median Family Income (1969)* | *Taxes per $1,000 of Assessed Valuation (1971)* | *Median Family Income (1979)* | *Taxes per $1,000 of Assessed Valuation (1980)* |
|---|---|---|---|---|
| Lawrence | 27,413 | 159.12 | 42,875 | 217.7 |
| Garden City | 21,221 | 154.12 | 40,139 | 162.7 |
| Manhasset | 19,864 | 130.69 | 34,415 | 180.13 |
| Jericho | 19,311 | 149.43 | 36,680 | 215.36 |
| Merrick | 17,518 | 167.10 | 32,155 | 253.87 |
| Plainview | 16,198 | 181.56 | 32,532 | 261.41 |
| **Nassau County**[2] | 14,632 | | 28,445 | |
| Uniondale | 13,356 | 149.70 | 23,819 | 216.49 |
| Levittown | 13,083 | 181.64 | 26,245 | 287.09 |
| East Massapequa | 12,728 | 151.04 | 30,881 | 234.37 |
| New Cassel | 12,013 | 196.16 | 21,382 | 224.13 |
| Roosevelt | 11,122 | 183.50 | 22,125 | 245.69 |
| Inwood | 9,444 | 152.30 | 17,809 | 210.09 |

*Source*: *Nassau County Data Book*, 1974, 152–54; New York State Department of Audit and Control, *Overall Real Property Tax Rates: Local Government in New York State: Fiscal Years Ended in* 1971 (Albany, NY: Bureau of Research and Statistics, 1971), 22, 63–64; New York State Department of Audit and Control, *Overall Real Property Tax Rates: Local Government in New York State: Fiscal Years Ended in* 1980 (Albany, NY: Bureau of Research and Statistics, 1980), 31–32, 87–88.

[1] Total tax burden includes county, town, city/village (where applicable), and school district taxes. I cannot add Suffolk County hamlets for comparison given distinct assessment practices.

[2] Countywide medians.

property owners in lower-income hamlets paid more than those in higher income hamlets. The tax was based on property assessments, not income. But the property tax did not align with ability to pay. As an award-winning *Newsday* study revealed in 1984, this could mean lower-income homeowners paid more. Property owners in wealthy Manhasset and Garden City paid around 1 percent of their homes' value in property taxes. Residents of Roosevelt and Wyandanch paid over 4 percent of their homes' value in taxes each year. In some instances, residents in poorer neighborhoods actually paid more in taxes than affluent homeowners. In Nassau, a $41,000 home in Roosevelt owed $2,144 in taxes in 1984. In Manhasset, a $175,000 home owed only $2,091. In Suffolk, a two-story Wyandanch home worth one-third of a West Babylon ranch received tax bills only $2 apart.[59]

Over-assessment and property wealth may seem abstract, but homeowners understood its burden when they wrote checks to their town and county each year. Saving for bills meant budgeting the household, and people suffered from the tax inequities. As the *Newsday* report contended, "over-assessment affects the way a family lives—the way people eat and dress and furnish their homes . . . whether they can plant grass or paint the kitchen or pay the phone bill." Individual stories illustrate this point. Elizabeth Milton bought a $36,500 Wyandanch home. It came with a $2,233.64 yearly tax bill, about $960 more than she should be paying based on her home's value. This tax burden contributed to her $616 in combined monthly mortgage and tax payments. When she fell ill and missed several workdays at her $5.45 per hour packer job ($15.00 in 2021), she couldn't pay her bills. To catch up, Milton ended Friday pizza nights with her daughters and forewent needed clothing. Such sacrifices paled in comparison to that of the Holman family. Glenda and William Holman fell behind on their mortgage and taxes, a combined $724 (including a $223 monthly tax bill, double the county's median tax burden). William tried working double maintenance shifts at a hospital while his wife asked relatives for money and braided hair for friends and neighbors. Nonetheless, the mortgage company foreclosed on their home.[60]

Frustration over property taxes was a national political issue in the 1970s. Historian Isaac William Martin describes property tax revolts as a social movement during the decade. For anyone who attended a heated county board meeting, watched homeowners turn over a mayor's car on the evening news, or heard about retirees burning assessment cards, tax protests surely looked like a movement. We may think of anti-tax protests as right-wing, but the right only seized tax anxieties by the 1980s. In the 1970s, tax protests just as often veered left. Working-class homeowners especially wanted relief from onerous property taxes, unfair assessment practices, and the high costs of funding local public schools. In other words, they wanted protection from the market, a more robust tax base to support public goods. Former National Welfare Rights Organization chair George Wiley's 1972 campaign to abolish the property tax altogether exemplifies the left-leaning anti-tax protests. The campaign had widespread grassroots support from Rochester, New York to San Bernadino, California, where both civil rights and local homeowner groups wanted public goods financed with progressive income taxes, not regressive property taxes. In the 1972 presidential campaign, Senators George McGovern and Edmund Muskie announced plans to federally fund schools or subsidize local taxes. Even President Nixon considered replacing property taxes with value added taxes.[61]

Property tax reform, or even its abolition, reached Long Island too. Nassau County executive Eugene Nickerson's press secretary, Paul M. O'Brien, exemplified the liberal case in the late 1960s, advocating that the state and federal government assume local service costs. As O'Brien argued, Washington and Albany "possess the most equitable means of taxation [but] refuse to pay for such functions as education, social services, courts, and the struggle to eliminate poverty and disease . . . sentencing local government to the penalty of paying for such functions out of unfair and oppressive tax devices, which are the only kinds of taxes most local governments have to draw on." County Executive Nickerson's Republican successor, Ralph Caso, thought abolishing the local property tax extreme, but nonetheless advocated a "circuit-breaker" law, a credit for lower-income homeowners when their tax burden reached a determined percentage of their income. Long Island school officials, meanwhile, launched the most far-reaching attack on local school finance in 1974. The Levittown school district, along with eleven other Long Island districts and another fifteen from around the state, sued New York's Education Department. They alleged that property wealth inequality among New York school districts harmed students. They demanded an end to using property values and taxes to fund schools.[62]

These solutions remained hypothetical in the 1970s, hashed out in state assemblies, Congress, and the courts. In the meantime, fair-share advocates targeted sites for public housing within Long Island's byzantine labyrinth of tax districts, with its acute consequences for local property values, school taxes, and public infrastructure. This was the material backdrop to the political battles around fair-share public housing: while the suburbs as a whole satisfied fair-share advocates, *which* suburbs to target mattered most to Long Islanders. Fair-share proponents also established the ideological context for political battles over suburban housing. They framed Long Island as affluent and mostly white, exceptional in the metropolitan area, and therefore able to bear the burden of metropolitan poverty. Local homeowners, particularly those in racially integrated or relatively poor suburbs, inverted the fair-share logic. They decried the heavily localized tax, property value, and public service implications of public housing projects. For Long Island's working-class homeowners, fair share was a social injustice imposed on them. This ideological conflict left the existing challenges of poverty, namely the exploitation surrounding it, unresolved.

Below then are three case studies, all detailed dives that lay bare both the programmatic and discursive limits of fair-share suburban housing proposals. None were fair to affected neighbors, and the battles established fault lines around who should, or could, accept responsibility for poverty. Most importantly, each example shows how opponents decried suburban poverty's exploitative mechanisms, and the fair-share concept offered little in response. The first case is a HUD-approved public housing project in the Town of Oyster Bay. It exemplifies the disconnect between the federal conception of affluent suburbia and its reality, as well as the burden public housing projects placed on some schools and not others. The second case grapples with Long

Island's long-standing welfare motel crisis and a fair-share solution imposed on a racially integrated and cash-strapped suburban hamlet. The last case is similar to the New Cassel vignette in the chapter's introduction. It covers a New York State-sponsored project in Wyandanch, a place long besieged by informal housing, which civic activists contended public housing would only worsen.

## Oyster Bay's Public Housing "Compromise"

The first case study originated as a response to the NAACP's *Fair Housing Development Fund Corp. v. Burke* suit against the Town of Oyster Bay. The town's housing authority tried to both satisfy local low-income housing demand and weaken the NAACP's case against them. In 1973, Oyster Bay unveiled a modest 172-unit public apartment complex. It was funded through HUD's Open Communities program, HUD chair George Romney's ambitious effort to penetrate the "well-to-do, indifferent white ring" choking cities. Oyster Bay selected the small hamlet of East Massapequa, which bordered Suffolk County in the extreme southeast of the town, as the project site. Viewed through the city–suburb framework, the location met Open Communities' goals: a mostly white hamlet near plentiful job opportunities without affordable housing. But the federal analysis exemplified Open Communities' crude formulation: East Massapequa was the most diverse place in Oyster Bay, and the local school district already educated a disproportionately poor student body. Oyster Bay was exploiting the city–suburb framework to further segregate and intensify local inequities.[63] Suburban homeowners wielded the local facts to portray fair share as racist. They claimed to oppose the project on anti-racist grounds in a shrewd defense of their material interests.

HUD's East Massapequa public housing project qualified for the Open Communities program because the hamlet was on Long Island, one of the twenty-five suburban metropolitan areas HUD targeted for public housing construction. East Massapequa was, in the aggregate at least, a microcosm of Long Island's affluence: a mostly white hamlet (16 percent of its residents were Black) with open space, a clean local environment, and near to "employment positions available to all types of applicants."[64] But general census numbers and town-wide labor market statistics belied more complex socioeconomic dynamics. Among the Town of Oyster Bay's neighborhoods, East Massapequa was only one of three with Black residents, and the only one with Black homeowners rather than tenants. Despite the census tract's white majority, East Massapequa residents attended the Amityville school district in neighboring Suffolk County. Nearly a fifth of students in Amityville's half-Black district received money from the Aid to Families with Dependent Children program, and 13 percent of school district families lived near the poverty line. While the town had jobs, retail employers struggled to stay open in East Massapequa's only employment center, the Sunrise Mall. Otherwise, residents had to travel over a mile for the nearest public bus stop or spend between 10 percent and 15 percent of their yearly income on a car to reach Long Island's industrial parks.[65]

East Massapequa's diversity, the relatively poor schools that residents attended, and HUD's white and affluent appraisal mobilized six civic associations and the Amityville school board to stop the project. They packaged together contradictory positions. First, civic association activists deployed a "color-blind" defense of their suburb that obscured decades of exclusionary housing policy. Second, activists drew on racialized ideas that tied the minority poor to public housing degradation. Last, they claimed East Massapequa achieved racial integration, and the housing project would resegregate the suburb.[66] David Behrman, the East Massapequa Civic Association president and de facto opposition leader espoused all three perspectives in a 1974 mass civic association meeting. He argued that the project would inundate the schools with poor kids "since sterilization is not a requirement" and upend an "already integrated and delicately balanced" suburb. Therefore, it should be placed somewhere better suited to absorb the costs of poor residents. Civic members embraced variants of each, from the racialized fears that "someone is going to get mugged" and how they worked long hours to "say I live in a nice neighborhood," to their disgust with "concentrating any subsidized housing in the same community."[67]

Of all the rhetorical arguments, the anti-racist claims caught on, largely because they labeled HUD as the agent of segregation. As the official opposition report noted, the project contradicted HUD's goals of integrating suburbs and increasing opportunity. By relocating Oyster Bay's low-income residents (estimated to be 65 percent Black), HUD would be lowering the racial balance of other hamlets while tipping the Black school population over 50 percent, forcing an already burdened school district to now educate the town's poor students. They presented evidence of blockbusting leaflets filling mailboxes as proof of further segregation. As both the school district board and residents made clear, the project contradicted the ideals of the civil rights acts rather than upheld them. The project would also isolate the poor from public services and job sites, accomplishing little aside from building public housing.[68] David Behrman labeled HUD a "partner with the leadership of the

Town of Oyster Bay in practicing racial segregation" in a strongly worded letter to *Newsday*. As he proclaimed, "the combined actions of HUD and Oyster Bay have done more to further racial segregation in southeastern Oyster Bay than any other single influence, and their actions would please the most ardent southern segregationist."[69]

Residents also contradicted HUD's claims that they were affluent. East Massapequa had the lowest median income in Oyster Bay, but residents paid a yearly school tax around the median (table 6.1).[70] The town already exempted many public properties within East Massapequa borders from taxes, foisting school funding onto homeowners. Meanwhile, HUD estimated the project would add fifty children to the district at an additional cost of $75,000. The town promised $10,000 from rents, though project opponents calculated HUD would only cover $8,700.[71] In light of the public costs, the projected increase in segregation, and the isolation from jobs, residents basically wanted to know: "Why East Massapequa?" If the town and HUD were both committed to affordable housing as a means of integration and expanding opportunity, as a town-sponsored planning report claimed, why not place the project in the "restrictive and exclusionary zoning of the North Shore of the Town of Oyster Bay"? Why not close to industrial parks in Plainview, Hicksville, Bethpage, or Farmingdale, with bus routes and all-white schools?[72]

Their critiques, the fiery town hall meetings, and a lawsuit pushed HUD to reduce the number of family units from thirty to ten. Elderly residents replaced them. While Behrman and the Amityville superintendent still opposed the project, the town board approved it in July 1974, and the lawsuit died in the state supreme court the next year. By the time the complex opened two years later, only twenty working-age adults and ten children filled the apartments. 182 senior citizens scattered across fourteen townhouses. *Newsday* interviewed the elderly tenants and neighboring residents. The article teased the project's opponents, detailing the "threat" of old ladies drinking coffee in the community center. David Behrman had to defend his actions, admitting he had "nothing against these [old] people per se." He reiterated his original argument: that the "whole thing was unconstitutional . . . the federal government is placing people here but not reimbursing the local community for schools and other services."[73]

Behrman's humiliating defense reflected both victory and failure. While the civic associations reduced the number of low-income units and could point to East Massapequa as retaining its racially integrated makeup, the property remained tax-exempt. Public housing was not a revenue-producing use of land. The fair-share concept proved a losing battle for HUD, but the inverse proved to only defend the existing unequal state of affairs. If anything, the Town of Oyster Bay won, exploiting HUD's vague rubric of "fair share" as a defensive maneuver in the NAACP suit. Opponents flipped the concept on its head, demanding that whiter and wealthier areas house their share of the poor. But that did not happen either. In the end, the town supplied little public housing, while the oppositional politics only defended the status quo in the name of racial "balance." Blockbusting still existed, and even Behrman admitted that "it takes only the slightest breath to throw [integration] off."[74]

## Ending Welfare Motels

Fair share was not only a novel approach for urban poverty; it offered new solutions to old suburban problems as well. Few challenges proved as irresolvable as sheltering suburban welfare recipients. It was a task assigned to counties with no land-use powers, forcing the poorest Long Islanders into the segregated private housing market or temporary welfare motels. The former sparked the explosive politics detailed in chapter 3 surrounding code enforcement and informal housing. The latter condemned the poor to deplorable living conditions at exorbitant public cost. Fair share offered a solution to both: equitably distribute the poor across the suburbs in decent public housing, rather than ad hoc motel rooms or informal single-family homes. But public housing was high-density, not widely dispersed across suburbs. In New York State, counties could only build on county-owned land, itself concentrated in some places and not others. Wherever they built public housing, local homeowners would pay the tax bills. In effect, fair share was only an abstract solution. In reality, fair-share projects had to find a suitable site in a segregated housing market and regressive tax system. Familiar battles, echoing informal housing conflicts, emerged. Now though, suburbanites, welfare tenants, and government bureaucrats fought over public housing, rather than public subsidy of private informal rentals.

The problem started in 1963, when Congress transferred ownership of Mitchel Field, a decommissioned air force base along the Uniondale, Garden City, and Hempstead borders to Nassau County. The site immediately housed Nassau Community College, and after five years of planning, Nassau unveiled the grand plan: a hotel, sports arena, office/retail complex, and most importantly, an eight-building, 1,200-unit housing project to replace the county's welfare motel network.[75] The housing proposal was a lynchpin for the entire project. Norman Blankman was its biggest proponent, a millionaire real estate developer and resident of Sands Point on Long Island's North Shore, one of the country's richest places. Blankman framed the project as a solution to informal housing: "We have at least 15,000 illegal double and triple occupancies in one-family houses starting to decay whole neighborhoods into eventual slums." Blankman even presented the members of Nassau County's legislature with a copy of Gilbert Osofsky's *Harlem: The Making of a Ghetto* to illustrate how informal housing begat slums. In Blankman's mind, only planned housing that met needs on a countywide basis could reverse this ghetto formation.[76]

Though presented as a countywide answer, the housing proposal concentrated welfare recipients into Uniondale. This unincorporated place was mostly blue collar, and sat just to the north of Roosevelt, the hamlet engulfed in blockbusting and informal housing conversion. Uniondale was majority white by contrast; 9 percent of its residents were Black. While Blankman argued the project would prevent ghettoes, a Black Uniondale resident countered that the county was welfare dumping, which already hurt Roosevelt to the south. As he claimed, "slums are made; they don't just occur, and the politicians are trying to make another Roosevelt in Uniondale."[77] To Uniondale residents, Nassau County threatened to fiscally burden their suburb, encouraging blockbusting and segregation all for the sake of other whiter places in Nassau. While the nearby Roosevelt Field shopping and industrial hub supplied Uniondale's tax base, this did not translate into low taxes (table 6.1), particularly as the number of students exploded in the late '60s. Residents voted down the school budget three years in a row, and the school system operated with temporary classrooms to accommodate increasing enrollment. Planners projected the public housing project would add one hundred children to the district, and residents were unconvinced that Mitchel Field's commercial space would increase tax revenues by 50 percent as project advocates claimed.[78]

Debates over the housing proposal between the Uniondale school district, the Town of Hempstead (charged with land use surrounding Mitchel Field), and Nassau County spilled into 1970. In the meantime, poor Long Islanders staged a protest for a right to housing. The Quaker-owned Friends World College, which had been using Mitchel Field's vacant military housing for classes, donated extra homes to sixteen families lodged in New Cassel's Mid-Island Motel, in what they called a "move-in." The families squatted in the vacant buildings, started vegetable gardens, and initiated their own home improvement projects. One of the residents admitted that the long-abandoned units were not ideal, but residents still considered "Mitchel Gardens" preferable to the kitchen-less single-room hotel rooms they previously inhabited. Crucially, the county saved money from the "move-in," collecting state and federal welfare reimbursements while avoiding any motel fees. The highly publicized move-in also worked to County Executive Nickerson's advantage, demonstrating the desire for adequate housing among Long Island's poor. But the county did not want to rehabilitate the units. County officials instead looked to demolish the units and place recipients in the undetermined public housing complex.

By September 1970, Uniondale schools had to decide whether to admit the twenty-seven children at the district's expense. The school board initially blocked the squatters, but a state judge quickly ordered the district to enroll the students.[79] Uniondale's reaction set off an intense response. *Newsday* columnist Martin Buskin called Uniondale's decision "one of the more sickening examples of the rotting civic conscience of suburbia . . . [a] selfish, narrow demonstration of local control."[80] Residents felt differently, flipping the fair-share concept around by asserting the county forced Uniondale to bear the burden of poverty to spare other wealthier and whiter districts. They framed their fight in spatial and class terms. They rallied around State Assemblyman and Uniondale resident Joseph Margiotta, who demanded the county place the welfare families "on the North Shore," the former Gold Coast and still home to Long Island's most affluent residents. Hempstead town supervisor Francis Purcell put it in blunter terms: "Why doesn't Blankman go over to Sands Point, where he lives, and the density is about 1.1 persons per acre, and do this in his backyard?" Residents repeatedly echoed the fair-share idea themselves, condemning the county for encouraging a "welfare ghetto" to the detriment of the poor and the Uniondale community. They believed scattering the poor across Long Island was fairer to both Uniondale and the recipients.[81] Of course, talk of deconcentrating the poor hinged around the costs of poverty for home-owning suburbanites, not the burden of destitution and homelessness on the poor, who requested funds to improve the existing Mitchel Field barracks.

The uproar pushed incoming Republican county executive Ralph Caso to remove any housing plans from Mitchel Field's future, and in 1971, Caso forcibly removed the squatters. The next year, Blankman, along with the SAI and the Long Island NAACP, sued the county for denying people of color and low-income residents affordable housing. Blankman demanded that "countywide interests . . . take precedence over those of communities."[82] District Court Judge Mark Constantino disagreed and sided with Uniondale residents. While admitting racism played a factor, Constantino contended that Uniondale could not resolve countywide problems because of the "loss of revenue [public housing] causes and the increased burdens it places on the community's resources."[83] Constantino judged this burden unfair "considering the availability of land throughout Nassau County that could be used to construct multifamily housing." In addition, Judge Constantino recognized that low-income housing in Uniondale would worsen segregation and not alleviate it.[84]

As both Uniondale residents and Judge Constantino made clear, one place could not resolve "countywide interests" within Long Island's segregated landscape and fragmented tax system. Real estate developer Norman Blankman pushed for public housing to prevent what occurred in Roosevelt and elsewhere. But Uniondale residents flipped fair share around to highlight the proposal's broader inequities. Fair share would concentrate poverty in a racially integrated suburb for the sake of relieving it elsewhere, inoculating some of the nation's wealthiest homeowners. But like in East Massapequa, the anti-racist moralistic veneer didn't address homeowner's property tax burdens or the needs of Long Island's homeless.

## Informal versus Public Housing in Wyandanch

Fair-share proposals proved ill-equipped to resolve suburban housing segregation and property tax inequities. Fair share proved no more suited to confronting exploitative informal housing, the means by which landlords already carved out low-income apartments in the suburbs. In New Cassel, informal housing was PCANC's primary concern with five prefabricated Turnkey units. The same held true for Wyandanch, the unincorporated suburb that by 1970 was neither affluent nor white. The Suffolk hamlet nonetheless became a flashpoint for a bold state new authority, the UDC, and its unflinching chair, famed planner Edward Logue. Armed with the power to override local zoning powers, Logue and the UDC looked to distribute public housing throughout New York's suburbs. But Wyandanch homeowners saw the project as another attempt to exploit the hamlet's segregation to further concentrate poverty, eroding Wyandanch's housing stock and tax base. In Wyandanch, more than elsewhere, the local politics of racial segregation and poverty shaped how supporters and opponents approached the public housing project. Both sides claimed to fight housing segregation and labeled their opponents racists. But only one side's racial appeal built a successful political coalition. Wyandanch's poor, living as tenants in single-family homes, lost either way.

Like other fair-share projects, Wyandanch's public housing efforts started locally. In 1969, residents, churches, and non-profits formed the Wyandanch Task Force, an organization devoted to "increasing industry, constructing low- and moderate-income housing, and strengthening Negro owned businesses in Wyandanch."[85] They had broad aims, from reducing informal housing demand to expanding the tax base and increasing job opportunities. The goals required land-use controls, but the larger Town of Babylon, white and relatively wealthier, held power over zoning in Wyandanch. The town was the obstacle, but the new UDC had a workaround.

In 1968, New York's liberal Republican governor Nelson Rockefeller formed the UDC to revive cities and build public housing throughout the state. The UDC was Rockefeller's antidote to the urban crisis. It was a state public benefit corporation that could override land-use laws usually reserved for the state's towns, villages, and cities. He handed the UDC's reins to planner Edward J. Logue, a liberal who cut his teeth on urban redevelopment in New Haven and Boston. Logue had long held a deep concern for inner-city decline, racial segregation, and the nation's dearth of affordable housing. The UDC gave Logue critical powers at a time when "fair share" was in the political zeitgeist, and Logue looked to use it. As Logue biographer Lizabeth Cohen writes, by the late 1960s, he was convinced that integrated communities along income, age, and race could revitalize cities and suburbs alike.[86] Redistributing the poor across metropolitan areas contributed to this goal. As Logue contended, low-income suburban housing would "create opportunities for low-income families to share in the good schools, the safe streets, the fresh air and open space other Americans like so well without unsettling or unbalancing the suburban communities."[87]

For the Wyandanch Task Force, the UDC's zoning override powers offered them the powers to circumvent the town's exclusionary land-use laws. For Ed Logue, Wyandanch's suburban location and grassroots support exemplified his "metropolitan" approach to urban problems.[88] The suburban location was ideal, like his "New Towns" effort to the north in Westchester County, New York. Though the task force originally envisioned a mass commercial, industrial, and residential redevelopment, the UDC settled on a 182-unit, twenty-nine-building garden apartment complex for an eleven-acre vacant lot on Wyandanch's main thoroughfare The UDC and Wyandanch Task Force then sought community input.

The battle lines took familiar forms, and the fair-share concept shaped how each side composed their support or disapproval. UDC project proponents appealed to a unified racial interest within Wyandanch, epitomized by the lead supporter, Reverend David Rooks, who celebrated the local effort as a community "trying to pull ourselves up by our own bootstraps." Politicians lined up on his side, including New York governor Nelson Rockefeller, Suffolk's county executive John V. N. Klein, and Babylon town supervisor Aaron Barnett. Homeowners dominated the opposition, particularly Wyandanch's well-organized civic associations, veterans of the informal housing battles. Hermann "The Griem" and his Joint Civic and Taxpayers' Council led the charge. They were joined by the Black-dominated Triangle Civic Association and white-dominated civic associations of neighboring Deer Park. And like in Uniondale and East Massapequa, the Wyandanch school board president, Alfred Bostic, longtime Black homeowner and Triangle Civic Association member, placed the school district firmly in the opposition's camp. Reverend Rooks framed both support and resistance in racial terms, presuming divided political interest between Black and white residents, in particular "outside whites" who "come into Wyandanch to stymie the efforts Blacks were making."[89]

But the Black/white, insider/outsider portrait did not capture the conflicting ideological positions and material interests of the opposition.[90] Project opponents deployed race for their own ends. School board president Alfred Bostic divorced race from class, lamenting how the idyllic integrated suburb of the 1950s became a "dumping ground for welfare cases," and how racial prejudice did not motivate his objection to the housing complex. Instead, Bostic interpreted the project as one of undeserved merit:

> The difference we are talking about is between people who see what they want and are ready to go out and work for it, and those who just sit back and expect somebody to give it to them. . . . I don't care whether they are black or white, I am against that kind of attitude. I am not against the kind of housing proposed by the UDC, but I do feel that the people who live in it should pay their way. Giving this kind of housing to people who have lived all their lives expecting something for nothing is not going to change those people. There's still a chance for the children, and that's why I spend as much time and effort as I do on the schools. But as far as I am concerned, most of the adults are already lost.[91]

Bostic deployed the old line about suburban homeownership as a badge of merit. This was written into the exclusionary tools of the FHA, local land-use laws, and various codes imposed on suburban housing. Suburbanites themselves likewise imbibed the belief's undergirding policy. Here, Bostic trotted out the suburbia-as-achievement trope to oppose the UDC project. It proved effective in uniting Black and white residents as homeowners, evident in the Deer Park civic leader's similar, if more direct line: "Why should the working people of this town support those who don't?"[92]

Suburbia as a place for the meritorious coalesced with an anti-racist claim: that the UDC's project constituted racism itself, further "corralling" poor Black people into Wyandanch and intensifying segregation. This thesis assembled a different coalition among Black residents in Wyandanch which overlapped with white allies within the hamlet and beyond. Black middle-class homeowners commonly deployed this argument against public housing.[93]

But to say they emulated other rhetorical arguments would miss the local homeowner activism informing this perspective. Local opponents cited two consequences of segregation that they feared the UDC project would exacerbate. First, the project would further burden Wyandanch's already stretched school district that activists had previously tried to dissolve altogether. The Triangle Civic Association calculated $30 to $40 per month tax increases. More consequentially, the Triangle Civic Association, Griem's Joint Civic and Taxpayers' Council, and others repeatedly demanded that the UDC address informal housing. As Triangle spokesperson Ted Williams argued, "what are they going to do with the substandard housing that the people who move to the project move out of?" After all, the UDC only committed to overriding local zoning ordinances, and the Town of Babylon had yet to adopt a housing code. Nearly everyone agreed that once locals moved into the project, the newly vacated homes would fill with low-income tenants, mediated by landlords, the county welfare department, and the persistent dearth of affordable housing elsewhere. While a few hundred would obtain clean public housing, others would potentially replace them in existing substandard and overcrowded homes. This would only intensify Wyandanch's dilapidated housing stock, high taxes, and segregation. Triangle Civic Association member Bernice Bostic concluded that "we already have enough [welfare] recipients"[94]

While proponents had the UDC and their zoning override powers on their side, the opposition had a broad-based alliance of homeowners across the town on theirs. In 1972, homeowners formed the ad hoc Babylon Citizens for Home Rule under the leadership of Judith Bernor, a Deer Park resident who contended "the only way to [win] is to behave like animals. Then use [political] blackmail." The group investigated the UDC's land-use override powers, even contacting Westchester County groups fighting the UDC's similar New Towns suburban public housing project there. Collectively, the Babylon Citizens for Home Rule gathered 4,931 signatures against the Wyandanch apartments. They, in tandem with Westchester homeowners, pressured state legislators to overturn the UDC's powers in 1973.

UDC project proponents now had to change tactics. They could no longer steamroll local land-use law but had to persuade a five-member town board, a level of government far more amenable to property owners. The UDC also now needed public support. At two public hearings in late July 1973, the last of which filled Wyandanch high school's gymnasium for over five hours, the two sides voiced their conflicting interpretations of fair share. Proponents defended the project in the Kerner Report's framework, that an "affluent society" had a responsibility to help the disadvantaged while downplaying the burdens on existing housing and taxes. They painted their opponents as racists, who then countered that the UDC were the racists, concentrating public housing in an already segregated suburb, further impoverishing a Black-dominated school district, and exacerbating informal housing.[95]

The project's fate ultimately rested with the five-member town board, pressured by home-owning voters and mindful of an upcoming November election. At a town board meeting in early August 1973, the only board member who openly supported the project, Sondra Bachety, called on her colleagues to pass a town-wide housing code. Babylon was one of Long Island's last towns without housing codes regulating proper occupancy. It was the only means to assure the UDC project would not perpetuate overcrowding and dilapidation in Wyandanch's existing rentals. But Town Supervisor Aaron Barnett claimed Babylon could rely on the county's unenforced health codes rather than develop their own. Bachety challenged Barnett's stance, but still approved the UDC project. Three of her colleagues did not, voting down the UDC project in August 1973.[96]

The project's local leader, Reverend Rooks, broke down in tears at the town board vote, citing "racial attitudes" for its defeat. UDC president Edward J. Logue remarked, "I know of no other instance where there has been such clearly demonstrated support for a development in a community . . . it is sad that the will of that community was disregarded." A *New York Amsterdam News* reporter lamented the "death a miniature civil rights movement in Wyandanch," further proof that white suburbanites "do not intend to allow Blacks, and other minorities to break out of the ghetto walls which the whites have built around them and spill over into neatly manicured lawns and tree-lined avenues which such whites have designated as belonging to them alone." Opponents meanwhile drew two distinct lessons from the victory. Some, like Triangle Civic Association member Bernice Bostic, celebrated the victory as a homeowner win, that "finally the taxpayers of Wyandanch have been heard." The most prominent opponents were less sanguine, seeing the win as one step against "welfare dumping" and illegal rentals concentrating poverty in their midst. As civic leader Hermann Griem put it, "I don't feel this is a victory . . . I'll call it a victory when those homes that are not up to date—not just in Wyandanch but all over the town of Babylon—have been refurbished." Fellow Joint Civic and Taxpayers' Council member Conrad Trigilio was more pessimistic, lamenting that "nothing's been resolved . . . we weren't just interested in throwing out the UDC. We don't feel now we can all say, 'The problems of Babylon are solved.' That's baloney."

The opposition's indifferent response to their victory reflected how little the UDC public housing project resolved. UDC proponents believed they were building an anti-racist project to help residents "break out of ghetto walls." But the project would intensify those "ghetto" walls, forcing suburban public housing on a sliver of Long Islanders and doing little to curb informal housing. In other words, the fair-share framework obscured Wyandanch's resource needs. Fair share viewed exclusionary land-use powers as the problem. Homeowners responded by pointing out the exploitative practices impoverishing Wyandanch: informal housing conversion and the regressive tax structure sensitive to minute cost changes. Fair share also drew political conflict along racial lines and in moralistic terms. This perpetuated a defensive homeowner politics concerned with concentrated poverty and its effect on their pocketbooks and quality of life. Ultimately, the homeowners only temporarily won. Informal housing, which cost homeowners tax dollars and property values, remained, as did the exploitative and life-threatening conditions that illegal-apartment living entailed. Project opponents would, as a *New York Times* editorial concluded, still "have to take upon themselves the unwelcome burden of coming up with something better."[97]

## Conclusion

The 1973 UDC project defeat in Wyandanch echoed what occurred in New Cassel three years prior. In both places, local civic associations used their clout with town boards to reject public housing proposals. And in both places, each side claimed to defend housing integration and social responsibility. Even where layers of governance differed, like in Uniondale and East Massapequa, similar rhetorical arguments appeared. In each case study, opposing homeowners crushed the housing proposals, save one neutered project tucked into East Massapequa.

In one way, we could read the defeats as a tragic loss for a more egalitarian society. The Kerner Report was the "last gasp of the progressive imagination," killed by a conservative counterrevolution.[98] The dispersal and fair-share proposals that followed Kerner's wake tried to dismantle the exclusionary barriers preventing non-white and poor people from enjoying suburban jobs, schools, clean air, and green spaces. But President Nixon, looking to preserve his suburban "silent majority" electoral coalition, stripped HUD of its powers to integrate suburban housing. The UDC faced similar constraints once New York's legislature defanged the corporation's zoning override powers. Other projects confronted formidable local resistance with land-use powers in their hands. The opponents hid behind "color-blind" defenses, or in the case of white and Black opponents in integrated suburbs, anti-racism, to defend their exclusionary privileges. In this dominant narrative, exclusion destroyed the egalitarian promise of the late 1960s.[99]

Dispersal and fair-share proposals were anything but egalitarian, however.

The belief that suburbs were exceptionally affluent, and exclusion the barrier, was both programmatically flawed and politically fruitless. Programmatically flawed because good-paying jobs did not flow from Long Island's industrial parks and housing segregation operated within Long Island's balkanized neighborhoods. Speculators already sheltered poor people in suburbs through informal housing conversion. Regressive property taxes and tightly bounded tax bases often placed public service burdens on a few thousand homeowners. In other words, exploitation stalked the suburbs.

Dispersal and fair-share housing projects were also politically fruitless because proponents took suburban prosperity for granted, which obscured the exploitation suburbanites actually wanted to stop. Appeals to social responsibility and the focus on exclusion only intensified conflict along class and racial lines. Suburban opposition appeared as parochial defenses of suburban privilege, but as scholars note, beneath the surface of NIMBY claims was a demand for social protections.[100] This was especially true for the suburban neighborhoods mentioned in this chapter, none of which were affluent or white-exclusive. These suburbanites needed the same things as the urban poor—good schools, well-funded public services, secure homes, and neighborhoods free of exploitation. The Black/white, poor/rich, city/suburb framing foreclosed the possibility of building potential coalitions across cities and suburbs. Thus, defeated projects were self-fulfilling prophecies. The city–suburb divide, rooted in racial exclusion, caused the problem, and intractable racial conflict to preserve exclusion doomed dispersed suburban public housing.

By embracing suburban exceptionalism, the Kerner Report's interpretation of America's social ills was not the "last gasp of the progressive imagination," but the first breath of a less social-democratic vision. No one can fault the efforts to open up the suburbs for lacking a moral imperative. The call to dismantle ghettoes was emancipatory. It was the means chosen that failed to liberate. Like the War on Poverty and Title VII, liberals assumed prosperity, that the market could be made just. They blamed discrimination, skill deficiencies, exclusionary zoning, and school district boundaries instead. Fair share and poverty dispersal was part of an impoverished antipoverty ideology that rested on dismantling the barriers to a more efficient labor and housing market, rather than altering the institutions responsible for distributing jobs and housing. It was part of a general political retreat from social-democratic ideas, including full employment and mass public housing where people already lived. Instead, liberal policymakers presumed affluence and looked to redistribute people to achieve equality.[101] Despite its failures, deconcentrating the poor would dominate the urban reform agenda for decades to come.

# 7

# The Long Island Miracle

## *Suburbia into the Next Century*

In November 2006, volunteer firefighters responded to a call in New Cassel on New York Avenue, two blocks from the Levitt-built Maplewood Avenue subdivision. From outside, it was a typical fire in a standard four-bedroom single-family house. But when firefighters entered the unit, they discovered the house had seven, not four bedrooms. Three were upstairs, as intended. Four more were in the basement, assembled with drywell, extra plumbing, and jerry-rigged gas pipes. Eleven people lived in the home, complicating efforts that night. The firefighters managed to save everyone. And the town charged the property owner for the illegal walls, heating system alterations, and unpermitted rentals. But the tenants were now homeless.[1]

Forty years after civic associations mounted their fight against New Cassel's informal housing, episodes like this one made clear the problem remained on Long Island. As in most suburbs, informal housing continues to serve as the "solution" to an enduring housing crisis. The fire prompted a blitz of code enforcement, which proved as contentious as the 1960s crackdowns. Even though the Town of North Hempstead, charged with enforcing housing codes in New Cassel, tried to avoid abrupt evictions, they happened anyway. A year before, the town condemned a nearby single-family house stuffed with thirty beds laid across hallways and under stairwells. They only gave tenants a week's notice and a few social workers to help. Unsurprisingly, people ended up on the street.[2] Town Supervisor Jon Kaiman admitted, "I am aware that we must not forget that the people we are displacing are moms and dads, sons and daughters, old and young, people like you and me . . . but this does not relieve us of our obligation to enforce our codes . . . it is inherently unsafe to crowd people into cramped and unsafe living quarters such as basements, attics, and sub-par structures built within a residence."[3] The New York Avenue fire proved the town needed to enforce its housing codes. But codes still didn't address the dearth of decent and legal housing.

The inhabitants of New Cassel's informal apartments were Latin American immigrants. Some were legal residents, others undocumented. Their place of origin differed from New Cassel's earlier southern Black migrants. But they came for similar reasons and labored in similar jobs. Like James Baxter, the horse groom from Jim Crow North Carolina, Salvadoran and Mexican immigrants escaped war-torn and violence-ridden towns starting in the 1980s. Like their predecessors from the postwar golden age, almost half of all New Cassel residents worked in construction, in retail shops, at restaurants, for cleaning services, or in low-wage industry. On any given day in the early 2000s, over 300 day laborers waited along New Cassel's main thoroughfare for a day's pay during the early twenty-first century housing boom. Most, whether factory worker or day laborer, earned less than the federal poverty threshold for a four-person family.[4] Like their suburban forerunners, they still built and maintained Long Island, and their wages still prohibited many from living in a decent and legal home.

Unlike their precursors though, scholars and journalists no longer overlook informal tenants and suburban day laborers. If anything, they are now at the center of America's urban narrative. Since 2000, suburbs have become the primary residence of America's poor. And since the 2008 recession in particular, journalists have publicized California's "gated ghettoes," "inner-ring" suburbs like Ferguson in the wake of the Michael Brown shooting, suburban gangs during President Trump's visit to the allegedly MS-13 plagued Suffolk County, and the purported revitalization of cities at the expense of their outlying areas.[5] Academics and policymakers deploy the postwar trope as a contrast to the ethnically and socioeconomically diverse "new suburb." The suburbs now have dropping labor market participation rates, families struggling to meet their basic needs, and a wide gulf between the suburban "haves" in their McMansions versus the "have-nots" in aging postwar ranches and Cape Cods.

Social scientists and journalists no doubt identify an important shift in metropolitan America. But the novelty of recent trends depends on suburban exceptionalism, the idea that suburbs in the postwar period were free of poverty, a myth historians perpetuate. In reality, the trends since 1980 differ little from the postwar years, despite the changed faces, aging housing stock, and new investments in cities. In the quarter century after 1945, policymakers failed to improve how people earned their livelihoods, how suburbanites satisfied their needs, and how the market provisioned housing. They supplied nothing to replace military Keynesianism, the foundation of Long Island's postwar prosperity, along with the rest of the gunbelt. Inequality then intensified. Once the post–World War II construction boom slowed, informal housing spread. Public officials now vacillate between embracing or rejecting informal housing units, as their predecessors did. And despite suburban distress, suburban exceptionalism still informs antipoverty projects. Policymakers recognize suburban poverty, but they still attack exclusion. Only now, they do so *within* suburbs, rather than *between* cities and suburbs. They rebuild the places where struggling suburbanites live, to absorb distressed suburbs into the surrounding affluence. They hope improving places might improve the prospects of the people living there. These are half-century-old ideas dressed up for suburbs: decent pay and housing trickle down through redevelopment, not policies that directly create jobs, boost wages, and create legal dwellings.

What follows is a history of Long Island's inequality since the 1960s, keeping suburbia's *longue durée* in mind. One place cannot explain all national trends, but neither can suburbs of any stripe. Echoing the insights of Harlan Paul Douglass's 1925 *The Suburban Trend*, Karen Beck Pooley notes that suburbs range widely in function, and that factors beyond a suburb's borders, namely regional economic strength, largely determine the local labor market, housing prices, and the magnitude of poverty. Scholars hinge their academic careers on typologizing recent suburbs, slicing demographic, income, tenure, and labor force statistics to categorize suburbs by age (i.e., mature suburbs, inner-ring suburbs, first suburbs, and first-tier suburbs), propensity for decline (i.e., developing, distressed, "at risk," etc.), or the relation between diversity, incomes, and property values, among others.[6] Using the categories laid out in Alan Berube and Emily Kneebone's influential *Confronting Suburban Poverty*, Long Island sits somewhere between the lower categories of "at risk" and "distressed." This is thanks to the bi-county's anemic job and population growth (0.6 percent and 0.4 percent from 2000 and 2010, respectively), as well as its steady poverty levels compared to the country's most hard-hit suburban areas. If anything, Long Island, and metropolitan New York generally, has been remarkably stable over time—affluent hamlets have remained so since their founding, as have poor enclaves.[7]

The primary shift on Long Island has not been rising absolute poverty, but rising inequality and corresponding relative poverty, mirroring the national chasm. In this sense, Long Island is indeed a representative case study, particularly as the problems from the postwar period—defense dependence for decent-paying jobs in an otherwise divided labor market, the squeeze between low wages and high housing costs, and the private market approach to addressing poverty—only intensified in the late twentieth and early twenty-first centuries. Defense money dried up, while growing diversity aligned with an expanding "informal" labor market. Wages couldn't keep up with skyrocketing housing prices, increasing "shelter poverty" and spreading housing informality. Market ideology forced more people to depend on their housing equity or meager means-tested programs for survival. Antipoverty policy, meanwhile, still focuses on expanding "opportunity" in an economy with fewer prospects. Long Islanders face what all Americans do.

### The Familiar Boom

Long Island was not immune to the economic stagnation of the 1970s. Job growth slowed to half its postwar rate, unemployment averaged higher than the postwar boom, and only the top half of families in Suffolk County saw any real income gains during the decade. In some respects, Long Island fared worse than the nation. Young people and retirees left the island, and Nassau County's population dropped 8 percent during the decade, a dynamic only repeated in other parts of New York State and Rhode Island. Poverty's trajectory bucked the national trend, growing rather than declining. More importantly, working-age families, particularly the nearly doubling of female-headed households, drove the rise (figure A.1).[8] A local union official summarized the general feeling in 1978: "I was a lot like other people who felt because of our growth through the '50s that Long Island would always prosper and grow, but our economic expansion has come to a halt. Considering our present unemployment figures and high costs, I have very little optimism for the immediate future of Long Island."[9]

In the postwar years, Long Island epitomized the nation's rising living standards; by the 1970s, the suburb symbolized America's declining material well-being. At the national level, both Republicans and Democrats did not restore growth, leaving Americans mired in high inflation and unemployment for the decade. Left with few options, Long Islanders weathered the decade in familiar ways. They doubled or tripled up in single-family houses, taking in roomers for some extra rent, or watching inflation shrink their mortgage debt. By the 1980s, Long Islanders rode Reagan's defense spending spree, the dizzying rise in property values, and the ascendance of the world's financial capital only a brief commuter train ride away. Without alternatives, the suburb relied on what had worked since 1940, even if it delivered the goods to fewer people.

While the inflationary spiral eroded living standards, Long Island homeowners felt some benefits, particularly because it coincided with a sharp decline in homebuilding. While there was no real increased housing value, inflation nonetheless doubled housing prices, helping incumbent homeowners whose real mortgage debt fell over time. But aspiring homebuyers confronted sky high interest rates, forced into the already constricted rental market.[10] Stagnant wages incentivized cash-poor homeowners, particularly middle-aged and elderly "empty nesters," to put their basements, attics, and extra bedrooms onto the market. They spread informal housing well beyond Long Island's racially integrated neighborhoods. As one landlord put it, "the couple hundred bucks I get help me make the taxes and the fuel costs. Otherwise, I couldn't afford to live here." By the early '70s, *Newsday* reported how "illegal apartments" had become "a preeminently white, middle-class suburban phenomenon." Real estate agents and owners openly advertised informal housing units in classifieds because they rarely faced any consequences. Nassau County formed a Priorities Commission to study informal housing in 1977, comparing census and county assessment data in nine unincorporated census tracts around the county's median family income. The commission found that property owners converted around 10 percent of all single-family housing into two-family dwellings. In Suffolk County, the Town of Babylon's Planning Department ran a more comprehensive survey. Planners ingeniously counted phone landlines on randomly chosen streets, then a sign of multiple residences in a single-family home. They found that 15 percent of the homes across the town, from Black-dominated North Amityville and Wyandanch to mostly white Copiague and Lindenhurst, had renters, though the street averages ranged from only 3 percent to 22 percent.[11]

As informal housing proliferated beyond Long Island's segregated neighborhoods, public authorities finally took note. Rather than call for enforcement, the Nassau Priorities Commission advised the county executive, town boards, and the public that it was "untimely" to clamp down on informality given "economic conditions and inflation." *Newsday*, which ten years prior shadowed code inspectors on their violation sprees, now penned editorials in support of legalizing informal dwellings. Building departments likewise came around. The Tri-State Regional Planning Commission found that 54 percent of department heads favored legalization if owners lived in the homes, paid their taxes, and obeyed local codes.[12] In 1979, the Town of Babylon was one of the nation's first suburbs to legalize informal housing as "accessory apartments" (or "accessory dwelling units," i.e., ADUs). Babylon's Building Department distributed permits to owner-occupiers and inspected the units so they were up to code and accurately reassessed. Within just two years, the town registered around one thousand ADUs, and judging from a major study conducted on the program, the effort worked as intended. Dwelling costs averaged $118 per month, a third less than regular rental units, making it the least expensive housing available. Lower-income homeowners and "empty nesters" nearing retirement generally took advantage of the new law.[13]

ADUs made only a small dent in the market, however. Only a quarter of the estimated 4,000 informal landlords in Babylon town emerged from the shadows, the rest avoiding the permit fees and property tax hikes. The ADUs did not substitute for low-income projects or federally subsidized rent either, instead helping renters and homeowners who earned around three-quarters of Suffolk County's median family income. They enabled blue-collar and clerical workers to live on Long Island, but cost-burdened families only indirectly benefited from new supply. White Long Islanders were also more likely to apply for permits and live in ADUs. Black homeowners did not subdivide their properties. This was partly a consequence of their younger average age (and higher likelihood of having young children in need of the space), but also because absentee landlords accounted for a disproportionate supply of informal housing. Absentee landlords did not qualify for the program. On the flip side, white owners rarely opened their ADUs to non-white renters, preserving segregated housing patterns. While a route to more affordable housing, white Long Island homeowners profited most, tapping the exchange value of rooms, garages, and basements as an alternative form of income generation and wealth building in a period of stagnant incomes.[14]

Informal rentals served incumbent homeowners well when President Ronald Reagan and Congress unleashed an economic boom on Long Island rivaling the postwar era. Reagan entered the White House thanks in part to an electoral coalition ranging from hawkish anti-communists to underemployed defense workers, who collectively supported an aggressive and uncompromising foreign policy supported by a strong and innovative military.[15] His massive arms buildup repaid his base. Long Island's Grumman hired over 6,000 workers between 1981 and 1987, "not World War II rates by any means, but considering the ballooning aircraft costs since then, a viable business," as Grumman president George Skurla put it.[16] Long Island bucked the downward trend of manufacturing evident throughout New York State and the "Rust Belt." Bi-county manufacturing surpassed its 1969 peak, reaching 180,000 jobs in 1986.[17]

A flood of credit followed the defense dollars as the old network that built suburbia—FHA guarantees and local savings and loan—gave way to a new system of mortgage financing: national and even international corporations transforming the most illiquid of assets into a standardized financial security, which could then be pooled together, converted into cash, and traded across the world. The Government National Mortgage Association began bundling FHA and VA loans in 1970, but reforms in the 1980s deregulated the industry and encouraged mass mortgage securitization. The Federal Reserve for its part dropped interest rates, drowning suburbia in credit.[18] For Long Islanders, this had two effects: a slew of Manhattan-based finance, insurance, and real estate jobs for dashing commuters, and an unprecedented surge in suburban housing prices, which climbed over 250 percent from 1980 to 1988. Long Island became the nation's most expensive housing market, the antithesis of its golden age affordability.[19]

The two stimuli intensified the contradictions that existed since the 1960s. Defense spending propped up a blue-collar working class, all while New York City finance jobs dispersed as far east as Montauk. Median family incomes climbed 20 percent in real terms in Nassau and almost a quarter in Suffolk County during the decade. Unemployment plunged to a record low 2.4 percent in April 1988, full employment even by heterodox standards (figure A.4). Fast-food restaurants offered double the minimum wage and still had difficulty finding workers.[20] The racial income gap narrowed by 1990 as affirmative action policies and suburban public sector expansion opened up new job opportunities. Black families went from earning 58¢ and 68¢ for every dollar a white family made in Nassau and Suffolk in 1960, to 80¢ and 75¢ for each county respectively by 1990. A 1986 study found Black Long Islanders better off on Long Island than in any other large metropolitan area, closest to white families in terms of home value, incomes, and occupational distribution. Key disparities remained, above all the fact that the Black homeownership rate barely budged, meaning fewer Black households built long-term wealth they could bequeath to their kin.[21] But the gains were real, especially because homeownership outperformed even the S&P and Dow Jones' dizzying gains during the decade. Speculators and house-flippers could expect five-digit profits in two months' time, while homebuyers doubled their down payment in equity growth within a year. As *Newsday* observed, "the value of residential real estate has soared beyond the wildest dreams of homeowners and even the perennially optimistic real-estate agents," hardening the constituencies wedded to the system.[22] In a decade of declining public services and a receding welfare state, a homeowner could depend on rising values as a pension, a college fund, or collateral in times of declining wages or bouts of unemployment.

But the boom obscured inequalities. Manufacturing roared back, but the steady march toward an unequal service economy continued. One had to work three retail or two service jobs to match what Grumman paid in the 1980s. But the retail and service sectors grew fastest during the decade. Working women also buttressed rising family incomes. The male breadwinner and female homemaker model had come to an end by 1990, as Long Island moms were as likely to work as any other in the nation.[23] As women joined the labor force, demand for people to clean homes, watch kids, cook, or tend to lawns only multiplied. Immigrants, primarily from El Salvador, arrived to fill them. Salvadoran immigrants were almost non-existent prior to 1980; by the early 1990s, an estimated 90,000, most undocumented, lived on Long Island. Echoing the earlier waves of poor suburbanites, Salvadorans escaped the brutal Salvadoran Civil War for a better life. Vividly narrated by Sarah Mahler in *American Dreaming*, Salvadoran migrants fled murder and forced conscription in their war-torn country, faced extortion, theft, and rape as they were trafficked across Mexico, evaded immigration enforcement at the US border, and then made their way to Nassau and Suffolk Counties through word-of-mouth contacts.[24]

Arriving with less than seven years of educational experience, little command of the English language, and with many lacking papers (especially problematic after the Immigration Reform and Control Act of 1986 made it illegal to hire undocumented workers), Salvadorans took the most marginal jobs. They worked in what scholars referred to as the "informal" job sector, cobbling together inconsistent incomes from day labor, housecleaning, child-rearing, waste management, or periodic factory jobs. Like their poor suburban predecessors, they lacked any of the labor protections afforded to Americans in the formal economy. Their undocumented status intensified exploitation, as deportation proved an effective threat against labor demands. Their incomes reflected their marginal status: they earned around half of Long Island workers in the late '80s and early '90s, below poverty for a family and slightly above for single migrants, who sent $200 to $300 per month to family in El Salvador.[25]

Shelter costs ate away at wage gains, blunting the '80s boom. As Long Island's average home price reached $190,000 in Nassau ($480,000 in 2021) and $157,000 in Suffolk ($396,000 in 2021) by the late '80s, Polytechnic University economist Thomas Conoscenti calculated that the average family could not afford the median priced home. Banks solved this by simply extending credit beyond old lending rules of thumb. By 1989, over a third of all households spent more than the new 30 percent income threshold that experts now agreed distinguished safe debtors from burdened ones. This was nearly one and a half times the national average. For those in white-collar or skilled blue-collar jobs, crossing the 30 percent benchmark signified what it always had: a slightly smaller home than one wished, perhaps a little further from work, but nonetheless an investment that could return more than the soaring stock market. But for households making less than half the region's median, costs were oppressive. Fifty-seven percent of relatively poor households devoted at least half of their income to housing in 1989, and only one in ten managed to find shelter under the "affordable" 30 percent threshold.[26]

High housing costs, low wages, informal jobs, and the undocumented migrants who filled them undermined Long Island's roaring eighties mirage. Between 1985 and 1990 alone, over 250,000 people left Long Island. Nearly 40 percent of working-age adults in their prime years (35–44) moved elsewhere.[27] The Long Island Regional Planning Board calculated that informal housing made up more than half of all new housing units in the 1980s.[28] Curiously, the bi-county suburb recorded its lowest poverty rate and fewest absolute number of poor people in 1990, a quarter drop from the previous decade (figure A.1). But activists accused the Census Bureau of undercounting the poor.[29] The bureau stood by their numbers, but Jill Winter, executive director for the Huntington Coalition for the Homeless, called the numbers "ludicrous." "There are thousands of people who are homeless or doubled up and tripled up in illegal residences. What we're seeing is an illusion." Local officials agreed that federal enumerators missed informal tenants. As Jack O'Connell of the Nassau County Health and Welfare Council put it, "most of the poor on Long Island live in illegal housing settings, and they are disinclined to be counted by any government entity."[30]

Evidence suggests they did indeed neglect to count thousands. The Long Island Lighting Company (LILCO) kept meticulous records of installed meters and building permits. LILCO's numbers indicated legal households. Census workers counted people regardless of their living arrangement. In 1970, the Census recorded 3 percent more households than LILCO did. Ten years later, the Census counted 10 percent more households, a possible reflection of proliferating informal housing during the decade. But in 1990 the numbers flipped: LILCO recorded 35 percent more households than the Census. Sarah Mahler's 1990 Alternative Enumeration for the Census Bureau revealed how the Census skipped the undocumented. Through an intense door-to-door canvass on a three-block area in a North Shore domestic enclave, Mahler found striking contrasts between the official count and her tallies. Where the Census found 116 people, Mahler counted 249. Entire households accounted for 86 percent of the misses, including a four-story boarding house with fourteen units for which a single census form sat in the mailbox. Many were undocumented Salvadorans, but the unrecorded included non-Hispanic Black and white Long Islanders, Puerto Ricans, and Colombians.[31]

Official poverty measures also ignored housing, the ever-present but increasingly relevant factor driving suburban deprivation and distress. Rising homelessness, the logical outcome of rising prices and trailing wages, revealed how shelter costs impoverished people. Though likely present throughout the postwar period, their numbers remained small enough that Long Island had no emergency shelters aside from the motel system. Applicants to Nassau and Suffolk's social services doubled in the mid-1980s. Working families making an average of $17,000 a year, above the poverty line for all but the largest households, made up a significant proportion of welfare clients. They included families like the Pettuses. James and Linda Pettus had met in Freeport High School, and following graduation, James worked as a security guard while Linda was a pediatric aide. Despite steady incomes, James and Linda decided to move to North Carolina for cheaper housing, like so many Long Islanders their age. But James had difficulty finding anything beyond fast-food counter jobs down South. They decided to head back to Long Island in 1988. While James easily secured a handyman job, finding a home proved impossible. The Pettuses quickly discovered they could no longer afford the apartments they rented only a few years prior. Humiliated, James moved Linda and the kids into a relative's home nearby while he lived in their car. He could only stand the arrangement for two hot summer months before the family turned to social services. The agency first placed them in a Roosevelt basement rental (likely informal), but the landlord cut off water and heat to drive them out. Then social services moved them into the Rosa Parks Shelter in Roosevelt, one of seven that the Interfaith Nutrition Network charity managed on Long Island. The organization opened Long Island's first shelters in 1988, joining the newly formed Nassau–Suffolk Coalition for the Homeless that same year, the bi-county's first organization devoted to counting and serving the suburban homeless.[32]

The disconnect between rising homelessness and declining poverty rates, between gains for Long Island's long oppressed residents and widespread exploitation for newly arrived poor suburbanites, and between rising home values versus fleeing young all reflected the intensifying contradictions of suburban prosperity. Long Island bucked the dominant trends evident across the Northeast, prospering from dynamics that long buttressed its affluence: a resurgent New York City, aggressive US foreign policy, and a revised mortgage structure juicing housing prices. It made for a good decade and an oppressive one all the same. As the Cold War waned and banks began to falter under the weight of indebtedness, questions about suburbia's future took center stage. Those in power drew on the recent past for solutions.

## The Last Peace Dividend

By the late 1980s, Long Island's boom went bust. While economic statistics depict the 1990 recession as "short and shallow," national data obscures regional severity. An outcome of the high interest rates following the savings and loan crisis, along with gunbelt-specific defense cuts, the recession hit the Northeast and West Coast most acutely. New York State lost more jobs in 1991 than at any time since 1945. Nassau–Suffolk shed just under 64,000 jobs between 1989 and 1991, second only to Manhattan's purge of 167,000. Whereas upstate regions or the city's manufacturing base commonly bore the brunt of downturns, this time was different. Contract losses got Long Island's slump started early, first with Fairchild Republic, then Grumman. After a canceled contract in 1985, Fairchild closed the Farmingdale plant and laid off the remaining 3,500 workers. Grumman, meanwhile, lost bids to produce the navy's next generation fighter. Job cuts started in 1988, and Dick Cheney, George H. W. Bush's defense secretary, canceled Grumman's F-14 and A-6 intruder contracts two years later. The corporate buyout vultures started circling. With housing values starting to plunge in 1989, regional economist Pearl Kamer identified the recession's local origins in 1988, two years before the national downturn.[33]

While Nassau and Suffolk had been through these kinds of crises before, the '90s were a "postwar decade" akin to 1919 and 1945. The threat of nuclear annihilation subsided, democracy was on the rise, and the developed world looked toward the possibility of another "peace dividend." For Long Islanders, this was a rehearsal of 1945, 1964, or 1969. Defense workers and politicians once again looked to reorient military Keynesianism to social ends. In the 1940s, it was about sustaining full employment. In the 1960s, harnessing industry to resolve domestic needs. The Cold War's end presented another chance to transform the garrison state into a social democracy. And because the peace dividend aligned with a recession, defense conversion offered the most immediate source of job creation compared to painful diversification or uncertain worker adjustment schemes. If there was ever a time to wean the US off military spending, this was it.

Defense conversion was particularly appealing in a political climate where few legislators advocated jobs programs and Congress preferred tax cuts to jumpstart growth. With already entrenched constituencies, converting defense factories to other uses was the one remaining avenue to preserve a strong domestic manufacturing base, employ people, and address the nation's ailing infrastructure and environmental challenges. The 1988 congressional elections propelled Democrats into Congress and suggested broad support for shifting military spending toward domestic programs. But the penchant for budget balancing pervaded Washington after Reagan's deficit hole all but precluded mass conversion. This was especially true once the Budget Enforcement Act of 1990 separated the defense and domestic budgets to prevent Congress from reallocating military cuts to social programs.[34]

Left without federal defense dollars, Long Island was truly at a crossroads. Late in 1989, Long Island congressional representative Thomas J. Downey called for a strategic meeting to determine how the federal government could aid Long Island's peace transition. Downey was a Democrat "Watergate" baby, elected in the 1974 blue wave to replace defense-friendly Republican James Grover. By the 1980s, he conversed in what had become bipartisan talking points in a conservative promarket era. His solutions to Long Island's recession ranged from streamlining "onerous layers of government" and providing tax relief, to grounding Long Island's economy in "emergent technologies." Downey planned to assemble local industrial representatives, politicians, real estate professionals, and residents to devise a roadmap for the bi-county future amidst economic turmoil. Congress finally heeded Downey's call in 1992. The Ways and Means Committee held a special hearing in Mineola, chaired by the committee's two New York members: Democrat Thomas Downey and Republican Raymond McGrath. Here local witnesses would voice practical means the federal government could take to promote recovery for Long Island's "severe long-term economic problems." But Downey and McGrath set the tone for the hearing: Downey talked up the congressional debate over whether a middle-class or capital-gains tax cut would best whip the recession, while McGrath warned that the national debt precluded anything but a "modest incentive at most."[35]

What followed revealed the contours of Long Island's future. Real estate stacked half of the panel. Members included Wilbur Breslin, Long Island's preeminent commercial developer, Arnold Gruber of the pro-development "Association for a Better Long Island," and former Suffolk County executive John V. N. Klein, who now chaired the Bi-County Temporary State Commission on Tax Relief on Long Island. The 1986 Tax Reform Act's various reforms dominated the conversation. Breslin, one of Long Island's most influential voices, claimed tax reform plummeted "real estate values by at least 20 percent or more" with a snowball effect on the banks and stock market. Gruber contended that reinstituting real estate tax incentives could spark recovery, while Breslin added that lowering interest rates and expanding credit was "probably the most important issue in the whole United States of America."[36]

The congressmen listened and debated the ins and outs of federal taxes, credit, and banking. Not until halfway through the meeting did James Larocca, president of the industry-aligned Long Island Association, interject:

> I think there is a danger in the discussion, with its focus on real estate, to not maybe fully address something perhaps more fundamental. We can do all the housing tax credits and IRA devices in the world, but unless people have a job

> they are not going to buy your house. We can rent out your office space, but what we don't have yet in any of this discussion and probably and really lacking still in the national discussions is a fundamental policy of industrialization in this country; where we fit in this post-defense era, how we diversify our defense industries.[37]

Congressman Downey followed with an abstract lecture about industrial planning in Germany and Japan, but then returned to real estate and taxes. He gave Breslin the floor to conclude that helping real estate, a third of Long Island's economy by his calculations, would help all Long Islanders.[38]

Citizen groups voiced quite different concerns than the elite panelists and their ideas, Larocca excepted. Reverend Reginald Tuggle of Roosevelt's Memorial Presbyterian Church shared vignettes of local people's struggles. They included a recently laid-off defense worker and single mother who had to rent her basement to make ends meet, but the tenant was then laid off and unable to pay. Another was a thirty-seven-year-old father with a factory job lacking health benefits, which forced the man to treat his child's illnesses with makeshift homemade remedies. A twenty-two-year-old young mother recently found a job that pushed her over the home relief threshold, forcing her to choose either rental subsidies and income poverty, or paid work and shelter poverty. Tuggle then questioned whether the proposed "trickle-down" ideas floating around the hearing would produce jobs, affordable housing, or decent healthcare.

Others laid out alternative solutions to Long Island's ills. Steven Harvey, director of the Long Island Progressive Coalition, asked the congressmen to pass a federal jobs program. He attacked the real estate industry for pushing homebuilding to create jobs. He called out Breslin for his own harsh words against the supposed NIMBY (not-in-my-backyard) environmentalists thwarting commercial projects, contending that more malls wouldn't help Long Islanders prosper. Harvey's own three-point platform included immediate extension of unemployment benefits, supporting Congressman Marty Russo's universal health care bill, and a jobs program to match every defense dollar that poured into Long Island to civilian uses. Keith Brooks, coordinator of the New York Unemployed Committee, added that with Democratic Party dominance and President Bush's popularity sinking, now was the time to extend benefits and pass a jobs program. He talked of the immense need for universal day care, affordable housing, and more broadly a "second bill of rights . . . that every worker who needs work has a right to a job." With bank bailouts and the Gulf War, Brooks noted the issue was not one of finances, but of will.[39]

The Congressmen listened but offered little commentary. Downey agreed to pursue unemployment extensions while reiterating his belief in tax reform. Congressman McGrath finished with a retort against universal health care. Then the hearing concluded.[40] By 1993, Long Island's recession hit its fifth consecutive year. From peak to trough, the bi-county region lost over 100,000 jobs, mostly in manufacturing, which shed 43 percent of its defense jobs. Housing values declined 30 percent.[41] The record low Census Bureau poverty numbers came out that year. Attendance in soup kitchens, homeless shelters, and unemployed organizations, all relatively new institutions on the island, swelled. The hope of any defense renaissance ended when California-based Northrop Corporation offered the highest bid for Grumman, concluding a dramatic bout of corporate maneuvering with a hostile takeover in 1994. Northrop cut Long Island's workforce to a bare minimum and sold Grumman's equipment in a fire sale.[42] Congressional representative Downey for his part sponsored three unemployment extensions, four jobs program bills, and two defense conversion bills in 1992. One offered grants for contractors to research peacetime work, the other tax breaks to small subcontractors making the transition. Of all the bills, only unemployment extension became law. In November of that year, Downey narrowly lost his seat to Republican Rick Lazio, who condemned Downey's economic efforts and promised steep tax cuts.[43]

## Suburbia in the Age of Inequality

Long Island recovered from its early '90s doldrums in what some called an economic "miracle." Though local boosters dreamed Long Island might become the "future Detroit of the East" on the eve of World War II, the suburb avoided Motor City's fate in the '90s. This was mostly thanks to New York City's resurgence. For all the conversion and diversification talk, it was Wall Street that pulled Long Island in when the suburb fell out of the federal orbit. But post–Cold War growth resembled the Gold Coast era. Housing prices spiraled higher, poverty rates marched upward, and the middle class has been slowly and steadily hollowing out. Unlike in the early twentieth century, when a relatively small and native-born white elite exploited the low-wage services of European immigrants and southern Black migrants, it is now a much larger, and more diverse cohort of suburban commuters and local professionals basking in an equally large and diverse "savannah of cheap labor."[44] Without military contracts flowing through Long Island, health care and local government are the only sectors leaning against the trend. Both are state-driven and heavily unionized variations of "eds and meds" that cities now hinge their fortunes on. But even hospitals and public sector jobs have wide disparities in pay and job quality.[45]

One can see the new Age of Inequality written across Long Island's physical landscape. Because land values quickly returned to their record highs and consumers were still flush with credit, vacant industrial property did not sit idle for long. Republic Aviation's former plant site went up for sale shortly after Fairchild shuttered the factory in 1988. None other than Wilbur Breslin, the developer who stole the floor at the 1992 congressional hearing, put in a bid to build a one million-square-foot mall on the site. Breslin pulled out in 1990 when Fairchild would not compensate him for any toxic cleanup, and Fairchild decided to enter real estate and develop the area themselves. "Airport Plaza" was born eight years after the last layoffs, a shopping center with a megaplex movie theater, Home Depot, Applebee's, and CompUSA, among other stores. A couple thousand cashiers, ushers, waiters, and managers replaced the 22,000 welders, assemblers, fabricators, and engineers who once hunched over plane fuselages and wings at the company's height. Six miles west, Northrop Grumman kept a few plants and a skeleton crew in Bethpage, selling off the sprawling Grumman property over time. It became a business park with a Goya food distribution center, the local cable provider, a for-profit college, an Amazon distribution center, and a public-private senior citizen housing cooperative.[46]

No area reflects the new Age of Inequality more than Suffolk's East End, where a Gold Coast formed that rivals its old counterpart in Nassau and western Suffolk. County Executive H. Lee Dennison's never lived to see an "absolutely duckless county," but his efforts to preserve land turned the East End into an appealing retirement and vacation spot. What started as an artist and middle-class summer retreat in the postwar era turned into a full-blown year-round wealthy enclave. A flood of urban professionals and New York elites built beach and country estates reminiscent of the early twentieth century. Real-life Gordon Geckos replaced the Gilded-Age elite of yore to create the world-renowned "Hamptons." New homes ranged from "modest" 3,000- to 7,000-foot ranches on former potato fields to enormous mega-mansions. Investor Ira Rennert's exemplifies the enormity: his 110,000-square-foot Sagaponack manse has nearly thirty bedrooms, forty bathrooms, a 164-seat movie theater, and an authentic reconstructed English pub. Like Long Island's North Shore decades prior, the Hamptons has become a venerable who's who, and their competition to live among one another pushes median housing prices into the millions, the most expensive estates reaching into nine digits.[47]

These transformations have skewed job growth toward low-wage sectors. Tourism and related leisure jobs have risen, offering mostly seasonal or sporadic work averaging around $30,000 per year. These sit alongside retail and restaurants, the more traditional low-wage jobs. While retail has been in decline since the 2008 Recession, restaurant work remains robust as Americans eat out more than ever before. Overall, just under a third of Long Island's jobs pay less than $18 per hour in 2021, compared to 43 percent of jobs offering "high wages" of around $32 per hour. These numbers don't include "informal" jobs. In what Jennifer Gordon aptly describes as "suburban sweatshops," the work may no longer be in factories (though low-wage immigrant workers now dominate Long Island's manufacturing base), but it is no less deadly. Informal domestic labor can top out at sixty-five hours per week, driving down wages below $5 per hour in 2021 for exhausting child-rearing and cleaning. A day-labor gig may expose a worker to toxic fumes from sanding a yacht or spraying pesticides on wine grapes. Restaurant workers or landscapers face the wrath of employers intent on speeding up their lawn or vegetable cutting at the risk of lost fingers or worse. Figuring out the magnitude of informal work is always challenging, especially because these workers rarely labor in a single job.[48]

Of course, as is true nationwide and across the previous century, employers continue to choose "races" and "genders" for particular jobs. Nearly 18 percent of Long Island's residents were born outside the United States as of 2013. Immigrants, like the poor, now make the suburbs their primary residence. They have reversed otherwise steady population declines on Long Island.[49] El Salvador is the top country of origin for Long Island's foreign born, with 73,000 residents. But others have joined them: 36,000 from India, 27,000 from the Dominican Republic, followed closely by Jamaica, Haiti, Ecuador, Italy, Colombia, and Guatemala, among others, over half a million in total. Skills, language proficiency, job-finding networks, employer preferences, and class-specific resources from their home countries determine where they fit in the metropolitan economy. Generally, though, they have aligned with the hollowed-out economy, diversifying both the suburban haves and have-nots.[50] Asian American Long Islanders reflect the more traditional suburbanization route—i.e., obtaining college degrees, securing employment in core industries, and translating their social mobility into a suburban single-family home. Central Americans parallel that of postwar Black and Puerto Rican Long Islanders. For some, Long Island has been a steppingstone to economic security. But over a third use suburbia as a site for work, taking advantage of low-wage worker demand and relying on parallel institutions in segregated immigrant enclaves for survival and stability.[51]

As poverty on Long Island resumed its hike after the 1989 plunge, Latinos have generally dominated its growth. They account for over a third of all

Long Islanders living below poverty, double their share of the population. But despite a new racialized class of low-wage workers, the poor are diverse, including white workers, a declining proportion but rising number of Black Americans, and a small but growing number of Asian Americans. Just as importantly, new "relatively" poor families and households have joined them, as the share of households earning below half of Long Island's median has risen in every census since 1990, all while the proportion of median-income households have shrunk and those earning twice the median have expanded at an even more striking rate (table A.1).[52]

But as has been true since the postwar period, income measures, and the federal poverty rate, do not capture Long Island's incredible living costs. It took a decade for Long Island's housing prices to recover from the 1989 recession, but they then rode the housing bubble, nearly tripling through early 2007 to a median price of $420,000 in Suffolk ($578,000 in 2021) and $502,500 in Nassau County ($692,129 in 2021), all while wages declined in real terms. With the advent and proliferation of "subprime" mortgages, the connection between wages and housing prices became irrelevant. Banks thrusted more people into home buying, bidding up prices and muddying the distinctions between homeowners and renters in terms of economic stability, socioeconomic status, and degree of exploitation.[53] Federal poverty thresholds are less relevant than ever because housing costs have plunged more Long Islanders into precarious living conditions than at any point since 1945. Nearly half of households spent over one-third of their income on housing as of 2015.[54]

A more accurate measure would consider living standards, including housing costs, as the Bureau of Labor Statistics (BLS) did in the mid-twentieth century. The federal government devised the supplemental poverty measure in 2010 to do just that, though it does not yet measure below the state level. The United Way charity provides a surrogate through its "ALICE" measurement: asset-limited, income-constrained, and employed households. Their statistic, which accounts for households earning low wages and lacking assets to carry them through an emergency, calculates the number of families who cannot afford the local costs of housing, childcare, food, health care, and transportation. It is a spartan budget with no luxuries like cable service, eating out, holiday gifts, or automotive repairs included. With a four-person "basic survival budget" of $54,684 for Suffolk County and $64,068 in Nassau as of 2014, over 35 percent of Long Island's households do not meet the minimum. And except for childcare expenses for young families, housing is the biggest expenditure, followed by taxes. While Long Island's poverty rate is only a fraction of the national rate, Long Island's ALICE households are only a few percentage points off the nation's overall state averages.[55]

Long Islanders have used familiar strategies in these tougher times. Some left for other states, which peaked right alongside the housing bubble's crest in 2006. Young "millennials" and "zoomers" simply hunker down in their parents' spare rooms or basements. Long Islanders intent on living independently work five more hours per week than the national average by one estimate. Others used subprime mortgages during the housing bubble, which accounted for 30 percent of all single-family financing at the bubble's peak. For those with low credit scores and little savings, Long Island's estimated 100,000 informal rentals are the most practical option, about one in five available units, especially because other affordable choice (Section 8, rent control, public housing, nonprofit) account for just 4 percent of housing stock.[56] The squeeze between low incomes and high housing costs remains, touching a wider swath of Long Islanders than ever.

## The New Suburban Renewal

Inequality grew across Long Island over the last fifty years. Wages stagnated and housing costs climbed ever higher, leaving even those above any poverty line distressed. While inequality is not a place-based problem, it does affect certain places. Poverty has concentrated in the same places because Long Island's most affluent and poorest hamlets have stayed that way since the postwar period. Black-white racial segregation has barely budged since 1980 (and little changed since 1960 really), and as of 2010, Long Island was still the nation's tenth most segregated metropolitan region.[57] Racial real estate steering and informal housing conversion still prevail, concentrating a new generation of poor and marginal homeowners into the same neighborhoods their predecessors inhabited in the postwar era.[58]

With suburban poverty's rise, policymakers have devised new suburb-oriented solutions. But the antipoverty agenda remains steeped in mid-twentieth-century ideas. Since the 1990s, "concentrated poverty" and its "neighborhood effects" have resurfaced to inform antipoverty policy. On Long Island, and in suburbs across America, "redevelopment" is the new watchword. Local authorities raze dilapidated homes and downtowns, while private developers woo new businesses and better-off residents to struggling suburbs with mixed-use apartments, affordable homeownership deals, or comprehensive pedestrian-friendly, mixed-use, and green projects. The goal is twofold. Redevelopment can improve *poor places* by filling the local tax coffers and attracting middle-class residents. The benefits then filter down to *poor people*, as middle-class "role models" bring positive cultural norms, useful social networks, and finally, more political power to demand clean, orderly suburbs. It is a permutation of mid-twentieth-century urban renewal schemes, premised on the idea that exclusion deprives the poor of opportunity. And old ideas, even when dressed in new clothes, produce familiar results. The new suburban renewal demolishes more units than it replaces, favors more profitable property uses over what's needed, reflects homeowner interests more than tenants, and doesn't improve the homes poor people already inhabit.[59] Projects in the four hamlets this book has followed—Central Islip, Roosevelt, New Cassel, and Wyandanch—offer glimpses into what renewal does, and does not, address.

James Northrop's Carleton Park, and the surrounding environ of Central Islip illustrate the most dramatic transformation. By the 1970s, "Long Island's Slumlord" had a $7 million real estate portfolio stretching from the Queens border to the Hamptons. Two companies and twenty-three employees serviced Carleton Park's units. Northrop did not rent all the units because eighty-three homes were either derelict, burned by vandals, or just bulldozed into weed-infested lots, around 35 percent of Carleton Park's properties (figure 7.1). With faulty plumbing, remaining tenants resorted to outdoor spigots for their water supply. The Suffolk County Department of Social Services still footed the bill, as Northrop collected nearly half a million dollars per year in welfare payments. He still avoided paying property taxes and ignored building permit fines to boost his earnings a little more.

Northrop's death in October 1981 sent shockwaves through Carleton Park. Tenants hoped for change. On the day of his death, Northrop's third wife sold off seventy properties for $850,000. But with scores of code violations and overdue tax bills, his widow had difficulty finding a buyer for most of the homes. Northrop's companies then stopped paying the mortgages altogether. By 1982, the Town of Islip auctioned forty-four houses and Suffolk County seized another eighty-four for tax delinquencies in 1983. Developer Donovan & Donovan bought 148 properties in a fire sale, planning to bulldoze them and build a middle-class subdivision in 1984. In the meantime, arsonists burned more homes down. The county considered fixing the places but then reneged, leaving the homes to further degrade. Donovan & Donovan started raising rents and evicting families. As former Northrop tenant Paulette Wolfe said, "I was looking forward to a few changes, if anything, it got worse."[60]

In the late 1980s, the Town of Islip combined local, state, and even federal Community Development Block Grant funds to buy the remaining properties, relocate tenants, and raze the homes. College Woods, then the nation's largest suburban affordable housing development, replaced the postwar subdivision by 1993. College Woods harkened back to Carleton Park's original purpose: a collection of 370 new and rehabilitated townhouses and detached

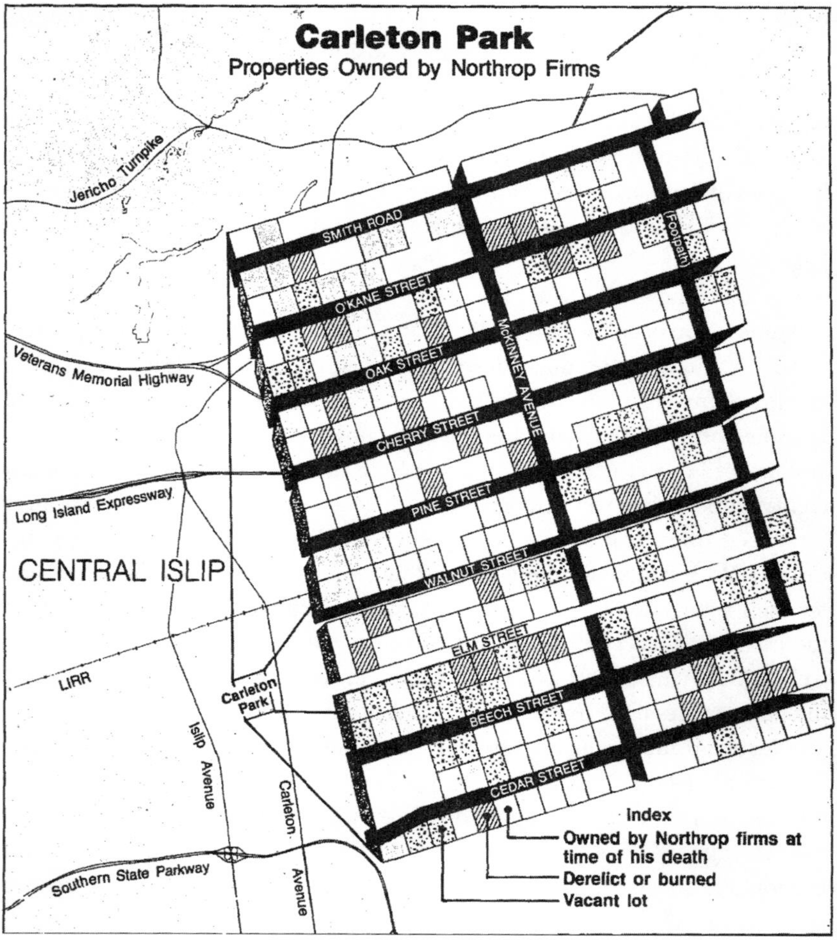


FIGURE 7.1. Northrop's Carleton Park properties as of 1984.
*Source*: "Legacy of a Slumlord: Enduring Legacy of Squalor," *Newsday*, July 1, 1984, 4. Courtesy of PARS International Corp.

units, available for first-time buyers who qualified for insured mortgages. But College Woods erased what Carleton Park became by the 1960s, a site for low-income housing: the developer set aside only thirty-six rental units for Section 8 subsidies. The Town of Islip distributed the affordable homes via lottery, names picked from drum and all, reserved for families earning between 50 percent and 80 percent of the county median.[61]

College Woods became what Carleton Park was originally supposed to be, single-family owner-occupied housing for working-class people. Now, residents enjoy quality homes on paved roads with proper drainage and sewage. Even more impressive is the fact that it is a mixed-income development, a rare instance of formal class integration on Long Island. Martha Dyson was a former Carleton Park tenant and food service worker. She lived in the Northrop-owned housing in the 1980s and came to work with the Central Islip Civic Council's self-sufficiency program. With their help, she stowed away pay raises for a down payment in College Woods. She achieved her goal in 1999 with a $40,000 subsidy from the town's housing fund and a first-time buyer mortgage, enabling her to reach what she described as her "best."[62]

But whether it improved upon what Carleton Park became by the 1960s, an exploitative but critical space for Long Island's poorest, is decidedly mixed. The thirty-six Section 8 units didn't meet low-income housing demand, and despite efforts to curb informal housing, bulldozing homes only intensified exploitation elsewhere. Just one mile north, a local Baptist minister carved twenty-two rooms out of a two-story house on East Suffolk Avenue. The rooms, partitioned using cheap plywood, averaged about twenty-eight square feet in size. Tenants navigated to their "apartments" across a sewage-soaked yard from the overflowing septic tank, and then through a maze of hallways lined with extension cords snaking around the house. The minister, himself a Central Islip resident, charged $200 per month per unit, and added another hundred if they received welfare. It was one of three properties he rented out in the hamlet; another down the block had forty-seven rooms before it burned down in 1989. Where College Woods offered thirty-six affordable units, one landlord with three single-family houses could supply at least seventy.[63]

The dearth of housing options remains, especially because College Woods kickstarted Central Islip's wholesale revolution in the twenty-first century. The Central Islip State Hospital was demolished to make way for a new federal courthouse, minor league baseball stadium, college campus, and other housing developments. Alongside these structural changes came Salvadoran, Puerto Rican, Dominican, and Honduran Americans, among other Latinos, who by 2010 turned Central Islip into a majority-Latino suburb neighboring Brentwood, Long Island's largest Latino suburb, complete with its own El Salvadorean consular office. In both suburbs, about two-thirds are homeowners, harking back to the earlier generations of suburbanites who used the area as a means to acquire property. But the racially segregated housing market, when mixed with language barriers, undocumented status, and the extremely low wages of some Latino immigrants, still encourages exploitative informal housing in the two hamlets. The Town of Islip's accessory dwelling permits, first enacted in 1992, brought some informal units into the legal market. But because inspectors cannot force their way into rentals, rooting out the worst offenders is still a game of cat and mouse. The failure to do so can and has proven deadly.[64]

Across the county line in Roosevelt, a less spectacular redevelopment began, favoring profitable property uses over what's needed. The three Stanley Phillips informal rentals, the same landlord targeted during the heavy code crackdowns in the late 1960s, followed different trajectories. Phillips sold off all three by 1970. 96 East Clinton Street rapidly deteriorated and became a Department of Housing and Urban Development (HUD) Turnkey project in 1973. Long-term homeowners eventually bought the house. Phillips sold 21 Rose Avenue and 62 Mansfield Avenue to fellow welfare landlord Herbert Mahler. 21 Rose Avenue burned down in 1980, and the town demolished the ruins two years later. The lot remained empty until 2012, when a developer purchased the property from the county.[65] Mahler held onto 62 Mansfield Avenue until 1981, and then it was sold to two subsequent owners. By the early 1990s, a burned-out husk was all that remained.

Activists targeted vacant houses like 62 Mansfield Avenue for renewal; by 1995, the Town of Hempstead secured federal funding to rebuild the homes. In total the town seized fourteen properties via negotiation or eminent domain. The absentee owner of 62 Mansfield refused the public offers. Eminent domain compensated the owner $12,000, about the going rate for Roosevelt homes in the 1960s and substantially less than the $52,000 mortgage still attached to the home. Then the town contracted with private builders to construct new single-family houses in the early 2000s. Like in Central Islip's College Woods, first-time buyers could qualify for low-interest mortgages. But the town deployed an old exclusionary tool to prevent rental conversion: each unit included a restrictive covenant prohibiting future multifamily use.[66] Single-family occupation was 62 Mansfield Avenue's original purpose, but the covenant dropped the Mansfield Avenue unit from the informal rental market.

Locals celebrated the reconstruction of formerly informal rentals, but proliferating subprime mortgages in the early 2000s undermined suburban renewal. In the postwar period, Roosevelt's Black homeowners were consigned to alternative financing schemes. By the early twenty-first century, the mortgage system took on a new discriminatory turn. Lenders disproportionately preyed on Black and Latino homebuyers even though many (judging from the median household income in the hamlet) qualified for conventional loans. Roosevelt had Long Island's highest share of subprime mortgages issued prior to the crash (60 percent in 2006), leading Long Island in foreclosures between 2008 and 2010, with a rate of 21 per 1,000 households, far higher than any other Nassau County hamlet.[67]

In addition, Roosevelt's Latino American population, mostly from El Salvador or descended from Salvadoran immigrants, has doubled every decade since 1980 (table A.3). As in Central Islip, most Latino Americans in Roosevelt are homeowners, though Roosevelt is still a haven for Long Island's low-wage and informal workforce. As of 2010, office work, followed by cleaning and maintenance, were the two most common occupations among Roosevelt residents. The former is a popular job among dual earners, the latter rarely offers more than minimum wage or basic worker safety. And because Roosevelt is within walkable distance to Freeport's major day-labor sites around the train station and Home Depot, day-labor commuters moved to Roosevelt's southern border, just as the earlier prewar generation had used Roosevelt as their home when Freeport was itself the job center. While Roosevelt's northern blocks—the old Hausch Manor development, for example—retain their quaint suburban feel with single-family home dominance, one in five residents live under the federal poverty line in Roosevelt's southern and western half.[68]

In contrast to the mostly housing-oriented changes in Roosevelt and Carleton Park, New Cassel has been at the forefront of comprehensive efforts to mix housing and commercial redevelopment. But while planners looked to include the "community" in New Cassel's revitalization, homeowner activists had disproportionate influence. New Cassel has undergone changes reflective of Roosevelt and Central Islip, becoming a Latino-majority suburb and informal housing enclave (tables A.3, A.4). The hamlet's main thoroughfare, Prospect Avenue, fell into disrepair in the 1970s and 1980s. The Town of North Hempstead bulldozed dilapidated buildings, leaving empty lots that further discouraged investment, while industrial waste seeped into the ground near housing tracts. The Progressive Civic Association of New Cassel (PCANC), among other groups, pressed hard for revitalization. With HUD money, the Town of North Hempstead's Community Development Agency established the "Prospect Avenue Corridor Urban Renewal Area," in the 1980s, buying dilapidated properties and constructing affordable single-family homes.[69]

Those property grabs, and the brownfields, served well when civic groups and local churches formed the Unified New Cassel Community Revitalization Corporation in 1999. They partnered with the town, county, and regional revitalization groups to develop the Vision Plan for New Cassel, a comprehensive redevelopment effort. They designed a new zoning overlay for New Cassel that offered flexibility from the usual suburban land-use laws. With outreach programs in three languages and over one hundred neighborhood representatives culled from around New Cassel, Vision New Cassel culminated in a three-day charrette with eight hundred stakeholders in July 2002, who collectively debated New Cassel's needs.[70]

Residents were divided between neighborhood safety and cleanliness versus affordable housing and jobs. Homeowners wanted stringent housing codes, especially limits on how many people could inhabit single-family homes. Tenants questioned whether New Cassel needed new codes or stricter enforcement. The Town of North Hempstead sided with homeowners, infusing suburban renewal with strict codes and enforcers. In 2004, the town's building department set up a 311 hotline for informal housing reports, pursued over one hundred illegal housing cases, and joined forces with the district attorney to hound absentee landlords. The New York Avenue house fire, mentioned in the chapter introduction, vindicated their tough tactics. To prevent future house conversions, the town rewrote New Cassel's zoning laws, targeting institutions, structures, and alterations associated with informal housing. The zoning overlay prohibited laundromats and public pay phones. For individual homes, basements could not have partitions more than six feet apart, bathrooms with more than two fixtures, or egress stairwells. Homeowners also could not build any additional garages, divide existing garages, or add kitchens or bathrooms to their garages.[71] Formal affordable housing came at the expense of informal housing.

Downtown renewal coincided with the code crackdowns, but New Cassel's renewal is still ongoing as of this book. Union troubles, shady contractors, and the arrest of a county legislator for bribery all slowed things down. Condemnation has been easier than rebuilding, and urban renewal has disproportionately evicted poor residents. Two hundred residential units, ranging from 50 percent to 80 percent of Nassau County's median household income, are available to rent or own, in addition to market rate housing that will eventually replace the empty lots.[72] More are on the way, but in the meantime, residents have vigorously debated the town's harsh zoning overlay district, desiring a game room, storage space, or just a bathroom in their basements, while those who support the code fear further influxes of "illegal" housing. In 2015, homeowners could request permits, provided they pay a $50 fee. The town, meanwhile, upped the fines for breaking violations. In 2021, opponents finally struck down the strict zoning codes, winning their right to renovate their basements and add bedrooms again. As one longtime resident admitted, the law never stopped overcrowding, which people already did illegally; it instead put further stress on homeowners.[73]

Like New Cassel, Wyandanch's renewal fit the redevelopment concept, with all its potential and pitfalls. Of all four case studies, Wyandanch declined the most since the failed Urban Development Corporation (UDC) public housing project in the 1970s (tables A.3, A.4). From 1984 to 1989, the county seized and auctioned 110 properties via tax defaults, and speculators turned the homes into rentals. In 1989, over one in five people lived in poverty hamlet-wide, and nearly 3,000 of Suffolk's 9,000 welfare clients lived there.[74] Drug users and prostitutes moved into derelict houses. Homeless individuals and addicts hung out in the "Living Room" and "Pork Chop Hill," two wooded areas near the hamlet's main thoroughfare. In winter months, they kept warm with barrel fires. The neighborhood made front page headlines when police arrested a ten-year-old who sold crack from his bicycle. To be sure, Wyandanch had a sizable Black homeowner class. Single-family rentals mostly blend in with owner-occupied homes, and activists sustained the long history of civic engagement.[75]

It was not until 2002, after the Wyandanch Democratic Committee looked to unseat the party's endorsed candidates, that the new Town of Babylon supervisor Steve Bellone made Wyandanch a top priority. Shrewd politics or not, Bellone's efforts started what is an ongoing renewal dubbed "Wyandanch Rising." The project checks all the boxes of twenty-first century redevelopment, as seen on a large scale in Chicago, Atlanta, and San Francisco. The town looks to transform the hamlet's downtown with high-density, mixed-income, mixed-use, walkable, and "green" development principles. This is known in planning circles as "new urbanism." Unlike the 1970s UDC plan, it includes no public housing, but rather a collection of public grants, tax incentives, and public-private partnerships to lure developers and commercial tenants to Wyandanch. Planners did however aim to include resident voices in the process, kicking off Wyandanch Rising with a five-day hamlet-wide conference in June 2003.[76]

Like in New Cassel, the meeting revealed those old divisions between homeowners and tenants, secure working class and poor. Initial plans also exposed the dissonance between planning principles and local needs. While some residents repeatedly called for affordable housing, planners nonetheless favored homeownership. They did so by applying planning principles related to "social exclusion." It is an amorphous idea, reminiscent of the culture of poverty thesis, which claims multiple exclusions—from the labor market, democratic decision-making, education, mainstream culture—compound to socially, even psychologically, marginalize people and the places where they concentrate.[77] The architects promoted the social and psychological benefits of homeownership for example, hoping to close the "homeownership gap" in Wyandanch with programs to help renters save for down payments. The planners intended to fill the downtown with mixed-use and mixed-income buildings, including units rented for 50 percent, 60 percent, and 90 percent of the county's median household income. The purpose was so Wyandanch could "benefit from the economic assets of middle and upper-income individuals." Planners cited academic research about how these better-off people would be positive "role models" to encourage "upwardly mobile behaviors" and, most importantly, a "work ethic" for poorer residents. In this formulation, glass and concrete could wipe away the poor's deficiencies.[78]

When the town completed the renewal plan in 2009, Wyandanch Rising would replace the old train station, its parking lot, and run-down vacant properties with 1,335 household units, a new park square, a renewed Geiger Park, 100,000 square feet of retail space, 150,000 square feet of offices, and over 50,000 square feet of nonprofit or other institutional services, all within easy walking distance to a rebuilt Wyandanch train station. Locals feared absentee landlords would benefit most. The town responded by earmarking funds from its Affordable Housing Trust Fund for the Wyandanch Rising Down Payment Assistance Program, which offered longtime renters down payment and closing cost grants. It was a symbolic gesture (as of 2016, only six families made use of the program) and still within the overall focus on homeownership. More consequential were the sixty housing units reserved for tenants making no more than 50 percent to 90 percent of Suffolk's median income, as well as the First Source Labor Agreement that compelled developers to hire sixteen local residents for union jobs. Erica Prince, an unemployed mother formerly living in a shelter with her youngest of three kids, received training through a county labor department program. She then worked installing insulation and wall board at the construction site as a member of Carpenter's Union Local 290. As she said, "it's not just a job, but a career . . . it's made me feel like I am . . . an example for my children." Similarly, Tyrone Davis Sr., formerly homeless, built housing units across the street from the train station he once slept in. As he exclaimed, "getting into the union was one of the best things that ever happened to me in my life." The job paid $35 per hour in 2016, twice Long Island's typical wages.[79]

The verdict is still out for Wyandanch Rising's effect on the hamlet. While it reflects revitalization's best practices, it is a small contribution to Long Island's affordable housing stock. With redevelopment producing only a few decent and legal units, the battles over informal tenants continue. Local schools still depend on small tax bases for their funding support, and the new racialized class dynamics reproduce the familiar contradiction between the need for housing near dispersed suburban job sites and the lack of safe, legal options. The recent battles played out on the national stage in Suffolk County's Farmingville, which briefly became a hotspot on nightly cable news programs and the source material for a documentary bearing the hamlet's name. As one of the last affordable places amidst the housing bubble, but also strategically located between the Hamptons and Suffolk's construction boom, speculators carved out informal housing for Latino workers in Farmingville. What unfurled would be familiar to postwar suburbanites: code violation "crackdowns," stringent housing code reforms, landlord arrests, and informal tenant activism. Here, though, the conflict turned violent as white supremacist groups joined the fray, locals hurled rocks and shot BB guns at day laborers while they waited for jobs, and young white men tried to murder two Latino Farmingville residents.[80]

Farmingville may have been the most high-profile example, but efforts to restrict the poorest Latinos' work and living conditions, and drive them out altogether, spread across the island, as they have throughout suburbs nationwide. In 2008, seven white teenagers brutally murdered Ecuadorian immigrant Marcel Lucero in Patchogue. In the Hamptons, code enforcers do routine housing raids. In 2009, a Town of Oyster Bay law prohibited day laborers from soliciting jobs on the street (struck down in 2015 on First Amendment grounds). These are a few examples of the ways Long Island reflects national suburban trends. Like elsewhere, Long Islanders harness local government powers to stabilize the historically constructed postwar suburban ideal—i.e., middle-class, single-family homeowners—in places undergoing the simultaneous process of socioeconomic decline and demographic transformation.[81] The suburban ideal never existed and won't return now. And the tools deployed to revive an idealized past, from code enforcement and suburban "renewal" to housing condemnation, merely move the poor around, as they have for the last sixty years.

## Conclusion

The 2006 single-family house fire in New Cassel was a tragic accident. But even if few realized it, the fire was also decades in the making. The eleven people living in the home were the latest generation of low-wage laborers undergirding suburban prosperity. The informal rental was their only housing option, just as it had been for their predecessors. The fire reflected the risks of informal housing. The local government's analysis, however, differed little from the failed approaches of the postwar era. And the fact that the house sat within the new zoning overlay, part of New Cassel's revitalization plan, illustrated the persistent belief that improving places might trickle down to helping people. In the 1960s, policymakers hoped to harness suburban places to end poverty. By the early 2000s, they recognized suburbs had poverty. But they continued to lean on market forces to attract richer people and businesses that would redound to the people beneath them. And that meant outlawing New York Avenue's informal units rather than prioritizing safe and secure dwellings where the poor already lived. As in the past, it has yet to yield the purported outcomes. That's because the solutions still depend on the market to resolve needs. Despite the social-democratic alternatives bubbling beneath the surface in the postwar period, market-oriented policies continue to predominate long after the golden age.

To say nothing changed would miss the headline story of the past half-century. The Latino workers inhabiting the New York Avenue home were part of the distinct shift that began in the 1980s. Poverty began growing faster in the suburbs than in cities. Investment has poured back into cities or out into far-reaching exurbs, skipping over the aging postwar suburbs with homes half the average size of twenty-first century suburban McMansions. The new money has inflated urban property values, making midcentury suburbs more affordable by comparison. And the suburbanization of jobs has attracted the poor and newly arrived as well. But the labor market's booms and busts hurt both immigrants and settled suburbanites alike.[82] Latino workers were the most exploited in a suburb of increasingly exploited residents. But what was once the experience of a small proportion of Long Islanders in the postwar years—informal housing, stagnant wages, high mortgage debts—has become a reality for many more over the last half-century. If the general pattern holds, the middle class, as defined by income, will no longer dominate Long Island by 2043, instead evenly split between the rich and poor.[83] Long Island is not insulated from broader economic change, but this more recent past reflects the unraveling of institutions that produced suburban prosperity in the decades after World War II. Exploitation has filled the vacuum. Long Islanders, and Americans, still need egalitarian policies that make jobs, daycare, healthcare, and housing, among other needs, public goods for all.

CONCLUSION

# Lessons from Long Island's Past

When Dorothy Daniels hopped into a van outside her James Northrop–owned rental in Carleton Park, she was taking part in a thoroughly suburban act. So was James Baxter, the horse groom turned plane builder. Or Bessie Jackson, the stay-at-home parent who returned to domestic service after her husband's illness. The unemployed Wyandanch residents queued up for defense jobs, or Edwin Dove sitting in a job counseling office, experienced an all-too-familiar bout of suburban joblessness. Even the property owner who converted their Levitt Cape Cod into an informal apartment created a ubiquitous form of suburban housing. And the Latino residents escaping from a burning informal dwelling survived a suburban catastrophe. All expose the popular image of postwar suburbs as a myth. Nestled among the white picket fences, and burrowed into suburban homes, were families living in poverty. The myth of poverty-free postwar suburbs nonetheless persists even as we recognize that the poor live in contemporary suburbs. That's because it serves political ends. For conservatives, suburbs conjure an idealized homogeneous, stable, and prosperous past, something we should resurrect to Make America Great Again. For liberals, suburbs have caused America's urban problems. Redistributing people to the suburbs, or resources from the suburbs, could rectify inequality.

The postwar suburban poor offer us a third perspective: suburbs were the manifestation of America's ersatz social democracy. When we talk of welfare states, social democracy is the gold standard. Social-democratic welfare states arose in mid-twentieth-century Europe, at their root a political compromise between capital and labor, farmers and workers, working class and middle class. Their architects used macroeconomic policy, social insurance programs, and labor rights to make jobs plentiful, wages and working conditions negotiable, and basic needs satisfied regardless of one's ability to pay.[1] Social democracies have done more to eradicate poverty than any other form of state-building. Generous welfare states (Finland, Denmark, and the Netherlands) have poverty rates that are between 70 percent and 90 percent lower than meager welfare states (United States, Canada, or Ireland).[2]

We tend not to think of America's welfare state as social democratic. Scholars have long debated whether the United States was ever a social-democratic welfare state.[3] The New Deal had many tools at its disposal to plan, build, and protect citizens from misfortune. Broadly, the New Deal married working-class progress and modernization.[4] But the political project produced what famed economist Thomas Piketty calls a "bargain-basement version of social democracy."[5] If we want to see America's imitation social democracy, postwar Long Island is the place to look. The ticky-tacky houses underwritten by the FHA and the factory jobs sustained by defense contracts lifted a million people into material comfort. Long Island reflected the best of what America's welfare state offered, social democracy's TJ Maxx to Scandinavia's Macy's. If we want to understand why the US welfare state was a discount social democracy, look again to postwar Long Island. One in six labored outside full welfare-state protection. One in nine earned too little to afford the suburban standard of living. One in ten could not afford to own or rent the FHA-insured homes around them.

By viewing postwar Long Island through the lens of a flawed social democracy, issues like suburban jobs, housing, taxes, and segregation are questions of social-democratic reform. From this perspective, we can draw new lessons about the institutional origins of affluence and poverty in the twentieth century. This history offers a clearer template for addressing twenty-first century challenges. Broader constituencies now live and labor in precarity. Climate change will also demand a mass mobilization that dwarfs what occurred on Long Island and elsewhere during World War II. Saving humanity will require us to redeploy the policy tools used to create unprecedented wealth on postwar Long Island for social-democratic purposes.

The first lesson is that the federal government produced Long Island's prosperity *and* poverty. The poor's living and working conditions did not have to exist; Long Island's prosperous working class proves that. On Long Island, the federal government transformed potato farms and neglected estates into airplane factories and single-family subdivisions through defense contracts and mortgage guarantees. Federal spending turned into private wealth for banks, manufacturers, workers, and households.[6] The state offered unprecedented material comfort to blue-collar workers: large homes on even bigger yards, enough money for a personal automobile, electronic gadgets, and vacations. It was the high-investment, high-profit, high-consumption, military spending path to the good life.[7]

But federal spending served only some white male breadwinners, and aside from World War II, it never tightened the labor market nor supplied enough affordable legal housing. Public provisions were means-based, reinforcing the exclusions carved into labor law and the municipal ordinances regulating housing occupancy. This encouraged exploitation. Low-wage employers hired the poor for suburban jobs. Speculative landlords skirted the law to profit from the poor's housing needs. In short, America's welfare state, forged through the New Deal, World War II, and the early Cold War, institutionalized poverty even as it compressed wages and distributed wealth more widely than ever before or since. This was not inevitable. It was a policy choice. Long Island demonstrates what federal spending achieved after 1945. The suburb also exemplifies what inegalitarian federal programs produced.

The second lesson relates to the first: Long Island's history also demonstrates how America's flawed social democracy encouraged exploitation in jobs and housing. And this contributed to racial and gender disparities in income, wealth, and poverty. Long Island employers and contractors filled low-wage jobs with oppressed southern Black workers, denied basic citizenship rights and excluded from the New Deal's landmark labor laws. When lawmakers killed day care and parental-leave programs, employers took advantage of gender oppression within the home to pack suburban sweatshops and retail stores with women. When those labor sources disappeared, employers tapped into migrant streams across the nation's southern border. Many migrants lacked citizenship and thus experienced the ultimate categorical exclusion.[8] In housing, Long Island epitomized the racist practices embedded in federal mortgage programs and the real estate industry. But that too encouraged exploitation. Real estate agents exploited racial housing segregation to flip white-exclusive suburbs to the segregated "Black" housing market. Speculative landlords, enterprising property owners, and even burdened homeowners subverted the institutional rules governing housing. They sheltered the diverse swath of people excluded from Long Island's formal housing market within informal apartments. Their tenants paid a lot of money, sometimes forcing them into shelter poverty, for a place to live.

As Long Islanders themselves learned, ending exploitation required enough jobs and homes to tip power away from the employers and property owners who controlled them. In other words, an expanded welfare state. During World War II, a tight labor market empowered workers and efforts to demand fair employment from defense manufacturers. When the job market was loose in the 1960s, fair employment efforts could not deliver the same benefits to Long Island's Black working class. Fair housing was never as effective or policed as fair employment. As recently as 2019, *Newsday* found Long Island real estate agents still pervasively discriminate.[9] Black and white homeowners demanded local governments end housing segregation to reduce exploitation in their neighborhoods. But that would only rearrange where exploitation might take place. More legal and affordable housing units could reduce the demand that encourages informal housing, predation, and blockbusting. But the FHA architects never envisioned housing for all despite its ubiquity across Long Island. In both jobs and housing, Long Islanders needed a decommodified, social-democratic right to jobs and housing. Otherwise, people played what sociologist Mark Rank analogizes to a game of musical chairs for a finite number of legal houses and well-paying jobs.[10]

This brings us to the third lesson: Long Islanders wanted the things social democracy could deliver. We interpret postwar suburbs as a tragic story for egalitarian politics. Scholars focus on what postwar suburbanites opposed, decrying their "narrow social responsibility" that only extended to their own privileges. And they rightly blame federal housing policy and a bipartisan political consensus for encouraging a "defensive localism" among suburbanites against egalitarian reform.[11] But if we consider what suburbanites wanted and demanded, we find bread-and-butter social-democratic policies: public jobs, services, and broad tax bases. Of course, Long Islanders wanted government to help them above all else; they did not want explicitly egalitarian policy for the many. But their self-interest nonetheless aligned with that of the majority of Americans. Mutual self-interest is at the core of social-democratic coalitions. In the postwar period, working Long Island parents fought for wartime day care centers to remain open. Defense workers believed the federal government had a responsibility to employ them beyond defense contracting. With every "peace dividend," they imagined domestic uses for federal spending. Suburban antipoverty activists and local politicians likewise understood the limits of federal and state minimum wage laws. Activists called for living-wage jobs. A suburban county executive recognized the value of a countywide job guarantee to reduce poverty and provide needed services outside the exploitative low-wage care market. Even in Long Island's ugly housing battles, similar needs came into view. These included school funding beyond the bounds of local property tax bases, ways to thwart the speculative pressure on segregated hamlets, and the implicit lesson that poverty cannot be solved by moving people around. All contradicted the very assumptions policymakers had of Long Island and places like it. What they advocated for might fit into a more egalitarian society for cities and suburbs alike, even when framed in unconventional terms.

These lessons matter because we can redeploy the policy tools used to create unprecedented wealth on postwar Long Island for social-democratic purposes in the twenty-first century. We cannot recreate the historical context of the postwar golden age. Nor should prosperity be contingent on permanent war, climate-destroying consumption, racial segregation, or glaring gaps in welfare-state coverage. But if we identify the institutional flaws, we can salvage the virtues for egalitarian purposes.

This means we must first dispense with suburban exceptionalism. It is a legacy of the 1960s that continues to inform urban antipoverty policy. The Kerner Report casts a long shadow, its thesis brandished as a prescient indictment of American inequality. Deindustrialization, and a federal retreat from public housing support, has revived scholarly and policymaking interest in "concentrated" poverty since the 1990s. Poverty dispersal remains a central goal, evident in federal program titles like Moving to Opportunity (MTO), Housing Opportunities for People Everywhere (HOPE VI), and Choice Neighborhoods. "New Regionalists" repackage the old idea of fair share. They devise programs to form regional mega-governments, or deconcentrate the poor living in "bad" places so they can move to allegedly "good" places.[12] In the twenty-first century, neo-liberal profit-seeking imperatives coalesced with the anti-racist thrust of dispersal programs. Policymakers promote public housing demolition and forced deconcentration. This took a grotesque turn after Hurricane Katrina in 2005, when academics and policymakers saw New Orleans's flooded downtown as a chance to disperse the poor and demolish public housing. Tenants just wanted their homes back.[13]

Like their 1960s predecessors, contemporary dispersal advocates oppose racial segregation, exclusionary land-use policies, and balkanized tax systems that allow the wealthy to hoard resources and pass advantages to their kin. But the redistribution they seek accepts the institutions that already distributed income and wealth. They instead aim to rectify the unequal outcomes by rearranging people, municipal lines, or local tax structures. This interpretation of suburban affluence produces a posture and policy framework "cloaked in egalitarian, emancipatory ideas" but with limited potential to liberate and equalize.[14] And fifty years of policy initiatives have only produced modest results.[15] Nonetheless, unlocking the suburbs is still the policy goal. In the wake of George Floyd's 2020 murder at the hands of Minneapolis police officer Derek Chauvin, Princeton sociologist Patrick Sharkey lamented urban inequality's resistance to decades of integration efforts. He doubted whether the rich would ever "send their resources over to the other side." For Sharkey, we must double down, starting a "large-scale demolition" of the barricades that separate the poor from the wealthy, a demand echoing the Kerner Report half a century ago.[16]

Policymakers can relate to Dr. Sharkey's frustration. But the "milk and honey" is not on the other side of those barricades. It is instead rooted in the way our federal government distributes needs like housing and the means to access food, clothing, or medical care. John Maynard Keynes once remarked that "anything we can actually do we can afford."[17] We need to debate priority, not cost. We can redirect federal spending toward universal programs that create more jobs than there are unemployed people, and more housing than there are unhoused people. Such programs would reduce exploitation, give antidiscrimination policy teeth, and disproportionately help people of color and women overrepresented among the poor. We live in a propitious time to reconsider federal priorities. The long-standing ideologies naturalizing the market and justifying austerity over the last half-century face increased scrutiny. Heterodox economic theories filter through Congress and public discourse, emphasizing the positive effects of federal spending.[18]

There are many routes to achieve these things, and policy solutions that cross metropolitan boundaries abound. Not all demand concrete, wood, or metal—real resources that would limit our goals and spark inflation. Contemporary job guarantee proposals echo what suburbanites needed half a century ago: elderly care, after-school activities, parks, playgrounds, water quality, and runoff projects, among others.[19] Scholars now recognize that informal housing is the most widespread form of "affordable" housing across the US. Informal housing cuts through the perennial debates between NIMBY (not in my back yard), YIMBY (yes in my backyard), and PHIMBY (public housing in my backyard), all of which either advocate new construction or the status quo. But homebuilding, no matter how green, adds to climate change. Instead, we should consider how people already inhabit housing stock, and how to improve unit quality, expand tenant protections, enforce rent control, or even socialize single-family housing.[20] Relatedly, the federal government, with the power to deficit spend and print money, can expand federal funding to local schools, which otherwise must take on debt or raise taxes to survive. Reorienting "fiscal federalism," which too often leans on subnational governments to fund needs services, would have several benefits.[21] For this book's purposes, it would dilute opposition to the suburban poor. New neighbors moving into the dormered attic next door would not jeopardize after-school programs or district-wide textbook purchases.

There is no shortage of ideas. The trick is the political and social movement to enact them. But the present context is perversely more fortuitous, because most Americans now face precarious work, onerous housing costs, and stretched tax bases in cities and suburbs alike. The issues suburbanites cared about during the postwar era poll high in suburbs today. Suburbanites want universal day care, higher minimum wages, even guaranteed jobs.[22] The claim that suburbanites are America's "vital center" rests on ideological assumptions, political consultant salesmanship, and the most active, economically secure suburban voters. The day laborers, retail workers, informal tenants, renters, indebted homeowners, and young people in their parent's basements benefit most from social-democratic housing and labor market policies. Getting them out to the polls and giving existing voters choices that improve their material well-being could make all the difference. This is the major distinction between the US electorate and those in social democracies. There have been indicators suburban voters have already done so: suburban voters propelled presidential candidate Bernie Sanders to his 2020 Nevada primary victory. Ilhan Omar and Rashida Tlaib represent suburban districts in the House of Representatives.[23]

Most importantly, political possibilities will shift further soon. Environmental collapse is upon us. As I write this conclusion, six hundred square miles of Oregon burn, bringing smoke that blots out the sun here in New York. Mass-transit riders held onto subway straps to avoid drowning in Zhengzhou, China as catastrophic flooding filled train tunnels. British Columbia recorded temperatures of 121 degrees Fahrenheit, a high once newsworthy for Jacobabad, Pakistan. By the time you read this book, dozens more events like these will have occurred. While no place is safe or free from responsibility, suburbs are both a major cause and victim of climate change. Affluent places like Long Island disproportionately spew carbon emissions. And as sprawling, low-density built environments, suburbs are acutely vulnerable to flooding, hurricanes, and forest fires. This is especially true for Long Island, which juts out into the Atlantic Ocean. Climate change will no doubt come to dominate the political landscape. Saving suburbs, cities, and humanity itself will require resilient suburban infrastructure, a lower suburban carbon footprint, and replacing material consumption with sustainable human services. To do any of these things, we must put people to work on a scale that will dwarf any effort in human history. Long Island's model of war mobilization, and its effects on full employment and equality, can serve as a model to stave off the worst possible future. Otherwise, Long Island's great equalizer may very well be the sea.

## *Acknowledgments*

As any author knows, writing is often a miserable slog. Acknowledgments really celebrate those who have either eased an author's agony or suffered alongside them—or both. What follows is a catalog of those who enlivened an otherwise solitary endeavor, who helped the author think and write clearly, and who reminded the author of life's more important things.

First, to those who made the book possible. I must begin by thanking the history professor who planted the seeds that grew into this book. Before college, I wasn't aware that the humdrum suburbia where I lived could be such an exciting and important field of historical inquiry. But Philip Nicholson at Nassau Community College changed that. His "Racism in the Modern World" course blew my mind, and this book attempts to answer a classroom tangent about Long Island's segregation from years ago. I hope it succeeds.

I could not have found any answers without the evidence librarians and archivists unearthed for me. The staff at the Long Island Studies Institute, especially Debra Willett, happily obliged my endless requests for microfilm, old newspapers, VHS tapes, and esoteric folders. Kristen Nyitray and Lynn Toscano of Stony Brook University's Special Collections not only retrieved material unknown to me but were so welcoming and friendly while doing so. I want to tailor my next book project to their archive. I would also like to thank others for lending their time. Elly Shodell of the Port Washington Public Library, Babylon town historian Mary Cascone, Edward Smith of the Suffolk County Historical Society, and Lawrence Feliu of the Northrop Grumman History Center were indispensable to the book's findings.

The generous support of nonprofit organizations funded research trips and photograph rights. The Larry J. Hackman Research Residency Program allowed me to spend a week in Albany, working with Jim Folts on uncatalogued records. My union, the Professional Staff Congress, provided needed research grants. The J. M. Kaplan Fund graciously awarded me the Furthermore grant in publishing, which paid for the image rights throughout the book. Finally, the CUNY Book Completion Award enabled me to do exactly what it purports: finish the last round of edits.

The team at the University of Chicago Press did the arduous labor that transformed the first draft into the finished book you are now reading. Former series editor Becky Nicolaides embraced the project from the start and never let go. Becky has a rare ability to balance constructive criticism with an infectious enthusiasm. One could not ask for better qualities in an editor. Current series editor Amanda Seligman picked up right where Becky left off, offering the same mix of suggestions and support in the manuscript's final stages. Susannah Engstrom answered my many image queries with grace. And Tim Mennel exhibited superhuman patience as I blew past deadlines. Finally, I must thank the anonymous peer reviewers. Each took the time to truly understand what I was trying to argue, suggesting ways I could better deploy my evidence and express myself cogently. This book's strengths are thanks to the editors and reviewers who made it so. The book's weaknesses are the outcome of not heeding their advice.

Many, many colleagues read the many, many drafts this book went through. Linta Varghese, Alexander Zevin, Stuart Parker, Emma Tsui, Jacob Apkarian, Carol Giardina, and Katherine Chen offered invaluable critiques during the CUNY Faculty Fellows program. The CUNY Graduate Center faculty, especially Thomas Kessner, Clarence Taylor, and Joshua Freeman, sharpened the book's loose concepts. And without developmental editor Margaret Puskar-Pasewicz, the thesis would have remained muddled. I owe Margaret for so much, but above all, for her clear thinking.

Friends went beyond. Former colleague Megan Elias took time from her busy writing schedule to offer insightful comments on early drafts. But more than that, she encouraged me to push further and embrace revisions. Nicholas Juravich did the same. I owe a special debt to Michael Glass. Our research intersects, as the many references to his work reveal. But they do not reflect his influence on this book's scholarly intervention. It would be a much weaker contribution without him.

I especially want to thank three friends who were in the trenches alongside me during revisions: Brendan Cooper, Michael Brenes, and Peter-Christian Aigner. They read the true garbage, the stream-of-consciousness first-draft drivel that leapt from my fingers onto the screen. I'm amazed they made sense of it and managed to edit the stuff! Without their insight and support, this book would have never crossed the finish line. Mike is a fount of knowledge on Cold

War political economy, but more importantly, someone I could turn to for advice beyond our shared historical interests. Brendan didn't just read and comment on my work, but also spent hours on the phone going over the book line by line. I think he missed dinner on several occasions. My apologies to Claudia.

Peter deserves his own acknowledgments altogether. He's read everything several times. He picked up the phone at whatever hour I beckoned him. When we hung out, he sat through my ruminations on urban history, poverty concepts, and economic theory. We should have been enjoying food or a movie, but he graciously entertained my self-absorption. Most importantly, he liberated me from the worst bouts of writer's block. It will take years to repay the debt.

Finally, we reach those who had the privilege of both easing my agony and suffering alongside me. No single scholar shaped my work more than my mentor, Judith Stein. Her scholarship is cited throughout the notes. She read repeated drafts, each returned with copious commentary, and all within a few weeks (or days) after I sent them. She never settled for generic claims, demanded I reconsider conventional interpretations, combed each sentence in every draft for assertions without evidence, and motivated me to probe deeper into the sources. Her rigor didn't deflate though; she instead matched it with exceptional encouragement. When she passed, the profession lost an intellectual giant. Anyone who knew her lost a pillar of support. I hope this book would make her proud.

My family took care of everything around the book. If not for my mom, dad, and brother, I literally could not have finished it. They kept the kids occupied so I could belch out a few hundred words in the local library, coffeehouse, or their basement if need be. The kids loved their days with Nana and Grandpa; I was thankfully the last thing on the kids' minds. My mother and father-in-law were saviors too. I pricked my fingers one too many times while writing in my mother-in-law's sewing room.

While I've contended all of the above people are important to this book (which they are!), none compare to the love of my life, Marie. When I needed time to write, she delicately balanced her career with caring for the kids, the house, mealtime, and most importantly, our children's bedtime routines. And after she finished all that and I sauntered downstairs all bleary-eyed, she commiserated about the trials and tribulations of revising. I couldn't have finished the book, satisfied our family's caloric needs, or kept my sanity without her. Now that we can hold the book in our hands, I'm looking forward to more fun and less work.

Last, but certainly not least, I want to thank my children for exhibiting a patience unusual for their age. Both were born at various stages of this manuscript. And both have been the greatest distractions a writer could ask for. I could barely stand sitting at a computer whenever Kieran burst into the room, smiling ear-to-ear, with a new gardening, building block, or holiday decorating idea. Kieran, I can't wait to jump into your bottomless joy and boundless energy. And Aila, to whom this book is dedicated, deserves the final thanks. In the time it took me to write one book, you wrote two dozen. Few things were more difficult than having to say "in a little bit" when you asked me to read your book, look at your painting, or play your video game. But you patiently waited every time. Now, I'll get to say "right away" whenever you finish your latest passion project. I cannot find the words to express how much I love you and your brother. Nor how much I'm looking forward to spending the rest of my days building basement city, drinking slushies, and mining deepslate.

# *Appendix*

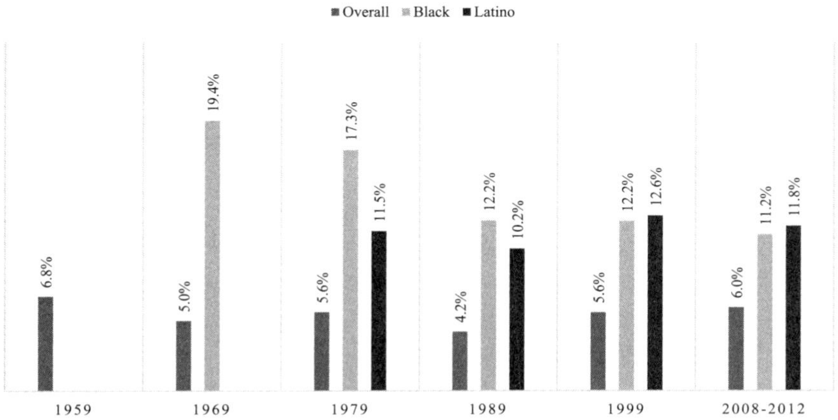


FIGURE A.1. Federal poverty rates by race/ethnicity, Long Island, 1960–2012.

*Source*: Manson et al., *IPUMS*; United States Census Bureau, “Historical County Level Poverty Estimates Tool,” Library, United States Census Bureau.

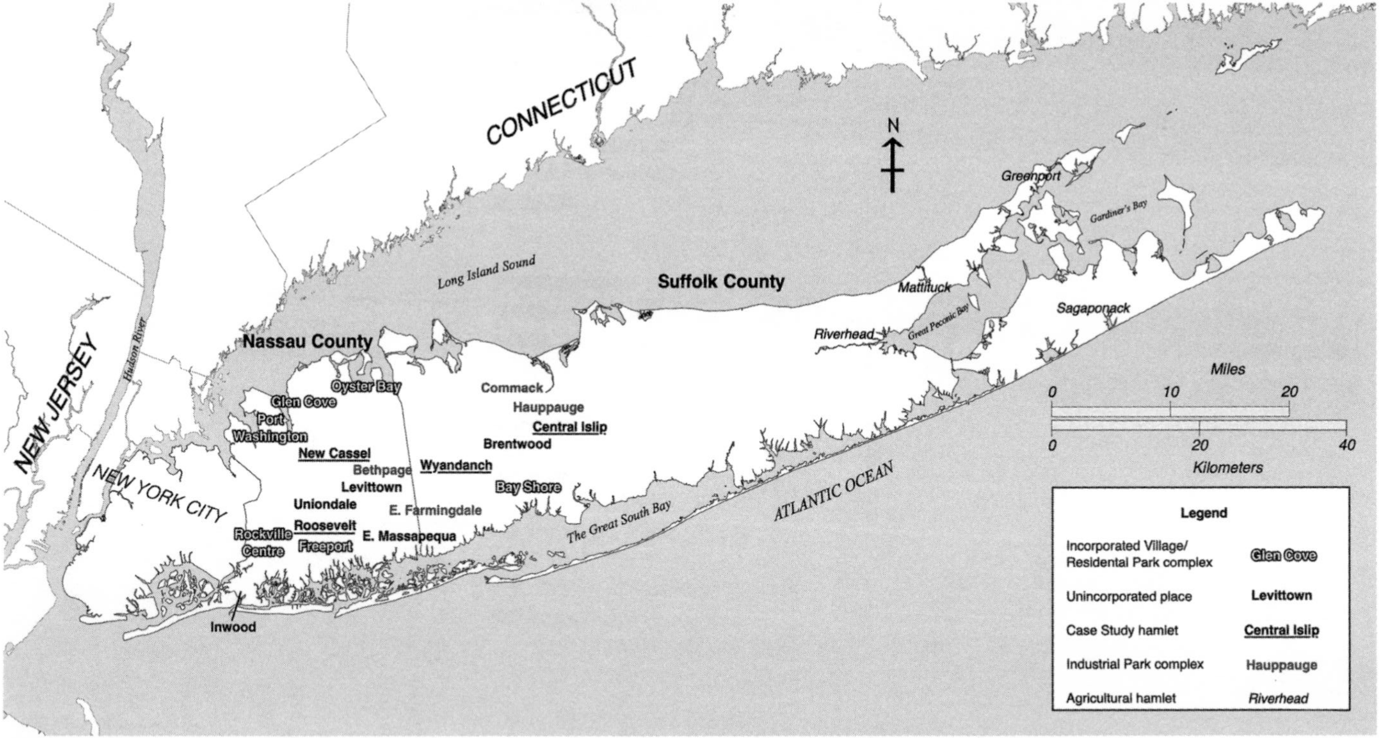


FIGURE A.2. Map of Long Island with references to key hamlets. Made with Mapdiva Ortelius 2.

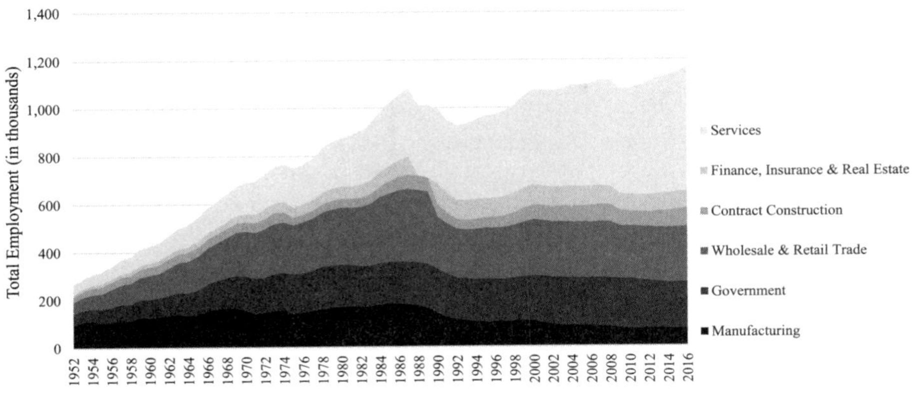


FIGURE A.3. Employment by sector, Nassau–Suffolk, 1952–2016.

*Sources*: NYS Department of Labor, *A Handbook of Statistical Data: Nassau–Suffolk Area* (Albany, NY: Department of Labor, 1970), 2, 3; NYS Department of Labor, *Employment Statistics: Volume 10* (Albany, 1973), 59–61; NYS Department of Labor, *Employment Review* 31, no. 2 (February 1978): 27; NYS Department of Labor, *Long Island Labor Area Summary* 7, no. 3 (March 1983): table 3; NYS Department of Labor, *Annual Labor Area Report, Nassau–Suffolk Fiscal Year 1988* (Albany, 1988), 22–23; NYS Department of Labor, *Annual Labor Area Report, Nassau–Suffolk Area, Fiscal Year* 1989 (Albany: NYS GPO, 1988), 20; NYS Department of Labor, *Labor Market Assessment, Occupational Supply and Demand, Nassau–Suffolk* (Albany, 1990): 14–15; "Current Employment by Industry, Current Employment Statistics," NYS Department of Labor.

*Note*: Data does not correlate between pre-1990 period and afterward. Prior to 1990, the New York State Labor Department collected their own data and then switched to Bureau of Labor Statistics data afterward. For the sake of continuity, I rely on the New York State records, and I define "services" after 1990 as professional and business services, health care and social assistance, and leisure and hospitality, because the numbers most closely match prior records. Hence, service growth is underestimated after 1990.

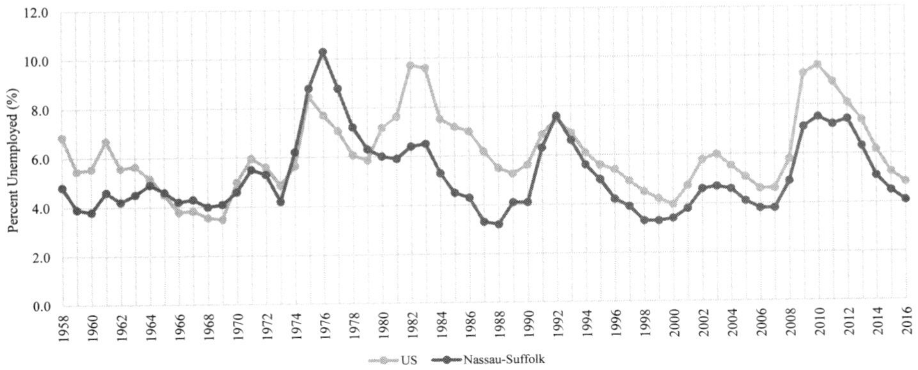


FIGURE A.4. Unemployment rate, Nassau–Suffolk and United States, 1958–2016.

*Sources*: NYS Department of Labor, *Employment Review* 20, 4 (April 1967): 19; NYS Department of Labor, *Employment Statistics Vol. 10* (August 1973): 5, 9, 13, 17, 21, 25; NYS Department of Labor, *Employment Review Supplement* (July 1976): 8; NYS Department of Commerce, *Business Statistics: New York State Annual Summary, 1973–1981* (Albany: NYS GPO, 1983), 9; NYS Department of Economic Development, *New York State Business Statistics Annual Summary, 1982–1989* (Albany: NYS GPO, 1990), 8; NYS Department of Labor, "Unemployment Rate, Local Area Unemployment Statistics Program, Nassau–Suffolk NY Metropolitan Division," NYS Department of Labor, accessed November 1, 2017, https://www.labor.ny.gov /stats/laus.asp.

TABLE A.1. Relative Poverty Rates of Families by Race or Ethnicity, Nassau and Suffolk Counties, 1950–2012

| | *1950* | *1960* | *1970* | *1980* | *1990* | *2000* | *2008–12* |
|---|---|---|---|---|---|---|---|
| **Nassau County** | | | | | | | |
| Total families | 162,915 | 326,420 | 359,638 | 355,437 | 346,790 | 349,694 | 340,577 |
| Relative poverty (%) | 11.9 | 10.1 | 12.8 | 15.5 | 16.4 | 18.4 | 20.5 |
| Black families | | 7,384 | 13,357 | 20,566 | 24,676 | 30,518 | 33,812 |
| Relative poverty (%) | | 37.9 | 36.7 | 33.9 | 28.5 | 27.9 | 28.0 |
| Latino families | | | 1,643 | 2,829 | 5,174 | 10,228 | 15,745 |
| Relative poverty (%) | | | 28.6 | 28.4 | 32.1 | 37.7 | 39.4 |
| **Suffolk County** | | | | | | | |
| Total families | 58,700 | 158,411 | 266,172 | 323,628 | 343,611 | 362,857 | 374,995 |
| Relative poverty (%) | 15.2 | 13.0 | 14.1 | 16.7 | 16.2 | 17.6 | 19.6 |
| Black families | | 5,844 | 10,301 | 15,621 | 18,086 | 21,418 | 24,476 |
| Relative poverty (%) | | 31.6 | 29.4 | 29.3 | 30.4 | 31.9 | 30.8 |
| Latino families | | | 742 | 2,884 | 4,494 | 8,709 | 16,365 |
| Relative poverty (%) | | | 20.8 | 22.3 | 24.8 | 30.2 | 34.7 |

*Source*: Manson et al., *IPUMS*, database, accessed October 31, 2017; United States Census Bureau, *1990 Census of Population: Social and Economic Characteristics, New York Section 1 of 3* (Washington, DC: US GPO), 565, 566, 574.

*Note*: These estimated relative poverty rates—half the county's median family income—are based on families, which underestimates the magnitude of poverty relative to households, but was chosen to compare over a longer period. In addition, I use linear interpolation within the Census Bureau's Pareto interpolated "bins" for consistency. The Census Bureau historically calculated median incomes using linear interpolation within intervals no wider than $2,500, using Pareto interpolation for some calculations beginning in the late 1970s.

TABLE A.2. Occupational Distribution of Employed Long Island Residents, 1940–70

| | *1940* | *1950* | *1960* | | *1970* | | |
|---|---|---|---|---|---|---|---|
| | *All* | *All* | *All* | *Non-white*[3] | *All* | *Black* | *Puerto Rican* |
| Employed civilians[1] | 206,262 | 349,275 | 688,358 | 31,831 | 958,177 | 43,168 | 8,613 |
| Professional and technical workers (%) | 11.4 | 14.1 | 15.9 | 4.3 | 18.7 | 9.3 | 9.5 |
| Managers, officials, proprietors (%) | 14.8 | 15.5 | 12.8 | 1.7 | 11.8 | 3.6 | 5.2 |
| Clerical and kindred workers (%)[2] | 22.2 | 14.9 | 15.7 | 5.2 | 20.1 | 16.0 | 16.0 |
| Sales workers (%) | | 8.8 | 9.5 | 1.2 | 9.8 | 2.6 | 3.4 |
| Craftsmen and foremen (%) | 13.0 | 17.4 | 15.9 | 6.1 | 13.6 | 8.3 | 13.2 |
| Operatives and kindred (%) | 11.7 | 11.6 | 12.0 | 14.4 | 10.6 | 18.2 | 25.3 |
| Private household workers (%) | 7.8 | 3.5 | 2.7 | 32.0 | 1.0 | 11.3 | 0.3 |
| Service workers (%) | 9.1 | 6.9 | 7.5 | 14.4 | 10.7 | 22.0 | 20.1 |
| Laborers and farm foremen (%) | 8.6 | 6.1 | 3.4 | 9.5 | 3.8 | 8.7 | 7.0 |

*Source*: Manson et al., *IPUMS*, database, accessed January 1, 2017.

*Note*: Sums do not equal 100 percent due to unreported occupations.

[1] In 1950 and 1960, the Census calculated all employed residents ages fourteen or older but raised the employed age to sixteen in 1970.

[2] In 1940, the Census combined clerical and sales categories.

[3] The Census did not record occupation by race prior to 1960. In 1960, African Americans were collapsed into the "non-white" category, though they comprised over 94 percent of all non-white inhabitants on Long Island.

TABLE A.3. Demographic Statistics for Four Case Study Hamlets and Long Island, 1960–2010

| | *1960* | *1970* | *1980* | *1990* | *2000* | *2010*[2] |
|---|---|---|---|---|---|---|
| **Central Islip**[1] | | | | | | |
| Total population | 16,607 | 36,391 | 19,734 | 26,028 | 31,950 | 34,450 |
| White (%) | 98.0 | 94.4 | 62.0 | 48.4 | 31.8 | 43.6 |
| Black (%) | 1.8 | 5.2 | 21.2 | 23.4 | 25.8 | 25.0 |
| Latino (%) | | | 15.5 | 26.2 | 35.8 | 52.1 |
| Federal poverty rate (%) | | 6 | 11.4 | 10.1 | 11.4 | 10.8 |
| **Wyandanch** | | | | | | |
| Total population | 6,930 | 15,716 | 13,215 | 8,950 | 10,546 | 11,647 |
| White (%) | 58.9 | 39.6 | 28.4 | 5.4 | 3.9 | 5.0 |
| Black (%) | 40.8 | 59.5 | 62.1 | 82.1 | 75.4 | 65.0 |
| Latino (%) | | | 7.5 | 11.5 | 16.3 | 28.2 |
| Federal poverty rate (%) | | 13.8 | 14 | 21.4 | 16.4 | 14 |
| **New Cassel** | | | | | | |
| Total population | 7,555 | 8,721 | 9,635 | 10,257 | 13,298 | 14,059 |
| White (%) | 63.7 | 37.9 | 22.9 | 15.3 | 9.0 | 6.0 |
| Black (%) | 35.6 | 61.4 | 68.0 | 64.7 | 45.7 | 37.2 |
| Latino (%) | | | 7.6 | 18.6 | 41.1 | 53.9 |
| Federal poverty rate (%) | | 10.7 | 16.6 | 9.2 | 14.8 | 17.8 |
| **Roosevelt** | | | | | | |
| Total population | 12,883 | 15,008 | 14,109 | 15,030 | 15,854 | 16,258 |
| White (%) | 82.3 | 31.5 | 7.8 | 4.6 | 2.9 | 2.0 |
| Black (%) | 17.4 | 67.5 | 86.6 | 86.4 | 77.6 | 63.1 |
| Latino (%) | | | 4.6 | 8.2 | 16.2 | 34.1 |
| Federal poverty rate (%) | | 12.1 | 15.1 | 11.3 | 15 | 14.9 |

*Source*: Nassau–Suffolk Regional Planning Board, *Census '70 Volume 2: Color and Race* (Mineola, NY: Nassau–Suffolk Regional Planning Board, 1972), 32–33, 34–35, 38–39, 42–43; State of the Cities Data Systems (SOCDS), Office of Policy Development and Research, US Department of Housing and Urban Development, accessed October 31, 2018, https://www.huduser.gov/portal/datasets/socds.html.

[1] Census tract changes account for Central Islip's population fluctuations.

[2] Racial/ethnic proportions do not add to 100% due to multiple racial/ethnic identifications. Poverty rate calculations based on five-year American Community Survey (2008–12).

TABLE A.4. Housing Statistics for Four Case Study Hamlets and Long Island, 1960–2010

| | *1960* | *1970* | *1980* | *1990* | *2000* | *2010* |
|---|---|---|---|---|---|---|
| **Central Islip**[1] | | | | | | |
| Total housing units | | 8,925 | 5,810 | 7,396 | 8,792 | 9,365 |
| Owner-occupied (%) | | 82.6 | 69.1 | 73.6 | 73.1 | 68.9 |
| Renter-occupied (%) | | 17.4 | 30.9 | 26.4 | 26.9 | 31.1 |
| Overcrowded[2] units (%) | | 8.7 | 5.9 | 8.5 | 10.8 | 10.9 |
| **Wyandanch**[1] | | | | | | |
| Total housing units | | 3,683 | 3,380 | 2,219 | 2,525 | 2,926 |
| Owner-occupied (%) | | 78.1 | 72.6 | 65.0 | 57.8 | 58.7 |
| Renter-occupied (%) | | 21.9 | 27.4 | 35.0 | 42.2 | 41.3 |
| Overcrowded units (%) | | 13.5 | 12.9 | 16.6 | 14.2 | 5.1 |
| **New Cassel** | | | | | | |
| Total housing units | 1,917 | 2,208 | 2,723 | 2,588 | 2,972 | 2,974 |
| Owner-occupied (%) | 84.3 | 73.6 | 66.4 | 67.7 | 62.4 | 61.6 |
| Renter-occupied (%) | 14.0 | 26.4 | 33.6 | 32.3 | 37.6 | 38.4 |
| Overcrowded units (%) | 8.9 | 10.1 | 9.2 | 16.2 | 24.8 | 22.9 |
| **Roosevelt** | | | | | | |
| Total housing units | 3,502 | 3,865 | 3,607 | 3,849 | 4,061 | 4,031 |
| Owner-occupied (%) | 79.8 | 76.4 | 75.7 | 75.5 | 73.8 | 70.0 |
| Renter-occupied (%) | 17.2 | 23.6 | 24.3 | 24.5 | 26.2 | 30.0 |
| Overcrowded units (%) | 6.7 | 10.5 | 11.0 | 12.8 | 14.2 | 7.7 |
| **Nassau–Suffolk** | | | | | | |
| Total housing units | 520,654 | 696,643 | 809,120 | 856,234 | 916,686 | 948,450 |
| Owner-occupied (%) | 84.2 | 81.8 | 79.4 | 80.3 | 80.0 | 79.3 |
| Renter-occupied (%) | 15.8 | 18.2 | 20.6 | 19.7 | 20.0 | 20.7 |
| Overcrowded units (%) | 5.7 | 4.6 | 2.4 | 2.7 | 3.5 | 2.3 |

*Source*: Nassau County Planning Commission, *Aspects: An Analysis of Social, Economic, and Housing Characteristics of Nassau County, N.Y. Part 7, Housing: Value and Density* (Mineola, NY: Nassau County Planning Commission, 1963), 31, 34; Nassau–Suffolk Regional Planning Board, *U.S. Census '70, Volume 4: Housing Inventory*, 71–80; State of the Cities Data Systems (SOCDS); Manson et al., *IPUMS*, database, accessed October 13, 2018.

[1] The Census Bureau did not demarcate Suffolk County census tracts along hamlet lines until 1970.

[2] I define overcrowding as >1 person per room in a housing unit, the standard benchmark of the US Department of Housing and Urban Development. See US Department of Housing and Urban Development, "Measuring Overcrowding in Housing" (September 2007), accessed January 21, 2019, https://www.huduser.gov/publications/pdf/measuring_overcrowding_in_hsg.pdf.

# *Abbreviations*

| | |
|---|---|
| AAH | African American Heritage Oral History Collection, PWP |
| AN | *New York Amsterdam News* |
| BD | *Brooklyn Daily Eagle* |
| CAM | Cradle of Aviation Museum, Garden City, New York |
| CRE | Departments and Related Organizations, 1946–67, Series 5, Papers of the Congress of Racial Equality, 1941–67 (Sanford, NC: Microfilming Corporation of America), microfilm |
| CSA | Records of the Office of Operations, Records of the Office of Opportunity, Records of the Community Service Administration, Record Group 381, NRM |
| CU | Columbia University Libraries, New York |
| EAA | Engineers Association of Arma Records, TRW |
| EG | Edith Gordon Papers, SB |
| ENP | Eugene H. Nickerson Papers, 1955–70, Rare Book & Manuscript Library, CU Columbia University Libraries, New York |
| FEP | Records of the Committee on Fair Employment Practice, Region II, Record Group 228, NNY |
| GCE | Gold Coast Estate Workers Oral History Collection, PWP |
| GR | Alphabetical Files, Northrop Grumman History Center, Bethpage, New York |
| HCB | Hofstra College Center for the Study of Business and Community Research Records, LISI |
| HLD | H. Lee Dennison Papers, Suffolk County Historical Society, Riverhead, New York |
| HSW | Historical Society of the Westburys, Westbury, New York |
| IB | *Islip Bulletin* |
| JJ | Senator Jacob K. Javits Collection, SB |
| LCM | Library of Congress, Manuscripts Division, Washington, DC |
| LISI | Long Island Studies Institute, Hofstra University, Hempstead, New York |

LWV League of Women Voters of Nassau County Collection, SB
MWP Migrant Workers Program State Files, 1966–72, Records of the Director, CSA
NCC Land Records Room, Office of the Nassau County Clerk, Mineola, New York
NCLR Nassau County Land Records Viewer
NCW Nassau County Emergency Work Bureau (microform), Microforms Reading Room, New York Public Library, New York, NY
*ND* *Newsday*
NNY National Archives and Records Administration, Northeast Region, New York, New York
NRM National Archives and Records Administration II, College Park, Maryland
NTU Public Hearings, 1937, vol. 1, New York State Temporary Commission on the Urban Colored Population (microfilm), SRB
NYA New York State Archives, Albany, New York
*NYT* *New York Times*
PCE President's Committee on Equal Employment Opportunity, 1961–63, RTC
PGC Comparative Analysis Summaries of Minority Employment, 1958–61, Records of the President's Government Contract Committee 1953–61, RTC
PNC Papers of the National Association for the Advancement of Colored People (Bethesda, MD: University Publications of America), microfilm
PWP Port Washington Public Library Local History Center, Port Washington, New York
RNCP Records of the National Association for the Advancement of Colored People, LCM
RTC Records of Temporary Committees, Commissions, and Boards, Record Group 220, NRM
SB Special Collections and University Archives, Stony Brook University Libraries, Stony Brook, New York
SCC Suffolk Community Council Collection, SB
SCH Historic Documents Library, Suffolk County Clerk Department, Riverhead, New York
SDR Scholarship, Education, and Defense Fund for Racial Equality Records (microfilm), SRB
SRB Schomburg Center for Research in Black Culture, New York Public Library, New York, NY
SWA Social Work Agency Library Collection, Social Work Library, CU
TBH Town of Babylon History Collection, Office of Historic Services, Town of Babylon, Babylon, New York
TFR Robert E. Lester, ed. *Task Force Reports of the Johnson White House, 1963–1969* (Bethesda, MD: LexisNexis, 2009), microfilm
TLN Tamiment Library Newspapers, TRW

TRW Tamiment Library and Robert F. Wagner Labor Archives, New York University, New York

WBT W. Burghardt Turner Collection, SB

WC New York State War Council, Committee on Discrimination in Employment Minutes and Investigations Files (Series A4278), NYA

WH Wheatley Heights—Civic Associations: Wheatley Heights Community Association, Inc. Papers, TBH

WMC Records of the War Manpower Commission, Region II, Record Group 211, NNY

# *Notes*

## Introduction

1. "Reliefers Living on Streets of Despair," *ND*, December 3, 1969, 10.

2. Anthony B. Stewart and Howell Walker, "Long Island Outgrows the Country," *National Geographic* 99, no. 3 (March 1951): 279–326; "At 45, Levittown's Legacy Is Unclear," *NYT*, June 28, 1992; "Take Protection in Own Hands over LI Burnings," *AN*, November 28, 1953.

3. Frank J. Cavaioli, "Ethnic Population Patterns on Long Island." in *Ethnicity in Suburbia: The Long Island Experience*, ed. Salvatore J. LaGumina (n.p.: Salvatore J. LaGumina: 1980), 16.

4. Michael B. Katz, *The Undeserving Poor: From the War on Poverty to the War on Welfare* (New York: Pantheon Books, 1990), 276.

5. Kenneth T. Jackson, *Crabgrass Frontier: The Suburbanization of the United States* (New York: Oxford University Press, 1985), 211.

6. Erik Olin Wright, *Class Counts: Comparative Studies in Class Analysis* (Cambridge: Cambridge University Press, 1997), 9–19.

7. Daniel Zamora, "When Exclusion Replaces Exploitation: The Condition of the Surplus-Population under Neoliberalism," *Nonsite* 10 (Fall 2013), https://nonsite.org/when-exclusion-replaces-exploitation/#foot_55-6493.

8. Jackson, *Crabgrass Frontier*, 15–19.

9. William H. Lacy and David L. Philips, *Confronting Suburban Decline: Strategic Planning for Metropolitan Renewal* (Washington, DC: Island Press, 2000); Myron Orfield, *American Metropolitics: The New Suburban Reality* (Washington, DC: Brookings Institution Press, 2002); Bernadette Hanlon, John Rennie Short, and Thomas J. Vicino, *Cities and Suburbs: New Metropolitan Realities in the US* (London: Routledge, 2010); Elizabeth Kneebone and Alan Berube, *Confronting Suburban Poverty in America* (Washington, DC: Brookings Institution Press, 2013), 16–20; Katrin B. Anacker, ed., *The New American Suburb: Poverty, Race and the Economic Crisis* (Farnham, Surrey: Ashgate, 2015); Bernadette Hanlon, *Once the American Dream: Inner-Ring Suburbs of the United States* (Philadelphia: Temple University Press, 2010); Alan Ehrenhalt, *The Great Inversion and the Future of the American City* (New York: Knopf, 2012); Leigh Gallagher, *The End of the Suburbs: Where the American Dream is Moving* (New York: Portfolio/Penguin, 2013); Scott W. Allard, *Places in Need: The Changing Geography of Poverty* (New York: Russell Sage Foundation, 2017); Alexandra K. Murphy, *When the Sidewalks End: Poverty in an American Suburb* (New York: Oxford University Press, forthcoming).

10. Becky M. Nicolaides, *My Blue Heaven: Life and Politics in the Working-Class Suburbs of Los Angeles, 1920–1965* (Chicago: University of Chicago Press, 2002); Andrew Wiese, *Places of Their Own: African American Suburbanization in the Twentieth Century* (Chicago: University of Chicago Press, 2004); Lizabeth Cohen, *Consumers' Republic: The Politics of Mass Consumption in Postwar America* (New York: Random House, 2008), 194–256; Matthew D. Lassiter and Christopher Niedt, "Suburban Diversity in Postwar America," *Journal of Urban History* 39, no. 1 (January 2013): 3–14; For exceptions, see Aaron I. Cavin, "The Borders of Citizenship: The Politics of Race and Metropolitan Space in Silicon Valley," (PhD diss., University of Michigan, 2012); Wendy Cheng, "The Changs Next Door to the Diazes: Suburban Racial Formation in Los Angeles' San Gabriel Valley," *Journal of Urban History* 39, no. 1 (January 2013): 15–35; Walter Greason, *Suburban Erasure: How the Suburbs Ended the Civil Rights Movement in New Jersey* (Madison: Fairleigh Dickinson University Press, 2014); Paul J. P. Sandul, *California Dreaming: Boosterism, Memory, and Rural Suburbs in the Golden State* (Morgantown: West Virginia University Press, 2014); Jerry Gonzalez, *In Search of the Mexican Beverly Hills: Latino Suburbanization in Postwar Los Angeles* (New Brunswick, NJ: Rutgers University Press, 2018).

11. Mozaffar Qizilbash, "Vague Language and Precise Measurement: The Case of Poverty," *Journal of Economic Methodology* 10, no. 1 (2003): 41–58.

12. US Census Bureau, "Historical County Level Poverty Estimates Tool," US Census Bureau Library, https://www.census.gov/library/visualizations/time-series/demo/census-poverty-tool.html.

13. John Kenneth Galbraith, *The Affluent Society* (Boston: Houghton Mifflin Company, 1958), 251; Peter Townsend, *Poverty in the United Kingdom* (London: Penguin Books, 1979), 31; Amartya Sen, *Development as Freedom* (New York: Oxford University Press), 87–110; For the value relative measure for Long Island specifically, see Leonard Gaines and Pearl M. Kamer, "The Incidence of Economic Stress in Affluent Areas: Devising More Accurate Measures," *American Journal of Economics and Sociology* 53, no. 2 (April 1994): 175–85.

14. Michael Stone, *Shelter Poverty: New Ideas on Housing Affordability* (Philadelphia: Temple University Press, 1993), 34–35.

15. Stephen Pimpare, *A People's History of Poverty in America* (New York: The New Press, 2011), 6.

16. This perspective draws inspiration from Alice O'Connor's call to examine the "political, economic, institutional, and historical conditions that create poverty." See Alice O'Connor, *Poverty Knowledge: Social Science, Social Policy, and the Poor in Twentieth-Century U.S. History* (Princeton, NJ: Princeton University Press, 2001).

17. David Brady, *Rich Democracies, Poor People: How Politics Explain Poverty* (New York: Oxford University Press, 2009), 3–19, 121–81; Pierre Bourdieu, *The Social Structures of the Economy* (Malden, MA: Polity Press, 2005).

18. David Rueda, *Social Democracy Inside Out: Government Partisanship, Insiders, and Outsiders in Industrialized Democracies* (New York: Oxford University Press, 2008); Jérôme Gautié and John Schmitt, eds., *Low-Wage Work in the Wealthy World* (New York: Russell Sage Foundation, 2010).

19. For some examples see Christopher Howard, *The Hidden Welfare State: Tax Expenditures and Social Policy in the United States* (Princeton, NJ: Princeton University Press, 2001); Jacob S. Hacker, *The Divided Welfare State: the Battle over Public and Private Benefits in the United States* (New York: Cambridge University Press, 2002); James T. Sparrow, William J. Novak, and Stephen W. Sawyer, *Boundaries of the State in US History* (Chicago: University of Chicago Press, 2016); for the role of 'privatism' in housing policy, see R. Allen Hayes, *Federal Government and Urban Housing:*

*Ideology and Change in Public Policy* (Albany: State University of New York Press, 1985); Gregory D. Squires, Capital and Communities in Black and White (Albany: State University of New York Press, 1994); Kevin Fox Gotham, *Race, Real Estate, and Uneven Development: The Kansas City Experience, 1900–2000* (Albany: State University of New York Press, 2002).

20. Harlan K. Ullman, *In Irons: U.S. Military Might in the New Century* (Washington, DC: National Defense University Press, 1995), 169–70; Nassau–Suffolk Regional Planning Board, "Economic Highlights," *Long Island Economic Trends* 7, no. 8 (August 1976): 1.

21. David M. P. Freund, *Colored Property: State Policy and White Racial Politics in Suburban America* (Chicago: University of Chicago Press, 2007), 189–90; Franklin National Bank of Long Island, *Statistical Abstract of Nassau and Suffolk Counties Long Island, New York* (Franklin National Bank of Long Island, 1962), 241–42.

22. Suffolk County Department of Planning, *Population* (Hauppauge, NY: Suffolk County Department of Planning, 1962), 3.

23. Nassau–Suffolk Regional Planning Board, *The Economy of Long Island: Employment and Income Trends*, 17, Table II-3, HCB.

24. John S. Hoyt, "Financing Long Island's Aircraft Industry, 1954–1965," in Kaiser and Stonier, *The Development of the Aerospace Industry on Long Island*, 130–33.

25. Raymond & May Associates, *Residential Market Analysis Progress Report Part I: Residential Supply Inventory* (September 1967), 31, Table 18–19.

26. Jennifer Mittelstadt, *The Rise of the Military Welfare State* (Cambridge, MA: Harvard University Press, 2015); Michael Brenes, *For Might and Right: Cold War Defense Spending and the Remaking of American Democracy* (Amherst: University of Massachusetts Press, 2020).

27. See David Rusk, "'Little Boxes' Must Act as One: Overcoming Urban Sprawl & Suburban Segregation," 2002, http://www.gamaliel.org/DavidRusk/Long%20Island%20overheads.pdf Internet; more recent numbers crunched in Olivia Winslow, "Dividing Lines, Visible and Invisible: Long Island Divided Part 10," *ND*, November 17, 2019.

28. Stone, *Shelter Poverty*, 88, 108.

29. Karen E. Fields and Barbara J. Fields, *Racecraft: The Soul of Inequality in American Life* (New York: Verso, 2012), 103.

30. This is borrowed most directly from Fields and Fields, *Racecraft*, 17–18, but also draws on the Marxist-inflected scholarship that understands the inextricable link between ascriptive ideologies and class exploitation. For examples, see Oliver Cromwell Cox, *Caste, Class, and Race: A Study in Social Dynamics* (New York: Monthly Review Press, 1959); Adolph Reed Jr., "Marx, Race, and Neoliberalism," *New Labor Forum* 22, no. 1 (2013): 49–57; For gender and exploitation, see Lise Vogel, *Marxism and the Oppression of Women* (Newark, NJ: Rutgers University Press, 1983).

31. US Census Bureau, *1970 Census of Population and Housing: Census Tracts, Part 14: New York, NY Standard Metropolitan Area* (Washington, DC: GPO, 1972), P-601, P-603.

32. Wiese, *Places of their Own*; Amanda Seligman, *Block by Block: Neighborhoods and Public Policy on Chicago's West Side* (Chicago: University of Chicago Press, 2005); Beryl Satter, *Family Properties: How the Struggle Over Race and Real Estate Transformed Chicago and Urban America* (New York: Henry Holt & Company, 2010); N. D. B. Connolly, *A World More Concrete: Real Estate and the Remaking of Jim Crow South Florida* (Chicago: University of Chicago Press, 2016); Todd M. Michney, *Surrogate Suburbs: Black Upward Mobility and Neighborhood Change in Cleveland, 1900–1980* (Chapel Hill: University of North Carolina Press, 2017); Keeanga-Yamahtta Taylor, *Race for Profit: How Banks and the Real Estate Industry Undermined Black Homeownership* (Chapel Hill: University of North Carolina Press, 2019).

33. Edgar L. Feige, "Defining and Estimating Underground and Informal Economies: The New Institutional Economics Approach," *World Development* 18, no. 7 (July 1990): 989–1002; For an overview of informal urban development, see Richard Harris, "Modes of Informal Urban Development: A Global Phenomenon," *Journal of Planning Literature* 33, no. 3 (August 2018): 267–86; For informality in the US, see Lisa Goff, *Shantytown USA: Forgotten Landscapes of the Working Poor* (Cambridge, MA: Harvard University Press, 2016); Jason Jindrich, "Squatting in the US: What Historians Can Learn from Developing Countries," in *Public Goods versus Economic Interests: Global Perspectives on the History of Squatting*, eds. Freia Anders and Alexander Sedlmaier (London: Routledge, 2016), 56–77; Noah J. Durst and Jake Wegmann, "Informal Housing in the United States," *International Journal of Urban and Regional Research* 41, no. 2 (March 2017): 282–97. Jacob Wegmann, "We Just Built It: Code Enforcement, Local Politics, and the Informal Housing Market in Southeast Los Angeles County" (PhD diss., University of California, Berkeley, 2014).

34. Irwin B. Kessman, *A Cost and Use Analysis of Single and Two-Family Housing* (Mineola, NY: Nassau County Commission on Priorities, 1977); Town of Babylon Department of Planning and Development, *Report on Illegal Two-Family Dwellings in the Town of Babylon* (n.p., 1979); Tri-State Regional Planning Commission, *Legalizing Single Family Conversions* (New York: 1981); "Planners Say LI Needs Its Illegal Apartments and Must Declare . . . Amnesty," *ND*, December 8, 1989, 3, 25.

35. O'Connor, *Poverty Knowledge*, 8–17; Brady, *Rich Democracies, Poor People*, 165–81; Katz, *Undeserving Poor*, 1.

36. O'Connor, *Poverty Knowledge*, 139–65; Margaret Weir, *Politics and Jobs: The Boundaries of Employment Policy in the United States* (Princeton, NJ: Princeton University Press, 1992), 68–73; Judith Stein, *Running Steel, Running America: Race, Economic Policy and the Decline of Liberalism* (Chapel Hill: University of North Carolina Press, 1998), 73–76; Gary Mucciaroni, *The Political Failure of Employment Policy, 1945–1982* (Pittsburgh: University of Pittsburgh Press, 1990), 53–62; Katz, *Undeserving Poor*, 102–19.

## Chapter One

1. James Baxter, interview by Hempstead High School Students, January 30, 1981, 1–10, LISI; "Robert L. Burton Dies after Stroke," *NYT*, July 19, 1927, 23; "Two Aiken Riders Unhorsed in Hunt," *NYT*, March 30, 1928, 24.

2. Wiese, *Places of their Own*, 5.

3. Robert B. MacKay ed., *Gardens of Eden: Long Island's Early Twentieth-Century Planned Communities* (New York: W. W. Norton, 2015), 10–11.

4. Baxter, interview, 1, 21.

5. Nicolaides, *My Blue Heaven*, 9–38; Wiese, *Places of their Own*, 11–28.

6. US Department of Commerce, *County and City Data Book Consolidated File: County Data, 1947–1977* (Ann Arbor, MI: Inter-university Consortium for Political and Social Research, 2012), https://doi.org/10.3886/ICPSR07736.v2.

7. Baxter interview, 25.

8. Claudia Goldin and Robert A. Margo, "The Great Compression: The Wage Structure in the United States at Mid-Century," *The Quarterly Journal of Economics* 107, no. 1 (February 1992): 1–34.

9. Cindy R. Lobel, *Urban Appetites: Food and Culture in Nineteenth-Century New York* (Chicago: University of Chicago Press, 2014), 40–44.

10. US Census Bureau, *1930 Census of the United States: Volume III, Part 2: Montana-Wyoming, section II - New Hampshire-New York* (Washington, DC: GPO, 1932), 298, 307–8.

11. Kara Murphy-Schlichting, "'Among the Ash Heaps and Millionaires': Shaping New York's Periphery, 1840–1940," (PhD diss., Rutgers University, 2014), 15.

12. Dennis P. Sobin, *Dynamics of Community Change: The Case of Long Island's Declining "Gold Coast"* (Port Washington, NY: I. J. Friedman, 1968), 40; Robert B. MacKay, Anthony K. Baker, and Carol A. Traynor, *Long Island Country Houses and Their Architects, 1860–1940* (New York: W. W. Norton & Company, 1997), 19–25, 35; MacKay, *Gardens of Eden*, 11.

13. Mackay et al., *Long Island Country Houses*, 30–31, 328; Elly Shodell, *In the Service: Workers on the Grand Estates of Long Island 1890's–1940's* (Port Washington, NY: Port Washington Public Library, 1991), xiii; Sobin, *Dynamics of Community Change*, 47.

14. Ella Beatrice Russell, interview by Glenderlyn Johnson, January 25, 1981, 5–30, AAH.

15. Hubert Goode, interview by Glenderlyn Johnson, March 17, 1981, 1–7, AAH.

16. Goode, interview, 7.

17. Evelyn Nakano Glenn, "From Servitude to Service Work: Historical Continuities in the Racial Division of Paid Reproductive Labor," in *Working in the Service Society*, eds. Cameron Lynne Macdonald and Carmen Sirianni (Philadelphia: Temple University Press, 1996), 115–32; John Bodnar, Roger Simon, and Michael P. Weber, *Lives of Their Own: Blacks, Italians, and Poles in Pittsburgh, 1900–1960* (Urbana and Chicago: University of Illinois Press, 1983).

18. Sobin, *Dynamics of Community Change*, 47; Alec Sucilsky, interview by Elly Shodell, January 13, 1984, 13, GCE.

19. Long Island Section, *BD*, September 8, 1910, 1–60; MacKay, *Gardens of Eden*, 7–19.

20. Elizabeth Clark-Lewis, *Living In, Living Out* (Washington, DC: Smithsonian Institution Press, 1994), 123–46; Vanessa May, *Unprotected Labor: Workers, Politics and Middle-Class Reform in New York, 1870–1940* (Chapel Hill: University of North Carolina Press, 2011), 113–15.

21. Quoted in May, *Unprotected Labor*, 116.

22. Marjorie Biddle and Florence Longworth Biddle, interview by Glenderlyn Johnson, January 1981, 23, AAH.

23. NYS Temporary Commission, "Public Hearing," 52, NTU.

24. NYS Temporary Commission, "Public Hearing," 65.

25. Perry Gangloff, "A Study of Community Organization in Glen Cove, NY," (MA thesis, New York School of Social Work, 1937), 5, 77–80, SWA.

26. Cindy Hahamovitch, "In the Valley of the Giant: The Politics of Migrant Farm Labor, 1865–1945" (PhD diss., University of North Carolina, 1992), 196–97, 228–29.

27. Dorothy Mealy, ed., "Meet the Seniors" Oral History Collection, Suffolk County Historical Society, Riverhead, New York.

28. Clarence Phillips, interview by Elly Shodell, January 23, 1981, 110, AAH.

29. Robin Cook Jacobsen, "Life in Cutchogue and Mattituck during the Great Depression," 55, "The Great Depression and the New Deal on Long Island: A Local History Curriculum Guide," *Hofstra University Faculty Page: Alan Singer*, http://people.hofstra.edu/alan_j_singer/294%20Course%20Pack/9.%20Depression_ND/124.pdf.

30. Michelle Mancuso, "Joseph Mancuso Remembers Life in Bethpage during the Great Depression," 59, "The Great Depression and the New Deal on Long Island: A Local History

Curriculum Guide," *Hofstra University Faculty Page: Alan Singer*, http://people.hofstra.edu/alan_j_singer/294%20Course%20Pack/9.%20Depression_ND/124.pdf.

31. Norton Sydney Ginsburg, Bruce Koppel, T. G. McGee, eds., *The Extended Metropolis: Settlement Transition in Asia* (Honolulu: University of Hawai'i Press, 1991).

32. Robert M. Fogelson, *Bourgeois Nightmares: Suburbia, 1870–1930* (New Haven: Yale University Press, 2005); Sara Stevens, *Developing Expertise: Architecture and Real Estate in Metropolitan America* (New Haven: Yale University Press, 2016), 22–63.

33. John C. Teaford, *Post-Suburbia: Government and Politics in the Edge Cities* (Baltimore: Johns Hopkins University Press, 1997), 15–24.

34. Daniels, "Bennington Park," 7, 9–14.

35. NYS Temporary Commission, "Public Hearing," 6–11, 95–96, NTU.

36. Minnie O. Daniels, "A Study of Community Conditions in the Bennington Park Area of Freeport, New York" (MA thesis, Columbia University, 1937), 5–11, SWA; NYS Temporary Commission, "Public Hearing," 6–11, 47–52, NTU.

37. Dorothy Eklund, "Impressionistic Study of the Life and Social Needs of the Negro Community in Inwood, Long Island" (MA thesis, New York School of Social Work, 1937), 20–27, SWA.

38. Nassau-Suffolk Regional Planning Board, *Study of Local Housing Codes and Practices* (White Plains, NY: Raymond & May Associates, 1967), 33–62.

39. NYS Temporary Commission, "Public Hearing," 4–27, NTU; Gangloff, "A Study in Community Organization," 64; Eklund, "Impressionistic Study," 25.

40. Andrew Wiese categorizes these suburbs as domestic-service and unplanned subdivisions. See Wiese, *Places of their Own*, 25–28. For an intimate and nuanced view of these categories, see Greason, *Suburban Erasure*, 129–40.

41. Nicolaides, *My Blue Heaven*, 9–38; Wiese, *Places of their Own*, 67–93; See also Gonzalez, *In Search of the Mexican Beverly Hills*, 15–28.

42. "Leave Out Politics, Says W.W. Cocks of Mayor's Tax Quiz," *BD*, October 4, 1918, 10; See also Deed Liber 3977, 384, NCC.

43. Hagstrom Company, *Hagstrom's Street, Road and Property Ownership Map of Nassau County, Long Island, New York* (New York: Hagstrom Company, 1939), map no. 3.

44. "Roosevelt," *Nassau County Review*, December 25, 1908, 8; "The Week's Contract News," *Municipal Journal and Engineer* 25, no. 21 (November 18, 1908): 732; Joseph A. Lawson and Jacob C. E. Scott, eds., *The State Department Reports of the State of New York: Decisions of the Public Service Commissions, Business Damage Commissions Nos. 1 and 2, Board of Claims, and Education Department* (Albany, NY: J. B. Lyons Company, 1913), 340–42.

45. "Roosevelt Wants 3D Rail," *BD*, May 27, 1909, 7; Ad, *BD*, September 8, 1910, 44.

46. Tax Sale Notices, *The Daily Review*, May 28, 1921, 18.

47. Marquita James, "Blacks in Roosevelt, Long Island," in *Ethnicity in Suburbia*, ed., Salvatore LaGumina (n.p.: Salvatore J. LaGumina, 1980), 92–94; Sheldon Parrish, *One Square Mile: The History of Roosevelt, NY from an Autobiographical Perspective* (Xlibris Corp, 2009), 21.

48. Bruce Boyd, "The Man—The Land—And the Dollar," *National Magazine* 35, no. 1 (October 1911).

49. "Geiger Farms in Wyandanch Sold to H. Levey," *BD*, April 6, 1930, D2; "For Long Island Farm Colony," *BD*, April 6, 1930, D7.

50. Verne Dyson, *Deer Park-Wyandanch History* (Brentwood, NY: Brentwood Village Press, 1957), 91–119; Roy Douglas, "Pine Barrens Pioneers Part I," *Long Island Forum*, 45, no. 10

(October 1982): 188–93; Roy Douglas, "Pine Barrens Pioneers Conclusion," *Long Island Forum*, 45, no. 12 (December 1982): 241–44.

51. US Census Bureau, *Sixteenth Census of the United States, 1940: Housing* (Washington, DC: GPO, 1943), 317–18, 325–26.

52. Sobin, *Dynamics of Community Change*, 52–53; "Report of Activities," June 1, 1932—May 31, 1933, 2–3, 7, NCW.

53. Anthony J. Badger, *The New Deal: The Depression Years, 1933-1940* (Chicago: Ivan R. Dee, 1989), 311.

54. "Report of Activities," June 1, 1932–May 31, 1933, 5–6, NCW; "Report of Activities," June 1, 1933–June 17, 1934, 18, NCW.

55. "Report of Activities," November 1931–June 1932, 11, NCW; "Report of Activities," June 1, 1932–May 31, 1933, 5–6, NCW; "Report of Activities," June 1, 1933–June 17, 1934, 16–18, NCW. The 30 percent is an estimate based on the 1930 male population.

56. Beatrice Nixon, interview by Glenderlyn Johnson, January 24, 1981, 2–3, AAH.

57. "Report of Activities," November 1931–June 1932, 51, NCW; "Report of Activities," June 18, 1934–June 30, 1935, 50, NCW.

58. David A. Watson, "Financing Long Island's Aircraft Industry (From the Beginning to 1928)," in *The Development of the Aerospace Industry on Long Island; Financial and Related Aspects, Volume II*, eds. William K. Kaiser, Charles E. Stonier (Hempstead, NY: Hofstra University Yearbook of Business, Series 5, Volume 4, 1968), 1–36.

59. Tom Lilley, "Conversion to Wartime Production Techniques," *The History of the Aircraft Industry: An Anthology*, ed. G. R. Simonson (Cambridge, MA: MIT Press, 1968), 135–36.

60. Richard Thruelsen, *The Grumman Story* (New York: Praeger, 1976), 17–91; Joshua Stoff, *The Thunder Factory: An Illustrated History of the Republic Aviation Corporation* (Osceola, WI: Motorbooks International, 1990), 12–33; John W. Thomas, "Financing Long Island's Aircraft Industry," 48-53; Lavern A. Wittlock Sr., "Fairchild's Engines," *Long Island Forum* 48, no. 3 (March 1985): 44–52.

61. Lewis, *Calculating Property Relations*, 3–35.

62. Wilson, *Destructive Creation*, 66–67; Stoff, *The Thunder Factory*, 39, 67.

63. Ann Markusen, Peter Hall, Scott Campbell, and Sabina Detrick, *The Rise of the Gunbelt: The Military Remapping of Industrial America* (New York: Oxford University Press, 1991).

64. NYS Department of Labor, "Survey of the Employment Situation in Farmingdale and Bethpage, New York, December 1940," 4, box 7, folder 297, WC; "Labor Market Report—New York Metropolitan Region—August 1942," box 7, folder 319, WC.

65. "Manager's Monthly Reports, June 25, 1941," 2, box 7, folder 297, WC; Edward Lawson to Will Maslow, October 27, 1943, box 25, folder 2-BR-146, Case Files 1941–1946, FEP; Edward H. Lawson, "Field Report, October 10, 1941," box 48, folder "Republic Aviation," Case Files 1941–1946, FEP; Edward Lawson, "Field Report, August 27, 1941—Grumman Aeronautical Corporation," box 44, folder "Grumman Aeronautical Corporation," Case Files 1941–1946, FEP.

66. New York State Department of Labor, "Survey of the Employment Situation in Farmingdale and Bethpage, New York, December 1940," 6–10, box 7, folder 297, WC; Thruelsen, *Grumman Story*, 142–43.

67. Thruelsen, *Grumman Story*, 144; Brooklyn Urban League Industrial Department, "Moving Toward an Equitable Distribution of Negroes in War Production," June–August 1942, 12, box 7, WC.

68. "Labor Market Developments Report—New York Metropolitan Region," 5, no. 1 (Dec 1944–Jan 1945): 35, box 7, folder 319, WC; Kennedy, *Freedom from Fear*, 778.

69. Charles A. Collier, "Memorandum: The Employment and Training of Negro Aviation Mechanics by the Republic Aviation Corp," January 10, 1941, box 7, folder 404, WC.

70. Beth T. Bates, *Pullman Porters and the Rise of Protest Politics in Black America, 1925–1945* (Chapel Hill: University of North Carolina Press, 2001); Paul Moreno, *From Direct Action to Affirmative Action* (Baton Rouge: LSU Press, 1997); Erik S. Gellman, *Death Blow to Jim Crow: The National Negro Congress and the Rise of Militant Civil Rights Activism* (Chapel Hill: University of North Carolina Press, 2012).

71. Joseph Abel, "African Americans, Labor Unions and the Struggle for Fair Employment in the Aircraft Manufacturing Industry in Texas, 1941–1945," *The Journal of Southern History* 77, no. 3 (August 2011): 598, 637.

72. W. E. Hendricks to F. D. Roosevelt, September 8, 1941, box 48, folder "Republic Aviation," Case Files 1941–1946, FEP; "Field Report," September 26, 1941, box 48, folder "Republic Aviation," Case Files 1941–1946, FEP; "Field Report," October 4, 1941, box 48, folder "Republic Aviation," Case Files 1941–1946, FEP.

73. W. E. Hendricks to Edward Lawson, undated, box 48, folder "Republic Aviation," Case Files 1941–1946, FEP.

74. Edward Lawson to Lieutenant Colonel Herbert J. Schwabacher, August 10, 1942, box 33, folder 2-BR-56, Case Files 1941–1946, FEP; W. E. Hendricks to Edward Lawson, October 27, 1942, box 33, folder 2-BR-56, Case Files 1941–1946, FEP; H. J. Schwabacher to Edward Lawson, September 7, 1942, box 33, folder 2-BR-56, Case Files 1941–1946, FEP.

75. Edward Lawson to Anna M. Rosenberg, October 21, 1942, box 33, folder 2-BR-56, Case Files 1941–1946, FEP; Edward Lawson to William L. Wilson, October 21, 1942, box 33, folder 2-BR-56, Case Files 1941–1946, FEP.

76. Edward Lawson to Myrtle Lebby, August 31, 1943, box 25, folder 2-BR-146, Case Files 1941–1946, FEP; Arthur Lindsay to President Roosevelt, October 30, 1943, box 25, folder "Grumman Aircraft Training, 2-BR-370," Case Files 1941–1946, FEP; Edward Lawson to Paul Gilbert, December 8, 1943, box 25, folder "Grumman Aircraft Training, 2-BR-370," Case Files 1941–1946, FEP.

77. NYS War Council, Committee on Discrimination in Employment, "Monthly Report," August 1942, 3–4, box 5, folder 257, WC.

78. "Lawson's Report—Republic Aviation Corporation, Farmingdale, Long Island," September 28, 1942, 2, box 48, folder "Republic Aviation," Case Files 1941–1946, FEP; John Beecher and James Fleming, "Employment Practices at Brewster, Republic, Grumman, and Otis Elevator," September 28, 1942, 2, box 44, folder "Grumman Aeronautical Corporation," Case Files 1941–1946, FEP.

79. Edward Lawson to Charles Berkley, May 8, 1943, box 44, folder "Grumman Aeronautical Corporation," Case Files 1941–1946, FEP; "Monthly Report," August 1942, 4, box 5, folder 257, WC; "Report," April–May 1943, 6, box 6, folder 265, WC; "Labor Market Development Report," June 1943, 48, box 6, folder 271, WC; President's Committee on Fair Employment Practice, "New York Regional Office Activity," April-May-June 1943, 4, box 4, folder 321, WMC.

80. United States Employment Service, "Labor Market Reports: New York Metropolitan Region," December 1942, 39, box 6, folder 271, WC; USES, "Labor Market Development Report," June 1943, 46, box 6, folder 271, WC; USES, "Labor Market Developments Report—New York Metropolitan Region," August–September 1943, 46, box 6, folder 273, WC; "Labor Market

Developments Report—New York Metropolitan Region," 5, no. 2 (Feb–March 1945), 30–32, box 7, folder 319, WC.

81. Letter from Edward Lawson, October 22, 1942, box 48, folder "Republic Aviation," Case Files 1941–1946, FEP; "Field Visit to Republic Aviation Corporation, Farmingdale, Long Island," June 18, 1943, 2, box 48, folder "Republic Aviation," Case Files 1941–1946, FEP.

82. "Final Deposition Report," October 21, 1943, box 33, folder 2-BR-56, Case Files 1941–1946, FEP; Edward Lawson to Anthony J. Grimaldi, September 1, 1943, box 33, folder 2-BR-56, Case Files 1941–1946, FEP.

83. Beecher and Fleming, "Employment Practices at Brewster," 1–3; "Final Deposition Report," March 9, 1944, box 25, folder 2-BR-369, Case Files 1941–1946, FEP; "Compliance Report," October 25, 1944, box 27, folder 2-BR-409, Case Files 1941–1946, FEP.

84. "Labor Market Reports, New York State Metropolitan Region, Nassau and Suffolk Counties," December 15, 1942–February 15, 1943, 52, box 6, folder 271, WC.

85. "Field Visit to United Auto Workers, CIO, Long Island Division, Farmingdale, L.I.," June 29, 1943, box 33, folder 2-BR-109, Case Files 1941–1946, FEP; "Field Visit to Ranger Aircraft Engine Division of Fairchild engine and airplane Corporation, Jamaica, L.I.," July 1, 1943, box 33, folder 2-BR-109, Case Files 1941–1946, FEP.

86. Handwritten survey, September 23, 1943, box 48, folder "Republic Aviation," Case Files 1941–1946, FEP; Sperry Gyroscope Company to Daniel R. Donovan, May 29, 1945, box 35, folder "Sperry Gyroscope Co. Inc., 2-BC-1255," Case Files 1941–1946, FEP.

87. Joan Robinson, "The Second Crisis of Economic Theory," *The American Economic Review*, 62, no. 1/2 (March 1972): 1–10.

88. Tim Barker, "Macroeconomic Consequences of Peace: American Radical Economists and The Problem of Military Keynesianism, 1938–1975," *Research in the History of Economic Thought and Methodology*, 37A (2019): 14–15.

89. "Tides of Change," *ND*, September 10, 1965, p. 6S.

90. John Gregory, interview by D. Hammond and T. Vincittorio, February 18, 1987, 3–6, GCE.

91. Jacobsen, "Life in Cutchogue and Mattituck," 55.

92. Mancuso, "Joseph Mancuso Remembers Life," 59.

93. "Table 3: Firms Appearing before FEPC at New York Hearings," box 12, folder "Statistics," Case Files 1941–1946, FEP; "Manager's Monthly Reports," June 26, 1941, box 7, folder 297, WC.

94. "Survey of Employment Practices of the Sperry Gyroscope Company, Lake Success, Long Island," May 29, 1945, box 35, folder "Sperry Gyroscope Co., Inc., 2-BR-1256," Case Files 1941–1946, FEP.

95. "Employment Practices of Sperry Gyroscope"; "Field Visit to Republic Aviation Corporation," June 18, 1943, 2, box 48, folder "Republic Aviation," Case Files 1941–1946, FEP; Thruelsen, *Grumman Story*, 55, 143–47.

96. "5 Nassau Units Granted Federal Child Care Cash," *ND*, April 28, 1943, 5; "Labor Market Developments Report," 5, no. 1 (December 1944–January 1945), 32, box 7, folder 319, WC.

97. Greg Hise, *Magnetic Los Angeles: Planning the Twentieth-Century Metropolis* (Baltimore: Johns Hopkins University Press, 1997), 117–48.

98. "Big Bethpage Tract for Development," *The Long Islander*, December 19, 1940, 7.

99. "Avert Housing Shortage Here," *ND*, July 17, 1942, 5; "FHA Plans 200 Housing Projects Here," *ND*, July 31, 1942, 11; "Housing Must Wait for War," *ND*, March 31, 1944, 2; For LA comparison, see Hise, *Magnetic Los Angeles*, 133.

100. US Census Bureau, *Census of Housing: 1950. Volume I, General Characteristics. Part 4, Michigan–New York* (Washington, DC: GPO, 1953), Table 20.

101. Subdivision Database Map Search, 1941–1945, NCC.

102. "Building up 13 P.C. in 6 Months," *ND*, July 18, 1941, 3; "Defense Housing Brings Row," *ND*, March 11, 1942, 3; "No Gas, Light for Defense Workers," *ND*, June 30, 1942, 5; "War Builders Get Tract in Nassau," *ND*, August 23, 1942, RE1; "Rush Work on Homes for Aircraft Workers," Untitled Newspaper, August 3, 1941, folder "Republic—Newspaper Clippings," CAM; "Labor Market Reports: New York City, Nassau, Suffolk, Westchester Counties," Vol. 2, no. 11, December 1942, 41, box 6, folder 271, WC; "Edelman Firm Buys 1,500 Lots on Long Island," *New York Herald Tribune*, May 4, 1941, folder "Republic—Newspaper Clippings," CAM.

103. "Survey of the Employment Situation in Farmingdale and Bethpage, New York, December 1940," 12–13, box 7, folder 297, WC; "West Suffolk Enjoys War," *County Review*, February 5, 1942, 18; "Labor Market Conditions and Employment Service Program," December 1941, box 6, folder 270, WC.

104. Jacobsen, "Life in Cutchogue and Mattituck," 56.

105. "Labor Market Development Report," 4, no. 4, June/July 1944, 24, box 7, folder 319, WC; "Labor Market Reports, New York State Metropolitan Region, Nassau and Suffolk Counties," December 15, 1942–February 15, 1943, 38, box 6, folder 271, WC; "Labor Market Report—New York Metropolitan Region—August 1942," 27, box 7, folder 319, WC.

106. For Chicago's housing shortage, see Laura McEnaney, *Postwar: Waging Peace in Chicago* (Philadelphia: University of Pennsylvania Press, 2018), 20–36.

107. Thruelsen, *Grumman Story*, 139; Lawrence Feliu, "Impact on Long Island, Grumman Aircraft Engineering Corporation" (unpublished paper (binder)), Table VI, NGHC.

108. Gregory Hooks, *Forging the Military-Industrial Complex: World War II's Battle of the Potomac* (Urbana: University of Illinois Press, 1991), 119; Wilson, *Creative Destruction*, 251–52; Steven Attewell, *People Must Live by Work: Direct Job Creation from FDR to Reagan* (Philadelphia: University of Pennsylvania Press, 2018), 143–44; Lewis, *Calculating Property Relations*, 30; Meg Jacobs, *Pocketbook Politics: Economic Citizenship in Twentieth-Century America* (Princeton, NJ: Princeton University Press, 2005), 179–220; Samir Sonti, "The Price of Prosperity: Inflation and the Limits of the New Deal Order" (PhD diss., University of California, Santa Barbara, 2017), 97–102, 122–30.

109. Jeffry A. Frieden, *Global Capitalism: Its Fall and Rise in the Twentieth Century* (New York: W. W. Norton, 2007), 297–300; Attewell, *People Must Live by Work*, 129–31.

110. William J. Casey, "Leonard W. Hall, R.I.P.," *National Review*, June 22, 1979.

111. "Seek Relief for 'Peace' Jobless," *ND*, August 21, 1945, 3.

112. Attewell, *People Must Live by Work*, 157–68.

113. "End of Federal Funds Perils Child Care Centers in Nassau," *ND*, September 21, 1945, 1–2, 17; "We Still Have Children," *ND*, September 28, 1945, 23.

114. G. R. Simonson, "The Demand for Aircraft and the Aircraft Industry, 1907–1958," *The Journal of Economic History* 20, no. 3 (September 1960): 377; Reginald M. Cleveland and Frederick P. Graham, "Aviation Manufacturing Today in America," in Simonson, *The History of the Aircraft Industry*, 182–86.

115. Stoff, *The Thunder Factory*, 67, 81; "Sperry Golden Anniversary Book," folder "Sperry Gyroscope Corp.—Brooklyn/Lake Success," CAM; Thruelsen, *Grumman Story*, 218–19.

116. Baxter, interview, 25, 32, 34.

117. Alan Brinkley, *The End of Reform: New Deal Liberalism in Recession and War* (New York: Vintage Books, 1996).

118. Minsky, *John Maynard Keynes*, 14–17.

## Chapter Two

1. Brett Williams, "Deadly Inequalities: Race, Illness, and Poverty in Washington, D.C. since 1954," in *African American Urban History since World War II*, eds. Kenneth L. Kusmer and Joe W. Trotter (Chicago: University of Chicago Press, 2009): 151–52.

2. Organization for Social and Technical Innovation, Llewelyn-Davies Weeks, Forestier-Walker and Bor, *Poverty in Spread City: A Study of Constraints on the Poor in Nassau County* (August 1969), 5.

3. "Requiem in Suburban Ghetto," *ND*, April 10, 1968, 31.

4. William G. Gale, Jonathan Gruber, and Seth Stephens-Davidowitz, "Encouraging Homeownership through the Tax Code," *Tax Notes* 115, No. 12 (June 2007): 1172.

5. Richard Walker and Robert Walker, "Beyond the Crabgrass Frontier: Industry and the Spread of North American Cities, 1850–1950," in *Manufacturing Suburbs: Building Work and Home on the Metropolitan Fringe*, ed. Robert Lewis (Philadelphia: Temple University Press, 2004): 16; Hise, *Magnetic Los Angeles*; Robert O. Self, *American Babylon: Race and the Postwar Struggle for Oakland* (Princeton, NJ: Princeton University Press, 2003), 25–32, 98–131, 170–76; Thomas J. Sugrue, *The Origins of the Urban Crisis: Race and Inequality in Postwar Detroit* (Princeton, NJ: Princeton University Press, 1996), 140–41.

6. Mark Wilson, *Destructive Creation: Business and the Winning World War II* (Philadelphia: University of Pennsylvania Press, 2016); Jennifer Klein, *For All These Rights: Business, Labor, and the Shaping of America's Public- Private Welfare State* (Princeton, NJ: Princeton University Press, 2003); Zachary Carter, "The Beginning of the End," in *The Price of Peace: Money, Democracy, and the Life of John Maynard Keynes* (New York: Random House, 2020), e-book.

7. Brenes, *Right and Might*, 7–22.

8. Constance Perin, "Poverty, Socioeconomic Status, Occupational Structure, and Educational Attainment in Metropolitan Areas," in *The President's Task Force on Suburban Problems Final Report: Statistical Papers*, reel 6, slides 37–39, TFR.

9. "L.I. Shakes the 'Boudoir' Complex," *ND*, January 31, 1948, B3.

10. Geoffrey Rossano, "Suburbia armed: Nassau County Development and the Rise of the Aerospace Industry, 1909–69," in *The Martial Metropolis: U.S. Cities in War and Peace*, ed. Roger W. Lotchin (New York: Praeger, 1984), 61–87; Markusen et al., *The Rise of the Gunbelt*; Roger W. Lotchin, *Fortress California, 1910–1961: From Warfare to Welfare* (New York: Oxford University Press, 1992); Bruce Schulman, *From Cotton Belt to Sunbelt: Federal Policy, Economic Development, & the Transformation of the South, 1938–1980* (Durham, NC: Duke University Press, 1994); Hise, *Magnetic Los Angeles*; Lisa McGirr, *Suburban Warriors: the Origins of the New American Right* (Princeton, NJ: Princeton University Press, 2000); Margaret Pugh O'Mara, *Cities of Knowledge: Cold War Science and the Search for the Next Silicon Valley* (Princeton, NJ: Princeton University Press, 2004); Kari Fredrickson, "The Cold War at the Grassroots: Militarization and Modernization in South Carolina," in *The Myth of Southern Exceptionalism*, eds. Matthew D. Lassiter and Joseph Crespino (New York: Oxford University Press, 2009), 190–209.

11. For an overview of scholarship on the warfare–welfare link, see Herbert Obinger, Klaus Petersen, and Peter Starke, eds., *Warfare and Welfare: Military Conflict and Welfare State Development in Western Countries* (New York: Oxford University Press, 2018), 1–17; For the US "military welfare state," see Suzanne Mettler, *Soldiers to Citizens: The G.I. Bill and the Making of the Greatest Generation* (New York: Oxford University Press, 2005); Mittelstadt, *The Rise of the Military Welfare State*.

12. Nelson Lichtenstein, *A Contest of Ideas: Capital, Politics, and Labor* (Urbana: University of Illinois Press, 2013), 79–99; Kate Andrias, "An American Approach to Social Democracy: The Forgotten Promise of the Fair Labor Standards Act," *Yale Law Journal* 128, no. 3 (2019): 616–709; David Stein, "Fearing Inflation, Inflating Fears: The End of Full Employment and the Rise of the Carceral State," (PhD diss., University of Southern California, 2014), 118–39; Sonti, "The Price of Prosperity," 94–138, 118–39.

13. I rely on the political–economic interpretation of the origins of the Cold War and the military-industrial complex. For examples, see Hooks, *Forging the Military-Industrial Complex*; Curt Caldwell, *NSC 68 and the Political Economy of the Early Cold War* (Cambridge: Cambridge University Press, 2011); Benjamin O. Fordham, *Building the Cold War Consensus: The Political Economy of U.S. National Security Policy, 1949–1951* (Ann Arbor: University of Michigan Press, 1998); James M. Cypher, "The Origins and Evolution of Military Keynesianism in the United States," *Journal of Post-Keynesian Economics* 38, no. 3 (2015): 449–76; Rebecca U. Thorpe, *The American Warfare State: The Domestic Politics of Military Spending* (Chicago: University of Chicago Press, 2014); Brenes, *For Right and Might*, 23–71.

14. President's Air Policy Commission, *Survival in the Air Age: A Report* (Washington, DC: US GPO, 1948), v, 48.

15. NYS Bureau of Research and Statistics, "Labor Market Review," 5, no. 1 (January 1952): 3–7, 18–19.

16. Bruce Cumings, *The Korean War: A History* (New York: Modern Library, 2010), 147–62.

17. "Republic Engineers Produced Korean 'Workhorse,'" *Long Island Daily Press*, January 17, 1955, 23A; Joshua Stoff, "Grumman Versus Republic: Success and Failure in the Aviation Industry on Long Island," *Long Island Historical Journal* 1, no. 2 (Spring 1989): 115; Stoff, *The Thunder Factory*, 8, 93.

18. Feliu, "Impact on Long Island," Table VI.

19. James Hund, "Electronics," *Made in New York; Case Studies in Metropolitan Manufacturing*, eds. Max Hall and Roy B. Helfgott (Cambridge, MA: Harvard University Press, 1959), 244–46, 312.

20. Arthur C. Kerrigan, "The Impact of Airframe Manufacturing on Satellite Industries," in Kaiser and Stonier, eds., *The Development of the Aerospace Industry on Long Island*, 247.

21. Cipher, "The Origins and Evolution of Military Keynesianism," 466–71.

22. Lorne H. Price, "Labor in the Aircraft Industry on Long Island, 1940 to Present," in *The Development of the Aerospace Industry on Long Island; Financial and Related Aspects, Volume II*, eds. William K. Kaiser, Charles E. Stonier (Hempstead, NY: Hofstra University Yearbook of Business, Series 5, Volume 4, 1968), 201; Vincent W. Gillen, "Union Activity on Long Island," Long *Island Business* 2, no. 1 (July 1955): 1, box 1, HCB.

23. NYS Department of Labor, *Employment Statistics, Vol. 3 Supplement* (Albany, 1968), 17–21; Hoyt, "Financing Long Island's Aircraft Industry," 133.

24. Leah Platt Boustan and Robert A. Margo, "Job Decentralization and Residential Location," *Brookings-Wharton Papers on Urban Affairs* (2009, no. 1): 15–17.

25. Long Island Association Research Council, *Quality and Stability of New Home Owners in Nassau County, Long Island, N.Y.* (Garden City, NY: The Long Island Association Industrial Bureau), 3–12; NYS Department of Labor, *A Handbook of Statistical Data: Nassau-Suffolk Area* (Albany, NY: GPO, 1970), 8; Price, "Labor in the Aircraft Industry," 221.

26. "Interim Memorandum on the Condition and Outlook for the New Home Sales Market of Western Long Island," December 10, 1948, 4–5, box 13, folder "Long Island, N.Y.," Reports of Housing Market Analysts, 1937–1963, Records of the Federal Housing Administration, Record Group 31, NRM.

27. "Sperry Survey Finds Employees Moving to Nassau and Suffolk," *NYT*, September 23, 1962, 117.

28. "Republic Crisis Threatens LI," *ND*, February 8, 1962, 1M-4M.

29. David Onkst, "The Triumph and Decline of the 'Squares': Grumman Aerospace Engineers and Production Workers in the Apollo Era, 1957–1973" (PhD diss., American University, 2011), 25–26.

30. "Republic Crisis Threatens LI"; Onkst, "Triumph and Decline," 25–26; John Thomas Liell, "Levittown: A Study in Community Planning and Development" (PhD diss., Yale University, 1962), 244–48; William S. Dobriner, *Class in Suburbia* (Englewood Cliffs, NJ: Prentice-Hall, 1964), 97–110.

31. US Census Bureau, *US Censuses of Population and Housing: 1960* (Washington, DC: GPO, 1962), 16, 18, 196, 198; US Census Bureau, *1970 Census of Population and Housing: Census Tracts, Part 14: New York, NY Standard Metropolitan Area* (Washington, DC: GPO, 1972), P-201, P-203, P-801, P-803.

32. Quoted in Stephen Raymond Patnode, "Labor's Love Lost: The Influence of Gender, Race, and Class on the Workplace in Postwar America." (PhD diss., Stony Brook University, 2008), 88–92.

33. Thomas A. Clark, *Blacks in Suburbs: A National Perspective* (New Brunswick, NJ: Center for Urban Policy Research, 1979), 81.

34. Kamer et al., *A Profile of the Nassau-Suffolk Labor Force*, 18–20; Pearl M. Kamer, "An Economic Profile of Commuter Relationships: The Nassau-Suffolk SMSA," *Long Island Economic Trends Quarterly Technical Supplement—Third Quarter 1974* (September 1974): 2–4.

35. "Ethnic Survey of Suffolk County Government Employees," VI Summary of Findings, box 5, folder 6, WBT; "Hospital, Blacks Agree to Talks," July 15, 1970, and "Blacks List Demands at Hospital Meeting," July 16, 1970, box 1, folder 7, WBT; For occupational distribution at mental hospitals, see "Central Islip State Hospital, Central Islip, New York," box 15, folder "C.I.S.H.—Various Fact Sheets," NYS Office of Mental Health Subject Files (Series B1973), NYA.

36. "Haves and Have-Nots," *ND*, Jan 8, 1966, 8W-9W.

37. That number is not definitive because state agencies didn't even keep track of ditchdiggers, farm laborers, seamstresses, and domestic workers

38. Manson et al., *IPUMS*, database; Lynn Y. Weiner, *From Working Girl to Working Mother: The Female Labor Force in the United States, 1820–1980* (Chapel Hill: University of North Carolina Press, 1988), 6–7; Dorothy Sue Cobble, "More than Sex Equality: Feminism after Suffrage," in *Feminism Unfinished: A Short, Surprising History of American Women's Movements*, eds. Dorothy Sue Cobble, Linda Gordon, and Astrid Henry (New York: Liveright, 2014), 38–44; Emilie Stoltzfus, *Citizen, Mother, Worker: Debating Public Responsibility for Child Care after the Second World War* (Chapel Hill: University of North Carolina Press, 2003), 65.

39. Richard O. Davies, *Housing Reform During the Truman Administration* (Columbia: University of Missouri Press, 1967), 118–21.

40. Isaac William Martin, "The Shackles of the Past: Constitutional Property Tax Limitations and the Fall of the New Deal Order," in *Capitalism Contested: The New Deal and its Legacies*, eds. Romain Huret, Nelson Lichtenstein, and Jean-Christian Vinel (Philadelphia: University of Pennsylvania Press, 2020), 136–51.

41. This contention rests on heterodox economic views of sovereign currency issuers (like the US federal government), who have the power to create money, which sparks the productive capacities, and therefore adds financial assets to the private (or local public) sector. For an overview, see L. Randall Wray, *Modern Monetary Theory: A Primer on Macroeconomics for Sovereign Monetary Systems* (New York: Palgrave Macmillan, 2012), 9–40.

42. "Employment Covered Under the Social Security Program, 1935–84," *Social Security Bulletin* 48, no. 4 (April 1985): 33–39; Ellora Derenoncourt and Claire Montialoux, "Minimum Wages and Racial Inequality," *Quarterly Journal of Economics* 136, no. 1 (February 2021): 169–228.

43. Larry DeWitt, "The Decision to Exclude Agricultural and Domestic Workers from the 1935 Social Security Act," *Social Security Bulletin* 70, no. 4 (November 2010): 49–68; Lee Alston and Joseph P. Ferrie, "Labor Costs, Paternalism, and Loyalty in Southern Agriculture: A Constraint on the Growth of the Welfare State," *Journal of Economic History* 45, no. 1 (March 1985): 95–117.

44. Andrias, "American Approach to Social Democracy," 684–88.

45. Examples of a vast literature include Rueda, *Social Democracy Inside Out*; Patrick Emmenegger, Silja Häusermann, Bruno Palier, and Martin Seeleib-Kaiser, eds., *The Age of Dualization. The Changing Face of Inequality in Deindustrializing Societies* (New York: Oxford University Press, 2012).

46. Rosalyn Fraad Baxandall and Elizabeth Ewen, *Picture Windows: How the Suburbs Happened* (New York: Basic Books, 2000), 126–30; Liell, "Levittown," 106–7.

47. "Non-Union Levittown Workers Walk Out," *ND*, August 24, 1948, 5; "Sample Houses Picketed as AFL Opens Drive to Unionize Levitt," *ND*, April 12, 1950, 5.

48. "Union, Levitt Firms at Odds on Pickets," *ND*, April 18, 1950, 5; "4 Labor Heads Quit AFL Trades Council," *ND*, August 15, 1951, 10; "Building Trades Council Gives Lie to Ex-Czar," *ND*, January 3, 1952, 3.

49. Robert Grey Reynolds Jr., *The AFL's Extortion of Long Island Building Contractors, November 1953* (n.p., 2016), e-book; US Senate, *Select Committee on Improper Activities in the Labor or Management Field Eighty-Fifth Congress, First Session, April/Nov 1957, Part 17* (Washington, DC: GPO, 1957), 7791–93.

50. "DA Calls Levitt on DeKoning Tie," *ND*, October 10, 1953, 3; "How Levitt Fought Bid to Kill L'Town," *ND*, October 1, 1957, 1; "DeKoning Sr. Dies in L.I. Hospital," *NYT*, October 20, 1957, 86.

51. US Senate, *Interim Report of the Select Committee on Improper Activities in the Labor or Management Field, 85th Congress* (Washington, DC: GPO, 1958), 404–12; Reavis Cox, Charles S. Goodman, and Franklin R. Root, *The Supply-Support Requirements of Homebuilders: A Study of the Relationships Between Operations and Supply Support Requirements* (Washington, DC: The Producer's Council, Inc., 1962), 17.

52. Thomas J. Sugrue, *Sweet Land of Liberty: The Forgotten Struggle for Civil Rights in the North* (New York: Random House, 2008), 118.

53. "Local Union Questionnaire—Brotherhood of Painters, Decorators, and Paperhangers 66," box 41, Local Union Questionnaires, 1963 New York, PCE; "Local Union Questionnaire—Bricklayers Union Local #30," box 42, Local Union Questionnaires, 1963 New York, PCE;

W. Burghardt Turner to the New York Advisory Committee to the US Civil Rights Commission, March 23, 1971, 1–2, box 2, folder 9, WBT.

54. W. Burghardt Turner to the New York Advisory Committee to the US Civil Rights Commission, March 23, 1971, 1–2, box 2, folder 9, WBT.

55. Sugrue, *Origins of the Urban Crisis*, 119–20.

56. "LI Powder Keg: Awaiting Jobs that May Never Come," *ND*, August 16, 1966, 4.

57. Sobin, *Dynamics of Community Change*, 54–64, 112–17; *US Censuses of Population and Housing: 1960*, 150–52.

58. Kim V. L. England, "Changing Suburbs, Changing Women: Geographic Perspectives on Suburban Women and Suburbanization," *Frontiers: A Journal of Women Studies* 14, no. 1 (1993): 25–26; See also Elaine Tyler May, *Homeward Bound: American Families in the Cold War Era* (New York: Basic Books, 1988), 162–82; Dolores Hayden, *Building American Suburbia: Green Fields and Urban Growth, 1820–2000* (New York: Pantheon Books, 2003), 153–73.

59. Mark J. Stern, "Poverty and Family Composition Since 1940," in *The "Underclass" Debate: Views from History*, ed. Michael B. Katz (Princeton, NJ: Princeton University Press, 1993), 237; Nelson Lichtenstein, "From Corporatism to Collective Bargaining: Organized Labor and the Eclipse of Social Democracy in the Postwar Era," in *The Rise and Fall of the New Deal Order*, eds. Steve Fraser and Gary Gerstle (Princeton, NJ: Princeton University Press, 1990), 144–45.

60. Manson et al., *IPUMS*, database; Lynn Y. Weiner, *From Working Girl to Working Mother: The Female Labor Force in the United States, 1820–1980* (Chapel Hill: University of North Carolina Press, 1988), 6–7; "Parents to Launch Own Nursery School," *ND*, March 21, 1946, 25; "Elmont Loses Fight for Child Centers," *ND*, June 27, 1946, 18; "Gay Yule for War Waifs at Child Center," *ND*, December 24, 1946, 1.

61. Premilla Nadasen, "Citizenship Rights, Domestic Work, and the Fair Labor Standards Act," *Journal of Policy History* 24, no. 1 (January 2012): 74–94.

62. This was true nationwide. See Donna Franklin, *Ensuring Inequality: The Structural Transformation of the African American Family* (New York: Oxford University Press, 1997), 113, among others; "Haves and Have-Nots," *ND*, Jan 8, 1966, 8W-9W.

63. "State Probing LI Job Agents," *ND*, September 27, 1957, 5; "Buy a Negro Maid—Get Plaid Stamps Free!" *AN*, June 16, 1962; For ads, see Classifieds, *ND*, January 30, 1959, 31C; Classified Ads, *Farmingdale Observer*, January 3, 1962, 11; Classified Ads, *Farmingdale Observer*, April 22, 1965, 15; "Directory of Local Services," *Bethpage Tribune*, December 18, 1969, 19.

64. "Oyster Bay Clerk Revokes Domestic-Agency License," *ND*, May 21, 1958, 39; "Court Upsets Glen Cove Ruling that Shut Maid-Service Firm," *ND*, March 8, 1962, 35.

65. Henry Holley, interview by James Levy, April 9, 2011, 34, Hofstra Suburban Oral History Project, LISI.

66. "My Girl is Here: Working for the Man in Wantagh," *ND*, August 22, 1970, 11W.

67. *Newsday*, "My Girl is Here," 11W.

68. "Our Temporary Maid Part II: Some Lunches are Better," *ND*, January 26, 1965, 1C.

69. "Negro Maid Threatened, Is Warned to Leave Town," *ND*, July 24, 1956, 5; "LIers Rally to Aid of Negro Maid," *ND*, July 25, 1956, 4; "Bigot Drives Negro Maid from LI, New Maid Hired," *ND*, July 28, 1956, 5.

70. Self, *American Babylon*, 96–132; William N. Leonard and Charles E. Stonier, *The Long Island Survey, Volume I: Industry Looks at Long Island: A Study of How Manufacturers Rate Nassau and Suffolk Counties as Homes for Industry* (November 1956), 11–15, 50–51, box 2, HCB; Michael LoGrande, *A Study of New York City's Industrial Out-Migration* (MS thesis, Columbia University,

1966), 56–64; "New Plants Keep Sprouting in LI's Industrial Parks," *Long Island Daily Press*, January 18, 1965; John Griffin, *Industrial Location in the New York Area* (New York: City College Press, 1956), 77.

71. NYS Department of Labor, *Employment Statistics Vol. 6* (Albany, 1970), 180–82; William N. Leonard, "Labor Costs on Long Island," *Nassau-Suffolk Business Conditions* 2, no. 6 (June 1955), box 1, HCB.

72. NYS Department of Labor, *Employment Statistics Vol. 2* (Albany, 1966), 62–75.

73. Gillen, "Union Activity," 1–2.

74. Pearl M. Kamer and the Nassau County Planning Commission, *Manufacturing in Suburbia: The Nassau-Suffolk Employment Experience* (Mineola, NY: Nassau County Planning Commission, 1970), 68–69, 73.

75. *Nassau-Suffolk Business Conditions* 1, no. 2 (June 1954), 14, box 1, HCB; Albert Levenson et al., "The Economy of Long Island, Employment and Income Trends," 37, box 3, HCB; T. D. Ellsworth, Dolores Benjamin, and Herman Randolph, "Impact of Long Island Centers on Shopping Habits," *Long Island Business* 5, no. 1 (January 1958), 15–23, box 1, HCB; "Nassau-Suffolk, 4th Largest Retail Market," *Long Island Daily Press*, August 30, 1964.

76. Dora L. Costa, "Hours of Work and the Fair Labor Standards Act: A Study of Retail and Wholesale Trade, 1938–1950," *International and Labor Relations Review* 53, no. 4 (July 2000): 651.

77. League of Women Voters of Long Beach, "Preliminary Report of a Survey of Employment Opportunities for Negro and Spanish Speaking Minority Groups in Long Beach, New York," box 8, folder 321, LWV.

78. Minna Ziskind, "Labor Conflict in the Suburbs: Organizing Retail in Metropolitan New York, 1954–1958," *International Labor and Working-Class History*, no. 64 (Fall 2003): 55–73.

79. Kamer et al., *Manufacturing in Suburbia*, 64–73.

80. US Census Bureau, *United States Census of Agriculture: 1945 Volume 1, Part 7: New York Statistics for Counties* (Washington, DC: GPO, 1947), 24; US Census Bureau, *1964 United States Census of Agriculture. Volume 1 [State and County Statistics]. Part 7, New York* (Washington, DC: GPO, 1966), 261.

81. "Ducks by the Acre," *Popular Mechanics*, October 1947, 171–74, 236, 240; Suffolk County Department of Planning, "Appendix A: Long Island Duck Farm History and Ecosystem Restoration Opportunities, Suffolk County, New York," February 2009, http://www.suffolkcountyny.gov/portals/0/planning/envplanning/liduckhistory/main_report.pdf.

82. "Testimony before the New York State Joint Legislative Committee on Migrant Labor," November 11, 1967, 1–2, box 2, folder 81, HLD.

83. Quoted in Alan Rosenthal, *The New Documentary in Action: A Casebook in Film Making* (Berkeley: University of California Press, 1971), 107.

84. "Analysis of Farm Labor," January 22, 1968, 2–3, box 2, folder "Dev. Human Resources," EG; "Report of Arthur C. Bryant," November 3, 1967, 4, box 11, folder "Interdepartmental Social Welfare Advisory Committee, 1967," SCC.

85. Suffolk County Human Relations Commission to Suffolk County Executive and Board of Supervisors, "Recommendations," 4, box 1, folder "SCHRC Housing Committee," EG.

86. This estimate is derived from: state labor market data for retail and textile, apparel, and food manufacturing workers; census records for domestic workers; migrant farm laborer studies for farmworkers. There is no historical data on casual construction laborers. See NYS Dept. of Labor, *Employment Statistics Vol. 6*, 180–82; *US Censuses of Population and Housing: 1960*, 150–52; "Testimony Joint Legislative Committee on Migrant Labor," 1–2.

87. Leon Keyserling, *Poverty and Deprivation in the U.S.: The Plight of Two-Fifths of a Nation* (Washington, DC: Conference on Economic Progress, 1962), 13–18.

88. NYS Department of Labor, *Employment Statistics Vol. 6* (Albany, 1970), 180–82; NYS Department of Labor, *Employment, Payrolls and Earnings in Establishments Covered by Unemployment Insurance, 1942–1962* (Albany: Research and Statistics Office, 1965), 9; Untitled document, NAACP and Labor, 1956–1965, Part 13 supplement, reel 12, slide 393, PNC; "Far-Rockaway-Inwood Bulletin November Edition" 2, Box III:C97, folder 4, RNCP; "LI Powder Keg: Awaiting Jobs that May Never Come," *ND*, August 16, 1966, 4.

89. Hyman Minsky, "Effects of Shifts of Aggregate Demand upon Income Distribution." *American Journal of Agricultural Economics* 50, no. 2 (May 1968): 328–39; Walter Korpi, "The Great Trough in Unemployment: A Long-Term View of Unemployment, Inflation, Strikes, and the Profit/Wage Ratio," *Politics & Society* 30, no. 3 (September 2002): 365–426.

90. Claudia Dale Goldin and Lawrence F. Katz, *The Race between Education and Technology: The Evolution of U.S. Educational Wage Differentials, 1890 to 2005* (Cambridge, MA: National Bureau of Economic Research, 2007), http://papers.nber.org/papers/w12984; Hyman Minsky, "The Role of Full Employment Policy," *Ending Poverty: Jobs, Not Welfare*, ed. L. Randall Wray (Annandale-on-Hudson, NY: Levy Economics Institute, 2013), 15; Kamer et al., *Manufacturing in Suburbia*, 18.

91. Charles C. Killingsworth, "The Continuing Labor Market Twist: A Further Look at the Relationship Between Employment Change and Labor Force Change, and Some Unanswered Questions," *Monthly Labor Review* 91, no. 9 (September 1968): 12–17; Barry Bluestone, "Economic Inequality and the Macrostructuralist Debate," *Political Economy for the 21st Century: Contemporary Views on the Trend of Economics*, ed. Charles J. Whalen, (Armonk, NY: M. E. Sharpe, 1996), 172; Gregory R. Woirol, *The Technological Unemployment and Structural Unemployment Debates* (Westport, CT: Greenwood Press, 1996), 104.

92. Steven Manson, Jonathan Schroeder, David Van Riper, and Steven Ruggles *IPUMS National Historical Geographic Information System: Version 13.0* (Minneapolis: University of Minnesota, 2018), database, http://doi.org/10.18128/D050.V13.0; US Census Bureau, Education (Non-white Population), 1960. Prepared by Social Explorer, http://www.socialexplorer.com/tables/C1960TractDS/R11103716; US Census Bureau, Educational Attainment for Black Population 25 Years or Over, 1970. Prepared by Social Explorer, http://www.socialexplorer.com/tables/C1970/R11103719.

93. *US Censuses of Population and Housing: 1960*, 16, 18, 196, 198; US Census Bureau, *1970 Census of Population and Housing: Census Tracts, Part 14: New York, NY Standard Metropolitan Area* (Washington, DC: GPO, 1972), P-201, P-203, P-801, P-803.

94. Wiese, *Places of their Own*, 114–25; James N. Gregory, *The Southern Diaspora: How the Great Migrations of Black and White Southerners Transformed America* (Chapel Hill: University of North Carolina, Press, 2007), 11–42, 98–100; James N. Gregory, "The Second Great Migration: A Historical Overview," in Kusmer and Trotter, *African American Urban History since World War II*, 29; Leah Platt Boustan, "Competition in the Promised Land: Black Migration and Racial Wage Convergence in the North, 1940–1970," *The Journal of Economic History* 69, no. 3 (September 2009): 773.

95. James P. Smith and Finis R. Welch, "Black Economic Progress After Myrdal," *Journal of Economic Literature* 27, no. 2 (June 1989): 522; Richard B. Freeman, "Changes in the Labor Market for Black Americans, 1948–72," *Brookings Papers on Economic Activity* 1(1973): 67–131; Clark, *Blacks in Suburbs*, 83.

96. Judith Russell, *Economics, Bureaucracy, and Race: How Keynesians Misguided the War on Poverty* (New York: Columbia University Press, 2004), 46–48.

97. Local 1412 Division of Employment Minority Group Service Senior Consultant to NY-NJ Region of ASCFME, AFL-CIO, November 5, 1962, NAACP and Labor, 1956–1965, Part 13 supplement, reel 12, slides 19–20, PNC; for USES discrimination, see Desmond King, *Actively Seeking Work? The Politics of Unemployment and Welfare Policy in the United States and Great Britain* (Chicago: University of Chicago Press, 1995), 98–102.

98. Correspondence, July 31, 1962, NAACP and Labor, 1956–1965, Part 13 supplement, reel 12, slides 14–16, PNC.

99. Ansley Erickson, *Making the Unequal Metropolis: School Desegregation and its Limits* (Chicago: University of Chicago Press, 2016), 93, 103–7.

100. Daniels, "Bennington Park," 26–33.

101. Helen Randolph, Claire Collier, and Morton Inger, *The Black Suburbanite and His Schools: An Interim Report on the Study of the Impact of Black Suburbanization on the School System* (New York: Center for Urban Education, 1970), 17–18, 27–28, 61–68.

102. Janet S. Toohy, "Just What Do They Think We Are? An Experiment in Probing the Teenager's Image of the Group Work Agency" (MS thesis, New York School of Social Work, Columbia University, 1953), 132, SWA.

103. "Jobs for All in Booming LI Defense Plants," *ND*, July 6, 1951, 7.

104. "Ask Care in Picking School Plan," *ND*, May 11, 1955, 17; "Suffolk Schools Ignore Job Training for Pupils," *ND*, April 6, 1955, 2.

105. NYS Department of Labor and Nassau County Board of Cooperative Educational Services, *Vocational-Technical High School Students in Nassau County, 1965–1969: A Follow-up Study* (Albany: NYS Department of Labor, Division of Research and Statistics, 1973), 5; "Percent Distribution of Public-School Students by Racial/Ethnic Origin, 1969–1970," Box V: 1527, folder 3, RNCP.

106. For a forthcoming book on the subject, see Michael R. Glass, "Schooling Suburbia: The Politics of School Finance in Postwar Long Island," (PhD diss., Princeton University, 2020).

107. *1970 Census of Population and Housing*, P-863, P-865.

108. Gordon M. Fisher, "The Development and History of the Poverty Thresholds," *Social Security Bulletin* 55, no. 4 (1992); Thomas Stapleford, *The Cost of Living in America: A Political History of Economic Statistics, 1880–2000* (New York: Cambridge University Press, 2009); Alice O'Connor, "When Measurements Matter: Poverty, Wealth, and the Politics of Inequality in the United States," *History of Political Economy* 52, no. 3 (2020): 589–98; Romain Huret, *The Experts' War on Poverty: Social Research and the Welfare Agenda in Postwar America*, (Ithaca: Cornell University Press, 2018); O'Connor, *Poverty Knowledge*, 152–55, 182–85; See also Katz, *Undeserving Poor*, 115–17.

109. Timothy Smeeding, Lee Rainwater, Gary Burtles, "United States Poverty in a Cross-National Context," *Center for Policy Research* 151 (May 2001): 25en1; Alice O'Connor, "Poverty Knowledge and the History of Poverty Research," in *The Oxford Handbook of the Social Science of Poverty*, eds. Linda Burton and David Brady (New York: Oxford University Press, 2016), 184.

110. US Census Bureau, "Historical County Level Poverty Estimates Tool"; *1970 Census of Population and Housing*, P-601, P-603.

111. Examples include "Requiem in Suburban Ghetto," *ND*, April 10, 1968, 31; "Heads and Tales," *ND*, March 21, 1960, 30; Alice Brazier, William Cosenza, Gerald I. Fantel, Leah Goldberg, Fay Kauderer, Mildred Reed, and Harriet Rosenbaum, "Descriptive Study of First-Time

Unmarried Mothers who Applied to the Nassau County Department of Public Welfare," (M. Social Work thesis, Adelphi College, 1966); Minutes of Workshop Program on Employment, October 1, 1964, 1, box 58, ENP.

112. Keyserling, *Poverty and Deprivation in the U.S.*, 13–18.

113. Mark Robert Rank, *One Nation, Underprivileged: Why American Poverty Affects Us All* (New York: Oxford University Press, 2004), 88–95.

114. Alice Diaz, Eleanor Kremen, Saul Gessow, Virginia Lerner, Dorothy Hechtman, Sheila Ruth Perlman, Morris Karmel, and Fanny Steinberg, "Economic Impact of Prolonged Unemployment on Families: Republic Lodge 1987 Unemployment Survey" (M. Social Services thesis, Adelphi University, 1959), 27–33.

## Chapter Three

1. Liell, "Levittown," 100–101; "Real Estate News," *Brooklyn Eagle*, June 6, 1947, 9; "All of it is Levittown—to Levittowners," *ND*, November 30, 1951, 4; Deed Liber 3409, 547–600, NCC; "Okay Change for 10 New Cassel Streets," *ND*, March 31, 1948, 28; Deed Liber 3366, 315–16, NCC.

2. Section 11, Block 117, Lot 64, NCLR; For property transactions, see Deed Liber 3411, 45; Mortgage Liber 3056, 184–86; Deed Liber 4744, 277–78; Deed Liber 4744, 280–82; Mortgage Liber 4459, 408–10; Deed Liber 6149, 119–20, NCC.

3. Deed Liber 7203, 193; Mortgage Liber 7411, 474–77, NCC; "Betty Jean King is Planning Bridal," *NYT*, July 16, 1972; Property Card, Section 11, Block 117, Lot 64, NCLR; Coles Publications, Inc., *Cole's Metropolitan Householders Directory, Nassau County, New York, 1971 Issue* (n.p.: Coles Publishers, Inc., 1971), 267; *Code of the Town of North Hempstead* (Rochester: General Code Publisher's Corp., 1996), §70-44.

4. Connolly, *A World More Concrete*, 6–7; Taylor, *Race for Profit*, 31.

5. Preston H. Smith, *Racial Democracy and the Black Metropolis: Housing Policy in Postwar Chicago* (Minneapolis: University of Minnesota Press, 2012), xiii.

6. Smith, *Racial Democracy*, xiii.

7. For an effective overview, see Alexander von Hoffman, "History Lessons for Today's Housing Policy: The Politics of Low-Income Housing," *Housing Policy Debate* 22, no. 3 (May 2012): 321–76; See also Davies, *Housing Reform During the Truman Administration*, 118–21; Allen R. Hayes, *The Federal Government and Urban Housing* (Albany: State University of New York Press, 1995); Kristin M. Szylvian, *The Mutual Housing Experiment: New Deal Communities for the Urban Middle Class* (Philadelphia: Temple University Press, 2015), 150–71.

8. David M. P. Freund, "Money is Productive, and Racist Institutions Create Money," Just Money.org, June 8, 2020, https://justmoney.org/d-freund-money-is-productive-and-racist-institutions-create-money/; Freund, *Colored Property*, 191–96.

9. Jackson, *Crabgrass Frontier*, 211.

10. Raymond & May Associates, *Residential Market Analysis Progress Report Part III: An Overview of Housing Costs* (September 1968), 13; Jackson, *Crabgrass Frontier*, 211; *US Censuses of Population and Housing: 1960*, 213.

11. Franklin National Bank of Long Island, *Statistical Abstract of Nassau and Suffolk Counties Long Island, New York* (Franklin National Bank of Long Island, 1962), 242.

12. John P. Dean, "Only Caucasian: A Study of Race Covenants," *Journal of Land & Public Utility Economics* 23, no. 4 (November 1947): 428–32.

13. For the pre-FHA mortgage practices available to working-class people, see Elaine Lewinnek, *The Working Man's Reward: Chicago's Early Suburbs and the Roots of American Sprawl* (New York: Oxford University Press, 2014), 93–100.

14. Paige Glotzer, *How the Suburbs were Segregated: Developers and the Business of Exclusionary Housing, 1890–1960* (New York: Columbia University Press, 2020); Freund, *Colored Property*, 6–12; Taylor, *Race for Profit*, 32–37; Chole N. Thurston, *At the Boundaries of Homeownership* (Cambridge: Cambridge University Press, 2018), 80–90.

15. "An Island of Superlatives," *ND*, April 29, 1973, 8F.

16. Nassau-Suffolk Regional Planning Board, *Study of Local Housing Codes*, 33–35, 40–43.

17. *Housing Constructed under VA and FHA Programs: Hearings before the Subcommittee on Housing of the Committee on Banking and Currency, House of Representatives, Eighty-second Congress, Second Session, Bay Shore Long Island*, February 13, 1952 (Washington, DC: GPO, 1952), 301–2, 326–28.

18. "Order Twin Federal Probes of FHA Procedures on LI," *ND*, April 27, 1956, 7; "FHA Bribe Trial Ends after 4 Days; Judge Weights His Decision," *ND*, March 20, 1958, 39.

19. *Housing Constructed under VA and FHA Programs*, 301–2, 342–46, 356–59; *Title I - Amendments of the National Housing Act*, Public Laws, ch. 94, April 20, 1950, Sec. 8, 48–51, https://www.loc.gov/law/help/statutes-at-large/81st-congress/session-2/c81s2ch94.pdf.

20. Nassau County Planning Commission, *Apartments: Their Past and Future Impact on Suburban Living Patterns* (Mineola, NY: Nassau County Planning Commission, 1963), 36, 62–65; Raymond & May Associates, *Residential Market Analysis Progress Report Part II: Households and Housing Units, 1960–1985* (September 1968), 33–34.

21. NYS Division of Housing, *Survey of Housing Conditions*, Selected Branch Files, 1940–1955, Part 26, Series B, reel 4, slide 640, PNC.

22. "Slums on LI: The Dark Side of Suburbia: Long Island's Ugly Ducklings," *ND*, September 16, 1957, 1.

23. "New Homes Get Tenants from Slum," *Suffolk Sun*, September 24, 1967, 1; Wiese, *Places of their Own*, 104–9; See also Connolly, *A World More Concrete*, 74–99; Gonzalez, *In Search of the Mexican Beverly Hills*, 38–44, 105–14.

24. "Public Housing Boom: Or is it?" Box V:1527, folder 9, RNCP; Nassau-Suffolk Regional Planning Board and Raymond & May Associates, *Better Homes for Better Communities* (Hauppauge, NY: Nassau-Suffolk Regional Planning Board, 1968), 96.

25. "LI Communities making Plans and Progress in War on Slums," *ND*, January 7, 1959, 10C-11C; "Urban Renewal: Progress by Inches," *ND*, May 15, 1969, 13.

26. Raymond & May Associates, *Residential Market Analysis Progress Report Part I*, 31–32; NYS Division of Housing and Community Renewal, *Survey Report on Rental Housing* (January 1969), 61, 65; Nassau County Planning Commission, *Apartments: Their Past and Future Impact*, 37–38; Raymond & May Associates, *Residential Market Analysis Part III*, 13, 18–19; Raymond & May Associates, *Residential Market Analysis Progress Report Part I: Residential Supply Inventory* (September 1967), 31, Table 18–19.

27. Raymond & May Associates, *Residential Market Analysis Progress Report Part IV: Study of Housing of Welfare Recipients* (September 1967), Nassau Table XVIII-A, Suffolk Table XVIII-A; "Statement of the Nassau County Council of the League of Women Voters," November 1962, box 8, folder "Department of Welfare," LWV; See Bureau of Labor Statistics, *Three Standards of Living for an Urban Family of Four Persons, Spring 1967* (Washington, DC: US GPO 1969), 16; Stone, *Shelter Poverty*, 32, 324–30.

28. Jake Wegmann explains the limitations in detail. See Wegmann, "We Just Built It," 326–28.

29. Kessman, *A Cost and Use Analysis of Single and Two-Family Housing*, 20, 71–80; Nassau-Suffolk Regional Planning Board, *US Census '70, Volume 4: Housing Inventory* (Hauppauge, NY: Nassau-Suffolk Regional Planning Board, 1972), 71–80.

30. "Sees Local Building a LI Industry Boon," *ND*, October 22, 1953, 39; Display Ad, *ND*, November 14, 1953, 55; "Central Islip Sites to Get $7,650 Homes," *ND*, May 3, 1953, R10; "FHA Opens Investigations of Lightless C. Islip Home," *ND*, September 17, 1954, 4; "Reliefers Living on Streets of Despair," 10.

31. *Grantee "T"- Islip, 1951–1969*, pages "G" 1956–1962, SCH; Want Ads, *Long Island Advance*, September 27, 1962, 14.

32. Deed Liber 3794, 412; Deed Liber 4490, 460; Deed liber 4920, 190, SCH.

33. *Housing Constructed under VA and FHA Programs*, 301–2.

34. See Satter, *Family Properties*, 4, 64–97 for a description of the process.

35. "Louis J. Modica dead at 92," *ND*, April 28, 2016; "Name Unit to Study Home Losses," *ND*, December 16, 1959, 47; Classifieds, *ND*, February 25, 1960, 34C; Classifieds, *ND*, March 16, 1962, 41C; Classifieds, *ND*, March 9, 1962, 41C; Deed Liber 5307, 38, 44, 50–53, 80–93; Deed Liber 5860, 385, SCH.

36. Deed Liber 3738, 50; Deed Liber 4554, 124; Mortgage Liber 3126, 342; Deed Liber 5284, 429, SCH; "Terror, Despair Enfold a Suffolk Slum," *ND*, December 7, 1964, 11; Vivian Kopf, "Central Islip Catchword," *IB*, June 18, 1964, 7.

37. For examples see Deed Liber 5200, 579–82; Deed Liber 5151, 369–74; Deed Liber 5445, 241; Deed Liber 5300, 63; Deed Liber 5408, 373; Deed Liber 5408, 393; Deed Liber 5495, 36; Deed Liber 5816, 220–31, 234–59; Deed Liber 5803, 188–247, SCH; Classified Ads, *ND*, April 13, 1963, 15C; Classified Ads, *ND*, April 14, 1961, 44C.

38. "Slum Owners are Cited for 112 Violations," *Suffolk County News*, December 31, 1964, 7; "Civic Leaders Frght [*sic*] Growing Area Blight in C.I. Carleton Park," *IB*, April 1, 1965, 2.

39. "From Ousted Educator to Millionaire," *ND*, July 1, 1984, 28; "Arrest Northrop in Street Fight," *ND*, March 23, 1954; "Like a Dead End: Poverty-beset Carleton Park has a Grim Past and Cloudy Future," *ND*, January 25, 1977, 1A; Deed Liber 5803, 188–247, SCH.

40. Deed Liber 5813, 493, SCH; Deed Liber 5847, 262, SCH.

41. Elsie M. Bond, *Public Relief in New York State: A Summary of the Public Welfare Law and Related Statutes with 1938 Amendments* (State Charities Aid Association, 1938), 27–30.

42. Minutes of Building Inspectors Association of Suffolk County, January 11, 1963, box 1, folder "Literature—Housing," EG.

43. Raymond & May Associates, *Residential Market Analysis Part IV*, 6.

44. "Confrontation in Carleton Park Pits Tenants Against Landlord," *ND*, February 18, 1970, 8.

45. "Complete Homes from $4990," *AN*, December 3, 1949; "Non-Racial Dwellings Opened at Wyandanch," *NYT*, March 11, 1951; Classifieds, *AN*, December 1, 1956, 31; "New Homes Built for Minorities," *AN*, May 5, 1956, 35; *Housing Constructed under VA and FHA Programs*, 348; Manson et al., *IPUMS*, database.

46. For Crowe's property holdings, see Deed Liber 5084, 221; Mortgage Liber 3746, 354; Deed Liber 5298, 209; Deed Liber 5499, 598; Deed Liber 5508, 429, SCH; "Portraits of a Housing Crisis," *ND*, November 12, 1972, 11; For Crowe's business and political activities, see "At 18th Annual Pontier Installation," *AN*, June 3, 1950, B4; "Crowe's Funeral Home, Inc.," *New York Age*, July 21, 1951, 12.

47. "Certificate of Title," Torrens Certificates 32791, 3859, 87429, SCH; For Cobb's car lien, see Lien Document no. 189267, SCH; For housing conditions, see "House Fire Kills 2 in Wyandanch," *ND*, December 18, 1972, 17.

48. Regional Plan Association, *The Future of Suffolk County: A Supplement to the Second Regional Plan, a Draft for Discussion* (New York: Regional Plan Association, 1974), 53.

49. "Civics in New Home Area Act to Get Curbs, Paving," *Nassau Daily Review-Star*, February 13, 1950, 12.

50. Randolph et al., *The Black Suburbanite and His Schools*, 47; Manson et al., *IPUMS*, database.

51. Mortgage Liber 6225, 276–79; Mortgage Liber 6864, 498; Mortgage Liber 6875, 593–94; Mortgage Liber 7723, 300, NCC; *Cole's Metropolitan Householders Directory, Nassau 1971*, 267.

52. "Class vs. Class in Long Island: The Negro Problem in Suburbs: Negroes at odds with Each Other," *AN*, December 24, 1966, 25.

53. Parrish, *One Square Mile*, 23–25; Baxandall and Ewen, *Picture Windows*, 182–83; Michael Glass, "Color Lines: Slum Clearance, Busted Blocks, and Suburban Dreams Deferred," (unpublished PhD diss. chapter, Princeton University, 2018), 44–48; For scholarship on blockbusting, see Seligman, *Block by Block*; W. Edward Orser, *Blockbusting in Baltimore: The Edmondson Village Story* (Lexington: University Press of Kentucky, 2014).

54. Deed Liber 6450 469; Deed Liber 7455 566; Deed Liber 8655, 78; Mortgage Liber 6376 405; Mortgage Liber 7497, 547, NCC; See also Section 55, Block 307, Lot 1375, Section 55, Block 286, Lot 1367, Section 55, Block 286, Lot 1360 NCLR; Compare with *Cole's Metropolitan Householders Directory, Nassau 1971*, 243; "Road Map to Squalor Shows LI Slums," *ND*, February 11, 1963, 1.

55. Mortgage Liber 6624, 94, 149; Mortgage 7410, 739; Deed Liber 6672 218; Deed Liber 7495 151; Lien Liber 187 79, 133, NCC; "Grab 25 as LI Welfare Cheats," *ND*, October 18, 1962, 3.

56. Deed Liber 5357 310; Mortgage Liber 4986 415, NCC; Section 55, Block 559, Lot 47, NCLR; Deed Liber 7755 121; Deed Liber 7907, 26, NCC; Section 55 Block 559, Lot 50, NCLR; "Building Aide, Landlord Skirmish over Housing," *ND*, March 18, 1969, 13; ". . . But 4 in 1 Seemingly Does," *ND*, May 19, 1972, 3.

57. Smith, *Racial Democracy*, 4–20.

58. Nassau-Suffolk Regional Planning Board, *Study of Local Housing Codes*, 16–18; Nassau-Suffolk Regional Planning Board, *New Tools and Agencies for Housing Code Enforcement in Nassau and Suffolk Counties: An Innovative Study* (Hauppauge, NY, 1970), 4–5; Seligman, *Block by Block*, 43–51.

59. Wiese, *Places of their Own*, 154–63; Michney, *Surrogate Suburbs*, 4–15; Smith, *Racial Democracy*, xiii; For homeownership as a racialized white political ideology, see Self, *American Babylon*, 98–99; For homeownership as a racialized class politics among black homeowners, see Connolly, *World More Concrete*, 241–49; See also Steven Gregory, *Black Corona: Race and the Politics of Place in an Urban Community* (Princeton, NJ: Princeton University Press, 2011), 145; Mary Pattillo, *Black on the Block: the Politics of Race and Class in the City* (Chicago: University of Chicago Press, 2010), 14.

60. Robert Jay Dilger, *Neighborhood Politics: Resident Community Associations in American Governance* (New York: NYU Press, 1992), 108.

61. "Negroes Fault Cops, Welfare Dept. on Crime," *ND*, November 29, 1966, 9; "Town Drops Protested Industrial Zone," *ND*, June 13, 1957, 21; "Downzoning Creates Slums, Negro Says," *ND*, December 15, 1965, 15.

62. "C.I. Social Whirl," *IB*, Mar 14, 1963, 17; "Two Civic Groups March on Town Hall to Protest Conditions near Homes," *IB*, June 18, 1964, 3, 8-B.

63. Randolph et al., *Black Suburbanites and their Schools*, 36–37; Baxandall and Ewen, *Picture Windows*, 189–90; For this strategy elsewhere, see Seligman, *Block by Block*, 163–82.

64. "The Little Nemesis of Town Hall," *ND*, February 26, 1970, 3B; "Gadfly to Rest His Wings," *ND*, September 5, 1982, 19; "Suffolk Co. Negroes Up in Arms," *AN*, June 1, 1963.

65. "Terror, Despair Enfold a Suffolk Slum," *ND*, December 7, 1964, 11; "Suffolk to Halt Rent Payments for Violations," *ND*, December 11, 1964, 15.

66. "Islip Probers Move in Slum Check Today," *ND*, December 14, 1964, 14; "Slum Probers Find Variety of Violations," *ND*, December 15, 1964, 4; "Town Launches Large-Scale Program to Wipe out Slum Conditions in 300-Home Carleton Park Area," *IB*, December 17, 1964, 1, 2-B; Wegmann, "We Just Built it," 186, 214.

67. "Cheers, Tears, Great Adoption of Anti-Slum Law," *IB*, December 24, 1964, 3, 11.

68. Minutes of the Town Board, Town of Islip, NY, March 30, 1965, 530, Town Clerk's Office, Town of Islip, New York; "Civic Leaders Fight [*sic*] Growing Area Blight in C.I. Carleton Park."

69. "Minutes—Executive Meeting, November 21, 1966," folder 1, WH; "Wy'danch Housing Shows Violations," *Babylon Beacon*, December 7, 1967, 19.

70. "Negroes Fault Cops, Welfare Dept. on Crime," *ND*, November 29, 1966, 9; "Housing Check Pledged for Welfare Cases," *ND*, January 19, 1967, 15.

71. "Racial 'Coordinator' Asked in Roosevelt," *ND*, May 22, 1967, 20; Baxandall and Ewen, *Picture Windows*, 189–90.

72. Nassau-Suffolk Regional Planning Board, *Study of Local Housing Codes*, 44–45.

73. "Probe Housing in Roosevelt for Violations," *ND*, June 30, 1967, 15; "Muster Support," *ND*, Sep 21, 1967, 36; "Rev. Beatrice Desvignes, 70," *ND*, Dec 24, 1986, 29.

74. "Roosevelt Plan Splits Town," *ND*, July 7, 1967, 9; Badger v. Barbaro, 68C 432 (1968), pg. 4, Exhibit A.

75. "Nassau to Hold Back Reliefers' Rent Cash," *ND*, July 19, 1967, 22; "Plan Drive Against Roosevelt Crowding," *ND*, July 22, 1967, 11.

76. "Available Data on Roosevelt Reflecting Poverty Conditions," 2, box 66, folder "Economic Opportunity Commission," ENP; "Status Report: The Roosevelt Project," January 10, 1968, box 59, folder "County Executive—Status Report #1," ENP; "Inter-Department Memo—March 11, 1968," 3, box 59, folder " 'Co Exec—Status Reports' [3 of 3]," ENP; "News Release from County Executive Eugene H. Nickerson," December 29, 1967, box 59, folder "County Executive—Status Report #1," ENP.

77. "High-Rent Poor a 500-G Issue," *ND*, November 22, 1968, 11; "Welfare Motel Use at New High," *ND*, June 11, 1970, 7; "Statement for the Nassau County Human Rights Commission," May 17, 1971, Legal Department Case Files, 1960–1972, Supplement to Part 23, Series B, Section 2, reel 9, slides 782–804, PNC; "How Nassau Subsidizes Motel Slumlords," *Long Island Free Press* 1, no. 5, December 1970, 1–4, box 233, TLN; "Genocide . . . Nassau County Style," *Black News*, August 1, 1971, 1, box 233, TLN.

78. Badger v. Barbaro, 1–5, Exhibit A; "Negroes Sue, Say Welfare Bars Move," *ND*, May 7, 1968, 6.

79. James J. Graham, "Civil Liberties Problems in Welfare Administration," *New York University Law Review* 43 (November 1968), 858–99; Hugh Wilson, interview by Tim Keogh, December 4, 2017.

80. "Civil Action for Declaratory Judgement and Injunction," May 2, 1968, 6–10, Badger v. Barbaro, 68C 432 (1968); See also Aaron Cavin, "A Right to Housing in the Suburbs: *James v. Valtierra* and the Campaign against Economic Discrimination," *Journal of Urban History* 45, no. 3 (May 2019): 427–51.

81. "Answer," June 8, 1968, 1–5, Badger v. Barbaro, 68C 432 (1968).

82. "Stipulation of Discontinuance," September 5, 1969, 1–2, Badger v. Barbaro, 68C 432 (1968).

83. "Building Aide, Landlord Skirmish over Housing," *ND*, March 18, 1969, 13; Deed Liber 8182, 245; Mortgage Liber 8692, 245, NCC.

84. Seligman, *Block by Block*, 60–67, 237fn5.

85. Harris, "Modes of Informal Urban Development," 277–78.

86. Smith, *Racial Democracy*, 41–65.

87. Raymond & May Associates, *Residential Market Analysis Progress Report Part IV*, 11, 22, Table XIII.

88. "The Making of a Black Ghetto," *ND*, August 24, 1968, 8W; "The Roosevelt Picture," *ND*, August 30, 1968, 4B.

89. "An Obituary for a Dream," *ND*, September 12, 1969, 5B.

90. Mary E. Pattillo, *Black Picket Fences: Privilege and Peril among the Black Middle Class* (Chicago: University of Chicago Press, 1999), 203–15; "Poverty Unit Seeks a Voice in Housing," *ND*, February 4, 1969, 23; "Nassau Housing Unit to Give Poor a Voice," *ND*, February 6, 1969, 23.

91. "Drive is Set on Crowding in New Cassel," *ND*, August 1, 1969, 15; "Found: A Site for Sore Eyes," *ND*, August 12, 1969, 15; "Fear Forces the Poor to Live with Housing Code Offenses," *ND*, November 3, 1970, 13.

92. Robert Koubek, *Wyandanch: A Case Study of Political Impotence in a Black Suburban Ghetto* (MA thesis, Queens College, 1971), 30–32, 38, 78–82; "House Fire Kills 2 in Wyandanch," *ND*, December 18, 1972, 17.

93. "Over $1 Million goes to Town for Renewal," *IB*, October 24, 1968, 1; "Fund to Give New Look to Islip Homes, Streets," *ND*, October 30, 1968, 15; "Tenants in Central Islip Say No Repairs, No Rent," *ND*, December 19, 1969, 19; "Reliefers Living on Streets of Despair," 10; "Confrontation in Carleton Park Pits Tenants Against Landlord."

94. "Demonstration Set after Baby Dies," *ND*, January 15, 1970, 15; "Confrontation in Carleton Park Pits Tenants Against Landlord"; "Order to Close Inn Called 'Scrooge Act,'" *IB*, December 16, 1971, 1.

95. "An Eviction because of a Conviction," *ND*, March 4, 1972, 7.

96. "HUD Project Dashes Hopes After 4 Years," *ND*, August 8, 1972, 6.

97. Richard L. Florida and Marshall M. A. Feldman, "Housing in US Fordism," *International Journal of Urban and Regional Research* 12, no. 2 (June 1988): 192–203; Alexander Von Hoffman, "A Study in Contradictions: The Origins and Legacy of the Housing Act of 1949," *Housing Policy Debate* 11, no. 2 (2000): 299–312; Adam Tanaka, "Private Projects, Public Ambitions: Large-scale, Middle-Income Housing in New York City," (PhD diss., Harvard University, 2018), 104–8.

98. Zamora, "When Exclusion Replaces Exploitation."

## Chapter Four

1. "But Why Grumman?" *ND*, April 16, 1966, 1W.

2. See David Onkst, "Triumph and Decline," 265–66; "Grumman Hires 28 in 2 Poverty Areas," *ND*, February 5, 1968, 15; "Hunt For 'Black Energy' Proves Boon for Grumman," *Long Island Press*, February 5, 1968, Alphabetical files, section A-12, cabinet "Com–Cu," folder "CORE," GR.

3. Nassau-Suffolk Regional Planning Board, "Economic Highlights," 1.

4. Brenes, *Right and Might*, 64–70.

5. Ullman, *In Irons: U.S. Military Might in the New Century*, 169–70.

6. This divide is admittedly simplistic. For "commercial" Keynesianism, see Robert Lekachman, *The Ages of Keynes* (New York: McGraw-Hill, 1966), 287; For the social/commercial divide, see Alan Brinkley, "The New Deal and the Idea of the State," in *The Rise and Fall of the New Deal Order, 1930–1980*, eds. Steve Fraser and Gary Gerstle (Princeton, NJ: Princeton University Press, 1989), 85–121; Margaret Weir and Theda Skocpol, "State Structures and Social Keynesianism: Responses to the Great Depression in Sweden and the United States," *International Journal of Comparative Sociology* 24 (March 1983): 4–29; For a more nuanced view, see Attewell, *People Must Live by Work*, 135–39.

7. Harold L. Wilensky, *Rich Democracies: Political Economy, Public Policy, and Performance* (Berkeley: University of California Press, 2002), 463–65, 470; Robert Pollin and Heidi Garrett-Peltier, "The U.S. Employment Effects of Military and Domestic Spending Priorities," *International Journal of Health Services* 39, no. 3 (2009): 443–60.

8. Fordham, *Building the Cold War Consensus*, 31–56; Cipher, "The Origins and Evolution of Military Keynesianism," 453–57; Lester Brune, "Guns and Butter: The Pre-Korean War Dispute over Budget Allocations: Nourse's Conservative Keynesianism Loses Favor against Keyserling's Economic Expansion Plan," *The American Journal of Economics and Sociology* 48, no. 3 (1989): 357–71; Edmund F. Wehrle, "Guns, Butter, Leon Keyserling, the AFL-CIO, and the Fate of Full-Employment Economics," *The Historian* 66, no. 4 (2004): 730–36; Michael Hogan, *A Cross of Iron: Harry S. Truman and the Origins of the National Security State, 1945–1954* (Cambridge: Cambridge University Press, 1998), 69–118.

9. Anthony S. Chen, *The Fifth Freedom: Jobs, Politics, and Civil Rights in the United States, 1941–1972* (Princeton, NJ: Princeton University Press, 2009), 51; Martha Biondi, *To Stand and to Fight: The Struggle for Civil Rights in Postwar New York City* (Cambridge, MA: Harvard University Press, 2003), 18–20, 99–106.

10. NYS Commission against Discrimination, *Annual Report of the State Commission against Discrimination 1953* (Albany, NY: State Commission Against Discrimination, 1954), 13; "Alleged Discrimination in Employment—Respondent: Republic Aviation Corporation (Randolph R. Ford)," February 21, 1962, 3, box 31, folder C-4-1-538, Complaint Files, 1961–1965, PCE.

11. "Comparative Analysis: Occupational Breakdown by Race," box 3, folder "Comparative Analysis—New York," PGC; 5.8 percent of Long Island's black labor force worked for the region's top defense employers, compared to over 7 percent of the white labor force.

12. Jessie Carney Smith and Carrell Peterson Horton, *Historical Statistics of Black America: Agriculture to Labor & Employment* (New York: Gale Research Inc., 1995), 1018–19; Herbert Roof Northrup, *The Negro in the Aerospace Industry* (Philadelphia: University of Pennsylvania Press, 1968), 21.

13. Hooks, *Forging the Military-Industrial Complex*, 229–48; Hogan, *Cross of Iron*, 7.

14. Eugene Gholz, "The Curtis-Wright Corporation and Cold War-Era Defense Procurement: A Challenge to Military-Industrial Complex Theory," *Journal of Cold War Studies* 2, no. 1 (Winter 2000): 35–75; Mark R. Wilson, "Making 'Goop' Out of Lemons: The Permanente Metals Corporation, Magnesium Incendiary Bombs, and the Struggle for Profits during World War II,"

*Enterprise & Society* 12, no. 1 (March 2011): 10–45; Wehrle, "Aid Where It Is Needed Most," 96–119; Brenes, *Right and Might*, 38–40.

15. Herman O. Stekler, *The Structure and Performance of the Aerospace Industry* (Berkeley: University of California Press, 1965), 17.

16. Onkst, "Triumph and Decline," 20–24; Stoff, *The Thunder Factory*, 144–56; Thruelsen, *Grumman Story*, 263, 333.

17. Roger E. Bolton, *Defense Purchases and Regional Growth* (Washington, DC: Brookings Institution, 1966), 118, 152–62.

18. "Fairchild Layoffs: A Canceled Contract Jolts LI's Economy: Is Fairchild Canceled Out?" *ND*, January 16, 1959, 1C.

19. "Republic Hits Stuy's Strike Role," *ND*, April 18, 1956, 7; "Officials Confer Today on LI Layoffs," *ND*, January 16, 1959, 20; "Pike vs. Ormsby," *ND*, October 22, 1962, 1C; "Derounian Name to NY Steering Unit," *ND*, January 11, 1963, 36; Brenes, *Might and Right*, 60.

20. Wehrle, "Aid Where It Is Needed Most," 103–11.

21. Quoted in Bolton, *Defense Purchases*, 141.

22. "Pentagon Tells NY Plants: 'Ideas' Get the Contracts," *ND*, February 25, 1959, 33.

23. "Comparative Analysis: Occupational Breakdown by Race—Republic Aviation," April 10, 1957–January 10, 1961, box 3, folder "Comparative Analysis—New York," PGC; Thruelsen, *Grumman Story*, 287, 333.

24. Bob Schmidt, interview by Elly Shodell, January 31, 1995, 43, Aviation Oral History Collection, PWP.

25. Harold Wattel, "Unemployment on Long Island," *Long Island Business* 4, no. 1 (November 1957): 1, box 1, HCB; William N. Leonard, "Business Outlook for 1958," *Long Island Business* 5, no. 1 (January 1958): 2, box 1, HCB.

26. *EAA Scope* 1, no. 1 (June 1952), 2, box 12, EAA; Thruelsen, *Grumman Story*, 320–21.

27. Republic Aviation Occupational Distribution by Race Report, November 15, 1961, box 31, folder C-4-1-538, Complaint Files, 1961–1965, PCE.

28. "Comparative Analysis: Occupational Breakdown by Race- Grumman Engineering Corporation," October 19, 1959, box 3, folder "Comparative Analysis—New York," PGC.

29. See Reeves Instrument January 4, 1960, and Fairchild Stratos October 25, 1960, Occupational Breakdown by Race forms, box 3, folder "Comparative Analysis—New York," PGC.

30. American Instruments Laboratories, American Bosch Arma, Fairchild Stratos, Fairchild Guided, Grumman, Reeves Instrument, Republic, Weksler Instruments, Potter Instruments; Comparative Analysis: Occupational Breakdown by Race forms, box 3, folder "Comparative Analysis—New York," PGC.

31. "Complaint Form: Norman Baskin," February 12, 1962, box 31, folder C-4-1-553, Complaint Files, 1961–1965, PCE.

32. Chen, *The Fifth Freedom*, 86; "Comparative Analysis—United Aircraft Corp. (Norden Div.—Ketay Dept.) Commack, NY," December 1, 1960, box 3, folder "Comparative Analysis—New York," PGC; "Comparative Analysis—Gyrodyne Company of America, Inc.—St. James, NY," September 27, 1960, box 3, folder "Comparative Analysis—New York," PGC.

33. Sugrue, *Sweet Land of Liberty*, 268; Hugh Davis Graham, *The Civil Rights Era: Origins and Development of National Policy, 1960–1972* (New York: Oxford University Press, 1990), 42, 51–53.

34. "Republic Corp. Biased in Promotions: NAACP," *ND*, November 30, 1961, 4; "US Probing Bias in 128 Companies," *AN*, December 9, 1961; "Republic Aviation Denies Color Bias,"

December 1, 1961, folder "Newspaper Clippings - Industry, Republic Aviation 1960–1961," The Archives at Queens Library, Jamaica, New York.

35. See case files C-4-1-516 to C-4-1-567 in box 31, folder "Republic Aviation, Farmingdale, New York," Complaint Files, 1961–1965, PCE.

36. "Alleged Discrimination in Employment—Respondent: Republic Aviation Corporation (Randolph R. Ford)," February 21, 1962, 2–4, box 31, folder C-4-1-538, Complaint Files, 1961–1965, PCE; Handwritten testimony - Randolph R. Ford, box 31, folder C-4-1-538, Complaint Files, 1961–1965, PCE.

37. "Alleged Discrimination in Employment—Respondent: Republic Aviation Corporation (John Diggs)," August 10, 1961, 2–5, box 31, folder C-4-1-538, Complaint Files, 1961–1965, PCE; "Exhibit A: Complaint," box 31, folder C-4-1-538, Complaint Files, 1961–1965, PCE; "Exhibit C: Disciplinary Notice," box 31, folder C-4-1-538, Complaint Files, 1961–1965, PCE.

38. "Alleged Discrimination in Employment—Respondent: Republic Aviation Corporation (John Diggs)," August 10, 1961, 5, box 31, folder C-4-1-538, Complaint Files, 1961–1965, PCE.

39. John F. Kennedy, "Statement by the President Concerning a Cost Reduction Program in the Defense Department," July 8, 1962, Gerhard Peters and John T. Woolley, *The American Presidency Project*, http://www.presidency.ucsb.edu/ws/?pid=8761; Wehrle, "Aid Where It Is Needed Most," 114–15.

40. Wilson, *Creative Destruction*, 280; Ronald J. Fox, *Defense Acquisition Reform 1960–2009: An Elusive Goal* (Washington, DC: Center of Military History, US Army, 2011), 35–36; Laurence E. Lynn, Jr., and Richard I. Smith, "Can the Secretary of Defense Make a Difference?" *International Security* 7, no. 1 (Summer 1982): 49–51.

41. Quoted in James L. Clayton, *The Economic Impact of the Cold War: Sources and Readings* (New York: Harcourt, Brace, and World, 1970), 115.

42. Richard Austin Smith, *Corporations in Crisis* (Garden City, NY: Doubleday, 1963), 171–204.

43. Clayton, *Economic Impact of the Cold War*, 99; "Cutback Perils 9,000 Republic jobs: Republic May Ax 9,000 by June 63," *ND*, February 1, 1962, 1.

44. Gerard Piel, "The Economics of Disarmament," *Bulletin of the Atomic Scientists* 16, no. 4 (1960): 117–26; Emile Benoit, "The Economics of Disarmament," *Challenge* 10, no. 9 (1962): 9–13; Leslie Fishman, "The Expansionary Effects of Shifts from Defense to Nondefense Spending," in *Disarmament and the Economy*, eds. Emile Benoit and Kenneth E. Boulding (New York: Harper & Row, 1963): 173–81; Seymour Melman, *Our Depleted Society* (New York: Delta Publishing Co., 1965).

45. Cipher, "The Origins and Evolution of Military Keynesianism," 464–66; Thomas E. Woods, Jr. "The Neglected Costs of the Warfare State: An Austrian Tribute to Seymour Melman," *Journal of Libertarian Studies* 22 (2010): 103–25.

46. Margaret Weir, "Full Employment as a Political Issue in the United States," *Social Research* 54, no. 2 (Summer 1987): 392–95; Stein, *Running Steel*, 32–35.

47. Lyndon B. Johnson, "Memorandum Establishing the Committee on the Economic Impact of Defense and Disarmament," December 21, 1963, Gerhard Peters and John T. Woolley, *The American Presidency Project*, http://www.presidency.ucsb.edu/ws/?pid=26554.

48. Bernard Udis, ed., *The Economic Consequences of Reduced Military Spending* (Lexington, MA: Lexington Books, 1973), 2; Boulding "The Impact of the Defense Industry," 237.

49. "Officials Voice Concern, Demand Action," *ND*, February 8, 1962, 2M; "Warns Areas: Don't Rely on Defense Jobs," *ND*, March 12, 1962, 11.

50. William Lee Baldwin, *The Structure of the Defense Market, 1955–1964* (Durham, NC: Duke University Press, 1967), 198–99.

51. "Republic Union Calls Strike Vote," *ND*, March 17, 1962, 1; "Strike is on at Republic: Production Halts, No Talks Set," *ND*, April 2, 1962, 1, 3, 82; John F. Kennedy, *Public Papers of the Presidents of the United States: John F. Kennedy, January 1 to December 31, 1962* (Washington, DC: GPO, 1963), 497–98.

52. Quoted in Brenes, "For Right and Might," 107.

53. "Republic Lays off 151 at L.I. Factory," *NYT*, February 24, 1962, 29.

54. US Arms Control and Disarmament Agency, *The Post Layoff Labor Market Experiences of Former Republic Aviation Corporation (Long Island) Workers* (Washington, DC: US GPO, 1966), 77.

55. "Tempera Plans to Seek more U.S. Job Aid," *ND*, October 27, 1964, 15.

56. Economic Report 1963, box 10, folder 6, International FTPE Local 66 Papers, TRW; "Labor Committee for Full Employment," box 10, folder 6, International FTPE Local 66 Papers, TRW; "Wanted: Jobs," box 10, folder 6, International FTPE Local 66 Papers, TRW; "Program," December 16, box 111, folder 12, Newspaper Guild of New York Papers, TRW.

57. US Senate, Committee on Labor and Public Welfare, *Hearings Relating to the Training and Utilization of the Manpower Resources of the Nation*, Eighty-Eighth Congress, First Session, November 15, 18, 19, 20, 21, December 4–5, 1963 (Washington, DC: GPO, 1964), 2970–75, 2990–3032.

58. "LI Unionists See LBJ, Ask Industry Aid," *ND*, February 19, 1964.

59. Congressman Seymour Halpern, speaking on H.R. 10623, on March 2, 1964, 88th Cong., 2nd Session, *Congressional Record 110, pt. 3*: 4023–24.

60. *Hearings Before the Committee on Commerce, United States Senate, Eighty-Eight Congress, Second Session, on S. 2274*, May and June 22, 1964 (Washington, DC: US GPO, 1964), 10, 17–20; Seymour Melman, *The Permanent War Economy: American Capitalism in Decline* (New York: Touchstone, 1985), 292–96; Brenes, *Might is Right*, 104–5.

61. "Wirtz to Study LI Job Problem: RFK Pledges Study of LI Job Problem," *ND*, October 26, 1964, 1.

62. "LI Labor Has 3-Pt. Plan to Make Jobs," *ND*, December 21, 1964, 1.

63. "Wirtz to Study LI Job Problem: RFK Pledges Study of LI Job Problem," *ND*, October 26, 1964, 1; Memorandum to Mr. Valenti, September 28, 1964, Part I, box 25, folder 15, Daniel Patrick Moynihan Papers, LCM; "Douglas Offer is Seen Attracting 400 LIers," *ND*, October 29, 1965, 33.

64. "U.S. Tour Lights Republic's Hopes," *ND*, August 2, 1965, 7.

65. NYS Department of Labor, *The Transferability of Defense Job Skills to Non-Defense Occupations: A Report* (December 1965), 2; "Mac to Visit LI Industry," *ND*, September 15, 1965, 4.

66. "McNamara Tells LI: Diversify Industry," *ND*, October 14, 1965, 1, 3, 60, 118.

67. "Ask Mac to Confer on LI Labor Search," *ND*, November 29, 1965, 21; Eugene Gholz, "Eisenhower versus the Spin-off Story: Did the Rise of the Military-Industrial Complex Hurt or Help America's Commercial Aircraft Industry?" *Enterprise & Society*, 12, no. 1 (March 2011): 46–95.

68. US Arms Control and Disarmament Agency, *The Post Layoff Labor Market Experiences*, 6–8, 11, 26–32, 71–73, 133–44; Kamer et al., *Manufacturing in Suburbia*, 18; US Bureau of Labor Statistics, *Three Standards of Living Spring 1967*, 16.

69. Mark Clodfelter, *The Limits of Air Power: The American Bombing of North Vietnam* (Lincoln, NE: Bison Books), 133–36.

70. "Grumman Denies CORE'S Charge of Employment Bias," *LI Press*, August 6, 1965, Alphabetical files, Section A-12, cabinet "Com–Cu," folder "CORE," GR.

71. "A Statement by Grumman Aircraft after Four Meetings with Long Island CORE," undated, Section A-12, cabinet "Com–Cu," folder "CORE," GR; "Draft," August 19, 1965, section A-12, cabinet "Com–Cu," folder "CORE," GR; "Hank" to Jack Rettaliata, Revision to Draft, August 19, 1965, section A-12, cabinet "Com–Cu," folder "CORE," GR.

72. Long Island Congress of Racial Equality to Grumman Aircraft Corp. et al., August 5, 1965, section A-12, cabinet "Com–Cu," folder "CORE," GR; James J. Hill to Robert Bradshaw, September 23, 1965, section A-12, cabinet "Com–Cu," folder "CORE," GR.

73. P. E. Viemeister, "Who's Who in Civil Rights," September 15, 1965, section A-12, cabinet "Com–Cu," folder "CORE," GR.

74. "Grumman OKs CORE Points," *ND*, August 28, 1965; Peter Viemeister to Jack Rettaliata, September 20, 1965, section A-12, cabinet "Com–Cu," folder "CORE," GR; P. E. Viemeister to L. J. Evans, October 13, 1965, section A-12, cabinet "Com–Cu," folder "CORE," GR.

75. "CORE Says It Will Stop Talking, Start Acting in Grumman Case," *ND*, November 1, 1965, 27; "A Statement by Grumman Aircraft after Four Meetings with Long Island CORE," undated, section A-12, cabinet "Com–Cu," folder "CORE," GR.

76. "LI's Lynch Moves up in CORE," *ND*, April 19, 1966, 7.

77. Graham, *Civil Rights Era*, 187–88, 283.

78. 1967 Training Folder, Alphabetical files, section A-19, cabinet "Stol-Tim," folder "Training," GR; "Hunt For 'Black Energy' Proves Boon for Grumman," *Long Island Press*, February 5, 1968, Alphabetical files, section A-12, cabinet "Com–Cu," folder "CORE," GR; "Statement of Purpose," undated, Alphabetical files, section A-10, cabinet "Dept. (O)," folder "Department—Equal Opport. Open Door council 68," GR.

79. "Grumman Reports Sharp Decline in Space Work, Sees New Gains," *ND*, December 2, 1967, 3; Employment Improvement Organization to Grumman Negro Employees, January 24, 1968, Leadership Development Files, Part 3, Series B, reel 4, slide 869, SDR; "Inter-office Memorandum," February 14, 1968, Leadership Development Files, Part 3, Series B, reel 4, slides 870–73, SDR; "Big Brothers Statement of Purpose," box 1, folder 2, WBT; "Outline—Complaints against Grumman Aircraft in Regard to Bias in Employment," box 1, folder 2, WBT.

80. "U.S. to Study Charge of Bias at Grumman," *ND*, April 1, 1969; "Blacks at Grumman List Complaints," *ND*, April 2, 1969; "Grumman Keeping Us Down: Blacks," *Interavia*, April 4, 1969; Onkst, "Triumph and Decline," 267.

81. "'Out of Proportion' Tempera Decries Grumman Probe," *Suffolk Sun*, April 7, 1969, "Tempera is Denounced for Grumman Position," *ND*, March 28, 1969, in Alphabetical files, section A-12, cabinet "Com–Cu," folder "CORE," GR.

82. "U.S. Begins Job Bias Study at Grumman," *ND*, April 15, 1969, "Grumman Inter-Office Memorandum," September 10, 1969, and "Grumman Inter-Office Memorandum," November 15, 1969, Alphabetical files, section A-10, cabinet "Dept. (O)," folder "Department—Equal Opport. Open Door council 68," GR.

83. See "CORE to file Grumman Suit," *Suffolk Sun*, May 19, 1969, "Blacks Sue to Halt U.S. Contracts to Grumman," *Long Island Press*, October 31, 1969, and "Action Against Grumman May be a Landmark Case," *Long Island Press*, November 3, 1969, in Alphabetical files, section A-12, cabinet "Com–Cu," folder "CORE," GR.

84. Onkst, "Triumph and Decline," 331, 343–49; "Layoff No Blow to Industry: Grumman," *ND*, May 21, 1969, 9.

85. See "Blacks walkout threatened at Grumman," *ND*, August 2, 1969, "Grumman Blacks to Fight Firings," *Long Island Press*, August 2, 1969, in Alphabetical files, section A-12, cabinet "Com–Cu," folder "CORE," GR.

86. "Black Organization Threatens to Shut Down Grumman," *Long Island Press*, June 20, 1969, "Grumman Charged Anew with Bias," *ND*, June 20, 1969, in Alphabetical files, section A-12, cabinet "Com–Cu," folder "CORE," GR.

87. "Grumman Blacks Demand Change," *ND*, July 17, 1969.

88. "Grumman Plant Picketed by Blacks over Layoffs," *New York News*, August 5, 1969, in Alphabetical files, section A-12, cabinet "Com–Cu," folder "CORE," GR.

89. " 'Black Monday' Protest off to a Slow Start," *Long Island Press*, September 29, 1969, " 'Big Brother' Pickets Grumman," *Long Island Press*, September 30, 1969, and "80 Pickets at Grumman Charge Discrimination," *ND*, September 30, 1969, in Alphabetical files, section A-12, cabinet "Com–Cu," folder "CORE," GR.

90. Onkst, "Triumph and Decline," 289–93, 298–315.

91. Feliu, "Impact on Long Island," Table VI; OFCC Grumman Statistics, March 31, 1971, Box V: 1532, folder 7, RNCP.

92. Onkst, "Triumph and Decline," 233–26; "You Can't Learn It All on Campus," *Ebony Magazine*, 1972, "Co-op Students View 'Work Break' as Valuable Step on Career Path," *Grumman Plane News*, September 22, 1972, and "Co-op Student to Resume Studies at Bennett College," *Grumman Plane News*, July 27, 1973, Alphabetical files, section A-12, cabinet "Com–Cu," folder "CO-OP Students," GR.

93. Nassau-Suffolk Regional Planning Board, "Economic Highlights," *Long Island Economic Trends* 7, no. 8 (August 1976): 1.

94. "Opening Statement," November 25, 1969, box 67, folder "Commerce & Industry [2 of 3]," ENP; Marvin Berkowitz, *The Conversion of Military-Oriented Research and Development to Civilian Uses* (New York: Praeger, 1970), 397–472; "Long Island Federation of Labor, AFL-CIO, Save-a-Job Committee," 2–4, folder 13, box 111, Newspaper Guild of New York, TRW; "Rally: The Works, not the Workers," *ND*, September 8, 1970, 13; For the national context, see Brenes, *For Might and Right*, 112–24, 132–38; Lily Geismer, *Don't Blame Us: Suburban Liberals and the Transformation of the Democratic Party* (Princeton, NJ: Princeton University Press, 2014), 156–72.

95. Mathew Forstater, "From Civil Rights to Economic Security: Bayard Rustin and the African-American Struggle for Full Employment, 1945–1978," *International Journal of Political Economy* 36, no. 3 (Fall 2007): 63–74; Stein, "Fearing Inflation, Inflating Fears."

96. *Report of the Committee on Economic Security*, Social Security Reports & Studies, Social Security History, https://www.ssa.gov/history/reports/ces/ces5.html.

## Chapter Five

1. "Matching Jobs with the Jobless," *ND*, May 22, 1968, 36; "Defense Contracts won by 2 LI Firms," *ND*, July 20, 1967, 27; "LI Firm Hires only 8 from Wyandanch in Day of Recruiting," *ND*, March 25, 1968, 11.

2. *Newsday*, "LI Firm Hires only 8," 11.

3. Alice O'Connor, "When Measurements Matter: Poverty, Wealth, and the Politics of Inequality in the United States," *History of Political Economy* 52, no. 3 (June 2020): 590–94.

4. "Matching Jobs with the Jobless," *ND*, May 22, 1968, 36.

5. Robert Collins, *More: The Politics of Economic Growth in Postwar America* (New York: Oxford University Press, 2002), 51–67; Attewell, *People Must Live by Work*, 180–93.

6. "Community Profile, New York, Nassau County," CP-008, box 254, folder 30, "Community Profiles 1967," Records of the Information Center, CSA; "Community Profile, New York, Suffolk County," CP-008, box 256, folder 52, "Community Profiles 1967," Records of the Information Center, CSA.

7. US Department of Commerce, *County and City Data Book [United States] Consolidated File: County Data, 1947–1977* (Ann Arbor, MI: Inter-university Consortium for Political and Social Research, 2012), https://doi.org/10.3886/ICPSR07736.v2.

8. "Suffolk County Public Information News Release," August 15, 1965, box 3, folder 119, HLD; "A Shining Example for All America," *Long Island Daily Review*, date unknown, box 63, folder "Anti-Poverty," ENP.

9. O'Connor, *Poverty Knowledge*, 123–32; Huret, *Experts' War on Poverty*, 144–60.

10. Katz, *Undeserving Poor*, 119–25.

11. Organization for Social and Technical Innovation et al., *Poverty in Spread City*, Figure 1A.

12. "The Welfare," *Tri-Cap Reflector* 1, no. 2 (May 1971): 13, Box "New Cassel," HSW; "SED-FRE Workshop Application—Edwin R Geyer," Leadership Development Files, Part 3, Series B, reel 4, slide 715, SDR; "Interview with Glenn Moody," *The Black News/Long Island Free Press*, July 1971, Periodicals 1, box 233, TLN.

13. Hugh Wilson interview.

14. Ryan LaRochelle, "Reassessing the History of the Community Action Program, 1963–1967," *Journal of Policy History*, 31, no. 1 (January 2019): 126–64.

15. Paul M. Arfin, *Unfinished Business: Social Action in Suburbia, Long Island NY 1945–2014* (n.p.: Paul Arfin, 2015), 99–100; "Communique from LI's Poverty Battlefield," *ND*, October 29, 1966, 1W; Untitled Note, folder 100, box 2, HLD; "The Designation of the Economic Opportunity Council of Suffolk, Inc.," 7, box 1, folder 3, WBT; "One Place where it Worked," *ND*, August 4, 1971, 5A; "Up Front in LI's Poverty War: What One Village Does-and Doesn't-Do for its Poor," *ND*, April 13, 1968, 1W.

16. "Surplus Food," box 66, folder "Donable Foods" folder, ENP; "News Release," June 19, 1969, box 66, folder "Donable Foods," ENP.

17. O'Connor, *Poverty Knowledge*, 158–65; For CAP histories, see Kent Germany, *New Orleans After the Promises: Poverty, Citizenship, and the Search for the Great Society* (Athens: University of Georgia Press, 2007); Annelise Orleck, and Lisa Gayle Hazirjian, *The War on Poverty: A New Grassroots History, 1964–1980* (Athens: University of Georgia Press, 2011); William S. Clayson, *Freedom Is Not Enough The War on Poverty and the Civil Rights Movement in Texas* (Austin: University of Texas Press, 2010) among others.

18. Alan J. Boram, Walter J. Kershaw, Jr., Mary Knuth, Beryl Thomas, Reva Tyree, Casto Rodriguez, Patricia Arnell, "Lawyer and Participant Perceptions of Legal Services at Nassau County Law Services Committee, Inc.," (MSW: Adelphi University, 1970), 18–22; Graham, "Civil Liberties Problems," 858–59.

19. "Shifts in Suffolk Poverty Setup Point Up a Maze of Problems," *NYT*, June 30, 1968, 26; "Communique from LI's Poverty Battlefield," *ND*, October 29, 1966, 1W.

20. "Farm Labor Annual Report, 1966," 21, box 511, folder "New York Clips," MWP; "Special for: Long Island Press, February 19, 1960," 4, box 3, folder 104, HLD.

21. "Suffolk County Public Information News Release," December 9, 1965, box 3, folder 119, HLD.

22. "Feasibility Study of the Utilization of Local Residents versus Migrant Workers in the Agricultural Industry of Suffolk County," August 28, 1967, 5–9, box 2, folder 72, HLD.

23. "Three Laborers Killed in East End Blaze," *ND*, January 15, 1968; "Poverty and Powerlessness USA," June 9, 1969, box 1, folder 3, WBT; Morton Silverstein, *What Harvest the Reaper?* (National Educational Television and Radio Centre, 1968), film.

24. "Migrant System Is Called Costly," *NYT*, February 11, 1968, 55; "Initial Cost Study for Subsidizing Agricultural Workers in Suffolk County as a Possible Method of Replacing Migrant Workers with Local Residents," box 2, folder 72, HLD.

25. "Final Report of the Subcommittee on 'Alternatives to Migratory Labor,'" 2–4, box 2, folder 84, HLD.

26. "Suffolk County Department of Social Services Responses to Questionnaire of the State Legislative Committee," April 1, 1969, 6–9, box 11, folder "Suffolk County Social Services Dept. 1969–1968–1967," SCC.

27. "Submitted for the Consideration of the Joint Legislative Committee on Migratory Labor," 5–6, box 2, folder 72, HLD.

28. "L.I. Hopes to Give Sea Legs to Farm Workers," *NYT*, February 14, 1966; "School for Fishermen Proposed in Greenport," *ND*, March 21, 1966, 27.

29. "Highlight Memorandum: Application for Grant under Title II-A," May 18, 1967, box 511, folder "Suffolk County Economic Opportunity Commission," MWP; "Office of Economic Opportunity—Community Action Program: Highlight Memorandum," May 9, 1969, 1–5, box 511, folder "Suffolk County Economic Opportunity Commission," MWP.

30. "Immediate Release: Suffolk County, New York, Council to Develop Migrant Worker Housing," *News from the Office of Economic Opportunity*, box 511, folder "Suffolk County Economic Opportunity Commission," MWP.

31. "Migrant Worker Poverty Program Gets Clean Bill," box 511, folder "Seasonal Employees in Agriculture, Inc.," MWP.

32. "Report on Services Available to Migrants and Resident Seasonal Workers," box 2, folder 84, HLD; "LI Anti-Poverty Unit Probed," *ND*, February 20, 1969, box 511, folder "Seasonal Employees in Agriculture, Inc.," MWP.

33. "Report of Arthur C. Bryant," November 3, 1967, box 2, folder 83, HLD; Rev. Arthur C. Bryant to the Joint Legislative Committee on Migrant Labor, December 11, 1967, box 2, folder 72, HLD; "Poverty and Powerlessness USA," June 9, 1969, box 1, folder 3, WBT; "Suffolk Migrants are Union Target," *ND*, June 1, 1969.

34. Cindy Hahamovitch, *The Fruits of Their Labor: Atlantic Coast Farmworkers and the Making of Migrant Poverty, 1870–1945* (Chapel Hill: University of North Carolina Press, 1997), 203.

35. Cindy Hahamovitch, *No Man's Land: Jamaican Guestworkers and the Global History of Deportable Labor* (Princeton, NJ: Princeton University Press, 2011), 145–71.

36. Quoted in Cromarty, "Suffolk County Farmland Preservation," 158; Eric Fauss, "The Postsuburban Development of Riverhead, Long Island: 1970–2000," *Long Island Historical Journal* 19, no. 1–2 (Fall 2006/Spring 2007): 149–51.

37. "Migratory Labor in New York State—are there alternatives?" 14–15, box 2, folder 72, HLD; US Congress, Subcommittee on Migratory Labor, Committee on Labor and Public Welfare, *Who are the Migrants?* (91st Cong., 1st and 2nd sess., June 9–10, 1969), 75.

38. Cromarty, "Suffolk County Farmland Preservation," 163–66.

39. "White House Aiding Urban Transit Programs to Make It Easier for Poor to Get to Jobs," *NYT*, March 20, 1967, 17; Tri-State Transportation Commission, *Public Transport Services*

*to non-CBD Employment Concentrations; Progress Report 1* (New York: Tri-State Transportation Commission, September 1967), 3, 5; Wendell E. Pritchett, "Which Urban Crisis? Regionalism, Race, and Urban Policy, 1960–1974," *Journal of Urban History* 34, no. 2 (January 2008): 269.

40. Nassau County Planning Commission, *Nassau County, New York Data Book* (Carle Place, NY: June 1974), 250; Pearl Kamer and the Nassau-Suffolk Regional Planning Board, *A Profile of the Nassau-Suffolk Labor Force* (Hauppauge, NY: Nassau-Suffolk Regional Planning Board, 1973), 46, 250; Organization for Social and Technical Innovation et al., *Poverty in Spread City*, 4–15.

41. Tri-State Transportation Commission, *People—Transportation—Jobs Report 1*, 5, 10, 21; Tri-State Transportation Commission, *People—Transportation—Jobs, Public Transport Services to non-CBD Employment Concentrations; Progress Report 4* (New York: Tri-State Transportation Commission, October 1969), 20–25; Tri-State Transportation Commission, *People—Transportation—Jobs, Public Transport Services to non-CBD Employment Concentrations; Progress Report 5* (New York: Tri-State Transportation Commission, December 1971), 32.

42. Kamer et al., *Manufacturing in Suburbia*, 18–19, 47–72.

43. Tri-State Transportation Commission, *People—Transportation—Jobs Report 4*, 9–10; Organization for Social and Technical Innovation et al., *Poverty in Spread City*, 18–19.

44. Tri-State Transportation Commission, *People—Transportation—Jobs Report 4*, 3, 9–13; "Building Supplier Counts on Suffolk Action," *ND*, May 15, 1967, 17A.

45. Tri-State Transportation Commission, *People—Transportation—Jobs Report 4*, 20–25; Tri-State Transportation Commission, *People—Transportation—Jobs Report 5*, 32; "Few Ride Bus, but It's Fun," *ND*, July 16, 1968, 10.

46. "No Takers for Jobs at End of Line," *ND*, May 16, 1967, 9; Tri-State Transportation Commission, *People—Transportation—Jobs Report 4*, 3–10.

47. "Bus Runs for Poor Facing Revamp," *ND*, September 13, 1968, 13; Tri-State Transportation Commission, *Progress Report 3*, 5, 14–16, 33–35; Tri-State Transportation Commission, *Progress Report 4*, 3–10, 20; Tri-State Transportation Commission, *Progress Report 5*, 14, 33–35.

48. Pimpare, *Poverty in America*, 7–8.

49. Mucciaroni, *Political Failure*, 58–69; Attewell, *People Must Live by Work*, 187–89; Jean Baptiste Fleury, "Poverty and the Scope of Economics in the Sixties," Working Paper, http://public.econ.duke.edu/~staff/wrkshop_papers/2008-2009%20Papers/FLeury_poverty1.2.pdf; O'Connor, *Poverty Knowledge*, 117–23.

50. David Vogel, *Fluctuating Fortunes: The Political Power of Business in America* (New York: Basic Books, 1989), 16, 24–26.

51. "A Record of Nassau County Government, January 1962-September 1964," box 58, folder "Co Exec–Status Reports" [3 of 3], ENP; "Guide to Public Manpower Programs Nationwide," 3–22, box 66, folder "Economic Opportunity Commission" [2 of 2], ENP; "Rights Groups: One Aim, Two Systems," April 28, 1970, box 1, folder 5, WBT; "Nassau County Commission on Human Rights—1968 Annual Report," 2–3, box 67, folder "Human Rights," ENP; "News Release," October 30, 1967, box 67, folder "Human Rights," ENP; "Application for Refunding Community Action Project Job Counseling and Development Project," June 1, 1968, 2–4, box 1, folder 1, WBT; "Job Counseling and Development Program, Summary: Job Program," box 11, folder "Suffolk County Human Rights Commission," SCC.

52. "Job Counseling and Development Program, Summary: Job Program," box 11, folder "Suffolk County Human Rights Commission," SCC.

53. "News Release," July 28, 1967, 2, box 66, folder "Employment," ENP.

54. "Job Search," box 1, folder 1, WBT.

55. "Status Report: Commission on Human Rights," August 1, 1969, 15, box 59, folder "Co Exec—Status Reports" [3 of 3], ENP; "Inter-Department Memo," January 15, 1968, box 59, folder "County Executive—Status Report #1," ENP.

56. "Job Counseling and Development Program, December 1968 Report," Attached no. 2, box 1, folder 2, WBT.

57. "Status Report: Economic Opportunity Commission," October 1968, box 59, folder "Co Exec—Status Reports" [3 of 3], ENP.

58. Economic Opportunity Commission of Nassau County, Manpower Division, "Monthly Manpower Placement Record, December 1967," box 68, folder "Jobs," ENP.

59. "Current Job Openings," *Suffolk County Human Relations Commission News*, January 1968, box 6, folder 19, WBT.

60. Organization for Social and Technical Innovation et al., *Poverty in Spread City*, 19–24.

61. "Minutes of Workshop Program on Employment—County Executive's Conference on Poverty," 2–3, box 58, folder "Poverty Program—Conference," box 58, ENP.

62. "Hard-Core Jobless Snub Low Pay: ND Closeup," *ND*, March 19, 1968, 9.

63. "The People Industry Needs are in Nassau," *Commerce and Industry News* 3, no. 1 (October 1968): 5, box 65, folder "Commerce & Industry," ENP; "JOBS Program," 3 box 68, folder "Jobs," ENP; "LI Poverty War Called Flop: More Reported Unemployed Now than 3 Years Ago," *Sunday News*, June 30, 1968, box 63, folder "Anti-Poverty," ENP; "Jobs for All," *ND*, May 23, 1968, 44.

64. David Vogel, *Fluctuating Fortunes: The Political Power of Business in America* (New York: Basic Books, 1989), 16, 24–26.

65. "Nassau's Goal: A Community of Opportunity," *Commerce and Industry News* 3, no. 1 (October 1968): 1, box 65, folder "Commerce & Industry," ENP.

66. "Unemployment/Underemployment versus Unfilled Jobs," 3, box 68, folder "Labor," ENP.

67. "For Immediate Release," March 18, 1968, box 66, folder "Economic Opportunity Commission," ENP; "Program Concepts and Philosophy," box 63, folder "Anti-Poverty," ENP; "Purcell Blasts Poverty 'Boondoggle,'" *ND*, March 16, 1967, 11; "Pilot Centers to Coordinate Unemployment Efforts," *Commerce and Industry News* 3, no. 1 (October 1968): 1, box 65, folder "Commerce & Industry," ENP.

68. "Job Counseling and Development Program, Summary: Job Program," box 11, folder "Suffolk County Human Rights Commission," SCC.

69. "Application for Refunding Community Action Project," June 1, 1968, 10–11, box 1, folder 1, WBT; "Job Counseling and Development Program, December 1968 Report," box 1, folder 2, WBT.

70. Job Counseling and Development Program Office Reports, January-April 1969, box 1, folder 3, WBT; Estelle Manfre to Mr. George Pettengill, July 2, 1969, box 11, folder "Suffolk County Human Rights Commission," SCC; Booker T. Young to Mr. George Pettengill, July 2, 1969, box 11, folder "Suffolk County Human Rights Commission," SCC; John P. Hogan to Mr. George Pettengill, July 25, 1969, box 11, folder "Suffolk County Human Rights Commission," SCC; Stanley R. Kase to Mr. George Pettengill, August 7, 1969, box 11, folder "Suffolk County Human Rights Commission," SCC.

71. Weir, *Politics and Jobs*, 104–5, 117; Stein, *Running Steel, Running America*, 124; Mucciaroni, *Political Failure*, 72–75; Attewell, *People Must Live by Work*, 182–209; Guian McKee, *The Problem*

*of Jobs: Liberalism, Race, and Deindustrialization in Philadelphia* (Chicago: University of Chicago Press, 2008), 137–210; Philip Harvey, *Securing the Right to Employment: Social Welfare Policy and the Unemployed* (Princeton, NJ: Princeton University Press, 1989), 4–5.

72. Quoted in Donald Rumsfeld, *Known and Unknown: A Memoir* (New York: Sentinel, 2011), 125; "Nick Asks U.S. to Back Job Plan for Reliefers," *ND*, August 8, 1968.

73. Frank Riessman, "New Careers: A Basic Strategy against Poverty," 3–8, box 68, folder "Jobs," ENP; Frank Riessman and Hermine I. Popper, "The Evolutionary Revolution," in *Up from Poverty; New Career Ladders for Nonprofessionals*, ed. Frank Riessman and Hermine I. Popper (New York: Harper & Row, 1968), 8–10; "The New Careers Training System: An Overview," *New Careers Newsletter*, undated, 1–2.

74. Jennifer Klein and Eileen Boris, *Caring for America: Home Health Workers in the Shadow of the Welfare State* (New York: Oxford University Press, 2012), 83–85; Mucciaroni, *Political Failure*, 75–78; Nicholas Juravich, "The Work of Education: Community-Based Educators in Schools, Freedom Struggles, and the Labor Movement, 1953–1983," (PhD diss., Columbia University, 2017), 331–54.

75. Claire Dunning, "New Careers for the Poor: Human Services and the Post-Industrial City," *Journal of Urban History* 44, no. 4 (July 2018): 669–90; Frank Riessman, "New Careers: A Vehicle for Radical Social Change," *New Careers Newsletter* 1, no. 3 (Winter 1967): 18–20.

76. "1969 Annual Report," box 58, ENP; "Guaranteed Employment Plan," *New Careers Newsletter* 3, no. 3 (Summer 1969): 4; "Proposal for Demonstration or Training or Research Grant," April 11, 1969, 13–16, box 66, folder "Economic Opportunity Commission" [2 of 2], ENP.

77. "Proposal for Demonstration," April 11, 1969, 5, 8–10, box 66, folder "Economic Opportunity Commission" [2 of 2], ENP; "Nassau Plans to Find Jobs for Reliefers," *ND*, July 2, 1969.

78. "Nick's Job Plan Backed at Hearing," *ND*, October 15, 1969, 15; Martin L. Gross, "Critic at Large: Horn to Solve Welfare Woes," *ND*, July 25, 1969; "Conservatives Score Dem Welfare Plan," *Manhasset Mail*, October 9, 1969, 2; "A Task Force to Tackle the Unemployment Crisis Created by the Nixon Administration," July 16, 1970, box 68, folder "Jobs," ENP.

79. "Welfare Job Assistance for Nassau Hits Delay," *ND*, September 18, 1969, 19.

80. "Application to Office of Economic Opportunity for Funding for a Demonstration Guaranteed Employment Program," box 68, folder "Jobs," ENP; "U.S. Shifts, Rejects Nassau Job Plan," *ND*, April 17, 1970; June Leonard, *Changing Values in the Civil Service Commission: Merit Employment Versus Employing the Disadvantaged; The Profile of Nassau County, New York* (MA thesis, Hunter College, 1972).

81. "Signs Point to No Return if Nickerson Fails Again," *ND*, February 19, 1970, 5; "Nickerson, English, and others Subpoenaed in Contract Probe," *ND*, October 27, 1970, 2; "Caso Names Hofstra Dean Welfare Head," *ND*, December 4, 1970, 11; "Dennison Switches Emphasis to Social Problems in Suffolk," *ND*, January 5, 1971, 2; "Dennison to Step Down: Dems Searching for Candidate," *ND*, June 3, 1971, 1.

82. "Suburbs Outstrip City on Welfare," *NYT*, December 7, 1967, 1; "Study Claims 130% Rise in LI Welfare Rolls," *ND*, December 8, 1967, 9; "Editorials: Bad News," *ND*, September 24, 1971, 54; "Nassau, in the Red, Oks Notes," *ND*, November 5, 1968.

83. For examples see Germany, *New Orleans after the Promises*; Hazirjian and Orleck, *The War on Poverty: A New Grassroots History*; Michael Woodsworth, *Battle for Bed-Stuy: The Long War on Poverty in New York City* (Cambridge, MA: Harvard University Press, 2016) among others.

84. McKee, *Problem of Jobs*, 111.

## Chapter Six

1. "Low Rent Public Housing Production Control Chart," April 30, 1971, Region II, sheet 6, Box V: 1527, folder 4, RNCP; "U.S. Aid Sought on Home Project," *ND*, February 3, 1970, 21.

2. Thurston, *Boundaries of Homeownership*, 184–201.

3. Charles M. Lamb, *Housing Segregation in Suburban America Since 1960: Presidential and Judicial Politics* (New York: Cambridge University Press, 2005), 70–71.

4. "Housing Plan stirs ire of New Cassel Homeowners," *Westbury Times*, July 16, 1970.

5. "Housing Plans for Poor Rejected on 2 Fronts," *ND*, July 15, 1970, 2; "Blacks on L.I. Kill Plan to House Poor Blacks," *NYT*, July 24, 1970; Harold Russell, "Alu . . . ," *Westbury Times*, July 23, 1970.

6. "New Cassel Villages Rap Housing Plan," *ND*, July 13, 1970, 11; "Communications: A Just Solution," *Westbury Times*, July 30, 1970.

7. National Advisory Commission on Civil Disorders, *Report of the National Advisory Commission on Civil Disorders* (New York: Bantam Books, 1968), 22; for policy recommendations, see pages 410–83.

8. David Imbroscio, "Urban Policy as Meritocracy: A Critique," *Journal of Urban Affairs* 38, no. 1 (February 2016): 85, 93; David Imbroscio, "The Perils of Rationalism in American Urban Policy," *Urban Affairs Review* 55, no. 1 (2019): 25.

9. Adolph Reed, Jr., "The Kerner Commission and the Irony of Antiracist Politics," *Labor: Studies in Working Class History of the Americas* 14, no. 4 (December 2017): 31–38.

10. For the political purposes of appeals to racial identity, see Judith Stein, "History of an Idea," *The Nation*, December 14, 1998; Jedidiah Slaboda, "Politicizing the Centrality of Race in Post War Urban Histories," *Nonsite* 30 (Winter 2020), https://nonsite.org/politicizing-the-centrality-of-race-in-post-war-urban-histories/.

11. Steven M. Gillon, *Separate and Unequal: The Kerner Commission and the Unraveling of American Liberalism* (New York: Basic Books, 2018), Introduction, e-book.

12. *Report of the National Advisory Commission on Civil Disorders*, 389–408.

13. See Self, *American Babylon*, 271–72.

14. See, *Report of the National Advisory Commission on Civil Disorders*, 392; See also John F. Kain, "The Spatial Mismatch Hypothesis: Three Decades Later," *Housing Policy Debate* 3, no. 2 (1992): 373–74; Edward L. Glaeser, Eric A. Hanushek, and John M. Quigley, "Opportunities, Race, and Urban Location: The Influence of John Kain," *NBER Working Paper* no. 10312 (February 2004): 7.

15. Gillon, *Separate and Unequal*, 193–206; Anthony Downs, *Opening Up the Suburbs: An Urban Strategy for America* (New Haven: Yale University Press, 1973), 28.

16. Roger B. Noll, "Central City—Suburban Employment Distribution," in *The President's Task Force on Suburban Problems Final Report: Statistical Papers*, reel 5, slides 991–1007, reel 6, slides 3–17, TFR.

17. National Committee Against Discrimination in Housing, *The Impact of Housing Patterns on Job Opportunities; An Interim Report of a Study on Where People Live and Where the Jobs Are* (New York: National Committee Against Discrimination in Housing, 1968), iii, 21.

18. Regional Plan Association, "Housing Opportunities: An Analysis and Presentation for the New York Urban Development Corporation," June 5, 1969, 14, box 67, folder "Housing," ENP.

19. Matthew V. Rao, "Paul Davidoff and Planning Education: A Study of the Origin of the Urban Planning Program at Hunter College," *Journal of Planning History* 11, no. 3 (August 2012):

227–32; Tom Angotti, *New York for Sale: Community Planning Confronts Global Real Estate* (Cambridge, MA: MIT Press, 2008), 14–16.

20. Quoted in Paul Davidoff, Linda Davidoff, and Neil Gold, "The Suburbs Have to Open their Gates," *Suburbia in Transition*, eds. Louis H. Masotti and Jeffrey K. Hadden (New York: New Viewpoints, 1974), 134; See also Geoffrey Shields and L. Sanford Spector, "Opening Up the Suburbs: Notes on a Movement for Social Change," *Yale Review of Law and Social Action* 2, no. 4 (Summer 1974): 301–2.

21. Regional Plan Association, "Housing Opportunities: An Analysis and Presentation for the New York Urban Development Corporation," June 5, 1969, box 67, folder "Housing," ENP; Chris Kristensen, John Levy, and Tamar Savir, "The Suburban Lockout Effect," Box V:1526, folder 3, RNCP.

22. Downs, *Opening Up the Suburbs*, 28.

23. Christopher Bonastia, *Knocking on the Door: The Federal Government's Attempt to Desegregate the Suburbs* (Princeton, NJ: Princeton University Press, 2006), 103; Florence Wagman Roisman, "George Romney, Richard Nixon, and the Fair Housing Act of 1968," *Poverty and Race Research Action Council*, http://www.prrac.org/pdf/RoismanHistoryExcerpt.pdf; Peter Siskind, "Growth and its Discontents : Localism, Protest and the Politics of Development on the Postwar Northeast Corridor," (PhD diss., University of Pennsylvania, 2002), 244–45; NYS Urban Development Corporation, *New York State Urban Development Corporation Annual Report 1969* (New York: Urban Development Corp, 1970), 1–2; "A Housing Development Corporation for Suffolk," 4, box 2, folder "housing," EG.

24. Patricia Sullivan, *Lift Every Voice: The NAACP and the Making of the Civil Rights Movement* (New York: New Press, 2009), 24–27; Wendell E. Pritchett, *Robert Clifton Weaver and the American City: The Life and Times of an Urban Reformer* (Chicago: University of Chicago Press, 2008), 141.

25. See Aaron Cavin, "A Right to Housing in the Suburbs," 3, 15–16 for *James v. Valtierra*; See also Douglas S. Massey, Len Albright, Rebecca Casciano, Elizabeth Derickson, and David N. Kinsey, *Climbing Mount Laurel: The Struggle for Affordable Housing and Social Mobility in an American Suburb* (Princeton, NJ: Princeton University Press, 2013), 33–34.

26. "LI Communities Make Plans and Progress in War on Slums," *ND*, January 7, 1959, 1C; "O. Bay Slum Housing Cleanup," *ND*, December 8, 1966, 15; Nassau County Planning Commission, *Aspects, An Analysis of Social, Economic, and Housing Characteristics of Nassau County, NY, part 3, age sex and color* (Mineola, NY: Nassau County Planning Commission 1962), 10; Nassau-Suffolk Regional Planning Board, *US Census '70: Race*, 19; "NAACP Aide Hears O. Bay Bias Plaints," *ND*, August 21, 1968, 15.

27. Oyster Bay Town Board Meeting Minutes, October 22, 1968, 23, in Legal Department Case Files, 1960–1972, Supplement to Part 23, Series B, section 2, reel 9, slide 136, PNC.

28. Frank J. Swit to James Davis, September 4, 1970, in Legal Department Case Files, 1960–1972, Supplement to Part 23, Series B, section 2, reel 13, slides 879–80, PNC; Interrogatory, 13–14, in Legal Department Case Files, 1960–1972, Supplement to Part 23, Series B, section 2, reel 16, slide 267–69, PNC; "NAACP May Start Building Houses," *ND*, October 23, 1968, 8; "O. Bay Board Cool to Plea on Bias Law," *ND*, November 20, 1968, 15.

29. "NAACP's Views on Zoning," *ND*, December 8, 1969, 3.

30. "Points in our Favor," Box V:1527, folder 1, RNCP; Untitled NAACP Oyster Bay Study, Legal Department Case Files, 1960–1972, Supplement to Part 23, Series B, section 2, reel 9, slides 473, 476, PNC; "L.I. Commercial Review," February 1969, Legal Department Case Files,

1960–1972, Supplement to Part 23, Series B, section 2, reel 9, slide 310, PNC; "Population," Legal Department Case Files, 1960–1972, Supplement to Part 23, Series B, section 2, reel 8, slides 87, 101, PNC.

31. "Team Confronts Suburbs," *ND*, December 31, 1969, 4; "Blacks Seek Share of Suburbs," *ND*, December 9, 1969, 5.

32. "History of the Case," Box V: 1526, folder 3, RNCP; "NAACP Official Defends Figures in O. Bay Study," *ND*, December 27, 1969, 8; "NAACP's Views on Zoning," *ND*, December 8, 1969, 3.

33. "At Issue: A Quiet Corner of Town," *ND*, December 12, 1969, 7; "Zoning Fears Aired," *ND*, January 8, 1970, 17; "Planners Back NAACP in O. Bay," *ND*, January 28, 1970, 4; "Meeting Draws Crowd, But Not Board," *ND*, February 17, 1970, 13; "Poll Report: 95% Oppose NAACP View," *ND*, July 17, 1970, 11.

34. "Bad Judgement," *ND*, December 19, 1969, 5B; "NAACP Presses Oyster Bay Fight," *NYT*, December 26, 1969, 14; "Letters to the Editor," *Farmingdale Observer*, January 22, 1970, 6.

35. R. Stephen Browning to Nathaniel R. Jones, December 14, 1970, Legal Department Case Files, 1960–1972, Supplement to Part 23, Series B, section 2, reel 13, slides 893–95, PNC; "Why Oyster Bay?" 7, Box V:1526, folder 3, RNCP; Quoted in Michael Danielson, *The Politics of Exclusion* (New York: Columbia University Press, 1976), 192.

36. "Search for Better Housing Unites NAACP Plaintiffs," *ND*, March 26, 1971, 2; Plaintiff Affidavits, January 1971, Legal Department Case Files, 1960–1972, Supplement to Part 23, Series B, section 2, reel 16, slides 877–85, PNC.

37. Nathaniel R. Jones to William Morris, January 9, 1970, Legal Department Case Files, 1960–1972, Supplement to Part 23, Series B, section 2, reel 13, slides 821–22, PNC.

38. "Defendant's First Interrogatories," August 20, 1971, Legal Department Case Files, 1960–1972, Supplement to Part 23, Series B, section 2, reel 16, slides 402–7, PNC; "Defendant's Second Interrogatories," March 27, 1972, Legal Department Case Files, 1960–1972, Supplement to Part 23, Series B, section 2, reel 16, slide 486, PNC; Cavin, "A Right to Housing in the Suburbs," 3; See also Matthew D. Lassiter, *The Silent Majority: Suburban Politics in the Sunbelt South* (Princeton, NJ: Princeton University Press, 2006), 307–8; Danielson, *Politics of Exclusion*, 180–86.

39. Residence survey for Grumman Employees, March 31, 1971, Box V: 1532, folder 7, RNCP.

40. Deposition of Plaintiff Edward Louis Underwood, August 5, 1971, Legal Department Case Files, 1960–1972, Supplement to Part 23, Series B, section 2, reel 13, slides 672, 675, 688, 726–27, PNC.

41. Deposition of Plaintiff William Joseph Johnson, August 5, 1971, Legal Department Case Files, 1960–1972, Supplement to Part 23, Series B, section 2, reel 13, slides 87–97, PNC.

42. Untitled NAACP Oyster Bay Study, Legal Department Case Files, 1960–1972, Supplement to Part 23, Series B, section 2, reel 9, slides 408–26, 466–67, 473–76, 488–89, PNC; "Industry," Legal Department Case Files, 1960–1972, Supplement to Part 23, Series B, section 2, reel 8, slides 146–57, PNC; "Defendant's First Interrogatories," August 20, 1971, Legal Department Case Files, 1960–1972, Supplement to Part 23, Series B, section 2, reel 16, slides 405–6, PNC.

43. Kamer, *Nassau-Suffolk's Changing Manufacturing Base*, 1.

44. Hartman L. Butler, Jr., George J. Podrasky, and J. Devon Allen, "The Aerospace Industry Re-Revisited," *Financial Analysts Journal* 33, no. 4 (July-August 1977): 22–35; George M. Skurla, *Inside the Iron Works: How Grumman's Glory Days Faded* (Annapolis, MD: Naval Institute Press, 2004), 98–118, 149–53; Stoff, "Grumman vs. Republic," 121.

45. Nassau County Planning Commission, *Roosevelt Field Area Development Guide* (Carle Place, NY: Nassau County Planning Commission, 1977), vi-17, 99.

46. Pearl Kamer, "An Economic Profile of Commuter Relationships: The Nassau-Suffolk SMSA," *Long Island Economic Trends Quarterly Technical Supplement—Third Quarter 1974* (September 1974): 7.

47. "Memorandum in Support of Defendants' Motion for an Order Compelling Plaintiffs to Provide Further Answers to Interrogatories," Legal Department Case Files, 1960–1972, Supplement to Part 23, Series B, section 2, reel 16, slides 692–93, PNC.

48. "Supporting Data for Application for Low-Rent Housing Program," 5, Legal Department Case Files, 1960–1972, Supplement to Part 23, Series B, section 2, reel 16, slide 282, PNC.

49. Deposition of Plaintiff Edward Louis Underwood, August 5, 1971, Legal Department Case Files, 1960–1972, Supplement to Part 23, Series B, section 2, reel 13, slide 712, PNC.

50. Deposition of Plaintiff William Joseph Johnson, August 5, 1971, Legal Department Case Files, 1960–1972, Supplement to Part 23, Series B, section 2, reel 13, slides 173–74, PNC.

51. Additional Responses of Plaintiffs, March 16, 1973, Legal Department Case Files, 1960–1972, Supplement to Part 23, Series B, section 2, reel 16, slides 586–87, PNC.

52. "NAACP's Suit Moves Slowly to a Hearing," *ND*, July 16, 1974, 9.

53. "NAACP Drops LI Zoning Suit," *NYT*, October 9, 1975, 37; Danielson, *Politics of Exclusion*, 168; "Burke Cites Zoning Battle Victory," *Bethpage Tribune*, October 16, 1975, 6.

54. Massey et al., *Climbing Mount Laurel*, 34–39; Cavin, "A Right to Housing in the Suburbs."

55. State of NY, County of Nassau Public Employee Relations Board, *Impasse between Nassau County and Nassau County Patrolmen's Benevolent Association*, March 19, 1976, 3, http://www.perb.ny.gov/pdf/ia1974-98/NassauCountyMini-Perb.pdf.

56. Horace Z. Kramer, "The Too Taxing Real Property Tax," *ND*, September 28, 1976, 45.

57. See Glass, "Schooling Suburbia."

58. Nassau Citizens Budget Committee, Inc., *The Property Tax in Nassau County: Alternatives and Consequences* (n.p.: Nassau Citizens Budget Committee, 1981); See also Michael Glass, "Industry Pays Its Way: Industrial Property, School Taxes, and Uneven Development," (unpublished PhD diss. chapter, Princeton University, 2018), 1–28.

59. Lawrence C. Levy and Robert Fresco, "Property Taxes: The Unbalanced Burden," *ND*, May 12, 1985, 4–5, 30, 34; Irene Virag, "Penalties for Those Who Struggle: Making the Struggle Harder," *ND*, May 13, 1985, 4, 21–22; Paul Vitello, "Overassessment Hits New Homes Hardest," *ND*, May 14, 1985, 5, 26–28.

60. Irene Virag, "Penalties for Those Who Struggle: Making the Struggle Harder," *ND*, May 13, 1985, 22.

61. Isaac William Martin, *The Permanent Tax Revolt: How the Property Tax Transformed American Politics* (Stanford, CA: Stanford University Press, 2008), e-book, chapter 4; Joshua Mound, "Inflating Hopes, Taxing times: Fiscal Crisis, the Pocketbook Squeeze, and the Roots of the Tax Revolt," (PhD diss., University of Michigan, 2015), 1–25.

62. Paul M. O'Brien to Dr. Paul L. Noble, November 19, 1968, 7, box 67, folder "Housing," ENP; Ralph G. Caso, *America's Cities and Suburbs: Cooperation and Conflict* (Mineola, NY: n.p., 1974), 28; Dennis Bires, "Board of Education, Levittown Union Free School District V. Nyquist: A Return to Federal Equal Protection in School Financing Cases," *N.Y.U. Review of Law and Social Change* 8, no. 1 (1978–79): 87–120; See also Glass, "Schooling Suburbia."

63. Taylor, *Race for Profit*, 113–18.

64. "Applicant's Environmental Information," 3, Series 10, subseries 3, box 14, folder "Housing, Oyster Bay 1974," JJ; Lamb, *Housing Segregation*, 69–84.

65. "Report of the United Massapequa Civic Council on Proposed Downzoning for Construction of Public Housing in Massapequa, New York," II-6, IV-25-IV-27, Series 10, subseries 3, box 14, folder "Housing, Oyster Bay 1974," JJ.

66. For the postwar homeowner-oriented "spatial" racial ideology, see Sugrue, *Origins of the Urban Crisis*, 209–58; Lassiter, *Silent Majority*, 119–222; Freund, *Colored Property*, 176–400; For the "racial democratic" vision among black elites and property owners, see Smith, *Racial Democracy*, 4–20; Connolly, *A World More Concrete*, 244–70.

67. "War Declared on housing project," *Massapequa Post*, February 28, 1974; "In E. Massapequa, 'We Don't Want It,'" *ND*, March 31, 1974, 19; "A Civic Diet of Regular Scraps," *Newsday*, Mar 20, 1974, 19.

68. "Report of the United Massapequa Civic Council on Proposed Downzoning," VII-3-VII-4, XII-5.

69. "The Supreme Court, HUD and Housing," *ND*, April 28, 1976, 63.

70. *Nassau County Data Book* 1985, 218–19; NYS Department of Audit and Control, *Overall Real Property Tax Rates: Local Government in New York State: Fiscal Years Ended in 1974* (Albany, NY: Bureau of Research and Statistics, 1975), 64.

71. "Report of the United Massapequa Civic Council on Proposed Downzoning," II-8, IV-28-IV-29, VII-9-VII-10, Series 10, subseries 3, box 14, folder "Housing, Oyster Bay 1974," JJ; "In E. Massapequa, 'We Don't Want it,'" *ND*, March 13, 1974, 19; "E. Massapequa Project Draws Fire," *ND*, March 27, 1974, 17.

72. "Report of the United Massapequa Civic Council on Proposed Downzoning," VII-3-VII-4, XII-5.

73. "The Housing Project No More a Civic Battleground," *ND*, March 5, 1977, 1A.

74. *Newsday*, "A Civic Diet of Regular Scraps."

75. "Report & Recommendations, Phase 1, Nassau Center," July 1969, box 69, folder "Mitchel Field" [1 of 2], ENP.

76. "Suit Planned to Compel Housing at Mitchel Field," *NYT*, November 7, 1971, A3; "A Personal Defeat on Mitchel Field," *ND*, August 29, 1972, 17.

77. "Why Uniondale Finally Said No to a Social Welfare Project," *ND*, June 22, 1970, 9.

78. "Mitchel Neighbors Rap Housing Plan," *ND*, May 27, 1970, 4; "Why Uniondale Finally Said No to a Social Welfare Project," *ND*, June 22, 1970, 8–9; "Suit Planned to Compel Housing at Mitchel Field," *NYT*, November 7, 1971, A3; "Two Views of Mitchel Field," *The Carman Chronicle Community Association Newsletter*, no. 18 (September 1969): 1–3, box 69, folder "Mitchel Field" [1 of 2], ENP; "Overcrowded Uniondale," *ND*, May 22, 1970, 5B; "Mitchel Plan Spotlights School Tax Pool," *ND*, April 5, 1969, 7.

79. "Welfare Activists Move 3 Families into Mitchel Housing," *ND*, May 25, 1970, 1; "Mitchel Gardens . . . ," *L.I. Black News*, September 1971, B2, Periodicals 1, box 233, TLN; "At Center of Dispute: Mitchel School Rift Doesn't Ring a Bell," *ND*, September 3, 1970, 1; "Uniondale District is Ordered to Enroll Mitchel Students," *ND*, September 4, 1970, 1.

80. "Fighting the Welfare Children," *ND*, August 29, 1970, 3A.

81. "Mitchel Field: New Foes, New Tactics," *ND*, February 3, 1972, 23; "Apts. For Mitchel Field Draw Margiotta's Ire," *ND*, March 22, 1969, 7; "Welfare Children," *ND*, September 10, 1969, 5B; "Letters," *ND*, June 2, 1970, 5B.

82. "Caso to Take Reins at Mitchel Field, Rules out Housing," *ND*, November 24, 1970, 1; "A Suit for Housing at Mitchel Field," *ND*, March 7, 1972, 17.

83. Quoted in Lamb, *Housing Segregation*, 235.

84. Acevedo v. Nassau County, 369 F. Su1384 (EDNY 1974), 1390; "Federal Supplement, Acevedo v. Nassau County, New York," 1390, Box V: 1375, folder 5, RNCP.

85. "Wyandanch Task Force—Proposal Form," folder 4, WH.

86. Lizabeth Cohen, *Saving America's Cities: Ed Logue and the Struggle to Renew Urban America in the Suburban Age* (New York: Farrar, Straus and Giroux, 2019), ch. 7, e-book.

87. Quoted in Cohen, *Saving America's Cities*, ch. 7, e-book.

88. NYS Urban Development Corporation. *New York State Urban Development Corporation Annual Report 1969*, 3; NYS Urban Development Corporation, *New York State Urban Development Corporation Annual Report 1971* (New York: Urban Development Corp, 1972), 10.

89. Regional Plan Association, *The Future of Suffolk County*, 54; "Wyandanch Residents Fight for Housing Projects," *AN*, October 14, 1972.

90. Cedric Johnson, "The Panthers Can't Save Us Now," *Catalyst* 1, no. 1 (Spring 2017), https://catalyst-journal.com/vol1/no1/panthers-cant-save-us-cedric-johnson.

91. Regional Plan Association, *The Future of Suffolk County*, 56.

92. "Housing Debate, One Last Time," *ND*, July 27, 1973, 20.

93. See Connolly, *A World More Concrete*, 266–70 for an example in Miami suburbs.

94. "Two Groups Fear Project to Hike Taxes," *ND*, July 24, 1973, 18; "New Housing Plan Rouses Wyandanch," *NYT*, July 26, 1973; "Once Again the Wyandanch Housing Debate," *ND*, August 8, 1973, 31; Regional Plan Association, *The Future of Suffolk County*, 55.

95. Regional Plan Association, *The Future of Suffolk County*, 54; *NYT*, "New Housing Plan Rouses Wyandanch"; "The Wyandanch Housing Fight," *ND*, July 26, 1973, 4; "1,000 in Wyandanch Turn Out to Debate U.D.C. Housing Plan," *NYT*, July 27, 1973.

96. "Once Again the Wyandanch Housing Debate," *ND*, Aug 8, 1973, 31; "Baby Officials Reject Wyandanch Housing Plan," *NYT*, August 17, 1973.

97. NYS Urban Development Corporation, *New York State Urban Development Corporation Annual Report 1973*, 60; "A Dark Victory," *AN*, April 1, 1973; "Wyandanch Vote Robs Blacks of New Housing," *AN*, August 17, 1973; "Housing for Wyandanch," *NYT*, August 17, 1973.

98. Matthew D. Lassiter, "Suburban Strategies: The Volatile in Postwar American Politics," *New Directions in American Political History*, eds. Meg Jacobs, William J. Novak, and Julian E. Zelizer (Princeton, NJ: Princeton University Press, 2003), 343.

99. Lamb, *Housing Segregation since 1960*; Bonastia, *Knocking on the Door*; Lassiter, *Silent Majority*.

100. Robert W. Lake, "Rethinking NIMBY," *Journal of the American Planning Association* 59, no. 1 (Winter 1993): 87–93; Mark N. Wexler, "A Sociological Framing of the NIMBY (Not-in-My-Backyard) Syndrome," *International Review of Modern Sociology* 26, no. 1 (Spring 1996): 91–110; Timothy A. Gibson, "NIMBY and the Civic Good." *City & Community* 4, no. 4 (December 2005): 381–401.

101. Adolph Reed Jr., "The Kerner Commission and the Irony of Antiracist Politics," *Labor: Studies in Working-Class History* 14, no. 4 (December 2017): 31–38; James DeFilippis, "On Spatial Solutions to Social Problems," *CityScape: A Journal of Policy Development and Research* 15, no. 2 (2013): 69–72.

## Chapter Seven

1. "Illegal Housing, Towns try to crack down, North Hempstead to Brookhaven, citations are up," *ND*, Dec 19, 2004, G32.

2. "Nassau Officials Try a Different Approach to House Filled with Immigrants," *NYT*, July 1, 2005.

3. Supervisor Jon Kaiman, "North Hempstead State of the Town: 2005," *Town of North Hempstead*, https://www.northhempsteadny.gov/filestorage/16281/16525/17981/2005.pdf

4. "National Boycott: Day without Immigrants, LI Businesses Close, Students Skip School as Part of Countrywide Demonstration of What U.S. Would be like without Foreigners' Contributions," *ND*, May 2, 2005, A07.

5. Kneebone and Berube, *Confronting Suburban Poverty*, 18; Alana Samuels, "From bucolic bliss to 'gated ghetto'," *Los Angeles Times*, March 30, 2012; Richard Rothstein, "The Making of Ferguson: Public Policies at the Root of its Troubles," *Economic Policy Institute*, October 15, 2014, https://www.epi.org/publication/making-ferguson/; Rafael Bernal, "Trump to Announce MS-13 Gang Crackdown in Long Island," *The Hill*, July 27, 2017, https://thehill.com/homenews/administration/344243-trump-to-announce-ms-13-gang-crackdown-in-long-island; Ehrenhalt, *The Great Inversion*.

6. Some examples include Orfield, *American Metropolitics*, 23–48; Katrin Anacker, *Analyzing Mature Suburbs in Ohio through Property Values* (Saarbrucken, Germany: Verlag Dr. Muller, 2009); Thomas J. Vicino, *Transforming Race and Class in Suburbia: Decline in Metropolitan Baltimore* (New York: Palgrave Macmillan, 2008); Karen Beck Pooley, "Debunking the 'Cookie-cutter' Myth for Suburban Places and Suburban Poverty: Analyzing their Variety and Recent Trends" in *The New American Suburb*, ed. Katrin Anacker, 39–80; Hanlon, *Once the American Dream*, ch. 3; Gregory Smithsimon, "Punctuated Equilibrium: Community Responses to Neoliberalism in Three Suburban Communities in Baltimore County, Maryland," in *The New American Suburb*, ed. Katrin Anacker, 187–212.

7. Kneebone and Berube, *Confronting Suburban Poverty*, 71–76; Hanlon, *Once the American Dream*, 87–89.

8. Long Island Regional Planning Board, *Population - 1980: Income* (Hauppauge, NY: Long Island Regional Planning Board, 1983), 7, 18; Center for Labor and Industrial Relations, *Labor Market Survey of Nassau County—78* (n.p., 1979), 116–20.

9. Quoted in "Economy: Job losses, cost increases, signal end of boom years," *ND*, March 19, 1978, A88.

10. Mark Blyth, *Great Transformations: Economic Ideas and Institutional Change in the Twentieth Century* (New York: Cambridge University Press, 2011), 149.

11. "The Illegal Apartment Boom: A Growing LI Housing Trend," *ND*, May 28, 1972, 11–13; "Illegal Rentals, a major problem and a major part of the solution," *ND*, March 27, 1978, 1; "2-Family Housing Called a Necessity By Priorities Panel," *ND*, April 9, 1978, Q23; Kessman, *A Cost and Use Analysis of Single and Two-Family Housing*, 20; Town of Babylon Department of Planning and Development, *Report on Illegal Two-Family Dwellings in the Town of Babylon* (n.p., 1979), 4–11.

12. Kessman, *A Cost and Use Analysis*, i-ii; "Editorial: This Housing Program is Illegal—But it Works," *ND*, April 13, 1978, 96; "Editorial: Learning to Live with Two-Family Houses," *ND*, January 19, 1979, 60; Tri-State Regional Planning Commission, *Legalizing Single Family Conversions* (New York: 1981), Question 11.

13. "Babylon Eyes 2-Family Houses," *ND*, October 3, 1978, 3; Christopher Niedt and Katrin B. Anacker, "Accessory Dwellings on Long Island: An Overview," National Center for Suburban Studies at Hofstra University Report (Hempstead, NY: 2016), 5; Thomas K. Rudel, "Household

Change, Accessory Apartments, and Low-Income Housing in the Suburbs," *Professional Geographer* 36, no. 2 (1984): 177–80.

14. Rudel, "Household Change," 177–80.

15. Michael Brenes, "Peace Through Austerity: The Reagan Defense Buildup in the 'Age of Inequality,'" in *The Cold War at Home and Abroad: Domestic Politics and US Foreign Policy since 1945*, eds. Andrew L. Johns and Mitchell B. Lerner (Lexington: The University Press of Kentucky, 2018), 247–54.

16. Skurla, *Inside the Iron Works*, 9.

17. Pearl Kamer, "The Quality of Jobs on Long Island: Manufacturing vs. Services," *Hofstra University Business Research Institute Occasional Paper* 2 (July 1985): 8.

18. "Pie Shrinks, Party Winds Down: Mortgage Banking Suffers Cuts as Higher Rates Depress Loan Demand," *ND*, May 6, 1989, 1; Kevin Fox Graham, "Creating Liquidity out of Spatial Fixity: The Secondary Circuit of Capital and the Subprime Mortgage Crisis," *International Journal of Urban and Regional Research* 33, no. 2 (June 2009): 355–71; Daniel Immergluck, *Foreclosed: High-Risk Lending, Deregulation, and the Undermining of America's Mortgage Market* (Ithaca: Cornell University Press, 2011), 34–46.

19. US Federal Housing Finance Agency, "All-Transactions House Price Index for Nassau County-Suffolk County, NY," Federal Reserve Bank of St. Louis, https://fred.stlouisfed.org/series/ATNHPIUS35004Q; "Status '87: Housing the Hidden Cost of Li's Bonanza," *ND*, January 26, 1987, 11.

20. NYS Department of Labor, *Labor Market Assessment, Occupational Supply and Demand: Nassau-Suffolk* (Albany, NY: GPO, 1990): 1–12; "Birth of a Bust: Long Island's Empty Nest breeds a Labor Shortage," *ND*, December 12, 1988, B1–B4.

21. "For L.I. Blacks, Prosperity Is a Relative Term," *NYT*, August 1, 1986, B1; "Blacks Better off on LI, Study Claims," *ND*, 6, 23; Michael B. Katz, Mark J. Stern, and Jamie J. Fader, "The New African American Inequality," *Journal of American History* 92, no. 1 (June 2005): 75–108.

22. "Homeowners Still Raking in Profits," *ND*, February 1, 1986, B1.

23. Kamer, "The Quality of Jobs on Long Island," 1–9; NYS Bureau of Economic and Demographic Information, *New York State: 1991–92 County Profiles* (Albany, NY: GPO, 1992): 52–56; "A Census Snapshot of Life on the Island: Incomes Up, but Families Working Harder," *ND*, April 16, 1992, 7.

24. Sarah J. Mahler, *American Dreaming: Immigrant Life on the Margins* (Princeton, NJ: Princeton University Press, 1995), 17–21, 31–57.

25. Mahler, *American Dreaming*, 106–31.

26. "Record Price Escalation," *ND*, February 7, 1987, B1; "The Forgotten Mortgages: VA has streamlined Paperwork, but Loans Still Carry Stigma," *ND*, June 1989, 1; "Househunters A Move to Long Island: A Step Up or Slide Down?" *ND*, September 3, 1988, 3; Manson et al., *IPUMS*, database.

27. Janice R. Fine, "Community Unions in Baltimore and Long Island: Beyond the Politics of Particularism," (PhD diss., Massachusetts Institute of Technology, 2003), 92.

28. "Illegal Apts. Up by 90,000 On LI Since '80," *ND*, November 1, 1988, 1, 3, 27.

29. Anthony P. Polednak, *Segregation, Poverty, and Mortality in Urban African Americans* (New York: Oxford University Press, 1997), 40.

30. "LI's Hidden Poor Flaws in Census, High Housing Costs and Recession Blur the Poverty Line," *ND*, July 20, 1992, 7.

31. *Newsday*, "LI's Hidden Poor Flaws in Census," 7; Sarah Mahler, "Alternative Enumeration of Undocumented Salvadorans on Long Island," *Ethnographic Evaluation of the 1990 Decennial Census Report Series Report # 26* (Center for Survey Methods Research, US Bureau of the Census, 1993): 1–8.

32. "Down & Out on Long Island: Some Working Poor Joining the Ranks of the Homeless," *ND*, January 29, 1989, 5, 26–29; Arfin, *Unfinished Business*, 237–38, 427–28.

33. Samuel M. Ehrenhalt, *Profile of a Recession: The New York Experience in the Early 1990s* (Albany, NY: Nelson A. Rockefeller Institute of Government, 1992); New York State AFL-CIO, *Toward a New Economic Strategy for New York State* (May 1993), 3, folder "New York State AFL-CIO: Pamphlets and Publications," box 11, AFL-CIO Collection, TRW; Stoff, "Grumman versus Republic," 116–23; Lee E. Koppelman and Pearl M. Kamer, "Anatomy of the Long Island Economy: Retrospective and Prospective," *Long Island Historical Journal* 6, no. 2 (Spring 1994): 146–54.

34. John J. Accordino, *The Struggle for Defense Conversion in American Communities* (Westport CT: Praeger, 2000), 1–8.

35. "Economy of Long Island, N.Y., and What the Federal Government Can Do to Help Revitalize the Stagnant Economy," *Hearing before the Committee on Ways and Means, House of Representatives, 102nd Congress, Serial 102-92*, Mineola, NY, February 10, 1992 (Washington, DC: GPO, 1992), 2, 7–8.

36. *102nd Congress*, "Economy of Long Island," 8–9, 25–26.

37. *102nd Congress*, "Economy of Long Island," 48.

38. *102nd Congress*, "Economy of Long Island," 52.

39. *102nd Congress*, "Economy of Long Island," 53–56, 56–63, 76–79.

40. *102nd Congress*, "Economy of Long Island," 82–87.

41. Lee E. Koppelman and Pearl M. Kamer, "Anatomy of the Long Island Economy: Retrospective and Prospective," *Long Island Historical Journal* 6, no. 2 (Spring 1994): 146–54; NYS Office of the State Comptroller, "Recent Trends in the Long Island Economy," Report 3-2002 (June 2001): 2.

42. Skurla and Gregory, *Inside the Iron Works*, 5; Jake Bussolini, *The Last Chapter: The Facts about Grumman's Last Days* (n.p.: Authorhouse, 2014).

43. See Bills H.R. 4073, H.R. 4175, H.R. 4416, H.R. 4727, H.R. 5219, H.R. 5235, H.R. 5260, H.R. 5846, H.R. 6051, "Representative Thomas J. Downey," *Congress.gov*, https://www.congress.gov/member/thomas-downey/D000471; Brenes, "Peace Through Austerity," 258–59.

44. Gregory DeFreitas and Lonnie Stevans, "Regional Job Growth and Wage Trends in 1998," *Regional Labor Review* 1, no. 2 (Spring/Summer 1999): 6–7; Pearl M. Kamer and Gary W. Wotjas, *Long Island Association Annual Business Fact-Book 2009–2010: A Comprehensive Guide to Business Activity on Long Island* (n.p.: Long Island Association, 2010), 2, 23–25; Gregory DeFreitas and Bhaswati Sengupta, "The State of New York Unions 2017," *Regional Labor Review* 20, no. 1 (Fall 2017): 5–24.

45. Gabriel Winant, *The Next Shift: The Fall of Industry and the Rise of Health Care in Rust Belt America* (Cambridge, MA: Harvard University Press, 2021).

46. "Republic: A Year Later, The Business Impact for Mall Developer, Site an Opportunity," *ND*, April 25, 1988, 1; "Signs of Life at Silenced Factory / Retail plaza to follow multiplex theater on Fairchild property," *ND*, October 23, 1996, A49; "Grumman's Bethpage site gets an array of new uses," *ND*, December 22, 1997, C08; "The Media Colossus: A Sprawling Site Offers Cable Giant Room to Grow," *ND*, February 8, 1999, C09; "Town Oks Housing for Seniors," *ND*, September 17, 1998, A46.

47. Corey Dolgon, *The End of the Hamptons: Scenes from the Class Struggle in America's Paradise* (New York: NYU Press, 2005), 52–62; Cromarty "Suffolk County Farmland Preservation," 156–209; R. Lawrence Swanson, Carolyn Hall, and Kristin Krams, "Suffolk County, a National Leader in Environmental Initiatives. Why?" *Long Island History Journal* 22, no. 2 (Summer 2011): 14–15.

48. Rauch Foundation and the Regional Plan Association, *Long Island Profile: A Summary of Demographic, Economic, and Environmental Trends* (April 2003): 6; Gregory DeFreitas, "Pay Patterns on Long Island since the Great Recession," *Regional Labor Review* 17, no. 2 (Spring/Summer 2015): 10; Jennifer Gordon, *Suburban Sweatshops: The Fight for Immigrant Rights* (Cambridge, MA: Belknap Press of Harvard University Press, 2005), 3–7, 12–16, 21–30.

49. Mariano Torras and Curtis Skinner, *The Economic Impact of the Hispanic Population on Long Island, New York, A Research Report*, Hagedorn Foundation, 2, http://hagedornfoundation.org/assets/downloads/Adelphi-Report.pdf; This is true across suburbs in the 100 largest metropolitan areas. See William H. Frey, "Melting Pot Cities and Suburbs: Racial and Ethnic Change in Metro America in the 2000s," *State of Metropolitan America series, no. 30, Brookings Institution* (May 2011): 1–15.

50. Gregory DeFreitas and Bhaswati Sengupta, "The State of New York Unions 2017," *Regional Labor Review* (Fall 2017): 13; Cynthia Feliciano and Yader R. Lanuza, "An Immigrant Paradox? Contextual Attainment and Intergenerational Educational Mobility," *American Sociological Review* 82, no. 1 (2017): 211–41.

51. Richard Alba, Glenn Deane, Nancy Denton, Ilir Disha, Brian McKenzie, and Jeffrey Napierala, "The Role of Immigrant Enclaves for Latino Residential Inequalities," *Journal of Ethnic and Migration Studies* 40, no. 1 (2014): 1–20.

52. Long Island Association Research Institute, *Long Island's Thinning Middle Class*, LIA Research Institute Reports, https://chambermaster.blob.core.windows.net/userfiles/UserFiles/chambers/2181/CMS/LIA-Income-Distribution-Report-3.pdf; United Way of New York, *ALICE: Asset Limited, Income Constrained, Employed: Study of Financial Hardship*, Research Center United Way of New York (2016), 88, https://www.unitedforalice.org/new-york.

53. Saskia Sassen, "When Local Housing Becomes an Electronic Instrument: The Global Circulation of Mortgages—A Research Note," *International Journal of Urban and Regional Research* 33, no. 2 (June 2009): 411–26.

54. Regional Plan Association, "Pushed Out: Housing Displacement in an Unaffordable Region," *A Report of the Fourth Regional Plan Association* (March 2017), 4, http://library.rpa.org/pdf/RPA-Pushed-Out-Housing-Displacement-in-an-Unaffordable-Region.pdf.

55. The United Way does not calculate a national rate, only state proportions; See United Way of New York, *ALICE*, 211, 212, 243, 266.

56. Jan Vink, *Nassau County Profile 2017: A Collection of Recent Demographic, Social, and Economic Data*, Cornell University Program on Applied Demographics (2017), 10, http://pad.human.cornell.edu/profiles/Nassau.pdf; Jan Vink, *Suffolk County Profile 2017: A Collection of Recent Demographic, Social, and Economic Data*, Cornell University Program on Applied Demographics (2017), 10, http://pad.human.cornell.edu/profiles/Suffolk.pdf; Gregory DeFreitas, "Millennials in the Long Island Job Market: Underpaid and Underemployed," *Regional Labor Review* 19, no. 1 (Fall 2016): 5–17; Regional Plan Association, "Long Island's Rental Housing Crisis," Regional Plan Association Library, 3–9, http://library.rpa.org/pdf/RPA-Long-Islands-Rental-Housing-Crisis.pdf; Lonnie Stevans, "Trends in Wages, Employment and Economic Attitudes: New Findings from the Hofstra/Newsday Poll," *Regional Labor Review* 1, no. 2 (Spring/Summer

1999), 9; State of New York Comptroller, *Foreclosures in Long Island* Report 6-2012 (June 2011), 2, https://www.osc.state.ny.us/reports/foreclosure/long-island-foreclosures.pdf; Elizabeth Moore, *Home Remedies: Accessory Apartments on Long Island: Lessons Learned*, Long Island Index (June 2017), 11.

57. ERASE Racism, *Housing and Neighborhood Preferences of African Americans on Long Island 2012 Survey Research Report* (February 2012), 9–10, http://www.eraseracismny.org/storage/documents/FINAL_ERASE_Racism_2012_Housing_Survey_Report_web_version.pdf.

58. See John Iceland and Melissa Scopilliti, "Immigrant Residential Segregation in U.S. Metropolitan Areas," *Demography* 45, no. 1 (February 2008): 79–94; Manuel Pastor, "Maywood, Not Mayberry: Latinos and Suburbia in Los Angeles County," *Social Justice in Diverse Suburbs: History, Politics, and Prospects*, ed. Christopher Niedt (Philadelphia: Temple University Press, 2013), 139.

59. For critiques of contemporary redevelopment, see Pattillo, *Black on the Block*; Lawrence Vale, Alexander Von Hoffman, "High Ambitions: The Past and Future of American Low-Income Housing Policy," *Housing Policy Debate* 7, no. 3 (1996): 423–46; Derek S. Hyra, *The New Urban Renewal: The Economic Transformation of Harlem and Bronzeville* (Chicago: University of Chicago Press, 2008); Robert J. Chaskin and Mark L. Joseph, *Integrating the Inner City: The Promise and Perils of Mixed Income Public Housing Transformation* (Chicago: University of Chicago Press, 2015), 24–39.

60. "Legacy of the Slumlord," *ND*, July 1, 1984, 1, 4, 27.

61. "1,300 Seek Chance at Home Lottery," *ND*, April 13, 1990, 29; "'Whooping Allowed,' 150 Lottery Winners in Islip Drawing get Home Sweet Homes," *ND*, June 7, 1990, 29.

62. "When She Worked on the Assembly," *ND*, August 10, 1999, A55.

63. "Crackdown in Central Islip: Minister Charged with Numerous Violations of Housing Code," *ND*, May 17, 1992, 1.

64. "Town Does its Home Work: New Law Allows More '2-families' But Sets Quality, Safety Standards," *ND*, August 30, 1992, 1; "ISLIP TOWN: Rental Inspections Halted," *ND*, June 21, 2013, A28.

65. Deed Liber 7977, 427; Deed Liber 8243, 52; Deed Liber 8354, 384; Deed Liber 8521, 375, NCC; Deed Liber 8182, 394, NCLR; Section 55, Block 559, Lot 50, NCLR.

66. Deed Liber 9325, 449; Deed Liber 9985, 809; Mortgage Liber 13052, 814; Deed Liber 11159, 81; Deed Liber (Misc. with Fee) 11650, 288, NCC; Section 55, Block 559, Lot 47, NCLR.

67. NYS Comptroller, "Foreclosures in Long Island," 2.

68. "Population in Poverty," Long Island Index Map, http://www.longislandindexmaps.org/.

69. "At Long Last the Blight is Gone!" *New Cassel News*, September 1979; "New Hopes for Reviving New Cassel," *ND*, June 30, 1980; "New Cassel to Get a Face-Lift—Blighted areas to receive $8 million for mini-mall, low-income housing," *ND*, February 16, 1992, 1.

70. Town of North Hempstead, "Vision Plan for New Cassel: Seeking a Shared Vision for New Cassel," http://www.northhempstead.com/filestorage/16281/17115/17134/17141/VisionPlanforNewCassel.pdf; Mary Ann Allison, "Community Revitalization in New Cassel, NY" (Hempstead, NY: National Center for Suburban Studies, 2008), iii, 7–17, https://www.hofstra.edu/pdf/academics/css/ncss_newcassel_monograph022409.pdf.

71. Allison, "Community Revitalization in New Cassel," 19, 30–31, 47–49; "Chapter 70, Article XXB: New Cassel Urban Renewal Overlay District," *Town of Hempstead, NY Code* (Adopted 12/12/2006), https://ecode360.com/9301365.

72. "Civic leaders prefer to focus on project progress," *Newsday*, July 23, 2010, A3; Dick Carpenter and John K. Ross, "Empire State Eminent Domain: Robin Hood in Reverse," *City Journal*, January 15, 2010, https://www.city-journal.org/html/robin-hood-reverse-10676.html.

73. "Civic leaders prefer to focus on project progress," *ND*, July 23, 2010, A3; "Easing home rules—Town reconsiders some New Cassel rules meant to prevent illegal housing," *ND*, January 1, 2014, A19; "New Cassel: Another Look at Basement Rules," *ND*, July 14, 2015, A17; "Rules Eased for Homes: New Cassel Residents Can Ask to Make Additions," *ND*, October 1, 2015, A16; "Changes to New Cassel Housing Law to Give Residents More Access to their Homes," *ND*, December 30, 2021.

74. "Bid to Delay Property Auctions Bill Aims at Helping Wyandanch," *ND*, July 4, 1989, 17; "More Than Their Share of Welfare in Poorer Communities—Critics Cry Dumping, but County Says Marketplace Dictates the Load," *ND*, June 30, 1991, 1.

75. "In a Separate Suburbia Proud but Often Powerless, Wyandanch Residents Try to Stabilize Their Community," *ND*, September 23, 1990; "Wyandanch Aims to Take Back Streets from Pushers and Prostitutes," *NYT*, August 22, 1993; "Wyandanch Seeks U.S. Help in Fighting Crime," *NYT*, October 7, 1993, B7; "Family Court Judge Finds 10-Year-Old Did Sell Crack," *NYT*, February 2, 1989.

76. Sustainable Long Island, "Wyandanch Rising: The Wyandanch Hamlet Plan" (2003), 7–8, 76–87, https://www.townofbabylon.com/DocumentCenter/View/16.

77. Jonathan Davies, "The Social Exclusion Debate," *Policy Studies* 26, no. 1 (2005): 3–27.

78. Davies, "The Social Exclusion Debate," 8, 76–87.

79. Town of Babylon, *Urban Renewal Plan for the Revitalization of Downtown Wyandanch: Appendix J* (April 2009), 4, https://www.townofbabylon.com/DocumentCenter/View/53; Town of Babylon, *Wyandanch Rising: A Community's Transformation* (April 2016), 16, 29–31, https://townofbabylon.com/DocumentCenter/View/2180; Long Island Business Report, "Wyandanch Rising: Long Island Business Report Special," *Public Broadcasting Service*, September 2016, https://www.pbs.org/video/long-island-business-report-wyandanch-rising-long-island-business-report-special-full/.

80. Edward Hernandez, "An Exploratory Study of Undocumented Immigrants in a Suburban Northeast Community," (PhD diss., Stony Brook University, 2009), 56–77, 89–91; Ben Darvil, Jr., "Neighborhood Preservation or Xenophobism? An Examination of the Issues Surrounding the Town of Brookhaven's Rental Occupancy Law," *Journal of Affordable Housing & Community Development Law* 13, no. 1 (Fall 2003): 122–43; Carlos Sandoval and Catherine Tambini, directors, *Building the American Dream: Levittown, NY* (USA: Camino Bluff Productions, 2004), DVD.

81. Southern Poverty Law Center, *Climate of Fear: Latino Immigrants in Suffolk County, N.Y.* (Montgomery, AL: Southern Poverty Law Center, September 2009), 7–8; Centro de la Comunidad Hispana de Locust Valley v. Town of Oyster Bay, no. 15-2914-cv, (US Court of Appeals, Second Circuit, 2017); Bernadette Hanlon and Thomas J. Vicino, "Local Immigrant Legislation in Two Suburbs: An Examination of Immigration Policies in Farmers Branch, Texas, and Carpentersville, Illinois," in Anacker, *The New American Suburb*, 113–32.

82. For early works, see Louis H. Masotti and Jeffrey K. Hadden, eds., *Suburbia in Transition* (New York: New Viewpoints, 1974); Peter O. Muller, *Contemporary Suburban America* (Englewood Cliffs, NJ: Prentice-Hall, 1981); Mark Baldassare, *Trouble in Paradise: The Suburban Transformation in America* (New York: Columbia University Press, 1986); see also Kneebone and Berube, *Confronting Suburban Poverty*, 17, 38–49; Hanlon, *Once the American Dream*, 47–53,

70; Alexandra K. Murphy and Scott Allard, "The New Geography of Poverty," *Focus* 32, no. 1 (Spring/Summer 2015): 19–23.

83. Long Island Association Research Institute, *Long Island's Thinning Middle Class*, 6.

## Conclusion

1. For basic definitions of social democracy, see Frieden, *Global Capitalism*, 230–35; Donald Sassoon, *One Hundred Years of Socialism: The West European Left in the Twentieth Century* (London: I. B. Tauris, 2010), xii-xiii; Tony Judt, *Ill Fares the Land* (New York: Penguin Books, 2014).

2. Brady, *Rich Democracies, Poor People*, 81–86.

3. Margaret Weir, Theda Skocpol, and Ann Shola Orloff, "The Future of Social Policy in The United States: Political Constraints and Possibilities," in *The Politics of Social Policy in the United States*, eds. Margaret Weir, Theda Skocpol, and Ann Shola Orloff (Princeton, NJ: Princeton University Press, 1988): 421–45; Gøsta Esping-Andersen, *The Three Worlds of Welfare Capitalism* (Cambridge: Polity Press, 1990), 26–27; Franz-Xaver Kaufmann, *Variations of the Welfare State: Great Britain, Sweden, France and Germany Between Capitalism and Socialism* (New York: Springer, 2013), 65.

4. David Plotke, *Building a Democratic Political Order: Reshaping American Liberalism in the 1930s and 1940s* (Cambridge: Cambridge University Press, 1996), 188–89.

5. Thomas Piketty and Arthur Goldhammer, *Capital and Ideology* (Cambridge, MA: Harvard University Press, 2020), 490–91.

6. L. Randall Wray, *Modern Monetary Theory: A Primer on Macroeconomics for Sovereign Monetary Systems* (New York: Palgrave Macmillan, 2012), 9–40; Freund, "Money is Productive."

7. Hyman Minsky, *John Maynard Keynes* (New York: Columbia University Press, 1975), 165–67.

8. Rogers Brubaker, *Grounds for Difference* (Cambridge, MA: Harvard University Press, 2015), 10–47.

9. Ann Choi, Keith Herbert, Olivia Winslow, "Long Island Divided," *ND*, November 17, 2019, https://projects.newsday.com/long-island/real-estate-agents-investigation/.

10. Rank, *One Nation, Underprivileged*, 75–82.

11. For major examples, see Sugrue, *Origins of the Urban Crisis*, 209–29; Self, *American Babylon*, 289–90, 333; Lassiter, *Silent Majority*, 2–3.

12. Edward G. Goetz, *Clearing the Way: Deconcentrating the Poor in Urban America* (Washington, DC: Urban Institute Press, 2003); Stephen Steinberg, "The Myth of Concentrated Poverty" in *The Integration Debate: Competing Futures for American Cities*, eds. Chester Hartman and Gregory D. Squires (New York: Routledge, 2010): 213–28; David Imbroscio, "Beyond Mobility: The Limits of Liberal Urban Policy," *Journal of Urban Affairs* 34, no. 1 (February 2012): 1–20.

13. Xavier de Sousa Briggs, "After Katrina: Rebuilding Places and Lives," *City & Community* 5, no. 2 (June 2006): 119–28; Geoffrey Whitehall and Cedric Johnson, "Making Citizens in Magnaville: Katrina Refugees and Neoliberal Self-Governance," in *The Neoliberal Deluge: Hurricane Katrina, Late Capitalism, and the Remaking of New Orleans*, ed. Cedric Johnson (Minneapolis: University of Minnesota Press, 2011), 75–77.

14. David Imbroscio, "From Redistribution to Ownership: Toward an Alternative Urban Policy for America's Cities," *Urban Affairs Review* 20, no. 10 (2013): 1–34; David Imbroscio, "The Perils of Rationalism," 85.

15. Robert J. Chaskin and Mark L. Joseph, *Integrating the Inner City: The Promise and Perils of Mixed-Income Public Housing Transformation* (Chicago: University of Chicago Press, 2015); Edward G. Goetz, *The One-Way Street of Integration: Fair Housing and the Pursuit of Racial Justice in American Cities* (Ithaca: Cornell University Press, 2018).

16. Patrick Sharkey, "To Avoid Integration, Americans Built Barricades in Urban Space," *Atlantic*, June 20, 2020, https://www.theatlantic.com/ideas/archive/2020/06/barricades-let-urban-inequality-fester/613312/.

17. Quoted in Donald Moggridge, ed., *The Collected Writings of John Maynard Keynes, Volume XXVII: Activities 1940–1946, Shaping the Post-War World: Employment and Commodities* (Cambridge: Cambridge University Press, 2013), 270.

18. Heterodox economist Stephanie Kelton served on the US Senate Budget Committee and as Senior Economic Advisor to Bernie Sanders in his 2016 and 2020 presidential campaigns. Her 2020 book was a national bestseller and has reflected the surge of pro-deficit ideas in public discourse. See Stephanie Kelton, *The Deficit Myth: Modern Monetary Theory and the Birth of the People's Economy* (New York: Public Affairs Books, 2020).

19. Pavlina R. Tcherneva, *The Case for a Job Guarantee* (Cambridge: Polity Press, 2020), 81–113.

20. Wegmann, "We Just Built It," 283–89; Jake Wegmann, Alex Schafran, and Deirdre Pfeiffer, "Breaking the Double Impasse: Securing and Supporting Diverse Housing Tenures in the United States," *Housing Policy Debate* 27, no. 2 (2017): 193–216; Nassau-Suffolk Regional Planning Board and Raymond & May Associates, *Better Homes*, 31.

21. Mariely López-Santana and Philip Rocco, "Fiscal Federalism and Economic Crises in the United States: Lessons from the COVID-19 Pandemic and Great Recession," *Publius: The Journal of Federalism* 51, no. 3 (Summer 2021): 365–95; Philip Rocco, "State and Local Austerity is a Death Trap—Rip it Up and Start Again," *Notes on the Crises*, July 16, 2020, https://nathantankus.substack.com/p/state-and-local-austerity-is-a-death.

22. For job guarantee support among suburban voters, see "Polling the Left Agenda," Data for Progress, https://www.dataforprogress.org/polling-the-left-agenda; For universal child-care, see Bryce Covert, "Democrats are Running on Universal Child care—and Winning," *The American Prospect*, July 29, 2020, https://prospect.org/health/democrats-are-running-on-universal-child-care-and-winning/; For minimum wage, see for example "New York State Voters Back $15 Minimum Wage," Quinnipiac University Poll, September 18, 2015, https://poll.qu.edu/new-york-state/release-detail?ReleaseID=2280.

23. Oly Durose, *Suburban Socialism (or Barbarism)* (London: Repeater Books, 2022).

# *Index*

Page numbers in italics refer to figures and tables.